Our Aust ... e

in

the 1990s

edited by

Veronica Kelly

Monograph No. 7 in the series

AUSTRALIAN PLAYWRIGHTS

SERIES EDITOR: VERONICA KELLY

Rodopi

AMSTERDAM – ATLANTA, GA 1998

Cover illustration: Song Ngoc Water Puppetry Troupe's *Water Stories* (detail) Photo: David Morrow, courtesy Canberra Youth Theatre. Cover design: Sue Gray.

∞ The paper on which this book is printed meets the requirements of "ISO 9706:1994, Information and documentation - Paper for documents - Requirements for permanence".

ISBN: 90-420-0299-9 (bound)
ISBN: 90-420-0289-1 (paper)

Printed in The Netherlands

CONTENTS

Foreword by the Series Editor iv
VERONICA KELLY

Acknowledgements v

Contributors vi

List of Illustrations viii

Old patterns, new energies 1
VERONICA KELLY

Boundary riders and claim jumpers: the Australian theatre industry 20
RICHARD FOTHERINGHAM

Plays about the Vietnam War: the agon of the young 38
ELIZABETH PERKINS

Dis/orientations: contemporary Asian-Australian theatre 53
JACQUELINE LO

Reconciliation? Aboriginality and Australian theatre in the 1990s 71
HELEN GILBERT

From gay and lesbian to queer theatre 89
BRUCE PARR

Recent Australian women's writing for the stage 104
HELEN THOMSON

Inter-referentiality: interrogating multicultural Australian drama 117
JOANNE TOMPKINS

Maintaining cultural integrity: Teresa Crea, Doppio Teatro, Italo-Australian theatre and critical multiculturalism 132
TONY MITCHELL

Theatre in education: dead or alive? 152
GEOFFREY MILNE

Community stories: 'Aftershocks' and verbatim theatre 168
PAUL MAKEHAM

Sidetrack Performance Group and the post-modern turn 182
TOM BURVILL

Melbourne Women's Circus: theatre, feminism, community 195
ALISON RICHARDS

Performing sexed bodies in physical theatre 213
PETA TAIT

WORKS CITED 249

INDEX of PROPER NAMES 261

ILLUSTRATIONS

FOREWORD by the SERIES EDITOR

Veronica Kelly

This volume is the seventh in the monograph series commenced by Ortrun-Zuber-Skerritt of Griffith University, Brisbane. Since 1985 six monographs and eight video interviews have been produced. The book studies are *Louis Nowra* edited by Veronica Kelly; *Patrick White* by May-Brit Akerholt; *Jack Hibberd* by Paul McGillick; *David Williamson* edited by Ortrun Zuber-Skerritt; *John Romeril* edited by Gareth Griffiths and *Alma De Groen* by Elizabeth Perkins.

This collection of essays on recent Australian theatre focusses more on industrial developments, contemporary theorisations and specific theatre companies than on the work of particular playwrights, mapping the cultural and industrial context in which Australian theatre writing occurs. It is meant to provide information about the general theatrical field and to document and analyse the work of specific groups. Such activity concentrates on the broad range of plays and physical theatre being currently devised for varied audiences both inside and outside the field of text-based or authored writing. The illustrations are a major feature of the series, allowing readers to glimpse theatre and its performers in front of their varied audiences.

Future plans for the 'Australian Playwrights' series include more author studies; particularly of the major playwrights Nick Enright and Jack Davis. To consolidate the broadening of the Series' focus marked by this volume there will however be further occasional thematic or survey volumes concentrating on major features of Australian theatre, drama and performance.

The following video programmes have been produced and are available from the Australian Film Institute, 49 Eastern Road, South Melbourne, Victoria 3205, Australia. They consist of interviews with the named playwrights where they speak about their work.

Louis Nowra (1985)	36 min
Dorothy Hewett (1986)	52 min
Jack Hibberd (1986)	42 min
David Williamson (1986)	50 min
Stephen Sewell (1986)	59 min
Alma De Groen (1990)	44 min
Michael Gow (1991)	49 min
John Romeril (1992)	54 min

My thanks are due to the founding editor, Ortrun Zuber-Skerritt, for initiating and tenaciously sustaining this Series, and to the playwrights and contributors for their scholarly work, patient collegiality, and above all their enthusiasm for Australian theatre.

Brisbane, December 1997.

ACKNOWLEDGEMENTS

Appreciation is due to the following organisations and individuals who have generously assisted in the search for illustrative documents: Matthew Abeline of Canberra Youth Theatre; Anne Craven of Rock'n'Roll Circus; Nicole Tunis of Doppio Teatro; Katherine Hoepper of Kooemba Jdarra Indigenous Theatre; Rosemary Herbert of La Boite; Wesley Slattery of Sydney Theatre Company; Tanya Angelini of Playbox Theatre: Hannah Jamieson of Queensland Theatre Company; Melbourne Theatre Company; Rose Wilson of State Theatre Company of South Australia; Dina Panozzo. Individual photographers and contributors who provided illustrations are warmly thanked, and their work fully acknowledged in the List of Illustrations. Sue Gray at Graphic Design, Prentice Centre, University of Queensland assisted with computer graphics. Annette Henderson and the office staff of the Department of English at the University of Queensland, provided, as ever, skilled and efficient backup.

Deepest appreciation is due above all to two exemplary and inspiring graduate research assistants, Tiffany Urwin and Toni Johnson-Woods, whose efficiency and enthusiasm for the project were essential to its completion. Thank you Tiffany for your picture research, and Toni for your picture-hunting and courageous computer skills.

THIS VOLUME IS DEDICATED TO THE MEMORY OF SUE CULLEN (1947-1997), LIBRARIAN AND SCHOLAR OF AUSTRALIAN THEATRE, LOVED BY ALL WHO KNEW HER

CONTRIBUTORS

TOM BURVILL teaches drama and Australian cultural studies in the School of English, Linguistics and Media at Macquarie University in Sydney. In addition to his interest in Australian community and political theatre, he has written on audience and reception and on rehearsal and production processes, based on research with theatre practitioners in the USA, Britain as and Australia. He has an ongoing connection with Sidetrack Performance Group in Sydney with whom he has worked as Dramaturg and co-writer.

RICHARD FOTHERINGHAM is Associate Professor in Drama at the University of Queensland. He worked for ten years as a professional actor, playwright, and director, and was a member of the Board of the Queensland Theatre Company from 1990 to 1995. He is the author of *Sport in Australian Drama* (Cambridge UP, 1992), a biography of the short-story writer and playwright Arthur Hoey Davis (*In Search of Steele Rudd*, UQP, 1995), editor of the volume *Community Theatre in Australia* (Methuen, 1987, revised ed. Currency, 1992) and co-editor of the journal *Australasian Drama Studies* (1982-).

HELEN GILBERT teaches in drama and theatre studies at the University of Queensland, Australia, and also directs experimental student performance work. Her most recent book, *Sightlines: Race, Gender and Nation in Contemporary Australian Drama* is due from Michigan University Press in 1998. She is co-author of *Post-Colonial Drama: Theory, Practice, Politics* (Routledge 1996), and has published numerous articles in Australian and international journals in the fields of Australian, post-colonial and indigenous theatre. She is currently editing and anthology of post-colonial plays and working on a research project on Australian/Asian cross-cultural collaborations in the performing arts.

VERONICA KELLY teaches in drama at the University of Queensland, and is co-editor of the journal *Australasian Drama Studies*. She has published on colonial Australian drama and theatre history, including an annotated edition of Garnet Walch's 1873 pantomime *Australia Felix: or, Harlequin Laughing Jackass and the Magic Bat* (UQP, 1988), and on issues of colonial orientalism, journalism, melodrama and performance history. She is theatre critic for the national *Australian* newspaper, has published widely on contemporary Australian writers, and is completing a study of the theatre of Louis Nowra for Currency Press.

JACQUELINE LO lectures at the Department of Modern European Languages, Australian National University, Canberra. She has published in the areas of postcolonial drama, Malaysian and Singaporean theatre, and contemporary Australian performance, and is the editor of *Theatre in South East Asia*, a special focus issue of *Australasian Drama Studies* (1994).

PAUL MAKEHAM lectures in Drama at the Academy of the Arts, Queensland University of Technology. He has a background as a professional actor and teacher, and was a researcher on the *Aftershocks* project; he also performed in the play's premiere season. His doctoral thesis, completed at the University of Newcastle, NSW, is on representations of landscape in twentieth-century Australian drama

GEOFFREY MILNE is head of the Department of Theatre and Drama at La Trobe University, Melbourne, where he teaches in contemporary Australian theatre and drama. He has been a theatre critic in the print media since 1985 and on ABC radio since 1991, and has published articles on many aspects of Australian drama and theatre. He has worked in theatre lighting for the Melbourne Theatre Company and as a writer/researcher for Magpie Theatre in Adelaide.

TONY MITCHELL is a senior lecturer in Writing and Cultural Studies at the University of Technology, Sydney. His translations of plays by Dario Fo and Dacia Maraini have been performed throughout Australia, and he is the author of *Dario Fo: People's Court Jester* (Methuen 1986) and numerous journal articles about Italian and Italo-Australian theatre, performance and music. His books *Popular Music and Local Identity: Rock, Pop and Rap in Europe and Oceania* (U Leicester P) and *High Art in a Foreign Tongue: Adelaide Ristori's 1875 Australian Tour*(Australasian Drama Studies Association) appeared in 1996.

BRUCE PARR is the editor of *Australian Gay and Lesbian Plays* (Currency Press, 1996) and the author of a number of articles on the plays of Peter Kenna. He has worked as an actor, director and arts administrator, and has taught theatre at the Universities of Queensland, Southern Queensland and New England (Armidale).

ELIZABETH PERKINS is an Associate Professor of English in the School of Languages, Literature and Communication at James Cook University, Townsville. She has published extensively in Australian literature and has a special interest in comparative contemporary drama, including Filipino drama in English. She has edited from manuscript the *Poems* of the Australian colonial writer Charles Harpur (Sydney, 1984) and his verse drama *Stalwart the Bushranger* (Sydney, 1987). She is the author of *The Plays of Alma De Groen* (Rodopi, 1994) and acted as dramaturg for De Groen's most recent play *The Woman in the Window* at the 1997 Australian National Playwrights' Conference. She has written over thirty playscripts, chiefly for community theatre, including twelve musicals for children.

ALISON RICHARDS is a Melbourne-based researcher and theatre activist. She worked extensively as a director and performer in Australia's engaged 'new wave' theatre of the 1970s before turning to academic pursuits. Her research interests centre on the dynamics of performance processes; she is currently working on a book with Back to Back Theatre, a professional company of actors with intellectual disabilities.

PETA TAIT is a senior lecturer and playwright at the Theatre and Drama Department, La Trobe University, Melbourne. She is author of *Converging Realities: Feminism and Australian Theatre* (1994) and *Original Women's Theatre* (1993), and co-editor of *Australian Women's Drama: Texts and Feminisms* (1997). Her recent collaborative performance texts include The Party Line's *Appearing in Pieces* (1993), *700 Positions*, co-winner of the 1996 Gay and Lesbian Mardi Gras Performing Arts Award, and *Whet Flesh* (1997).

HELEN THOMSON is a Senior Lecturer in the English Department of Monash Univesity, Melbourne. She has edited several volumes of the work of the nineteenth-century South Australian writer Catherine Helen Spence, and published a number of book chapters on other colonial Australian women writers. Her other publications have been in the areas of eighteenth-century women's writing, Australian literature and drama, including the 'Drama' section of the *Oxford Literary History of Australia.*

She has been a professional theatre critic for nearly twenty years; for the *Australian* and presently the *Age* (Melbourne).

JOANNE TOMPKINS teaches drama and Australian literature at the University of Queensland. She has published widely in the area of post-colonial theory and drama, including, with Helen Gilbert, *Post-colonial Drama: Theory, Theatre, Practice* (Routledge, 1996). She has edited a special issue of *Australasian Drama Studies* on Canadian drama, titled *Theatre and the Canadian Imaginary* (October 1996). She has co-edited, with Julie Holledge, *Performing Women/Performing Feminisms: Interviews with International Women Playwrights* (ADSA, 1997), a collection of interviews with women who employ a variety of performance techniques. Her current research interests include the areas of multicultural theatre and theory in Australia and Canada, as well as women's intercultural theatre.

LIST of ILLUSTRATIONS

Fig. 1 Adam Broinowski, Daniel Witton, Teresa Blake (top); Michael Newbold (bottom) in Magpie's *Verona*. at Glen Street Theatre, Sydney, 1996. Photo: Branco Gaica, courtesy State Theatre Company of South Australia.

Fig. 2 Zen Zen Zo in *Unleashed* at Princess Theatre, Brisbane, 1996. Photo Rachel Konyi, courtesy Zen Zen Zo.

Fig. 3 Song Ngoc Water Puppetry Troupe's *Water Stories* at Canberra Youth Centre, 1997. Photo: David Morrow, courtesy Canberra Youth Theatre.

Fig. 4 Merlinda Bobis in *Cantata of the Warrior Woman Daragang Magayon* at Asian Theatre Festival, Belvoir Street Theatre, Sydney, 1994. Photo: John Borthwick, courtesy Merlinda Bobis.

Fig. 5 Denice Kickett, Ta Duy Binh, Kerry Cassey in Ta Duy Binh's *Conversations With Charlie* at Asian Theatre Festival, Belvoir Street Theatre, Sydney, 1996. Photo courtesy Ta Duy Binh.

Fig. 6 William Yang in *Sadness*, Performing Lines national tour, 1992. Photo: Peter Elfes, courtesy William Yang.

Fig. 7 Margaret Harvey, Bill Sandy in Jack Davis's *The Dreamers*. Kooemba Jdarra Indigenous Theatre at Festival Space, Brisbane, 1996. Photo: Michael Taylor, courtesy Kooemba Jdarra.

Fig. 8 Jaylene Riley in Sally Morgan's *Sistergirl*. Black Swan Theatre & Melbourne Theatre Company, 1992. Photo: David Dare Parker, courtesy MTC.

Fig. 9 Deborah Mailman in Kooemba Jdarra's *Seven Stages of Grieving*, 1995. Photo: Tracey Schramm, courtesy Kooemba Jdarra.

Fig.10 Lillian Sansbury, Paul Kelly, Kate Roberts, Wayne Anthoney in Roger Bennett's *Funerals and Circuses* by Magpie Theatre at Theatre 62, Adelaide, 1992. Photo Lisa Tomasetti, courtesy State Theatre Company of South Australia.

Fig. 11 Helen Moulder, Caroline Kennison in Sarah Hardy's *Vita! A Fantasy* at La Boite, Brisbane, 1993. Photo: Christabelle Baranay, courtesy La Boite.

Fig. 12 Wadin Dona (above) and Paul Capsis in Nick Enright's *Playgrounds*. Sydney Theatre Company at The Wharf, 1996. Photo: courtesy Tracey Schramm.

Fig. 13 Reg Livermore in *Red Riding Hood, the Speed Hump and the Wolf* at Ensemble Theatre, Sydney, 1996. Photo courtesy Steve Moorehouse.

Fig. 14 Glen Ryman and Philip Ross in Jill Shearer's *Shimada* at Queensland Theatre Company at Cremorne Theatre, Brisbane, 1990. Photo: Chris Ellis, courtesy QTC.

Fig. 15 Natasha Herbert, Mark Pegler, John Diedrich in Tobsha Learner's *Wolf* at Playbox Theatre, Melbourne, 1992. Photo: Jeff Busby, courtesy Playbox.

Fig. 16 Dina Panozzo in *Varda Che Bruta...Poretta.* Sydney Festival at Stables Theatre, Sydney 1992. Photo: Sandy Edwards, courtesy Dina Panozzo.

Fig. 17 Doppio Teatro's *Pane e cipolla* at Adelaide Italian Club, Ruggero Centre, © 1995. Photo: Peter Heydrich, courtesy Doppio Teatro

Fig. 18 Antonino Gorgone, Eva Di Cesare, Antonino Lo Giudice, Andreas Constantinou in Doppio Teatro's *Una festa di nozze* at Newcastle, Australian National Tour, © 1996. Photo: Peter Heydrich, courtesy Doppio Teatro.

Fig. 19 Crosswinds Theatre in the Community in *Blurgon the Bunyip*, 1979. Photo courtesy Geoffrey Milne.

Fig. 20 Steven Smith, Irene Jarzabek, Josie Eberhard in Arena Theatre's *Three Stories High*, 1990. Photo: Jeff Busby, courtesy Geoffrey Milne.

Fig. 21 *Aftershocks* at Civic Playhouse, Newcastle, 1991. Photo courtesy Paul Makeham.

Fig. 22 Sidetrack Performance Group's *Adios Cha-Cha* (rehearsal). Sydney 1986. Photo courtesy Tom Burvill.

Fig. 23 Sidetrack Performance Group in *The Measure.* City Square, Melbourne, 1994. Photo courtesy Tom Burvill.

Fig. 24 Women's Circus in the 'Women and Sport' show, Melbourne 1993. Photo: Viv Mehès.

Fig. 25 Women's Circus as the Bitches from Hell, Moomba River Pageant, Melbourne, 1994. Photo: Viv Mehès.

Fig 26 Kareena Oates, Steve Brown in Rock'n'Roll Circus's *Body Slam*, Sydney, 1994. Photo: courtesy Angela Bailey.

Fig. 27 Thor Blomfield, Gavin Robins, Kirsty Hilhouse, Bernie Regan in Legs on the Wall's *Temptation*, Sydney. Photo: Scott Barnett, courtesy Legs on the Wall.

Fig. 28 Kareena Oates, Matt Wilson, Rudy Mineur in Rock'n'Roll Circus's *The Dark* at Princess Theatre, Brisbane, 1995. Photo Ponch Hawkes

Fig. 29 Annabel Lines and Matt Wilson in Rock'n'Roll Circus's *The Dark.* Princess Theatre, Brisbane, 1995. Photo: Ponch Hawkes.

Fig. 30 Celia White and Anni Davey of Club Swing at Southgate, Melbourne International Festival, 1996. Photo: courtesy Angela Bailey.

Fig. 31 Anni Davey and Simone O'Brien in Club Swing's *Appetite.* Metro, Melbourne, 1996. Photo: courtesy Angela Bailey.

Fig. 32 Mia Mason and Grayson Millwood in Meryl Tankard's *Furioso* at Adelaide Festival Centre, 1995. Photo: Régis Lansac, courtesy Meryl Tankard Australian Dance Theatre.

Old patterns, new energies

Veronica Kelly

Periodising such a dynamic and inconsistent enterprise as live theatre is at best a dubious historiographic business, yet the desire to offer an account of recent Australian developments seems to justify at least an attempt. The rare opportunity for millennial speculation, moreover, requires some stock-taking and taxonomy of contemporary trends. As a historical period the 1990s decade looks simultaneously backwards and forwards. It is situated between two provocative public anniversaries: the 1988 Bicentenary of white settlement and the first centenary of Australian Federation in 2001. Questions of national direction are crystallised around the unresolved issues of Aboriginal land rights and the problematic and uncertain advent of an Australian republic. As Ken Stewart (1996) discerns of the Australian 1890s, the two periods share such features as national self-examination and utopian dreams, prolonged economic recession and the challenge of feminism; plus debates about Australia's international alignments, the persistence of empire, fantasies of a primordial white ethnic purity and responses to an internal Asian presence. Hence 1990s Australia, while increasingly bound into the economic and social patterns and modes of consciousness occasioned by globalised 'post-national' and 'post-historical' mass culture, yet shares some of the radical and questioning nationalism of the 1890s and some of its apocalyptic fragmentation.

History, and historical revisionism, are in the Australian late nineties hotly-contested and politicised sites of public discussion (McQueen 1997), mobilising such topics as the alleged collapse of the socialist project and the seeming inevitability of globalisation, managerial corporatism as government style and the privatisation of the public sector. More specifically, nineties debates are dominated by Australia's public dealings with its Aboriginal peoples: the on-going struggles to secure the legal principle of native title and government acknowledgment of the injustice done to the stolen generation of children. The policy of multiculturalism, the official success story of the 1980s whose social viability remains credible, is now coming under attack as populist politicians seek to scapegoat NESB migrants for the social costs of deregulation and privatisation. Theatrical interrogations of such a haunted 'history' now originating from smaller companies arguably both share and contest the quests for historical understanding and future paths displayed since the 1980s by such mainstage plays as the didactic discussion dramas of David Williamson, the gothic dystopias of Stephen Sewell or Louis Nowra's continued investigations of Aboriginal stories or public follies.

More pertinently to the present study, the 1990s marks the third decade of government-subsidised and culturally-visible Australian theatre since the writer-driven theatrical 'new wave' of the early 1970s put local playmaking firmly on the national cultural agenda. Theatre, a highly reactive, economically conditioned and opportunistically pro-active cultural form, has responded with remarkable energy to the cross-currents of public life and to the specific exigencies of its own industrial patterns. While this study does not claim revolutionary or evolutionary canonicity for recent forms of playwriting or performance practices, it charts significant activities and debates within a firmly-established but internally fissured industry. The historiographic narrative of a coherent national project here co-exists with those of regional and identity-based secessional activities, characterising the recent years through consolidation of distinctive industrial, theoretical and dramaturgical developments. George Bernard Shaw, more cautiously pluralistic, named his 1932 collection of commentary on English theatre's remarkable theatrical decade *Our Theatres in the Nineties* (Shaw 1932).[1] Appropriating the title of Shaw's collection, I suggest it is still possible in the 1990s to speak in the singular about our Australian 'theatre'; as a fairly coherent if internally dialogic enterprise.

Industry and repertoire: the 1970s and 1980s inheritance

Australian theatre in the late 1990s displays a varied and evolving range of address. Over the broad field of style and subject matter this activity differs in its forms of expression from the theatre which rose to prominence with the exuberant nationalism of the 1970s (Fitzpatrick 1979; Holloway 1981, 1987). The playwriting of the 1980s maintained a strong sense of public mission and a frequently disturbing urgency, as evidenced by David Williamson's investigatory dramas *Sons of Cain* or *Top Silk*. Intertextual, mythic and even apocalyptic dimensions were developed in the plays of Alma De Groen (*The Rivers of China*), David Malouf (*Blood Relations*), Michael Gow (*The Kid, 1841*), and particularly in the epic projects of Louis Nowra and Stephen Sewell (Kelly 1987b). The Bicentennial year of 1988, with its plethora of plays critiquing or celebrating various versions of Australian nationalism, appears to have marked some sort of determining moment in the subsequent confidence of playwrights in interpolating a unified or inclusive national narrative. The challenge of Aboriginal land-rights claims and the presence of a large migrant multicultural population has rendered problematic older versions of Australian history. A renovated historical paradigm of nationhood has not re-established itself on major stages in any authoritative way, but rather lives a productive and provocative underground life where it undergoes continuous contestation, fragmentation and recombinations. In the following decade more regionally-based and identity-focussed work has come to the fore, and Aboriginal writing and theatre-making have become major components of a theatrical endeavour which adopts new modes of historical enquiry.

There are of course hard economic and political reasons for recent mainstage theatre's apparent turning away from public matters. The state companies have been increasingly impelled by governmental policies to seek corporate sponsorship, with resultant reining-in of risk-taking or critical plays attacking the social outcomes of public corporatism, or presenting to mainstream audiences dystopian versions of Australian history. As subsidies decline, box office is expected to comprise an increasing component of total income. While remaining responsive to the 1970s social equity imperatives demanded by the Australia Council with its requirement to produce Australian work, annual seasons of major state companies must carry the burden of pursuing cultural mission with a judicious admixture of commercial hits and (decreasing) classical revivals. National and international touring and inter-company production-sharing have been responses to this drive for economy: an industrial situation in rapid evolution which in fact contains as many opportunities as drawbacks (see Fotheringham). Nonetheless such nineties audience 'suck-out factors' as Celtic dancing, the lavish international franchise musicals, state-run casinos, cable television and the internet — not to mention increasing job insecurity and prolonged economic recession — threaten to erode the big companies' box office and increasingly see them managing huge late-decade deficits (Morgan 1996a). The circumspection occasioned by the variegated repertoire responsibility of the state companies with their large pre-sold subscriber economic base is unlikely to alter greatly in the foreseeable future.

The dominance of this mixed repertoire pattern has been confirmed by a recent brave initiative by Chris Westwood, then executive producer of the State Theatre Company of South Australia, who proposed five years of 'National Repertoire' seasons comprising purely Australian revivals planned to culminate in the year 2000, the eve of the centenary of Federation (Westwood 1995). In mid-1997 this all-Australian focus was abandoned as economically unviable, though it did reveal audience loyalties through the company's invitation to the general public to nominate plays they saw as indispensible to an Australian theatrical repertoire (McCallum 1996).[2] At least as ideal and as vision, an

Australian canon of dramatic literature remains very much alive, but the major revivals so necessary to the establishment of a secure and visible national tradition are not routinely undertaken.[3] In current industrial circumstances new 'classics' are as likely to be nurtured on the theatrical and social margins as in prestigious mainstage premieres or revivals. As the contributors to this study argue, women's, gay and lesbian, community, Aboriginal and multicultural theatre over the last decade has moved from the theatrical margin to credibly inhabit, if not dominate, a centre undergoing various challenges to its centrality, and to affect some of its performance and dramaturgical practices.

In its plural modes of address and its more concentrated political focus the theatre of the last decade evolved from the 1980s industrial pattern, which saw consolidation of the subsidised state companies with the commencement of concomitant devolution of disaffected groups and writers servicing the specific energies of regional, women's, community, youth, gay and lesbian, multicultural or Aboriginal theatre. Australian playwriting for all kinds of companies has demonstrably flourished extraordinarily in the past two decades, confirming that dramatic writing is now established within the broad spectrum of national cultural life. This playwriting is exciting and considerable in its range, displaying the survival into the late nineties of many authors from the New Wave 1960s and 1970s, as well as the subsequent emergence of numerous important figures. Of the seventies playwrights, David Williamson and Louis Nowra — 'one-man repertoire machines' as McCallum (1996) terms them — are the great survivors, annually producing significant mainstage plays with national productions and numerous revivals. Jill Shearer and Stephen Sewell continue to write for major companies, while Nick Enright's prolific career since his 1991 play *Mongrels* has made him a commanding national figure. Commencing in the earlier 1960s were Dorothy Hewett and Jack Hibberd, who while largely retired remain major names, while Alex Buzo, John Romeril and Alma De Groen continue to produce occasional fine plays. Although these veteran playwrights' recent output is reduced their critical prestige remains high, as does that of the late Patrick White. Jack Davis, Janis Balodis and above all Michael Gow were late-seventies or early eighties starters who are still creating exciting mainstage and small-company work: Gow's 1986 hit play *Away* continues to dominate repertory and curriculum choices. More recent mainstage writers with important plays produced nationally include Andrew Bovell, Robert Hewett, Ron Elisha, Tes Lyssiotis, Michael Gurr, Joanna Murray-Smith, Hannie Rayson, Hilary Bell, Katherine Thomson, Daniel Keene, Tobsha Learner, Beatrix Christian, Tes Lyssiotis, Timothy Daly, Elaine Acworth, Peta Murray,

Alex Harding and the late Timothy Conigrave. Although much Aboriginal theatre, like multicultural and community work, is collaborative with musical, dance and performer-driven emphases, Eva Johnson, Jimmy Chi, Wesley Enoch and Deborah Mailman, John Harding and Roger Bennett have recently devised influential indigenous texts which have made it to published form.

This theatre writing has had to respond to rapidly altering social patterns and industrial circumstances. Remarkable production achievements such as Neill Gladwin's acrobaticly physicalised *Verona* for Adelaide's Magpie (see Milne, Tait), Neil Armfield's acclaimed direction of his 1994 *Hamlet* for Belvoir Street, or the continuously-funded international troupe Circus Oz (see Tait), tend to throw the mainstream industry's safety net of small-cast 'literary' shows into perhaps unfair focus. Economically viable casts have in fact diminished over this recession period and this has necessarily impacted on subject matter. A summary of cast sizes for the plays of Louis Nowra, a continuously-working writer professionally attuned to industrial constraints, will serve as a brief example. Nowra's mainstage premieres for various companies in the early 1980s were able to employ up to fourteen actors, where necessary doubling up to thirty-seven characters. The cast reduces to eight by the mid-eighties, and six to eight by the beginning of the 1990s. His 1993 play *Radiance* for Belvoir Street, written for three Aboriginal women performers and using no doubling, thus appeared to accommodate mainstage expectations of tightly-focussed psychological realism. By contrast, for *The Jungle*, an epic-scale collage of metropolitan Sydney life premiered in 1995 by the Sydney Theatre Company's New Stages programme, twenty-nine characters were played by five actors.[4] Increasing overheads and rentals have altered the perceptions of companies and writers of what is viable, and also affect content. As Nowra discerned (1989b, 13), while such industrial constraints may sometimes focus and sharpen writing, as in Stephen Sewell's claustrophobic 1988 thriller *Hate*, small casts mean that artistic risk-taking and radical provocation are increasingly at a discount. The eighties 'epic' vision is in danger of being lost: 'somehow there has to be a way of presenting a world on stage that is larger, deeper than the vision of a nuclear family in a living room, a way of presenting the dynamics of groups, individuals, class and power'.

Dissident observers periodically charge Australian established theatre with thematic safeness and stylistic unadventurousness, particularly compared with the innovation and brilliance of Australian hybrid arts, image and physical theatre and dance companies. Is theatre in the nineties sufficiently distinguishing its craft and audience from that of film and television, and can it win audiences from the ubiquitous international musicals? Many plays by Williamson, Rayson or Nowra, Bryce Hallett (1995) believes, could as easily have gone straight to screenplay form. Indeed, many recent stage plays have been speedily filmed: Rayson's *Hotel Sorrento*, Nowra's *Così* (1994b) and *Radiance*; Enright's *Blackrock*, Nicholas Parsons' *Dead Heart* and Williamson's *Emerald City*, *Travelling North* and *Brilliant Lies*. As Hallett sees it, echoing Jack Hibberd's long-held vision of a vigorously surreal Australian anti-naturalism, such dramas lack 'reality-distorting scenes, extravagant gestures, the economy and force of fantasy and invention', and he indicts playwrights as being 'no longer alert to our fantasies and dreams'. Influential practitioners maintain this anti-naturalist critique. In a well-publicised onslaught, the avant-garde opera and festival director Barrie Kosky lambasted text-based theatre and what he sees as the 'market-driven, masterpiece-sofa sort of mediocrity' dominating Australian stages, along with our provincial desire to be acclaimed as 'world class' (Wynhausen & Scott 1996, Kosky 1996). This programme of spectacle, textual overturning and deconstructive performance makes for exciting well-funded festival fare, but ignores the economic and social realities under which quotidian mainstream Australian theatre operations labour, let alone the determined shoestring operations of the regionals and profit-sharing radical groups. It discounts more or less entirely the craft and creative adaptability of contemporary playwriting and company-initiated script development programs, which inventively seek to contravene these circumstances or to address non-mainstream communities.

Without acceding to all of Kosky's cultural analysis, such provocations do in fact highlight the growing dichotomy between a more or less literary and text-based mainstage and an excitingly innovative and hybrid physical theatre flourishing on its sometimes near, sometimes remote outskirts, wherein middle-class old-Australian or 'Anglo-Celtic' voices are easily matched by queer, indigenous or new-migrant visions. While they remain largely precarious community ventures and prey to economic uncertainties, many of the companies documented in this study — Women's Circus, Rock 'n' Roll Circus, Doppio Teatro, Sidetrack, Body Slam or the programme of the Mardi Gras Arts Festival — display the erotic spectacle, physicality, multi-arts hybridity, communal responsiveness and informed critical attack which Kosky and Hallett find lacking in the current mainstream.

Centre or periphery?

It is to the second-rank — the community and regional theatres — with their hungry management structures, keen audience sense, and frequently critically-informed agenda, that much of the energies of repertoire innovation and stylistic renewal has relocated in the 1990s. Regional and specialist script development bodies, like Brisbane's Playlab or Sydney's Playworks dedicated to women's playwriting, generate and sustain new work, as do the development arms of the major companies or the long-established Australian National Playwright's Centre with its annual workshops and conferences. Indeed some observers predict that, while the recession 'certainties' of Shakespeare and David Williamson dominate mainstage repertoire planning, community-based 'grassroots theatre' expressing the 'values, insecurities and aspirations of its constituency' is likely to be the growth area of the future (Morgan 1996). The viability of such a forecast is attested by recent achievements, but its continuance is fraught with material difficulties. It is these smaller groups which are coming under economic pressure through the limiting of on-going Australia Council grants to big companies ensconced within the Major Organisations Fund, and the placing of the second-tier theatre and dance groups on a discontinuous regime of project funding. This policy impacts most severely upon such fertile and innovative regional companies as Doppio Teatro (Adelaide), Freewheels (Newcastle), Deck Chair (Perth), Kooemba Jdarra Indigenous Theatre (Brisbane) or even Neil Armfield's prestigious Company B ensemble at Sydney's Belvoir Street (Travers 1997). That these companies can generate material of wider than local success is evidenced by the national exposure of such modestly-originated plays as Newcastle's verbatim community piece *Aftershocks* (see Makeham); Graham Pitts' *Emma*, adapted for Fremantle's Deck Chair Theatre in 1991 from the life story of an Abruzzi immigrant (see Mitchell); or Nick Enright's *A Property of the Clan* (1992), originally a theatre in education piece for young people based upon a famous rape-murder case, written for Newcastle's Freewheels and subsequently revised for mainstage audiences as *Blackrock.*

Australian subsidised theatre, and also municipal and regional venue management perhaps in conjunction with commercial managements, have turned to entrepreneurial ventures designed for interstate and international touring in the South East Asian region and further abroad (see Fotheringham). But the portability of small-scale experimental shows also appeals to international festival programmers. In contrast to the success of Dein Perry's industrial grunge extravaganza *Tap Dogs*, a high-concept dance piece entrepreneured and now internationally toured and franchised by the Sydney Theatre Company, modestly resourced but widely-toured performer-driven shows have brought the experiences of migrant and Aboriginal Australians to national and overseas audiences. These include William Yang's *Sadness* and *The North* (see Lo) Erin Hefferon's *The Geography of Haunted Places* from the Perth Institute of Contemporary Arts, or Deborah Mailman's *Seven Stages of Grieving* for Kooemba Jdarra (see Gilbert, Tait), which have toured to Canada, New Zealand, the United Kingdom, South East Asia and the USA. These budget-price chamber pieces, with their visual sophistication and quizzical intertextuality, autobiographical or community story content and focus on the materiality of bodily presence, display fertile cross-currents between theatrical discourses and the practices of performance art. Yang's *Sadness* and *The North*, where the author narrates his family story and displays his compelling photographic images to the accompaniment of Colin Offord's Celtic and Pacific-influenced music, might with equal validity be claimed for performance art or for gay, Asian or multicultural theatre (see Lo). Such performances tend to privilege historical fragmentation and contingency, the exploration of gender, ethnic and regional identities, communal stories and personal memories, adapting their effects from story-telling, performance art and post-modern epistemological scepticism.

Thus the last decade has seen a partial dissolving of the central theatrical narrative of 'national identity' and its simultaneous re-inscription as indigenous, regional and new ethnic and gay voices continue to erode distinctions between mainstream and 'alternative' repertoire. As both Tompkins and Burvill (below) suggest, this is a selective and very post-colonial type of postmodernism; one which deploys bricolage and self-referentiality as strategies to map the rich — and richly confused — social grid of Australia's multicultural society. Arguably, such recession-age theatrical postmodernism appropriates its metatheatrical stylistics from current discourses of identity politics, but reinscribes these performance elements with communal stories. Recent Australian work is not afraid of fragmentation, self-division or incompleteness but uses them as strategy and subject for exploration rather than as ends in themselves. Although with pared-down and more self-reflective use of dramaturgy and mise-en-scène, such theatre in its way continues the eighties dramaturgical project of historical reclamation. Since the Bicentennial year of 1988 with its plethora of ambitious historical shows (Gilbert 1994b; Tompkins 1994b) the desire — and opportunity — to inscribe a broad public national narrative appears largely superseded by a more interrogatory and self-reflexive project exploring the silent voices and concealed histories at the margins of the older narratives.

Recent critical and historical studies

The need for a systematic overview of contemporary Australian theatre is apparent. Though its historical scope is necessarily limited, Fitzpatrick's *After the 'Doll'* (1979) remains the standard account of that New Wave writing renaissance against which much recent theatre defines itself. The most recent broad-scale history is Leonard Radic's *The State of Play* (1991a) which offers a more up-to-date but impressionistic reviewer's account commencing from the late 1960s. Dennis Carroll's *Australian Contemporary Drama* (1994), a revision of his 1985 study, commences its examination of twentieth-century writers in 1909 with Esson and Palmer but includes recent material on Sewell, Nowra, Gow and Davis, with some consideration of multicultural and Aboriginal theatre. The last authoritative critical essay collection remains Peter Holloway's substantially revised *Contemporary Australian Drama* (1987), updating much of the material selected for its 1981 original. Holloway's chronological reach goes beyond the much-mythologised late 1960s to the crucial 1950s, and analyses industrial factors and significant productions as well as dramaturgical concerns. Elizabeth Webby's study of recent Australian plays (1990) presents to students challenging ways of reading influential texts and productions. Fortunately, while comprehensive studies of the contemporary field are scarce, sustained results have been produced since the 1980s in the areas of reference, theatre-historical and documentary research, particularly evident in a wide-ranging and overdue recuperation of colonial theatre's remarkable cultural influence. Comprehensive accounts of theatre's occluded theatrical past have now been visibly reclaimed — an important task for any self-aware postcolonial society which requires coherent narratives of cultural traditions as informed grounding for contemporary practice. Harold Love's edited collection *The Australian Stage* (1984) assembles pictorial and literary documents from settlement to the early 1980s, including valuable essays on modern theatre history. More recently Currency Press's monumental and historically inclusive *Companion to Theatre in Australia* (Parsons & Chance 1995) documents and references a wide range of currently-active themes, personnel, repertoire and companies. Readers are referred to the *Companion*'s individual entries and its essays on 'Research and Scholarship' (Fotheringham 1995), 'Repertoire' (Webby, Love, Fotheringham, Radic 1995), and 'Playwriting' (Brisbane 1995a) for detailed information on recent dramatic and theatrical activity in this country.

In the place of panoptical overviews, studies of particular aspects of contemporary theatre have flourished, offering much-needed theorised accounts of areas of significant activity. Maria Shevtsova's *Theatre and*

Cultural Interaction (1993) contains sophisticated and important sociological research on the audience address and self-positioning of Australian theatre companies, using as samples the Sydney Theatre Company and Melbourne's anti-naturalist and European-influenced Australian Nouveau Theatre. Peta Tait's *Converging Realities* (1994) is the first comprehensive and feminist-informed account of contemporary Australian women's performance. Gilbert and Tompkins' *Post-Colonial Drama* (1996), theorising the contemporary theatre of numerous decolonising societies, offers penetrating readings of recent Australian work. A historical and contextual account of gay and lesbian theatre activity, and its negotiations with queer theory, appears in Parr's edition of *Australian Gay and Lesbian Plays* (1996b). Aspects of community theatre have been summarised and analysed in Fotheringham (1987, 1992), while Queensland's radical agitprop and community companies of the 1970s and 1980s are celebrated and documented in Capelin (1995).

Author studies in monograph form have also flourished in the last decade: a welcome development which accords important Australian writers the full-length analyses their output requires. This activity has produced two theatrical studies plus an updated biography of Williamson (Fitzpatrick 1987, Zuber-Skerritt 1988, Kiernan 1990, 1996) and two of Hibberd (Hainsworth 1987, McGillick 1988); and one each of Buzo (McCallum 1987), Nowra (Kelly 1987b), White (Akerholt 1988), Sewell (Fitzpatrick 1991), Hewett (Williams 1992), Romeril (Griffiths 1993), Davis (Turcotte 1994) and De Groen (Perkins 1994). Such major contemporary figures as Gow, Enright and Balodis still require their own full-length studies. Article-length accounts and analyses of writers or companies dealing in performance work or circus, and Aboriginal, multicultural or bilingual theatre are thickly scattered throughout the scholarly and journalistic literature, but await systematic synthesising. The establishment in 1982 of the bi-annual journal *Australasian Drama Studies* provides a forum for scholarly work on theatre history, drama and performance undertaken in this region. The dramaturgical erosion of grand historical narratives, noted above as a nineties characteristic, has seemingly been accompanied by diffusion of scholarly energies into more focussed or richly theorised studies of playwriting and theatrical practice. During this same time, ironically, detailed and comprehensive historical documentation and analysis of Australian theatre's social and theatrical contexts were embodied in these decades' encyclopaedic monuments: Love's *The Australian Stage: A Documentary History* in 1984 and the 1995 Currency *Companion.*

The scope of this collection

Some of the work of prominent mainstage Australian writers is discussed in this volume; particularly in Thomson's evaluation of opportunities for women playwrights, Parr's account of the burgeoning of gay and lesbian theatre and Gilbert's analysis of discourses of Aboriginality. But this study is not a complete chronicle or comprehensive analysis of contemporary Australian playwriting as such, necessary and important as such a study would be. It aims rather to consider the social circumstances and discursive underpinnings which have made recent theatre in this country such an innovative but fascinatingly fragmented project, and to chart the incursions of postmodernism and physical theatre into mainstage and text-based assumptions. While this collection cannot provide a historical or thematic account of the recent evolution of Australian theatre work, companies or writing, it aims rather to produce a symptomatic map of significant contemporary activity in its multiplicity and vitality: a list of orienting markers. Multicultural, bilingual, community, circus, women's and physical theatre are analysed through overviews and through case studies of the work of particular companies, and the communalities of techniques and subject matter between these groups, no less than their specific and immediate focus, will be evident to the enquirer.

Although the focus of the contributors to this volume is primarily on the work of the last ten to fifteen years, the collection is framed by a challenging long-range overview of evolving Australian subsidy policies and their effects on the contemporary industrial field, and by a chapter on political thematics whose chronological reach touches the mid-1960s. Richard Fotheringham argues that 'the very concept of a theatrical field, or of an industry, a profession, or any other organising term, has been ideologically produced by vested interests concerned as much to exclude as to include.' He gives a national taxonomy of paratheatrical organisations and structures (training institutions, academic associations, subsidy bodies) and analyses the self-positioning of the subsidised theatre industry vis-à-vis its commercial, amateur, profit-share and project-funded competitors. Marketing, touring and entrepreneurial activity by venue managements, Fotheringham discerns, are activities increasingly encroaching on the monopoly of 'nationally' significant theatre held since the 1970s by the subsidised companies. This shift is not all loss, since much of the activity documented in this volume originates in the 'experimental, hybrid and lively work' which exploits the fissures in changing economic and policy paradigms.

Elizabeth Perkins provides an account of theatre occasioned by Australia's involvement in the Vietnam war: an event of immeasurable social and political impact on Australian society whose echoes continue to reverberate either metaphorically or explicitly in practically all succeeding plays dealing with war, state violence, neo-colonialism or our relationship with Asia. Comparison of the theatricalisation of the Asian other in Hopgood's 1966 protest drama *Private Yuk Objects* with Lo's account of the theatre produced by Asian-Australian artists indicates that Australian society has over three decades absorbed significant populations and potential audiences from the once-feared Asian 'others', with impact on both theatrical manner and matter. The strategies for the encoding of Asian-ness have been influenced by the upsurge of intercultural exploration of Asian theatre forms. The *Hearts and Minds* Project in Wollongong in 1992 utilised local Vietnamese-Australian and old-Australian actors to explore community attitudes to Asian immigration with the co-operation of the Vietnamese Veterans' Counselling Service (Copeman 1994). This fusion of narrative realism with traditional Vietnamese water puppetry may be compared with the 1997 collaboration in *Water Stories* (1997) between the Canberra Youth Theatre, the Canberra Youth Wind Ensemble and the Song Ngoc Water Puppetry Troupe from Vietnam, indicating how intercultural hybrid performance modes are emerging as alternatives to the realist monolith of European-influenced mainstage style. Perkins' account of the moral dilemmas expressed in the on-going project of 'Vietnam' theatre frames that renovated questioning of Australian 'identity' which has long been held as the prime undertaking of our national stages.

In her account of contemporary Asian-Australian theatre work, Jacqueline Lo indicates the theatrical impacts of the past fifteen years' commercially-driven and government-sponsored 'drive into Asia', as well as the emergence of Australian multicultural theatre work produced by Asian-Australians. Merlinda Bobis' feminist reclamation of Filipino epic in her solo performance *The Cantata of the Warrior Woman Daragang Magayon* and Ta Duy Binh's *Conversations with Charlie* are the work of recent immigrants, while William Yang's *Sadness* and *The North* are created by an artist from a family long settled in Australia. Assumptions of unitary cultural and gender identities are challenged in these highly theatricalised diasporic performances, which unpick the totalising of national identity upon which simplistic formulations of inter- and intra-cultural artistic and social relations depend. Lo insists that 'it is vital that both the production and reception of Asian-Australian performances focus on the historical conditions and specific trajectories from which hybrid identities are enunciated.' Such negotiations with identity representations, theatrical form and sites of address are of vital importance to the project of Australia's vigorous

Aboriginal theatre, and the discourses of Aboriginality which pervade both mainstream and more specialised company work. Helen Gilbert queries the political valency of 'the incorporation of Aboriginal elements into mainstream art forms' to ensure the 'Australianness' of those forms. She sees resistant practices employed in hybrid theatrical forms and performances creating an 'in-between' space where indigenous presence can be declared and renewed. Questions of authenticity and ownership are important ones for mainstream and Aboriginal-white collaborators to negotiate, particularly as Aboriginal stories and texts increasingly find a place in mainstage companies. Black theatre's preference for non-naturalistic forms and its sophisticated intergeneric theatricality and appropriations of international popular culture are evident in such major shows as Jimmy Chi's musical *Bran Nue Dae*, Roger Bennett's *Funerals and Circuses*, or Ningali Lawford's solo show. Is this activity where Jack Hibberd's 1976 program for a Brechtian and antinaturalist indigenous Australian 'popular theatre' grounded on modernist international practice and informed by urgent audience address (Pierce 1987, McGillick 1987) may currently be located? While his concepts of 'Australian' and 'popular' have long been under interrogation (Burvill 1983, 28-30), arguably Hibberd has posed an enduringly crucial challenge and one which our more progressive theatre practice endeavours to explore or to reframe.

Gender questions and sites of address are central to Bruce Parr's account of Australian gay and lesbian theatre, activity focussed and brought to visibility partly through the high profile of Sydney's annual Gay and Lesbian Mardi Gras arts festival. Queer theatre, fabulous and dangerous, also (as Parr speculates) responds to calls by Hibberd and others for a expressive radicalised and physicalised Australian performance practice. Parr stresses the urgency, humour and fun of such important plays as Alex Harding's *Blood and Honour*, which answers both to immediate gay community concerns and to the destabilising theatrical energies of queer. Gay themes have informed prestigious recent mainstage plays by Michael Gow, Nick Enright and Louis Nowra, and David Williamson provides the occasional lesbian or gay character, as in his controversial sexual-harassment piece *Brilliant Lies*. Actual lesbian-identified theatre however has not to date been as successful in establishing itself in a still largely male-dominated industry; however the lesbian vision has achieved a strong Australian writing and performance tradition whose presence may as vitally inform physical theatre, cabaret, dance or performance art as 'straight' literary theatre. The discourse of queer, Parr argues, will increasingly provide a fertile critique for re-evaluating the Australian canon and for denaturalising

Australian readings and performance practices. As Melbourne artist Linda Sproul sees it, postmodernism has changed the gender economy of the mainstream. 'There isn't a singular truth or singular base from which things can be considered normal or otherwise [...] if once upon a time it was difference, now its differences. There's the notion of the mainstream not being in the middle any more but everyone hanging out at the edge and being part of a whole' (Litson 1997a). Nonetheless the perceived loss of radical and oppositional edge caused by widespread acceptance continues to concern gay and lesbian theatre workers.

Feminist theatre, Helen Thomson shows, remains 'firmly marginalised' within Australian production practices. Yet the women's movement, like the anti-Vietnam war movement, is one of the most valuable legacies of 1970s social radicalism which originally manifested itself in women's collectives and agitprop theatre practices. Debates about how feminist theatre intersects with plays written by women, and the strategic uses of naturalist and anti-naturalist styles, remain relevant to the overall concerns of Australian practice. Many mainstage Australian writers of recent years, like Jill Shearer, Hilary Bell and Therese Radic, deal with the 'public' themes of history and Asian relations, and both Beatrix Christian (*The Governor's Family*, 1997) and Elaine Acworth (*Solitary Animals*, 1996) have developed a confronting critique of Australian and international historical violence. Dorothy Hewett's poetic drama is now confined to revivals, but Alma De Groen pursues her examination of the role of the artist and her daring experiments with metamorphic form. Tobsha Learner's and Beatrix Christian's haunted poetic fairytales interrogate eroticism, historical agency and gender constructions. Hannie Rayson, Joanna Murray-Smith and Peta Murray have achieved mainstream success in Australia and abroad with comedies of manners and bourgeois dramas, while Katherine Thomson's writing for mainstage audiences keeps alive issues of region, class and power. The complex intersections of women's writing with multicultural, lesbian and feminist theatre, performance art, Aboriginal, migrant and community theatre are themes introduced by Thomson's chapter and are taken up by other writers in this volume, especially Tait and Richards.

The 'unattainable authenticity that multiculturalism seems to still require' is under interrogation in Joanne Tompkins' account of the 'stalled' situation of current Australian discourses and their 'rhetoric of authenticity'. The cynical — or genuine — confusions surrounding the categories of 'culture' and the 'ethnic' prevalent in public quarters are exemplified in the decision of the City of Sydney Cultural Council to change the name of Sydney's long-established annual Eisteddfod to the

'McDonald's Performing Arts Challenge' — this being explained as a change from an 'old-fashioned' name to one which better reflects 'Australia's multicultural society' (Morgan 1994b). Through examination of two productions by NESB writers, Noëlle Janaczewska's *In the Winter Garden* and Dina Panozzo's *Varda che Bruta*, Tompkins reveals that identity and ethnicity are being considerably more ironically and thoughtfully negotiated in small-scale performance work than in such corporately sponsored civic events. Story-telling, such a strong feature of community, Aboriginal or migrant-experience theatre, is used in these performances with consciously post-modern irony and with a sophisticated use of theatricality. While the official discourse of multiculturalism continues to totalise 'Australian' and 'migrant' identities and experience, the discursive confinement of such hybrid work to the multiculturalist performance 'ghetto' avoids the more extensive repositioning of Australian practise which twenty years' of official definitions seem to demand. In this transitional and uncertain climate, Tony Mitchell's case study of the work of Teresa Crea and Adelaide's bilingual Doppio Teatro provides a detailed account of one influential group, the sole survivor of the bilingual companies started in the 1980s. Immigrant stories, feminist recuperation and community involvement have been some of the focuses of Doppio's work, but Crea as a professional worker has refused enclosure in the ethnic or community theatre 'ghettos'. While responsible to her Italian-speaking or migrant-descendant audiences through devising theatre for 'social clubs, schools, [and] outdoor festivals', Crea also accessed a complex postmodern musical performance idiom for the 1993 *Filling the Silence*. Crea's activity within Australian company structures operating as a free-lance professional director indicates the current opportunities open to (in this case, Italian-Australian and female) theatre professionals.

Young peoples' theatre (including circus, musicals and puppetry) appears a notable locus of the 1990s mobility of field definition. Geoffrey Milne demonstrates the subsidy and discursive shifts from theatre in education (TIE) to youth theatre, but suggests also that TIE is perhaps not so much 'dead' as mutated. The activity initiated in the early-seventies derived from British-influenced practice, whose educational agenda examined 'social and developmental issues', producing a plethora of school shows where the topics of drugs, safe sex and gender roles enjoyed a prolonged vogue. Withdrawal of State Government subsidy and the squeezing of the public sector with concomitant school closures has dissipated the energy of this original educational missionary project, with its slim-line presentation and maybe earnest issues-based formats. Schoolchildren both primary and secondary, Milne believes, are now increasingly habituated to polished professional product and seek it in theatre designed for their consumption. An example is Adelaide's Magpie company, once a TIE stalwart but more recently the originator of the widely-acclaimed clown-piece *Verona* which impressed and delighted adult audiences when touring on the venue-based national circuits described by Fotheringham.

In April 1992 *Australasian Drama Studies* ran a focus issue 'Theatres for Communities', in which David Watt discerned that community theatre, as hitherto understood, was likewise undergoing a process of structural crisis and definitional parameter shift. In 1990 he detected 'the coexistence of three generations of community theatre workers with very different senses of what the movement was about' (1992, 4), of which the most recent display little sympathy with the radical politics or the wide understanding of international practice evident in such late 1960s Australian groups as Melbourne's Australian Performing Group or Brisbane's Popular Theatre Troupe (see Capelin 1995). Community theatre, fuelled by graduates of proliferating tertiary training courses, was coming to be seen as merely another funded career option. The initiative for field-definition and theorising passed to the subsidy bodies with their desiderata of 'cultural difference' and 'excellence', risking an undertheorised and product-driven enterprise; shrinking subsidy and project-funding patterns also took their toll. Milne (1993) resumed this threnodic theme in his subsequent account of recently-extinguished community theatres in Victoria.

Watt documents informed practitioners' concern that official privileging of pluralism and postmodernist 'difference' has the effect of occluding power relations and controlling the critical discourse of the Other (13). However, the flourishing of such companies as Sydney's Death Defying Theatre, whose *Blood Orange* and *Cafe Hakawati* dramatised, inter alia, stories of bodily and cultural perceptions of young women from dozens of ethnic backgrounds, suggests the creative mutations of community theatre and its present ability to address 'target communities within geographic locations' (Winning 1993). *Aftershocks*, by contrast, is an outstanding example of verbatim theatre mobilising an older, more class-defined and locality-based paradigm of 'community'. Paul Makeham's study of *Aftershocks*, in both its original community form and its metropolitan production, documents its circumstances and methodology which privileges the experience of working-class people in the face of catastrophe, countering the media constructions of the 1989 Newcastle earthquake. His account of the prestigious Belvoir Street remount, directed by Neil Armfield, suggest how 'different reading formations [...] produce different, and in some cases disabling, readings of texts'. While documenting one of the remarkable achievements of recent Australian community theatre, Makeham voices unease at the universalising and recuperative impulses of mainstage theatre discourses faced with the committed radicalism and informed theoretical position of the *Aftershocks* project.

A contrast is Sydney's Sidetrack Performance Group, in suburban operation since 1979 with a dynamic and musically-oriented physical style and sophisticated use of venue and space. Sidetrack has pre-eminently and necessarily been aware of discourses of multiculturalism, with a broad multicultural participant basis and migrant audiences reached in workplaces, community venues and schools. Tom Burvill charts its trajectory from community theatre to more performance-art work as an example of the incursion of postmodernism into older Australian radical theatre practice. As Burvill points out, 'the term "community" was always a paradoxical label for a movement which actually foregrounded the contradictions and exclusions of the mainstream society'. Ongoing renegotiation of their overall project can, in the case of Sidetrack, accommodate with renewed sophistication that radical and oppositional drive correctly perceived by Watt to be under threat. Subjectivity, language and representation are postmodern concerns reclaimable for deconstructive theatrical practice, Burvill argues. This 'postmodern' period may itself be in transition, since the replacing of the company's operating grant with project funding compromises the retention of their vital ensemble structure and hence of a coherently evolving project. In a national situation where the term 'community theatre' has been appropriated, American-style, by the powerful interstate associations of amateur groups who mount ambitious contemporary scripts with $100,000 budgets — Kushner's *Angels in America* is programmed for 1997 by Sydney's Phoenix (Litson 1997b) — the future for radical community work remains optimistic but the direction of its next transformations is at best uncertain.

Melbourne's Women's Circus, in operation since 1991, is as Alison Richards claims 'one of the few good new stories to emerge in Victoria's "other theatres" in the 1990s'. She documents its achievements, working methods and philosophy as an on-going feminist community theatre project with its roots in the radical 1970s, whose shows have delighted and astounded audiences as well as empowering non-professional performers. Richards introduces the primacy of the female performing body as seen through the Circus's training program and hard-disciplinary skills base, and provokingly questions whether the '[over] preoccupation with language and textuality' which postmodern discourses push to the forefront of performance agenda is indeed the only way forward for radical community work. This emphasis on the body as text is more broadly examined in Peta Tait's chapter on Australian physical theatre whose recent work seeks to 'redefine the cultural meanings of "sexed" bodies'. She documents and analyses the intersections of postmodernism and new circus, with accounts of the work of the long-established Circus Oz and such newer groups as Sydney Front, Theatre Physical, Legs on the Wall, Rock 'n' Roll Circus, Club Swing and Open City. The adjoining disciplines of dance (Meryl Tankard) and small-scale theatre such as *The Seven Stages of Grieving* are adduced for the cross-fertilisation in performance modes which occur when issues of race, gender and physical presence are explored across a wide range of performance options and practices. This account of companies which deal innovatively and variously with feminism, community, gender, queer sexuality, postmodern performance and spectacle rounds off this volume's mapping of significant contemporary theatrical practices. It could suggest that Hibberd's (et al's) two-decades-old program for a spectacular, enthralling and radical Australian theatre may be renewing and informing itself, not only through international postmodern self-reflexiveness, but by recourse to the older pre-modernist local popular traditions of circus, vaudeville and foregrounded theatricalism.

Notes

1 This is a reprinting in three volumes of Shaw's previous selected criticisms from the London *Saturday Review* 1895-1898 titled *Dramatic Opinions and Essays* (New York: Brentano's, 1907).

2 The results of the call for play favourites reflect secondary and tertiary curriculum staples and continuing 'first-wave' loyalties amongst middle-aged readers of the national daily the *Australian*, rather than actual repertoire leaders or current company choices. The readers' fifteen most popular plays were, in order, Alan Seymour's *The One Day of the Year* (1960), Peter Kenna's *A Hard God* (1973), Michael Boddy and Bob Ellis's *The Legend of King O'Malley* (1970), John Romeril's *The Floating World* (1974), Michael Gow's *Away* (1986), Ray Lawler's *Summer of the Seventeenth Doll* (1955), Katharine Susannah Prichard's *Brumby Innes* (1927), Jimmy Chi's *Bran Nue Dae* (1990), Betty Roland's *The Touch of Silk* (1928), Dorothy Hewett's *The Man from Mukinupin* (1979), Ron Blair's *The Christian Brothers* (1975), Jack Davis's *No Sugar* (1985), David Williamson's *Don's Party* (1971), Patrick White's *The Season at Sarsaparilla* (1962), and David Williamson's *The Removalists* (1971). However by adding the votes by author rather than play, Williamson emerges as top playwright, followed by Louis Nowra, Michael Gow, Stephen Sewell, Jack Hibberd, Nick Enright, Patrick White, Alma De Groen and Dorothy Hewett — a list more closely reflecting actual repertoire exposure over a sustained period (McCallum 1996).

3 There are of course outstanding exceptions; major renovatory productions of Australian classics by creative directors include Neil Armfield's production of Patrick White's *The Season at Sarsaparilla* (1983), *The Ham Funeral* (1989) and *Night on Bald Mountain* (1996); Jim Sharman's *A Cheery Soul* (1979); or Makato Sato's production of John Romeril's *The Floating World* for Playbox Theatre (1995) under the Japan-Australia Cultural Exchange Programme (Sawada 1996).

4 This material on Nowra's theatrical career is developed in the author's forthcoming study *The Theatre of Louis Nowra* (Sydney: Currency).

Boundary riders and claim jumpers: the Australian theatre industry

Richard Fotheringham

One of the most distinctive features of official culture in nation states in the twentieth century has been the decisions by many governments, in widely differing political systems, to attempt to preserve declining nineteenth-century art forms by offering various kinds of assistance that placed those arts at least partially outside the laws of the marketplace. The reasons for such intervention, though by no means stable across time, have always been couched in terms of the preservation of certain values supposedly embodied in those arts, and appeals have been made to the assumed superiority of high-art forms, to their potential educational role, to their alleged ability to provide 'universal' cultural experiences, and (paradoxically, though no-one seemed to notice) to their asserted ability to resist the globalisation of culture by representing and promulgating national icons and differences.

It is usual, in thinking of the provision of such support in countries such as Britain, Canada, and Australia, to begin with, and concentrate on, the direct financial assistance to arts organisations and individuals provided by the Arts Council of Great Britain, the Canada Council, and the Australia Council respectively. This is not, however, where government assistance began, nor where in many cases it is concentrated in terms of the impact on society or the monies committed. In prosperous market economies with unused resources and with surplus goods and services which can be redirected without this appearing in the balance sheet, 'in kind' support — free or cheap rental of unused property, and piggybacking arts need onto existing transport, infrastructure, personnel, and advertising activities — have been for many years ways of allowing arts organisations to work in ignorance of the fully-costed nature of their operations. In 1923 the Allan Wilkie Shakespeare Company was granted discount rail transport in Queensland and eventually free rail travel and exemption from entertainment tax throughout Australia and New Zealand (Wilkie 1984, 167); today some large and small state-subsidised theatre companies still enjoy subsidised or even peppercorn rental rates for some or all of their premises and equipment.[1]

More significantly in terms of the financial impact on the level of arts activities, the decisions by governments at all levels to provide buildings such as libraries, galleries, theatres, and concert halls, in which and through which arts products are made and disseminated, has further worked to conceal the real costs of producing those arts. The decision in 1954 to build what eventually became the Sydney Opera House was taken by the New South Wales state government independently of, but simultaneously with, the beginnings of the formalisation of federal government arts patronage through direct grants and tax deductibility for business and private donations. Although the establishment of national and state opera, dance, and theatre companies was undoubtedly influenced by the belief that these groups would be the major users of the venues which were being built in most capital cities, there was a dispersal of decision-making power and control between venue design and management and the performing arts producers. One of my major arguments here is that potential contradictions within this dichotomy are now starting to fundamentally reshape the performing arts throughout the country.

In Australia the kinds of support offered to various art forms have differed according to the nature of that art. We can see this by taking two extremes; books and opera. In literature, support began with the establishment of public libraries, moved on in the early years of this century to providing literary pensions for old, distinguished but no-longer-working authors, then to subsidies for the publication of books of 'literary merit' whose worth might not be reflected in popular sales, and in the last twenty years 'Public Lending Right' payments to authors whose books were borrowed from public libraries, as well as direct grants to major (but commercially unsuccessful) authors, and experiments with various fringe contributions to the book, magazine, and newspaper publishing industry in order to publicise and guide responses to 'quality' literature. But because the book trade exists as a major international commercial industry, the actual total monies outlaid by governments have been very modest, and are intended to distort the marketplace in favour of 'quality' literature, but not challenge or compete with the major commercial companies. Nor, until recently, have there been any attempts to teach the skills required for successful literary authorship. Opera in Australia, in contrast, has had since the 1920s no commercial industry, and so governments have been much more interventionist at all levels: building major opera houses costing hundreds of millions of dollars; funding elite training institutions for singers, musicians, etc; and establishing organisations such as the Australian Opera (from 1997, Opera Australia) which require several million dollars in direct annual subsidy on top of their expensive ticket prices.

One of the interesting dilemmas of live theatre in Australia is that, although there has always been some commercial theatre — and much more now than there was even ten years ago — it was decided to follow the opera-funding model and set up major non-commercial theatre companies rather than subsidise commercial companies to undertake high-risk or additional non-commercial activities. However the advent of a reactionary federal government in 1996, and recent decisions such as providing touring funds to take a commercial production of *Run For Your Wife* to regional centres, may soon render such analysis obsolete (Ward 1997). Government subsidy is for both individuals and organisations. Playwrights receive individual grants, and theatre companies all the forms of major support outlined above: use of government-built theatre buildings, organisational funding for major companies, specific project grants, in-kind support through the use of government facilities and infrastructure, and grants to individual artists. However there is no overarching plan, rather intersecting and competing interests and agents working within broad policy guidelines. So a playwright may get a writing grant but no guarantee that their work will be performed, a choreographer a personal development grant but no dancers to work with, a theatre company use of a venue which is destructive to their artistic policy and repertoire. Competing federal, state, and local government arts departments, and festival, touring, and special-interest organisations fund a variety of arts activities for different reasons and under different programs. While there has been some coordination between the national arts body, the Australia Council, and some of the six state and two territory governments, it is still true that nearly all theatre companies and artists are engaged in a continual process of grant application, representing themselves in radically different ways in order to fulfil different grant criteria, being forced to redirect resources away from preferred, developmental or core activities in order to respond to new policy directions and sources of funding, and presenting their work in venues designed with quite other entertainments in mind.

How then, we may ask, can we begin to analyse such an industry? Is its shape and direction clearly visible, or is it the random result of a resolution of unequal but differing forces? Who are the key agents, in what given circumstances do they operate, and (given their often covert relationship to market forces) to what extent is it an 'industry' at all?

The field of Australian theatre

Following Pierre Bourdieu, it has become customary to begin analysis of such cultural institutions or cultural practices by assuming that these phenomena can be considered part of a 'cultural field' of inquiry and, following on from that assumption, that there is a degree of commonality and coherence which justifies such a geographical cliché.

For such a concept to have any point or purpose, common conditions, pressures, and/or external agents must be able to be identified and must affect all phenomena if not identically or equally, at least in recognisably interconnected ways, while participants in that cultural field must, to some degree, have their actions informed by shared beliefs or habitual practices. That is, having defined cultural activity as a field, one must be able to argue within it deductively rather than inductively: what can be perceived in general ought to operate, and be able to be applied, in particular. So, for example, if we could identify commonalities within the sub-field of 'Australian theatre', these would have recognisably similar manifestations in commercial theatre, in the major government-subsidised state companies, and in regional, community, student, and experimental groups. Any differences, whether of the aesthetic avant-garde, political opposition, local knowledge, or competitive challenge, would be essentially reactions to an acknowledged centre (even when denied), or products of particular, explicable, and only partial differences.

Further, the use of a field metaphor for cultural activity leads to an assumption that the significant boundaries are between that field and other areas of social behaviour, and that differences within a field are defined by prominence. Like a hill in the landscape, a major theatre company is one made up of essentially the same material, only with more of it in one place. The imagery cannot cope with different kinds of noticeable lumps, particularly if some of them can move about (what are we funding here?), and never go to one side of the field at all but jump quite easily over the fence into the next paddock. The attempts by the Australia Council to define and locate 'Hybrid Arts' as a category for funding is one manifestation of the fact that history, not ontology, has given us different arts activities which are categorised together and made to compete financially, and that the vested interests and aesthetic assumptions of those who have power, however well-intentioned they may be, are inevitably reflected in the categories they create and the judgments they make, while simultaneously producing anxiety at their inadequacy (Anon 1996). The categories are usually presented as mechanisms to *enable* funding, but they also exist to *exclude* those who 'don't fit', either aesthetically or economically.

Four agents of influence

A further complication within the concept of Australian theatre as a field of cultural activity is that what have been widely assumed to be the main shaping and controlling factors are the sources of direct funding: the federal government through the Australia Council, and the states through their Arts Departments. However, if we look at the initiatives which have during the second half of the twentieth century distorted the practices of the performing arts away from commercial economic activity, we can identify not one but four types of agency, often working in incoherent opposition to one another. These are:

1. State and federal government grants to arts organisations and individuals, designed to enable what are assumed to be non-commercially-viable performances;
2. Building programs by state and local governments, usually not for the organisations funded in (1) above but in response to perceived community interest in attending shows in large commercial theatre spaces;
3. Festival organisations at state and local levels, aiming to promote in an entrepreneurial manner shows and events often of a 'uniqueness' and 'significance' unachievable by (1) above (a tour by Britain's Royal Shakespeare Company, say, rather than a state theatre company Shakespeare production), or of an experimental or innovative nature not achievable without specialised festival funding and marketing.
4. Tertiary education institutes, departments and centres, and commercial training colleges, themselves spread along a spectrum of classification of their work between formal 'training' and less-narrowly-focused 'education', and consequently operating with widely differing relationships to the arts industries they monitor, analyse, and in some cases service.

Often there are few or no direct contacts, either individually or in terms of cross-agency representation, between civic and state administrations, who conceive of the building of theatres as part of the role of public administration to provide public leisure spaces (parks, gardens, theatres); the theatre profession with its own internal value-structures and habituated craft practices; entrepreneurs, both public and private, promoting festivals and national and international touring; and the tertiary sector educating and training future artists and audiences.[2]

What we need to do therefore, rather than assume some commonality of purpose and practice, is to go back one step, and to ask a basic question: on what grounds, and with what validity, do we identify and group theatrical activity in Australia, and how does the consequently-defined theatre industry organise itself as a system of inclusion and exclusion in order to provide a sense of both essential existence and artistic and industrial purpose? We have to examine Australian theatre both in economic terms and from within various discursive frames which, because of these various types of intervention, were until recently significantly different from those which obtained in commercial industries. In an environment where economic viability was not the principal goal (or at least was not acknowledged as such) and where the various agencies were engaged in deeply contradictory and in some cases mutually destructive behaviour, various interest groups have mobilised themselves to create and defend various powerful hegemonies — over government funding, over training and employment, over access to venues and the conditions of touring, over the aesthetic criteria for good acting, good plays and good productions, and over what constituted professionalism.

Their principal strategy has been to use weapons of inclusion and exclusion to define the practice of professional theatre itself; that is, promulgating and preserving a dominant ideology which produces a boundary not around the wider field (at least as others would see it) but within it. In opposition to this control, those fighting for inclusion have exploited disjunctions and absences within the system, the sluggishness of the powerful institutions to respond to change, and both the peculiarity of theatre as economic activity and the peculiar distortions within that activity caused by the contradictory patterns of government intervention. But again, the fight has not been waged just in terms of economics or aesthetics, it has been also a matter of asserting a different, much narrower definition of the field. In short, the very concept of a theatrical field, or of an industry, a profession, or any other organising principle or term, has been ideologically produced by vested interests concerned as much to exclude as to include.

Forces *within* the field

As an alternative to shaky global and totalising concepts such as 'field' or 'theatre industry', we might begin instead by examining the dilemmas facing any one institution or group within more broad, loosely-defined theatre practices within Australia, and assume that it exists not within a community of similarity and support, but a hostile environment of suppression by asserted difference. In *A Textbook of Wisdom* Edward De Bono offers a simple diagram, something like this:

B \ A

which can be adapted to our purposes. De Bono invites the reader, as a first exercise in the pursuit of wisdom, to think of as many ways as possible to prevent B crossing the boundary and getting to A: by giving A incorrect directions; by explaining how high the fence is; by suggesting that A is so like B, or so different from B, that the journey isn't worth it; or, more viciously, by privileging A or disabling B (De Bono 1996, 2-3). Approaching Australian theatre in such a way reverses our conceptual framework: instead of seeking similarities and assuming common identity and common purpose, we look for mutual exclusions, appropriations, rejections, and denials; instead of focusing on the generalised hegemonic/economic power that operates from without, we examine the immediate competition within.

Consider, for example, the two organisations which make claims to representing tertiary education and training institutions: the Australasian Drama Studies Association (ADSA), and the Australian Theatre Training Conference (ATTC). Both run annual conferences, yet the cross-over of personnel is almost non-existent; A and B ignore one another. ADSA members offer few papers on training or technical theatre, nor on commercial theatre (unless distanced by history), the major state-subsidised companies, the economics or structure of the arts, nor performing arts policy, but instead examine, support, and work with alternative, experimental, lifestyle and exotic companies, artists, and training techniques. The reverse is true of the ATTC, which courts 'mainstream' industry professionals and is insistently concerned with servicing 'the profession', defined in the most conservative (commercial/state theatre company) terms. ADSA barely notices that such a profession exists.

This invisible yet uncrossed wall between 'education' and 'training' runs not just between institutions but within them, affecting what is taught and how it is taught. The Victorian College of the Arts in Melbourne (VCA — the second largest training institution after Sydney's NIDA — the National Institute of Dramatic Art) is dedicated to the one-on-one training of elite artists, but also runs a 'sixth school' organised more like a university arts degree. Conversely some university drama centres, such as Flinders in Adelaide or Monash in Melbourne, offer arts degrees with major studies in drama but supplement this for a few auditioned students who receive additional small-group 'professional training'. What is taught as training can also reveal the division: at the Academy of the Arts at the Queensland University of Technology in Brisbane (QUT) staff are divided between those who favour mainstream voice and movement studies and performances of European 'classics', and those trying to introduce alternative skills and experimental performance work. Since the power to offer or not to offer courses with different syllabi, in different modes, and with different educational and training goals, is dispersed across different institutions, denying control to any one institution or practice, A and B try to ignore one another unless they are competing for student time and effort within the one institution,[3] or for funding between institutions.

The establishment of the Australian Theatre Training Conference, which has no formal existence between conferences, offers an example of the complexity of boundary-riding and claim jumping which can occur behind the facade of unity. NIDA, set up in 1958 as *the* 'national' theatre-training institution, is funded at more that $20,000 per student, compared to the more recently-established state-based schools, in particular what is called 'the Studio Five': the VCA (Melbourne), QUT Academy (Brisbane), Western Australian Academy of the Performing Arts (WAAPA, Perth), the Helpmann Academy (Adelaide, a loose amalgamation of different art-form training schools at different universities and campuses), and the University of Tasmania School of Visual and Performing Arts at Launceston, which are each funded much less generously ($7000-$9000 per student). These five organisations each have financial reasons therefore to claim parity with NIDA, which has a vested interest in denying their existence and preventing their growth. Further, during the twenty years it was the only training school, NIDA developed close links with the subsidised state companies, and established a nexus which operated to privilege its own graduates and to exclude directors and actors who came from other backgrounds and training experiences. This worked to institutionalise a certain kind of performance style (realism) within an overall aesthetic (plays from the British tradition) and economic structure (the English provincial repertory theatres). Conversely however, since these other training schools do exist, NIDA has a contrary interest in maintaining its control over what acting is and what the profession is, and so wants to adopt a leadership role in relation to these other institutions. Consequently NIDA and the Studio Five all send representatives to the Australian Theatre Training Conference (in order to get it to attend, NIDA was invited to host the first conference) and then the two groups ignore one another for the rest of the year, while carefully siding with one another against the many other university drama courses with less-obviously 'training' profiles, and even lower funding indices.

The same aesthetic and practical disagreements exist amongst professional artists and companies, but here the inequalities of power cause A to try to destroy B by taking it over. The Sydney (STC), Melbourne (MTC), South Australian (STCSA), and Queensland Theatre (QTC) Companies, the four major state-subsidised organisations in Australia, were all established before 1970, and each has a virtual monopoly over large-scale state and federal theatre funding within their region. In spite of their declared role as 'flagship' companies, not only have they established an aggressive and competitive dominance in their own market, but they have colonised and/or suppressed other areas such as youth or community theatre as soon as that other activity became a significant area of energy and influence. Their interests are against diversity; they seek to destroy alternatives, not to assist or lead them; not to sail proudly guarding a fleet of smaller ships, but to blow them out of the water (Fotheringham 1993). By way of contrast, one only has to look at the recent entrepreneurial activity of venue managements and arts festivals, who must find and promote a *diversity* of performance products, and so have been keen to help small, innovative groups to establish themselves as viable organisations.[4]

Clearly then it is the particular position of an institution within a field, and its power relationships with its immediate neighbours, that determine its actions and goals and the discourses it chooses to argue its case. Further, because the four major agencies mentioned earlier (governments, companies, festivals, and tertiary education) are often working at odds or in direct competition, each institution can gravitate towards that agent most responsive to its agenda.

Two conditions of live performance

We also need to consider, in examining Australian live theatre, at least two conditions characteristic of theatre generally in the late twentieth century which do operate on, or at least set parameters for, all the agents in the field. The first comes from the fact that live theatre's relationship to the cash economy is singularly problematic, because its usual creative materials are primarily human bodies. A refusal to measure a theatrical production in terms of what its participants might earn in other arts or non-arts activities elsewhere places that production more-or-less outside the world of economics. Indeed, for some artists who come into theatre, this initially is its precise virtue: that it is possible to make significant aesthetic, lifestyle, and/or political statements without raising a loan, investing in capital equipment, establishing ongoing infrastructures, or needing to think in any way about payroll tax, workers' compensation insurance, or long-term economic viability; let alone confronting the organised hierarchies of, say, the film and television industries (which really are industries in a way almost all live theatre is not). Take the salary bill out of a production budget, and be prepared to work with dangerously inadequate insurance cover, and a far less critical measure of financial success is required to achieve a surplus. (Indeed, given its reliance on second-hand clothing, borrowed props, re-used materials, and venues available free or hired at subsidised rates, theatre is one of the most successful of fund-raising activities available; the musical is the backbone of the annual fund-raising effort at many high schools.) A talented group of artists, working together without payment and developing a show under a cooperative profit-share agreement, can produce high-quality productions which can then be promoted and presented, by festival entrepreneurs in particular, in the same venues and with similar ticket prices to plays produced at great expense by major companies.

The second unique factor affecting theatre is that the point at which the acquisition of skills merges into questions of aesthetic taste and tradition is relatively low, with no assured and agreed training structures. One actor may be NIDA-trained in the British-United States tradition, another a physical theatre graduate of the Lecoq Mime School in Paris, a third may have come into the profession from an adjacent area such as acrobatics or circus, while a fourth may have acquired speech, singing, and movement skills through private classes, and/or the numerous commercial acting colleges which have come into existence to teach singing and dancing and/or acting for film and television. Beyond requiring certain basic vocal and physical skills and qualities, it is doubtful if the average audience member perceives differences in performing style, or discriminates on the basis of taste for or against the differences they do perceive. While 'the profession' produces its own self-encircling aesthetic, this is always under challenge from other shows performed by artists using other skills. By comparison a career in, say, music is built on perhaps fifteen to twenty years of regular technical, interpretative, and intellectual/dogmatic training, and technical incompetence is evident to any listener. Perhaps because of this shared and agreed formal basis for performer and teacher alike, in music the line between educator and professional is much less marked, with at least some mutual respect on both sides: the biographical notes for most singers and instrumentalists will always list the distinguished teachers with whom they have studied, and many conservatorium teachers also undertake concert engagements and/or combine to form ensembles of the highest calibre. Music teaching staff are expected to be practitioners as well as teachers, whereas in theatre this is not a qualification for many university teaching posts, while conversely those teachers who have professional training and/or experience but choose to move into educational institutions are quickly frozen out of the profession. No-one uses the term 'academic' with greater contempt than professional actors and theatre directors.

These two conditions of theatre — flexible costs and a diversity of useable talents and skills — have produced a wide and growing field of activity. This ranges from amateur activity relying on voluntary labour and minimal and concealed costs, through a wide variety of profit-share, project-funded, and specialised groups, to fully commercial theatre paying real cost and profit rates for theatre rentals, costume and set constructions, negotiating through agents for copyrights (scripts, music, choreography) and for artists (with their fees often based on crowd-drawing appeal from other media appearances such as in TV serials), using unionised labour with strict demarcations between jobs (performers do not move the sets, must have dressers), and engaging in major nation-wide publicity and advertising campaigns, including tie-ins with airline companies, hotels, restaurants, and media institutions.

Strategies and struggles

One of the strategies of exclusion activated by the government-subsidised theatre industry is to deny the importance of and to omit from consideration both economic extremes: non-subsidised commercial theatre at one end of the spectrum, and amateur, profit-share, and project-based theatre at the other. There are however important economic and ideological reasons for including them, beginning with the fact that this assertion of a primarily non-commercial yet professional industry is just that, more assertion than reality, as well as the way in which work at both ends of the capital-categorised spectrum impacts both economically and ideologically on the major subsidised companies.

Relatively little theatre in Australia is genuinely commercial in the sense that the J. C. Williamson organisation once was: buying or renting land and building or leasing and managing theatres, as well as having to create or import enough product to fill them year-round and make a profit, on top of paying both production costs and real commercial rental rates, or the capital and interest repayments on their own land and buildings. One major wild-card in Australian theatre in the last forty years, as mentioned earlier, has been the actions of state and local governments (and in some cases, private sector companies)[5] in building major arts/cultural centres and other large theatre spaces, suitable primarily for large-scale musicals, dance shows, concerts, and school speech nights, and charging rentals designed only to recover the operating costs of those venues. The importance of 'the performing arts' was reflected first and foremost in Australia (particularly between 1955 and 1975) by the cargo-cult strategy of creating spaces for then non-existent product. The long-delayed but spectacular success of this policy can be seen in the last decade, with Australia joining in the global phenomenon to which Andrew Lloyd Webber has been central, but which also includes *Les Misérables*, *Miss Saigon*, and revivals of the American musical works of Cole Porter, Rodgers and Hammerstein, and others. In

January 1997 the Gordon Frost organisation has just announced that it will not be proceeding with a planned production of *The Sound of Music* because it could not secure bookings in venues including the Victorian Arts Centre and the Queensland Cultural Centre; clear evidence of the dependence of even large 'commercial' managements on government-built, financed, and managed venues.

Conversely, the existence of these venues, and the popularity of this kind of product, has started to erode the boundary between commercial and state-subsidised theatre. In England, co-production deals between the Cameron Mackintosh organisation and the Royal Shakespeare Company, and the decision of the Royal National Theatre to mount its own large-scale productions of shows like *Carousel* and to tour them internationally, indicate the shift of those large government-subsidised theatre organisations into this market. In Australia similar attempts have been made, although less successfully, such as the South Australian, Melbourne, and Queensland Theatre Companies' relatively low-capital and not-particularly-successful staging of *High Society* in 1992, and the Victoria State Opera's aesthetically successful but financially disastrous *West Side Story*. What is clear nevertheless, is that the challenge to the state theatre companies is coming from above, not below. Having spent much energy policing the boundary between their self-defined field and that occupied by the 'B' companies, the A team — the state companies — failed to notice the activity in the commercial paddock on the other side, or realise its consequences.

This major redefinition of the economic field of theatre activity is something that the Sydney, Melbourne, South Australian, and Queensland Theatre Companies did not expect. The first three of these had already experienced the near-financial disaster of attempting to take a classic/high-culture repertoire into the expensive, large-seating-capacity arts centres; indeed the survival of both the MTC and STCSA is still threatened, while in Brisbane the QTC, recently going into debt for the first time since its inception in 1969, is about to move from a 600-seat theatre, in which they play to audiences of on average four hundred, into a new and more expensive 850-seat venue. To date only the Sydney Theatre Company has recognised that it is no longer a large player protecting its home ground, but a modest-sized organisation in a much larger field, and developed a viable strategy for dealing with the new challenges: firstly, by opting out of exclusive playing in the expensive Opera House and centring its operations in The Wharf, a relatively low-cost venue, and secondly by expanding its own entrepreneurial activities, sensibly concentrating them in the niche market for smaller-cast commercial shows, of which the national and international tour of *Tap Dogs* is the most successful example.

A second major consequence of the disjunction between the provision of *venues*, undertaken directly by state and local governments, and financial support for theatre *companies*, provided indirectly by the federal and state governments through the Australia Council and the six separate state and two territory arts departments, has been the radical shift, apparent only in the last five years, in the control of the commissioning, advertising and marketing of shows. Traditionally, venue managers simply took bookings, and were reliant on product supplied by performing arts companies. The QTC, STC, MTC, and STCSA each performed at one or two regular venues, and ran subscription schemes and advertised their work with the company name strongly foregrounded; it was not primarily the play, nor in many cases the actors, who were used to draw audiences. However in recent years the Queensland Cultural Centre has started mounting productions of musicals both new (*The Secret Garden*) and old (*The King and I*, starring Hayley Mills), and touring them world-wide, while the Festival Centre in Adelaide has set up a subscription scheme based on shows imported into that venue, thereby competing with the STCSA's own subscription season. Throughout Australia the pattern is the same: venue managers, dissatisfied with either the quantity, cost or type of show being offered for tour, have moved into entrepreneurial mode, increasing the level of activity at their theatre and its visibility and profitability, but not necessarily to the advantage of existing companies who traditionally used those venues and assumed primary responsibility for creating, performing and marketing their own work in a near-monopoly situation.

This approach has been successful not only in the major cities; it has also proved particularly appropriate in regional areas neglected by the metropolitan-focused companies. A notable example is the Northern and Regional Performing Arts organisation (NORPA) centred in the town of Lismore (population c40,000) in northern New South Wales. Rather than try to establish a professional theatre company in the style of several which had already failed, NORPA's driving force, the international opera and film star Lyndon Terracini, decided to focus on providing multi-arts activities at two venues, the City Hall and a local picture theatre purchased by a private sponsor and refurbished with local council support. NORPA has structured itself in imitation of what Terracini (1996) calls 'the German model where you have a ballet company, a theatre company, an opera company and an orchestra all under one umbrella. So an audience can see an opera one night, a play the next'. By taking over the marketing and property-management activities previously considered part of the work of different groups in the area, NORPA has aided local theatre, music, and dance groups who can focus on developing major projects for inclusion in NORPA's subscription program, while Terracini's contacts have enabled him to attract to Lismore major touring shows (*Tap Dogs* was one) and international stars such as soprano Emma Kirkby. The economic logic of this reallocation of marketing power from production companies to venue managements is inescapable, but it is something new in the field of the Australian performing arts, and it is by no means certain that the Dimboola Diaghilevs will necessarily want the same kinds of shows as before, nor accept them under the old industrial conditions or through the pre-existing organisational structures. The loss of authority by theatre company artistic directors over both repertoire and the direction of the industry will not be achieved without heat, nor will new touring and marketing organisations be welcomed by the Arts Councils which in several states have for some fifty years organised such activities without opposition.

If we draw back to reconsider this alteration in the power relationships within the field of theatre in Australia, we can note firstly that, as far as I am aware, no-one writing about the industry before about 1990 even bothered to mention venues as anything more than being suitable or unsuitable, expensive or accessible.[6] They were seen as conditions, not agents. Secondly, what has characterised much of the discussion since is reaction from those whom we might term boundary riders — those who are resisting the reshaping or redefinition of *their* sphere of influence, their 'field'. Proposals for new venues have been met by calls either for them to be provided at low cost as 'homes' for existing companies, or for the money to be given instead to artists. Entrepreneurial activity by arts/cultural centre management has been met by anger, outspoken opposition, and paranoia. There are good reasons for the major subsidised companies to be concerned, for their power base undoubtedly is being eroded. But before examining some examples of the consequences of this, we need to look more closely at the discourses of theatre in Australia: the language and underlying ideologies which have been used as weapons by both boundary riders and claim jumpers.

The discourse of professionalism

Whether a sub-field stops at a particular point in the cultural landscape or continues, is then neither natural, self-evident, nor incontestable, and the forces that shape it can be contradictory and even at times unperceived. Traditionally however a number of discourses have been mobilised to inform the very different activities of groups which we might assume would be considered to lie within the field of Australian theatre, ranging from the *cheerful philanthropy* of the amateur theatre, to the *professionalism* in the commercial theatre. Neither extreme entirely escapes the ideology of the other: amateur groups will talk about 'achieving professional standards', commercial artists will appear regularly without payment in charity and benefit performances. Between these extremes lie groups ranging from amateur companies who see their mission as being 'more' than 'mere' 'entertainment', to nearly fully-commercial organisations. Such groups will adopt, to a greater or lesser extent, both discourses, but because of their marginal economic situation and their claim to greater symbolic capital than the commercial theatre, will add to them a third ideology of purpose: the discourse of the *virtuous poverty* of a proudly cottage industry.[7] Actual practices however shift in their ideological ascription: it is interesting to note that 'the show must go on', fewer than twenty years ago a dogma associated with both professionalism and virtuous poverty (acknowledging theatre's precarious finances) has now become a sneered-at 'amateur' way of thinking. Virtuous theatres cancel if the show isn't ready (artistic preciousness increases symbolic capital); commercial artists go on strike if their industrial demands aren't met.

The assumptions on which government subsidies for theatre have been based were quite different: non-commercial/commercial, high art/low art, Australian/non-Australian. These old binaries assumed stability and ease of definition, and that ideally all the first terms (non-commercial, high art, Australian) would line up against the second (commercial, low art, non-Australian); an example of what Bourdieu is referring to when he speak of cultural production being 'the economic world reversed' (1993, 27). Discourse based on these beliefs is still mobilised when required by a particular interest group, but increasingly has been over-ridden by the discourse of professionalism which has become the dominant force operating to centralise or marginalise particular artists, companies and shows.

Professionalism too always has been a contested term, since, as noted earlier, actual economic structures vary from profit-share companies which may spend tens of thousands of dollars upfront on theatre hire and set and costume design and construction, but close before paying their actors anything, through several other types of company structure, to the fully-unionised commercial and state companies with full-time administrative staff and artists and technicians working to negotiated contracts and agreed job descriptions. In some states (e.g.

South Australia) close ties between the funding bodies and the actors' union mean that only groups recognised by the latter body qualify for possible subsidy; in other states substantially lower wages and conditions are the norm. Australia Council resolutions in 1981 and 1983 established that only 'professional' artists and organisations would be funded, but this has had to be modified in some cases, notably for the Darwin Theatre Company, where the obvious limits to the size of potential audiences virtually rules out fully-professional activities. As Terracini has argued in relation to Lismore:

> [A] problem I've found is that if you're doing a production in regional Australia you're paying Equity rates but you can only charge $25 a ticket. You're paying the same rates as in Sydney where you can charge at least twice that. We can't do that. No-one would come. [...] The STC has 20,000 subscribers. [...] I'd like to have 600 subscribers next year. (36)

In some cases the inflexibility of both government policies and union-negotiated wages and conditions lead to outright duplicity in order to achieve 'professional' status. One recent case involved a provincial theatre company which, in order to be able to qualify for subsidy as a professional organisation, misrepresented what were in fact two amateur shows for which it acted as umbrella, as having been directed professionally by its youth director. Many theatre-in-education groups 'aim' to pay their artists wages comparable to union rates, but fail; the demise of the long-running Toe Truck Theatre in New South Wales in 1996 has been attributed to competition coming from small profit-share groups of actors devising shows for the same secondary-schools market. Such actors are often 'employed' by a company organiser but, midway between profit-share partners and employees and having no other source of work, they perceive that it is the economic system which limits their income rather than the nominal employer, often a fellow-actor who clearly isn't benefiting excessively. Further, such artists too have a vested interest in defining the company they are working for as 'professional'; the symbolic capital of being a 'professional artist' is more closely tied to the economics than to the culture of the arts.

Consequences: the world right side up

Professional theatre in Australia then no longer claims a privileged distance from the marketplace; instead it tries to pretend its economic viability is greater than it is, and asserts its own symbolic importance on this exaggerated measure. But by turning the field right side up, and establishing economic discourse as well as practices as the primary value system, theatre has suddenly found that the 'old' discourses have in turn been upended. Having abandoned its asserted special place in promoting and representing high art and Australian national culture, professional theatre is now told that there is no other reason why it should not share in the national pain of public spending reductions. Embracing the idea of theatre as an industry, artists are now told to be economically rational. Even the old battlefield of national companies and activity versus state-based institutions no longer generates significant opposition if financial failure can be demonstrated. The collapsed Western Australian Theatre Company has been replaced by a system of importing product generated elsewhere; the Sydney-based Australian Opera has taken over the debt-laden Melbourne-based Victoria State Opera with remarkably little fuss. Within states too the bottom line is drawn over struggling independent organisations; the Queensland Philharmonic Orchestra has been subsumed as a resident division of its host cultural centre.

As long as professionalism was a term centrally defined by the training institutions and the major state companies whose practices, repertoire, and control of the market was the perceived goal, ragged edges could be ignored or at least minimised. The emergence of both venue managers and of annual festivals as entrepreneurs challenged this hegemony, and the rise of independent or sub-contracting organisations which tour artists and shows further eroded it (Litson 1996). What matters for such entrepreneurs is the quality and marketability of the product, not the industrial structure or provenance of the company which produces it. This has created new opportunities for artists (particularly young artists) and companies to shift the boundaries even further. Whereas once a young actor might aspire to find work with a major company after graduation and gradually move inwards towards the centre of the NIDA/state-company-defined and controlled system, increasingly such artists, and many with no formal training or training in other disciplines, are coming together to create remarkable experimental, hybrid, and lively work which festivals in particular find attractive. Whereas a decade ago a NIDA hegemony/state theatre monopoly seemed the most accurate way to characterise the dominant force in Australian theatre, the different agendas of other major agents are starting to reshape the field, not principally from without but from within.

Notes

1 One difficulty the Queensland Theatre Company experienced in 1990-91, while I was a Board member, was the decision by the state government to withdraw the long-standing provision of a technical workshop in a warehouse in the suburb of Salisbury at no cost to the company.

Commercial rates of hire in the order of $40,000 per annum were subsequently charged, leading to the decision to vacate the premises soon afterwards.

2 Two examples from Brisbane illustrate the government/theatre profession separation. For some years the Queensland Theatre Company staged popular open-air Shakespeare productions in Albert Park, using the natural environment to great effect. In 1982, without consulting or even informing the QTC, the City Council built a large covered concrete stage on this site which proved unsuitable and has hardly been used since. More recently a new theatre in the Queensland Cultural Centre was announced. Although initially described as a 'home' for the QTC it took strenuous lobbying by that company before any consultation process was established. Its preferred model was a 600-seat auditorium. This didn't please the Centre management which wanted 1200 seats for commercial shows. Without reference to either party, the then Minister for the Arts decided on a 850-seat house, pleasing nobody.

3 An interesting attempt to change this has come from the establishment of Industry Advisory Boards in different states, which conceive of theatre in technical education terms and have tried to control the numbers of courses on offer, and the number of students enrolled. At present their direct influence extends only to the Technical and Further Education (TAFE) sector of Australian tertiary education, but they have been very destructive of the variety of courses on offer in that sector: see Hunter & Fotheringham (1993), 3.2.2. Their threats to 'take over' tertiary drama education in general have so far been unsuccessful.

4 An example is the Zen Zen Zo physical theatre troupe, which receives no federal or state funding but survives on festival grants, and has been assisted in establishing itself organisationally and administratively by the Queensland Performing Arts Trust management.

5 This has occurred particularly where the redevelopment by non-government or semi-government organisations of the sites of existing theatres, such as Sydney's Theatre Royal or Brisbane's Albert Hall, has been allowed only on condition that a replacement theatre be incorporated within or adjacent to the new structure.

6 See, for example, my own previous writing in this area, including the 'Introduction' to Fotheringham (1987), 11-29; (1992), pp. 66-83; (1993), 45-66; (1997), pp.36-53.

7 I once rang the artistic director of a professional theatre company only to be told that the theatre had sprung a leak in a downpour and they were up on the roof fixing the drains. The difference between cheerful philanthropy and virtuous poverty is that the obstetrician painting the set at the amateur theatre will stop and rush to the hospital; the professional theatre worker fixing the drains will send a message saying they'll ring back later, and then forget.

Plays about the Vietnam War: the agon of the young

Elizabeth Perkins

Australian stage plays dealing directly or indirectly with the Vietnam conflict tend to focus on different issues to those treated in plays written in the United States. All American plays, according to Nora M. Alter, 'seek to assign responsibility and guilt' for the war, 'rarely confronting deeper levels of causation', and almost all are 'extremely hesitant about presenting the point of view of the Vietnamese and Vietcong "other'' (Alter 1996, xi). Responsibility and guilt are significant elements in Australian plays, but most examine responsibility and guilt as they affect individual private citizens, so that collectively they enact the personal *agon* experienced by men young enough for conscription. Beginning in 1966 with Alan Hopgood's *Private Yuk Objects*, a number of Australian plays do attempt to represent the Vietnamese and Vietcong 'other.' Where Alter (113) suggests that American plays represent the 'other' 'only at the moment of voyeuristically witnessing that 'other's death or mutilation', Australian plays attempt to imagine an 'other' with more dimensions. More than most political issues in Australia, the Vietnam issue was characterised by hypocrisy, misinformation, betrayal of personal standards and mistaken motives. A few docu-dramas and political farces from the period deal with the role of the Australian and American governments, but most plays centre on the conflict within individuals, especially the young.

The bitter contention surrounding the undeclared war and its aftermath at first seems unexpected considering the 46,000 Australian military who participated and the official number of 402 (some official sources give 494) killed or missing in action. American accounts of the war pay minimal attention to Australian involvement; Linda Reinberg's comprehensive glossary, *In the Field: The Language of the Vietnam War* (1991) includes no item or acronym related to Australia; and American accounts of stage plays centred on Vietnam, although they may mention European or Canadian scripts, omit Australian plays. Vietnam, however, had a profound effect on Australian society. The plays, the majority written after the conflict, show that the decade of Australia's involvement in Vietnam and her attempts to come to terms with it created a generation asking more mature questions about the motives and heroics of warfare. Underlining uncertainty about the justice of the American-led conflict was the introduction in 1965 of the birthday-ballot conscription of twenty-year-old men for National service in Vietnam, and the arrival of the first conscripts in Phuoc Thui within a year. Hopgood's *Private Yuk Objects* in 1966 was the first play to introduce this crucial issue, and subsequent plays reveal complex motives for objections to, and compliance with, the conscription ballot. Penelope Curtis's *A Time to Kill* (1969) is one of the few extant plays depicting the honourable motivation that took many men and women to Vietnam.

This encounter with the so-called Orient disoriented both the military and the citizen at home. Robin Gerster indicates the travel metaphors of the Vietnam engagement, and the imperialism implicit even in metaphors like 'tour of duty': 'Vietnam remains the crucial destination in the cultural destination of an entire generation. Hanoi, Da Nang, Hue, Nui Dat, Saigon — these are the talismanic names of the 1960s, carved on the collective memory' (Gerster 1992, 223). But in Australian stage drama the impact of Vietnam is more than a shared cultural experience and can in no sense be dismissed as a bad trip. The Vietnam experience began for most young men and their families before the soldiers reached Vietnam, and in many plays it becomes an interior journey where frustration and moral complexities find no resolution or absolution. Even a play as late as Louis Nowra's *Così* (1994b), first produced in 1992 but set in 1971, struggles to weigh the anti-Vietnam demonstrations of the student protestors, Nick and Lucy, against the private project of the graduate Lewis who directs a version of Mozart's opera as therapy for patients in a mental institution. Several theatre projects on Vietnam have been undertaken specifically to raise awareness of the problems facing veterans and Vietnam migrants. The Darwin Theatre Group's *Dust Off Vietnam* (1988), four short pieces written in collaboration with Vietnam veterans and Vietnamese refugees, was an attempt to reach some kind of reconciliation and catharsis for those who participated. *Hearts and Minds*, written and directed by Peter Copeman at Theatre South (Wollongong) in 1982, was a bilingual play using Australian, Vietnamese and other Asian actors with Vietnamese water puppets. 'To win the hearts and minds' of the people through pacification programmes was the official mission of the American presence in Vietnam. Danny, the son of the veteran Skip, falls in love with Mai, daughter of Phuong, a Vietnamese refugee, and near-tragedy follows. Copeman's research with the Vietnamese community and the Vietnam Veterans' Counselling Service revealed 'the similarity of emotional legacy for both the refugees and the veterans' (Copeman 1994,

170), and he made this the point of contact and sympathy between the groups.

From 1962 when the first twenty-nine members of the Australian Army Training Team Vietnam arrived in Saigon, until the withdrawal of the last servicemen in December 1972, the Australian operations, apart from the work of the Training Team, were centred on the province of Phuoc Thui to the south-east of Saigon. Phuoc Thui was heavily occupied by Viet Cong (communist) guerrillas, and for five years Australians were almost wholly engaged in fighting guerrilla forces supported for varied reasons by the inhabitants of the province who were indistinguishable in appearance from the 'enemy.' The plays dealing with Vietnam thus pose problems of survival and ethical warfare different from those of drawn battlelines. One perspective available to the individual soldier is presented in Rosemary John's *Luck of the Draw* (1985) by the veteran John:

> What did we get when we came home? We got spat on. We got blamed for killing those cunts, but we didn't know who the enemy were. Those bastards didn't put on uniforms like us [...] If they're not V.C. today, they will be tomorrow, so why not kill them all, wipe their silly fucking smiles off their faces for ever. (John 1986, 28)

John's brother-in-law Richard, also a veteran, in retrospect sees it differently:

> Why do you hate them so much? How do you think they feel about us? Did you ever ask that? No, you'd never bother. They'd be better off if we'd never gone in there. Did the VC do any more damage than we did? We used the herbicides, defoliated, burned, bombed the place off the map — (John 1986, 18)

The political and social context of Australian involvement is dramatised by its effect on individuals. There were the suspected 'imperialist' motives of the American intervention, which began, as Hibberd's *Commitment* recalls, with America's assisting the North Vietnamese communist leader Ho Chi Minh to regain Vietnam after the defeat of the French at Dien Bien Phu in 1954. By the early sixties America began a massive attempt to control the spread of communist influence south of the agreed boundary of the 17th parallel and supported the non-democratic republican government in South Vietnam. Many Australians doubted the motives of their government which at the time feared primarily the communist power in Indonesia and, by supporting America's effort in Vietnam, hoped to secure its support if a conflict arose with Indonesia.

This is succinctly evoked in Mike Giles's *Rest and Recreation* (1973) when Jack and Dave, Americans on leave in Kuala Lumpur, meet up with Ben, an Australian economic adviser in Malaysia:

> JACK: Well, ... it's good to bump into you like this. Chance to talk with an Australian. Your boys are appreciated up there, you know.
>
> BEN: (*briskly*) Have to do our bit. Insurance policy, we reckon.
>
> JACK: Yeah ... I guess so. Though Dave and me, we don't aim to be any kind of premium. (Giles 1983, 47)

The plays also present characters still traumatised by Cold War anti-communist ideology, and others for whom fear of communism was a greater threat to democracy than communism itself. The specific ethical problems posed by foreign participation in guerrilla warfare are shown in several plays, like John's *Luck of the Draw*, which suggest that most soldiers could not understand the kind of warfare in which they risked their lives and came to regard the whole Vietnamese population as their enemy. This belated understanding of the conflict in which they were engaged questioned the hope nurtured by some, like the Soldier in Curtis's *A Time to Kill*, that if they could not obey the commandment 'You shall not kill', they were at least helping to prevent the slaughter perpetrated by the Viet Cong and obeying another commandment 'You shall not let be killed —' (Curtis 1969, 20). As the war dragged on there were reservations about the use of napalm and defoliants, and fear that the low morale and drug dependency of some of the American troops would infect the Australian army. *Luck of the Draw* and Rob George's *Sandy Lee Live at Nui Dat* include Australians cynically pursuing illegal commerce in Vietnam, and these, without exonerating the dealers, tend to be associated with American interests. Helen Gilbert's analysis of *Sandy Lee* and Barry Lowe's 1989 play *Tokyo Rose*, 'a refracted and displaced Vietnam narrative' set during World War 2 (Gilbert 1997), demonstrates the ambivalences of Australian and American relationships which Vietnam brought to crisis.

One of the most shameful aspects of Australian involvement criticised sharply in several plays was the treatment of the returned men. Public opinion began to strengthen against the war after the Tet offensives in January 1968 proved the extent of Vietnamese support for the Viet Cong, and as media reports on specific incidents of the war, including the My Lai massacre in March 1968, became more frequent. When phased withdrawal of Australian troops began in 1971 the returning servicemen were seen as an embarrassment even by the 'government who had sent them, and National Service conscripts were demobbed and shuffled back into civilian life sometimes within a day of arriving in Australia.

Plays engaging with one or more of these issues fall roughly into four groups. The first includes plays which treat Australian involvement in Vietnam allegorically, as a symbol of military invasion and destruction and of power operating for its own preservation; like Alan Seymour's *The Gaiety of Nations* (1965), the first anti-Vietnam play staged in London; and Thomas Keneally's *Childermas* (1968). Some, like Leonard Radic's *The General* (1965) and *Sideshow* (1971), deal with war generally, or with earlier wars, or are shadowed by the possibility of a third world war, but would probably not have been written without the impetus of Vietnam. Even the dramatic form of John Romeril's *Chicago, Chicago* (1969, revised 1970) surveying the American context of the 1968 Democratic convention in Chicago significant for its eventual effect on Australia's participation in Vietnam, evokes the uncertainty and confusion of the Vietnam era.

In the second group, plays make direct references to Vietnam and its effect on the lives of characters, including boys too young for conscription. In John Summons's *Lamb of God* (1978), Harry Reade's *The Naked Gun* (1981), Stephen Sewell's *The Blind Giant is Dancing* (1983), Michael Gow's *Away* (1986), Louis Nowra's *Così* (1994b), and Nick Enright's *St James' Infirmary* (1992), Vietnam is a presence or a point of reference. Relevant themes include political duress, family pressure (usually but not always patriarchal), the confused motivation of supporters and opponents of the war, grief at family members lost in a doubtful conflict, and the sanction of violence implied by the war.

The third type of play centres on the experience of Australian servicemen in Vietnam; whether as a serviceman in the field with scenes set in Vietnam, or as a civilian at home including flashbacks and vivid evocations of Vietnam conditions. Beginning with Alan Hopgood's *Private Yuk Objects* (1966), they include David Williamson's *Jugglers Three* (1972, rewritten as *Third World Blues* 1997); Rob George's *Sandy Lee Live at Nui Dat* (1981) and Rosemary John's *Luck of the Draw* (1985).

Political satires, farces and quasi-documentaries (including street theatre) critical of war and the real and ostensible motives of American and Australian involvement comprise the fourth type of play, and were not always published. The scripts of many performed plays and revues are now lost, as is Alan Seymour's *The Gaiety of Nations*, one of the first Australian plays on the subject performed in 1965. On the same theme, but also unpublished, is *Pearls Before Swine* (1988), a satirical survey of the 1960s by Dennis Watkins and Chris Harriott. Published pieces include Jack Hibberd's short farce *Asian Oranges* (1983) which uses ridicule to critique the diplomatic missions of Henry Kissinger and the use of the defoliant Agent Orange in Vietnam (Hibberd 1984a). Hibberd's 1968 documentary piece *Commitment* (1984b), 'a play for teachers and students', juxtaposes the actual words of the North Vietnamese leader Ho Chi Minh, the American presidents Johnson and Nixon and the Australian Prime Minister Menzies, with a semi-farcical display of the responses of a group of sixties ockers one of whom is called up for National Service in Vietnam.

This survey chapter shows that many obvious critiques are available for analysing the plays at greater depth: American and Australian imperialism and the patriarchal ethos informing it; the Australian 'Orientialist' perspective on Vietnam; Australian feminisation and 'othering' of the Vietnamese people with its implications of misogyny (and desire) and racism; the persistence and the questioning of the mateship myth; the reinforcement and devaluing of martial heroism; critiques of aggression and violence; and the nexus between war, violence, sex and sado-eroticism. These issues arise as individual characters attempt to make sense of the situations into which they are forced, and to understand their own responses.

Keneally's *Childermas* (1968) is set in an allegorical landscape against which several Christian myths are interwoven as a metaphor for what the play sees as the essential nature of that Vietnam engagement which is not mentioned overtly. Commissioned by the Australian Committee of Responsibility for Children of Vietnam, *Childermas* centres on the 'Search and Destroy' missions characteristic of the anti-guerrilla strategies in Vietnam, which would be the mission entrusted by Herod to the play's three wise men had they not been warned in a dream. The search for the seventy-fifth holy child or 'lama' represents the search for peace (that is, peaceful democracy) which was the ostensible motive for western intervention in Vietnam. The Herod story is rendered in its basic terms: the attempt of one power to destroy another that it sees as a rising threat. The set represents a desolate charred landscape haunted by the off-stage voices of wandering bands of children. The play questions the righteousness of the three wise men figures; Colonel Salamander, Major Oldfield and Lieutenant Young, knights of the Regiment of Noble Artists and Genial Thinkers, who represent levels of experience and survival under fire and an inheritance of bourgeois humanism. The action emphasises the role of Young, the present generation, whose innocence is lost and ideals corrupted by participation in killing, but Young is also the bearer of a faint hope of a better future. As their personal unfitness for a holy mission is revealed under interrogation by the Herod figure, the Chaplain-General (who is also the Comptroller-General of the Criminally Insane), the play questions the fitness of individuals or nations who set out on some Holy Grail mission to save the world for their preferred ideology. After exposing the weakness and shameful secrets of the three men, Herod, the chief mentor figure in the play, offers a mocking, hypocritical absolution which leaves them no alternative but compliance. When Herod's '49 millimetre mortars' kill the seventy-fifth and last holy child, and a blood-red conflagration silences the singing children, the 'quavering voice of one child' in the final darkness leaves a faint hope that the epoch of peace has not been utterly destroyed. The nexus between possession of armaments and promotion of a crusade is asserted by Herod in one of the play's many allusions to the context and the strategies of the Vietnam war: 'You can't always kill an epoch with high explosives, but when one has such facilities at hand, the temptation is to try' (75). The poem written by Judith Wright for the singing children ends with the lines 'No year will forgive you/ That innocence dies.' As other plays reiterate in many different ways, a certain innocence was lost to Australia in the Vietnam experience.

Alan Hopgood's *Private Yuk Objects*, like *Childermas* still unpublished, is one of the most significant plays concerned with this loss of innocence. 'Yuk', says Hopgood, means 'years of undisturbed kipping' and alludes directly to years of complacency on the part of ordinary people about their responsibilities as Australian and world citizens. The first scenes are set in March 1966, the year in which the play was produced. Hopgood (1995) called the play 'A comment on Vietnam' and felt that it could only be revived 'as an historical piece to remind us that in March 1966 people marched in the streets to protest but by November they were ready to vote the Government back in with a record majority. The play got lost somewhere between these huge swings of public opinion.' *Private Yuk Objects* moves from the Yuks' farm on the top of the Baw Baws to the middle-class Melbourne home of the MLA Henry McKay and to the Vietnamese jungle. Hoth Yuk sets off for Melbourne with his draft letter and the off-hand encouragement of his war hero father: 'You just go and do your job ... and nip back here in time for the next crotching' (Hopgood 1966, 2). Pastoral comedy changes to the realism of Melbourne anti-Vietnam demonstrations and to the McKay home, where Yuk has been sent by his father who saved

McKay's life on the Kokoda trail. Captain Peter McKay is serving in Vietnam but his younger brother Tony, who has also been called up, and his sister Jeannie support the demonstrations. The family arguments lay bare all the main issues of Australia's involvement in Vietnam and conscription, and the crux of the situation for many mothers is voiced by Phyllis:

> Look! I have one son fighting in Vietnam, and the other fighting in Swanston Street. And I haven't a clue which one is right. And I'm not going to take sides until I find out! (9)

Tony's and Jeannie's rejection of paternal authority is shown as partly responsible for their opposition to the war, just as Peter's and Hoth's willing enlistment is partly due to unquestioning acceptance of their fathers' digger tradition. Hoth Yuk, who is sharper than his semi-illiterate state suggests, is led by Jeannie's arguments and his admiration for her to re-evaluate the Vietnam situation, and after learning of the laws under which former war leaders were condemned at Nuremburg, he decides that 'I ought to be allowed to say . . . my conscience tells me not to obey the orders I been given to go to Vietnam. So . . . I *object*!' (53). But like Tony, who eventually yields to his father's arguments, Hoth is persuaded to go off 'as happy as Larry' when Daddy Yuk marches into Melbourne to reason with his son.

Meanwhile in Vietnam Peter is captured by the Sydney-educated Vo Lai who attends to his wounds and keeps him alive in the hope of hearing why Australia, which Vo Lai considers 'a wonderful country' which appreciates 'the position of the underdog in most things' and should therefore understand the position of the guerrillas, has entered the war: 'I could not share the common opinion that Australia had simply obeyed the command of the United States' (27). Peter, defiant and sceptical, avoids Vo Lai's attempts to discuss the issues in Vietnam from any point of view other than the one he is convinced he already 'knows.' He deflects Vo Lai's thoughtful arguments with crude flippancy, and when the woman guerrilla Chi tries to get him to respond more seriously, he insults her with a tirade of coarse insinuations. Peter's monologue reveals his shallow thinking and basic racism:

> They used to tell us ... trouble with going to Vietnam is, after a while they stop looking like Asians and start looking like women. But, whatever ya do ... don't marry 'em. Don't forget what they'd look like walking down Collins Street. (49)

Chi, revealing that she understood everything Peter has said, sums him up: 'He is very intelligent. But I think he is becoming confused.' Peter's confusion and frustration at the kind of war he is fighting, and his anger at the death of his mates by home-made Viet Cong weapons, only complicate the uncertainty that underlay his decision to fight in Vietnam. Tony, ironically, is rejected by the army on medical grounds, but Hoth with Tony's friend and formerly committed demonstrator Skite, meet up with Peter in Vietnam after their patrol has killed Vo Lai and Chi. 'What did ya have to do that for?' asks Peter, and to Hoth's question 'Hey, did you know them?' Peter answers: 'Yeah ... in a funny sort of way. Yeah ... I knew 'em' (59).

The play ends here, with complete lack of resolution or satisfaction for supporters and opponents of the Vietnam involvement. Phyllis warns Hoth that her daughter's opposition to the war 'looks very much like rebellion for rebellion's sake' (53), but her father admits he cannot answer Jeannie's question 'Can anyone prove to me, that we don't use one set of rules for ourselves, and a different set for other countries?' (54). He justifies the necessity of obeying the orders of one's government by refuting as irresponsible (because it would lead to anarchy) the legal argument of Nuremburg; that individuals should follow their conscience. The parents win, not because their arguments are the right ones but because there do not seem to be any better ones. As Daddy Yuk later tells his cloud-covered God: 'None of them in that big house was really wrong. But at the same time, none of 'em was really right.' Yuk's pastoral Christianity, not any call to military glory or patriotic duty, finally persuades Hoth:

> Well, I told him. Forget about the medal. Forget about God and the mountain ... if you want to [...] it looks like you gotta play it according to their rules now, to have any chance to change the rules tomorrow or the next day. (57)

Yuk's honest temporising and Old Testament concept of Christianity are the play's way of explaining the result of the November elections in 1966. A hard and tragic response to the Yuk position is given at the end by Peter (played by Hopgood himself in the first production): 'My God, what did ya have to [...] Why ... why [...] Yeah ... I knew 'em.'

The effect of Vietnam on men even younger than Hoth and Tony is shown in two plays, one set in a Catholic working-class family, and the other in a Catholic upper middle-class school. John Summons's *Lamb of God* (1978) centres on the difficulties faced by Jim, a sensitive fifteen-year-old growing up in a patriarchal masculinist society. The time is 1968 and the Vietnam war and the ethos that conscripted young men are explicitly presented. In a fantasy scene at the end of the play Jim answers an Authoritarian Voice which draws from him a catechism that is masculinist, militaristic and nihilistic:

> I fear love, gentleness, sex and life. I cannot love because I cannot be vulnerable. I cannot be gentle because that is unmanly [...] My anger has grown homicidal and is ready for your use. I have learnt to turn my anger against those you call my enemy because I must obey and win your approval to fill my emptiness. You have made me feel worthless and given me a uniform to make me feel important. You have made me feel powerless and given me a gun to make me feel strong. I will work in your service and like a sheep follow the leader to the slaughter. (Summons 1979, 93)

Jim is witty and imaginative and his friend Mick is a 'typical' boy, who shoots his pigeons on the pretext that '[t]hey were costing too much to feed' (9). He intends to join the army and acts out the killing of a Viet Cong as told by his veteran cousin. Both boys are in the cadets, and Mick already shows unhealthy enthusiasm for mock-killing. Jim's father Jack, a New Guinea veteran and semi-invalid, spends much of his time at the RSL club, but tells his wife: 'I hope to Christ this Vietnam thing's over before Jim's old enough. I didn't bring up a son to be killed in a bloody war' (27).

The masculinist brutality of the education system itself is pointed up in the recollections of both boys of punishments experienced now and at Catholic primary school, the prototype of tortures they dream up in military situations. Act Two opens with the boys playing a Vietnam interrogation scene with Jim as the Viet Cong prisoner. In the background a speaker on radio condemns Australia's continued involvement in Vietnam and expresses doubt that allegations of Australian troops practising torture can 'be brushed aside lightly, for the actions of our soldiers reflect on us all. Our soldiers are what we have made them' (63). The authoritarian Church teaching and school regime are challenged by Jim in his friendship with the young teacher, Brother John, who has been influenced by the more liberal edicts of Vatican II. But this is soon interpreted by the other boys as a 'poofter' relationship. They beat Jim up, and Brother John is declared ill and sent away; another victim of a refusal to conform to the patriarchal regime.

Lamb of God deals with other aspects of Jim's family, but everything in the play points to the entrapment of ordinary people in a series of patriarchal and authoritarian systems. Jim escapes through fantasy and tall stories, many of them witty and accepted as routine by his patient mother Ruth, but his suppressed anger is great and he tells her 'I must be a psychopath underneath. That's someone who likes to kill' (84). When possible service in Vietnam looms Ruth's refusal to face the ugly reality of war, which her son confronts openly, is characterised by her consoling suggestion: 'You mightn't have to kill. Not every soldier kills, you know. Anyway, if you get conscripted you could shoot your gun into a bush or something' (84). *Lamb of God* exposes the social pressures, often posing as moral issues, which operated on young people in the late sixties, and perhaps it could only have been written some years later when distance allowed young men to see themselves as scapegoats, or as lambs led to slaughter. At the time the Vietnam issue was complicated for them by patriarchal and masculinist pressures which lacked a name and specific identity, and which have since been identified as social forces integral to the imperialist project which involved the United States and Australia in the Vietnam conflict.

In Nick Enright's *St James' Infirmary*, set in 1967, the student artist Dominic Connolly, a boarder at the Jesuit St James College, faces much the same problems as Jim. Like Jack in *Lamb of God*, Dominic's father has been hospitalised for war trauma and finally shot his wife and himself. Father D'Arcy, the art teacher who wants to preserve and encourage Dominic's undoubted talent, urges the eighteen-year-old to compromise the anti-Vietnam principles he acquired during a vacation school so that he can win a travelling scholarship available within the closed militaristic world of the College. Opposing both D'Arcy and Dominic is the young school matron Jenny Walsh, whose husband, a former student at the school and recipient of the scholarship, has recently been killed while serving as a doctor in Vietnam, where she also served. Dominic becomes Jenny's patient when he falls from a ladder while painting anti-war scenes on the walls of the school drill-hall where a passing-out parade is to be held. Dominic's anti-Vietnam stance includes a hatred of the war-induced violence that led his father to kill his mother, and his painting of the blood-stained Vietnamese woman and child is also an image of his mother. Finally he rejects all his mentors, including his artistic friend Tim, his militaristic friend Bowker, Father D'Arcy, Jenny and St James, and escapes across the river that isolates the college from the mainland, burning his dinghy behind him.

In a short piece first performed in 1966, the present writer attempted to represent the confusion and desperate search for guidance observed in my students. *A Squeaking of Rats* shows Andrew, a young man escaping from conscription in an unofficial shelter managed by two voluntary social workers, the ex-digger Carew and a Czechoslovakian nurse, Libby. The middle-class Andrew is not treated sympathetically by the play, and when a destitute Aboriginal girl is brought in and he feels that the tone of his private refuge has dropped, he returns home with some acquired courage to face his mother. In the sixties, opposition to Vietnam did not always include a similar opposition to racism. However Andrew reveals to Cathy, another refugee, the genuine and deep-seated dismay of many young men faced by parental attitudes. He admits that he is afraid of killing others and of being maimed or killed himself, but what he cannot understand and fears most is the attitude of his mother who lost a brother in 1943 and who was 'thrilled' when Andrew was called up: 'God, you should hear her. She wants *me* to go out and be a hero. Dead or alive it doesn't matter much. I *am* afraid. I'm afraid of living at home' (Perkins 1970, 107). The ambivalent title refers to the young peoples' gnawing anxieties and to Carew, a former Rat of Tobruk, whose coolly anti-war stance questions Andrew's contemptuous enactment of a typical Anzac Day school address. *A Squeaking of Rats* represents the confusion of the young and their desperate attempt to escape responsibility, but also a willingness to accept it once they know where their responsibility lies. As Cathy says: 'It's a relief not to be able to blame someone else. There's somewhere to start from if you *know* you're responsible.' Andrew and Cathy are looking for answers that seem to be more than 'Opinions' (109).

Jim, Dominic and Andrew, like Hopgood's Tony, are young men whose natural aggressive instincts are displayed when a situation which they recognise as 'appropriate' arises. Nevertheless their anti-war slogans and whatever pacificism they profess are not hypocritical; nor do the plays criticise the confusion of their opposition to American imperialism, government duress, or church and parental authority. Instinctively they, and all the other conscripts in these plays, know what Tony articulates: 'you only have to conscript, when you can't get enough volunteers. And if this were a just war, there'd be any number of volunteers' (Hopgood 11). Some plays, like Nowra's *Così* (1994b), question the personal credibility of protestors, and in George's *Sandy Lee Live at Nui Dat* the professional student Peter sees Vietnam politics as a game, but another student protester, Pat, is shown as absolutely sincere in her stance. Most plays indicate that protestors' confused and sometimes dubious motives are mainly due to the moral chaos of the social and political situation. The responses of conscripts who did not protest are also confused. In his 1968 play *Commitment* Hibberd's ocker draftee Len, ironically the only one of his mates with a steady job, drowns his feelings about Vietnam in beer, sex and bravado. After claiming that he is not depressed about Vietnam, actually looking forward to it, he admits Vietnam is 'a civil war. A kind of war of independence. It's none of our business. Or the Yanks. Napalm. Kids and old ducks ending up like rissoles' (Hibberd 1984b, 144). He finally collapses in Cheryl's arms: 'I'm scared shitless' (150).

Williamson rewrote *Jugglers Three* in 1997 under one of its earlier discarded titles, *Third World Blues*, in an attempt 'to be more balanced and honest in the characterisation' and after consulting with the Vietnam Veterans' Counselling Service so that the play could reproduce more accurately the conditions of the war and its effects on young soldiers (Williamson 1997, ix). The play, an interesting study of male mateship and heterosexual relationships, centres on five middle-class ockers, one of whom, Graham, served as a conscript in Vietnam, giving Neville opportunity to take over his wife Keren and her apartment. His more proletarian Vietnam mate Dennis also loses his wife and child to another man. Graham exaggerates his stories about Canungra training-camp and his service in Vietnam during which he initially claims to have shot an American colonel in the back, describing the man's death throes in graphic detail. The stories represent Graham's response to the war, which includes self-disgust at his own crude aggression, but in the 1997 version the context of his emotions is spelt out more carefully. He confronts Neville who proudly carried a North Vietnamese flag in a protest march: 'Ever been ambushed in a jungle Neville? Ever seen an arm cartwheeling through the air towards you — all bloody and shattered? It gets really exciting when your little commie pals are detaching the odd limb or two around you [...] Little fucking yellow slant eyed bastards [...] You learn interesting things about yourself in situations like that. You learn that you can become just as full of hate as the most stupid prejudiced mindless prick in your battalion' (Williamson 1997, 15).

Dennis, distressed by his homecoming 'twenty-four hours back from hell' (14) abducts his baby daughter and farcically robs a service station, but avoids arrest when Graham and the yuppie lawyer Jamie give the arresting officer a share of the loot. Describing violence, threatening Neville with his bayonet and reminding him that 'I've been trained at Canungra,' Graham is a comic parody of the uglier version of the veteran represented by the drug dealer Karl in Harry Reade's *The Naked Gun*, for whom Vietnam was 'one genuine, rock and roll, video-taped, gumchewing, cocksucking conflict,' and who boasts that he was photographed urinating into the mouth of a Viet Cong whom he had just killed (Reade 1982, 22). Ugly characters exploiting the war and their less experienced 'mates' include the conscript Gordon Clarke in George's *Sandy Lee Live at Nui Dat* and the black marketeer Dancer in John's

Luck of the Draw. Gordon sells drugs for the Americans and continues his trade back home after the war and Dancer, a civilian driving petrol tankers for the Americans, profits from the black market goods imported on American ships. He boasts 'indirectly, I killed off quite a few nogs myself' by selling ersatz penicillin to North Vietnamese hospitals (John 1986, 23).

Sandy Lee Live at Nui Dat, like the later comedy musical *Pearls Before Swine*, also satirises the exploitation by entertainers touring the Vietnam 'circuit' as an audition or preliminary try-out for their shows, or to boost a flagging career. The sensitive and naive Bruce, whose Vietnamese girl Lai Dai was killed just after her immigration papers arrived, tries to interest the Country and Western singer Sandy Lee in his own songs. It is possible that Sandy has appropriated one of his lyrics, but in Melbourne she dismisses his attempts to work with her: 'I'm not an employment agency' (George 1983, 57). Bruce, exploited by Gordon in Vietnam and at home, finally kills the drug-dealing veteran and then turns his gun on himself.

Plays that sympathetically represent Vietnamese voices include Hopgood's *Private Yuk Objects*, Darwin Theatre Group's *Dust Off Vietnam*, Nowra's *Sunrise* and Copeman's *Hearts and Minds*. The angry grief at the effect of the communist government on his country expressed by Nowra's south Vietnamese refugee gardener, Ly, is contextualised by the passing of fire-fighting helicopters overhead. Ly, courted by both the housekeeper Peggy and the cancer specialist David, fares better than Khan in *Luck of the Draw* who also sings a lament for the fate of his homeland. *Luck of the Draw* ends when Richard tries to stop the crazed veteran John threatening Khan with a gun and is accidentally killed. At the final blackout John is about to shoot Khan, urged on by Dancer as a cover-up for Richard's death. 'He's the enemy,' says Dancer, 'He's not in his jungle, he's in yours. You don't have any choice.' As the stage darkens, John says 'It's just like before . . . you didn't have any choice there either' (John 1986, 48).

War seldom offers easy choices to citizens. The undeclared Vietnam war offered hard choices to the young represented in these plays, but Australian society offered few principles based on reliable facts, no standards of personal conduct, and no arguments with integrity to guide their choice. Enright's Father D'Arcy tells Dominic 'The subversive thing, the truly subversive thing, would be to make use of the system in order to challenge it,' but Matron Walsh counsels 'I think you either live within a system, believing in it, or you take yourself out of it' (Enright 1993, 47, 48). Neither mentor tries to weigh up the issues involved in the Vietnam conflict, leaving Dominic to express his frustration in slick graffiti on the art-room wall: 'Old soldiers never die. Not while they've got young ones to do it for them' (10). Crossing the river that separates the college from the outside world and burning his dinghy is a more effective action, but it does not answer the Vietnam question for Dominic, nor for the other young men in these plays.

Dis/orientations: contemporary Asian-Australian theatre

Jacqueline Lo

'Asian culture and values will, in a very short time I believe, begin to work their impact on mainstream Australian culture.' (Paul Keating, 15 February, 1995)

By the eighties, Australians were increasingly encouraged to view themselves as part of Asia rather than identifying with their European heritage; that is, to privilege geography over history. This gradual shift in perspective is related, amongst other factors, to the republican movement, multiculturalism and the realisation that the success of our economic future is tied to the economies in Asia. Today, the phrase 'Australia in Asia' has become almost a cliché. While most of the 'Asia' rhetoric has been dominated by diplomatic and economic considerations, there has been a significant flow-on effect into the arts in general. Examples of this so-called 'Asianisation' of Australian arts include the Brisbane Asia-Pacific Triennial of Contemporary Art, the 1994 Asia-focused Adelaide Festival, the annual Asia-Pacific Film Festival in Sydney, and the Asian theatre festivals organised by Playbox in Melbourne and Belvoir Street in Sydney.

Artistic trade in the region has also proven to be increasingly lucrative with organisations such as Asialink, Export Oz and the Australia Council's Visual Arts Export Strategy working to tap into the Asian market. According to Nicholas Jose, 'because so much Australian theatre is text-based English it doesn't really work in Asia... But music, dance and the visual arts are particularly well received. The visual arts are both able to cross the cultural gap and explore joint possibilities, [and] so are one of the greatest growth areas of Asian-Australian exchange' (McCulloch 1996, 1). Language and cultural difficulties notwithstanding, Australian performers, playwrights and directors have received a greater degree of support to engage with Asia than ever before. From the early to mid-nineties the Performing Arts Board of the Australia Council devoted up to half of its international arts funding budget to the Asia-Pacific region. Cross-cultural exchange was encouraged by enabling Australia to host Asian artists, and Australian arts practitioners to develop non-Western performance skills in Asia. Both forms of exchange still figure prominently in current performing arts practice even though policy imperatives have altered slightly with the 1996 change in the federal government. Examples of Asian-

Australian cross-cultural performances range widely in form and cultural influences from Tadashi Suzuki's direction of *The Chronicles of Macbeth* (1992), Sally Sussman's *Orientalia* (1995), and Zen Zen Zo's *The Cult of Dionysus* (1996), to the collaboration between the Canberra Youth Theatre, the Canberra Youth Wind Ensemble and the Song Ngoc Water Puppetry Troupe from Vietnam in *Water Stories* (1997).

Interest in Asia has also begun to permeate the mainstages of Australian theatre. Playbox has been a pioneer in conducting intercultural exchange programs with major Asian countries since the late seventies and has a history of producing performances with Asian influences. The company has stepped up its Asia profile in recent times, running the Asian-Australian theatre festival since 1991 and in 1995 initiating the annual playwriting competition with an Asian-Australian focus in association with Asialink. Belvoir Street Theatre's annual Asian Theatre Festival started in 1993 as part of the Celebration of Australian-Asian Artists Festival. The company, in partnership with the New South Wales Carnivale, launched its inaugural Asian-Australian Young Playwrights Award in 1996. It is also planning to run regular writing laboratories to develop Asian-Australian theatre. Smaller companies such as Entr'acte have been experimenting with Japanese and Indonesian performance traditions since the early nineties while an increasing number of plays dealing with various aspects of Australian-Asian relations have emerged on the mainstages of Australian theatre. These include Jill Shearer's *Shimada* (1987), Michael Gurr's *Sex Diary of an Infidel* (1992), Peter Copeman's *Hearts and Minds* (1992) and *Sinakulo* (1995), Anna Broinowski's *The Gap* (1993), Noëlle Janaczewska's *The History of Water* (1992) and *Madagascar Lily* (1997), Hilary Bell's *Fortune* (1993), Deborah Pollard's *Mother Tongue Interference* (1995) and Julie Janson's *Lotus War* (1995).[1] That Asia is a 'fashionable' topic is beyond dispute, and yet all too frequently 'Asia' is presented in public and artistic discourses as a politically and historically neutral concept. In this essay I would like to briefly dwell on how 'Asia' as a discursive formation has been made meaningful in the public domain before moving on to an examination of responses to this phenomenon by Asian-Australian performance practitioners.[2]

One of the most commonplace assumptions made about Asia is that Australia's future lies in 'enmeshment' with the region. The use of the term 'enmeshment' usually refers to economic relations though diplomatic and security considerations are also important. To avoid giving our Asian neighbours the impression of a purely economically driven motive , the discourse of enmeshment has tended to stress the goodwill and cultural benefits deriving from a regional identity. The rhetoric of cultural engagement however functions at a relatively superficial level. Since the mid-eighties there has been a burst of domestic public discourse which paint a picture of an economically depressed Australia and the opportunities abounding in the expanding Asian economies. According to Stephen Frost, these public statements and reports such as Ross Garnaut's *Australia and the Northeast Ascendancy* (1989) underlie and inform Australia's push into Asia. 'They demonstrate the priority given to 'enmeshment' as legitimated by 'Australian economic crisis'. In doing so, a multiplicity of other kinds of 'enmeshments' forged through 'immigration, professional contacts, cultural exchanges, tourism both ways, non-government organisations activities [...] and sporting exchanges are ignored or marginalised in the process' (1994, 26). Frost goes on to argue that the privileging of economic enmeshment is legitimised by the notion of the nation in crisis with the maintenance of Australian living standards being dependant on closer relations with Asian nations. 'Perhaps what is occurring here is that "enmeshment", for all its fine sounding Asia rhetoric, is after all a version of "protecting our way of life". In other words, a new way of remaining the same' (1994, 27).

The general view appears to be that the greatest single impediment to our enmeshment with Asia lies in the lack of understanding of cultural difference. There have been a host of programs set up to 'orientate' Australians to Asian cultures ranging from boardroom behaviour to communication and social skills. Whilst these attempts to encourage 'Asia-literacy' are laudable, there is also the risk of rushing into a simplistic and opportunistic approach to cross-cultural relations. The idea of comprehending 'Asian values', for instance, not only implies that such a definitive object exists but also suggests a degree of homogeneity which overlooks the complexity and diversity of value systems operating within the region.[3] The economic imperative behind the Asia push also presents an interesting paradox which the following quote by Ross Garnaut exemplifies. 'I look forward to the day when economics appears less often on the front pages, and when the deeper seams of cultural and political values fuel Australia's Asia-Pacific journey. But we will not reach that point until the Australian economic base has been built anew' (Frost 1994, 32). In other words, cultural and political understanding is developed not just through cultural exchanges, immigration or geo-political relations, but more importantly through trade and economic ties. This view is similar to Robert Mackie's who claims that 'until we have much stronger commercial connections with our neighbours [...]

most Australians [will] see little point in learning Asian languages or coming to grips with Asian cultures when these have no meaning or relevance to them' (Frost 1994, 31). There appears to be a catch-22 situation: unless we learn to be more culturally aware of Asia, we will not succeed in Asia, but unless we work on trade links, cultural and political relations will be limited.

The symbiotic relation between trade and culture as presented by the prevailing Asia discourse has a significant impact on the production of knowledges about Australia's relation to its near North. In a recent collection of essays from the Australian-Asian Perceptions Project initiated by the Academy of Social Sciences in Australia, Anthony Milner is careful to disassociate the project from the traditional Orientalist methodology: 'Today, in explaining cultural difference, we are more concerned about learning to develop an effective way of operating in Asia' (Milner 1996, 9). Thus, knowledge of cultural differences is desirable because it enables one to maximise the gains to be made from engaging with Asia. In a similar vein, Jeremy Eccles in his review of the month-long Celebration of Australian Asian Artists in 1993 argued that he would have preferred 'if more of the performances offered this month actually came from Asia — surely the proper presentation of its cultures first hand is the only true path to understanding' (Eccles 1993, 6). Eccles' statement is revealing on two counts. Firstly it clings to an essentialist notion that 'authentic' Asian culture can only be experienced from its 'source', and that performances by local Asian-Australians are therefore only corrupted versions of the original. Secondly, artistic engagement with Asia is perceived to serve a higher objective beyond cultural exchange and the empowerment of local Asian-Australians: a statement implicitly dovetailing with the dominant discourse of economic enmeshment with Asia.

The dominance of this orthodoxy has also lead to a form of policing of alternative views on Asia. 'At a range of sites in Australia there exists a politics that cannot be articulated; one that is fully able to criticise the policies of neighbouring regimes while at the same time asserting that it is neither Orientalist or Eurocentric in doing so. *It may in fact be as (or more) sympathetic to enmeshment with Asian cultures*' (Frost 1994, 43, emphasis added). The uproar caused by the 1980s ABC television series *Embassy*, for instance, is one example of how the promoters of enmeshment with Asia have aligned themselves with the Asian ruling elite by claiming that the representations of Asia (more particularly, Malaysia) in the show were culturally insensitive and Orientalist.[4] While aspects of the show were offensive, particularly the casting of Greek and Italian actors to play 'Asians' and the stereotyping of Asian society, nonetheless *Embassy* dealt with issues such as racial inequalities and government repression which are not widely known in Australia. In the quest to placate the Mahathir government, the 'pro-Asia' orthodoxy has attempted to silence a form of cultural critique which articulates the concerns of many people in both Malaysia and Australia.

It must be stressed that the issue here is not that awareness of Asian cultural difference should be discouraged or that enmeshment with Asia is a 'bad' thing. Rather, it is the mode of communicating and conducting this orientation which requires further scrutiny. The attention to cultural sensitivity and difference may reinscribe alterity even as it seeks to dismantle Australia's past history of Orientalist prejudice.[5] According to Rey Chow, 'Because the image, in which the other is often cast, is always distrusted as illusion, deception, and falsehood, attempts to salvage the other often turn into attempts to uphold the other as the non-duped — the site of authenticity and true knowledge' (Chow 1993, 52). In other words, overcompensation may end up reifying and essentialising the apparent differences between Self/Other, Australia/Asia, and/or Western/Eastern. The concept of 'authenticity' as it has been mobilised in dominant discourses can also hamper critical and artistic engagement which may be more effective, in the long-term, in dismantling the colonialist premises that continue to haunt Australian-Asian relations. Trevor Hay argues against the pressures to conform to the pressures of political correctness. 'Being anxious about "Asian" culture, respecting it all the time, guarding its indigenous purity, and scrutinising the arts for paternalism, orientalism and ethnocentrism, can make people very insensitive. It robs them of the raw curiosity and imagination needed for sifting through stereotypes and finding odd traces of truth, or for simply looking at them afresh and finding inspiration' (Hay 1996, 12).

The overcompensation of observations to cultural sensitivity and the reification of Asian differences as promoted by the pro-Asia orthodoxy has meant that the emphasis in current arts programming privileges bilateral relations *with* Asia rather than a consideration of how local Asian-Australians may contribute to our Asia-literateness. As Sneja Gunew puts it, '[h]ere are Australians uniquely qualified to act as cultural mediators but the focus still appears to be concentrated on bringing European-Australian artists to residencies there in order to educate them into non-Western aesthetic sensibilities' (Gunew 1994, 8). The implicit premise operating in the current practice appears to be that artists from Asian-Australian backgrounds are unreliable sources of knowledge about

Asia because they are no longer 'authentic', that is, their culture has been miscegenated. Thus in order to truly understand Asia it is necessary to refer back to the 'origin'. Eccles' call for the 'proper presentation of [Asian] cultures first hand' is just one of the many examples of the prevailing discourse of 'authenticity' underlying current thinking about cross-cultural exchange.

It was not until the late seventies, after the demise of the White Australia policy and the gradual implementation of a policy of cultural diversity, when Asian-Australian[6] writers and performers emerged as a presence on the national stage. Up till then, roles for Asian actors were predominantly stereotypes (Fitzpatrick 1985) and there were no mainstage plays written by Asian-Australians. John Joo-For Lee's *The Propitious Kidnapping of the Cultured Daughter* was one of the first plays by an Asian to be staged in 1978 by Playbox. An interpretation of the Patty Hearst story in Chinese opera style, its mixture of Asian and Western elements confused many critics who responded with headlines such as 'A Chinese Puzzle' and 'Never the Twain Shall Meet' (Broinowski 1996, 213). Kai Tai Chan, who comes from Malaysia, founded the One Extra Company in Sydney in 1976. This multiracial dance company integrates Asian, Aboriginal and Western contemporary traditions in performances which deal with a range of social and cultural issues including domestic violence (*Family Portrait,* 1978), homosexuality (*Jacaranda Blue*, 1983), the migrant experience (*Ah Q Goes West*, 1984) and cultural identity (*People Like Us*, 1991). Chan explored Australia's colonial history in an adaptation of *Othello* in 1989 whilst *Two Wongs* in 1995 used mimicry and parody to foreground race as the boundary of the national imagination[7] by having the First Fleet originating in China and colonising an Australia composed of Aboriginal and European Australians. Malaysian-born Chandrabhanu founded the Bhatalaya School of Indian Classical Dance in 1980 and established the Bharatam Dance Company six years later. The Melbourne-based group's style reflect the ethnicity of its members — an amalgam of Chinese, Indian, South American and European performers. According to Chandrabhanu, 'a fundamental aim of the Company is to evolve a contemporary dance style which combines its original cultural roots with other Asian and Western influences, as a means of further nurturing the art form and contributing to the development of dances in Australia' (Anon 1991, 103). Both Chan and Chandrabhanu have shifted from an early emphasis on pure dance to dance-theatre employing a range of performance codes including verbal language and the use of multimedia.

Chan's work, in particular, could be described as 'hybrid art' — fusing text, image and movement in performance.

It is not surprising that the initial entry of Asian-Australian performance should occur in dance and non-text-based theatre, since facility with the English language, and the Anglo-Australian accent in particular, has been a marker of membership into the national imagining. Movement, as a signifying system, is more ambiguous and less specific than verbal language. It can facilitate some degree of cross-cultural communication which 'neither denies difference nor appropriates representation for the dominant culture' (Gilbert 1992a, 139). This is not to suggest that the communication is unproblematic however, since the physical body of the performer is always already racially marked as Other. It is not enough for Asian-Australian performers to be merely present on stage, consideration must also be given to what they do (both textually and contextually) to subvert the codes which cast the Asian body as either Orientalist fantasy and/or economic commodity. By the nineties, more Asian-Australian artists were developing work which demonstrate a greater confidence in using both movement and verbal language in a range of performance modes. The repertoire includes the dance theatres of Chin Kham Yoke (*Inflamed*, 1995) and Padma Menon (*Relations: Of Mothers, Aunts and Other Memories*, 1995), the poetic and abstract works of Ta Duy Binh (*The Return*, 1994), Sawung Jabo (*Time's Journey*, 1996) and Suneeta Da Costa (*Blood is Blue,* 1996), and realist texts by Teck Tan and David Zhu (*Black Eyes*, 1993), Nicholas Jose (*Dead City*, 1994) and Merlinda Bobis (*Ms Serena Serenata*, 1995).

Despite the range of forms and the diversity of thematic concerns represented in contemporary Asian-Australian theatre, the concept of 'hybridity' is characteristic of most of the work. According to Homi Bhabha, hybridity is the construction of a political object that is new, '*neither the One ... nor the Other ... but something else besides* which contests the terms and territories of both. This does not necessarily involve the formation of a new synthesis, but the negotiation between them *in medias res*, in the profound experience or knowledge of the displaced, diversionary, differentiated boundaries in which the limits and limitations of social power are encountered in an agonistic relation' (Bhabha 1988, 13). The remainder of this essay will focus on four recent Asian-Australian performances as paradigmatic examples of ways of intervening in the prevailing discourses of Asia. The emphasis on hybridity — either through the use of form or/and the construction of subjectivity — functions as critique of the economic imperative and essentialist assumptions underlying the enmeshment orthodoxy.

Contrary to popular applications of the term,[8] hybridity is different from 'fusion' which usually suggests an unproblematic synthesis. Rather, the hybridisation which results from cross-cultural contact/integration is characterised, as Bhabha points out, by an agonistic relation which has to be continually reconfigured. Asian-Australian hybrid theatre dislocates and deterritorialises assumptions concerning the homogeneity and fixity of either an Asian or an Australian identity. Rather, to paraphrase Trinh Min-ha, the challenge of the hyphenated reality lies in the hyphen itself: the *becoming* Asian-Australian; the realm in-between, where pre-determined rules cannot fully apply (Trinh 1991, 157).

The Cantata of the Warrior Woman Daragang Magayon by Filipino-born writer/performer Merlinda Bobis has been performed in various versions since 1992 in Australia, the Philippines and France. It is a reworking of a Filipino myth with all the familiar stereotypes — the Beautiful Maiden (Daragang Magayon), an evil warlord, and the heroic male lover. Bobis recasts the tale in an epic poem which she performs using elements of monologue, chanting, lyric poetry, dance and music. In the Philippine indigenous epic tradition, the female is usually represented as war booty and/or victim. In Bobis' feminist text, the Beautiful Maiden transforms into the Warrior Woman; Daragang Magayon rejects patriarchal control of her fate and recuperates agency by taking arms in defence of herself and her tribe. Paradox underlies the very heart of the text; the Warrior Woman fights against those who glorify war and conquest yet she damns the consequences of every bloody encounter, including her own forthcoming battle. Although the text is mythic in scope, the critique of war and violence also function as metonymic references to contemporary Filipino history. The *Cantata* was written in the period between 1991 and 1993 when the writer was still coming to terms with the Australian environment and her status as a 'migrant' and a 'Filipina'.[9] The hybrid nature of the text reflects the author's own process of cultural negotiation. As Bobis says, 'I [...] attempted to unname/rename my Self and my chosen literary form by breaking restrictive traditions. I refused to be 'fixed' under absolute definitions of gender and ethnic background' (Bobis 1994, 118).

The *Cantata* not only challenges the masculine epic tradition in Filipino culture, it also subverts conventional artistic boundaries. The epic poem defies categorisation — it contains elements of lyric, dramatic and epic forms.[10] Similarly, as a performance text the *Cantata* is an amalgam of performance poetry, story-telling, indigenous chanting, monologue, and contemporary and folk dance. It is a translation and transformation of elements from the writer's postcolonial background which includes Filipino, Spanish/Latino, American and Australian cultures. The hybrid counter-energies resulting from the process of dialogisation produces 'a radical heterogeneity, discontinuity, [and] the perpetual revolution of form' (Young 1995, 25). The female hero Daragang Magayon breaks with the iconic definitions of female subjecthood by rejecting the names given to her by patriarchy. As 'The Nameless One Who is All Names', Bobis claims for her hero a provisional and partial identity which has to be continually re-invented as the occasion demands.

> Woman. Hunter. Warrior.
> Names only of a moment
> as other words rang
> more possibilities. Lover.
> Mother. Earth. Bird. Fish. (1993, 71)

Like the poetic metaphors of multiple subjectivities which she chants into being, the shadow sequence in Act Two is a visual manifestation of this play of partial and provisional selves. Two full-length screens which form the backdrop are lit at different times from the back and the front to create the illusion of multiple body-forms as the performer weaves her way around them. The shadow-form behind the screen is both 'neutral' in its one-dimensionality and yet still marked by an Othered accent which weaves its mesmerising incantations in Filipino and English languages. At other times we see Bobis' body dancing with her Self-Same Other. Daragang Magayon as the performer's alter-ego perhaps, or another Self yet unrealised but in the process of becoming? By hybridising the body in performance, a body that is at once real and representational, the *Cantata* challenges the codes of race and gender which essentialise and fix the signifying waywardness of the Filipina-Australian as Other.

> The back of my hand
> curves on my palm:
> one dance, one life. (1993, 17)

For Bobis, the co-existence of the back of the hand and the palm represents the combination of two worlds. The *Cantata* dances are a synthesis of traditional Filipino and contemporary forms. She 'adopted the contemporary spirit of dance: freedom... [and] reworked some of the softer and graceful folk movements along sharper and stronger lines' (Bobis 1994, 126). On a return visit to the Philippines she received some formal training in southern Philippines indigenous dance and blended these classical movements with contemporary ones: 'I allowed the body to shift between tradition and contemporaneity' (1994, 126).

The chanting in the performance is based on the ritualistic epic chanting by Philippines indigenous tribes but like the dancing, it too has undergone similar processes of grafting and hybridisation. In was whilst in Australia that Bobis first became acquainted with the concept of epic chanting as a form of story-telling. Her early untutored experimentations reflected the influences of the Gregorian chants and the *Misa Kantada* (sung Mass) from her Catholic background. Later, an audio tape of 'authentic' indigenous chanting transformed the rhythmic arrangement of the hybrid form. There is no space for entertaining notions of purity in this artistic process. Even when Bobis did get the chance to learn from an indigenous chanter in the northern Philippines the process was marked by appropriation and simulacra. According to Bobis, 'because [she] did not grow up within a tribal group that has preserved its roots from Western colonisation, [she] can only approximate the spirit of chanting among tribal peoples and their extraordinary vocal techniques' (Bobis 1994, 126).

It is important to remember that discourses of cultural purity and authenticity are not the sole preserves of the West or, in this context, of Australia. Nationalist efforts to recuperate a postcolonial identity often risk the replication of the manichean binaries of Self/Other and East/West by valorising the 'native' side of the equation. A noted Manila critic argued, after watching a performance of the *Cantata* in Australia, that the warm reception to the performance indicated that the text had already been co-opted by the West (Bobis 1994, 127). In other words, the fact that the Australian audience could identify with the performance was held as proof of its cultural impurity — its non-Filipino-ness. Bobis' own efforts to rectify this apparent 'error' by returning to 'native sources' draw attention to the fallacy of this myth of authenticity. 'I had searched for indigenous modes of performance', 'neo-ethnic [forms] ... indigenous rites and dances for the contemporary stage. These were hybridised forms as well, ones already touched by the West. It was almost impossible, after three hundred and forty years of Spanish and then American colonisation, to find something "truly Other" to the West' (Bobis1994, 128). Hence, although the chanting, dancing, the use of Filipino language and other ritualistic elements in the *Cantata* function as metonymic signifiers of Othered knowledges which cannot be fully captured and appropriated by the dominant culture, this is not to suggest that there is an essential Filipino, much less a Filipina-Australian, cultural identity. Rather, the discussion on the various modes of hybridising tradition and form foregrounds the strategic use of alterity as a means of countering any discourse of 'authenticity' and 'typicality'.

Ta Duy Binh defected to Australia in 1988 while representing Vietnam at the Interplay Festival for Young Playwrights. *Conversations with Charlie*, his second play to premiere at the Belvoir Street Asian Theatre Festival in 1996, is an abstract play about homelands, self-knowledge and love. The multiracial cast of three represent differing relationships to Australia. Charlie Chaplin is played by the Caucasian actor, Kerry Casey, and Ta himself plays the role of the Young Artist. The Aboriginal actor Denice Kickett plays the roles of Woman, Mother, and the Spirit of the Land. Charlie Chaplin is a popular icon among the Vietnamese people who see themselves reflected in his characterisation as the 'little tramp'. Charlie represents the underdog who, through his own wit, skill and cunning, overcomes adversity from not only powerful external social forces, but also the dark impulses from within. The young Vietnamese-Australian artist conjures up Charlie as his mentor to help him reconcile himself to the past and to integrate into the new Australian environment. The Aboriginal Spirit of the Land is also called up as another source of wisdom to aid in this process.

> THE MOTHER: Come here, son! I want to hold you like when you were a child.
>
> *The* YOUNG ARTIST *goes to his* MOTHER. *He lies on the floor and puts his head on her lap. The* MOTHER *becomes an Aboriginal* WOMAN *and sings an Aboriginal lullaby to him. Silence.*
>
> THE WOMAN: You are a new child of this land
> You will learn how to jump like a kangaroo
> You will learn how to find your way in the bush
> You will be told all of the Myths and the Legends
> The Land will embrace you warmly
> Feeding you all the food from her body...
>
> YOUNG ARTIST: Where am I? Where is here?
>
> THE WOMAN: Australia. Your new country.
>
> YOUNG ARTIST: Australia? The name sound strange, but everything else is familiar. Your voice, your warmth. The smell of the air. The sky is exactly the same. Look at the cloud, Mother. There are two dragons fighting each other.
>
> THE WOMAN: I am the spirit of this Land. This Land has more than forty thousand years of history. Come here my new child. Come here and I will teach you all the secrets of the Land.

THE WOMAN *shows him some ritual actions with a song. The* YOUNG ARTIST *follows ... There is a sense of him learning a new culture in the land. Aboriginal music. Lights fade down.*[11]

The transformation from the Vietnamese mother to the Aboriginal woman/spirit by the Aboriginal actor undermines the fixity of race as represented through the conventions of corporeal signifiers and verbal language. Whilst admittedly the use of the Aboriginal female actor to play a range of 'feminine' roles (Mother, Land, Spirit of Aboriginality) runs the risk of reinscribing gender essentialism, it could also be argued that the image of an Aboriginal (m)Other nurturing the Vietnamese new-comer displaces and dialogises the conventional binary representations of Self/Other, White/Black and West/East. This trope is repeated later in the play when the Woman becomes the love interest of the Young Artist. Urged on by Charlie, the shy youth is encouraged to court the Woman. In a live performance with the racially marked bodies of the Vietnamese and Aboriginal actors, the embrace which almost ends in a kiss presents a moment of *frisson* at the prospect of cross-racial coupling. As Robert Young reminds us, hybridity as a cultural description will always carry with it an implicit politics of heterosexuality since the offsprings of cross-racial intercourse are the 'embodied, living legacies' of such unions (1995, 25). In this respect, the iconic representation of the union of the Vietnamese man and Aboriginal woman defies not only colonialist attempts to divide and rule but also suggests the long (but hidden) history of miscegenation between Europeans, Asians and Aboriginals in Australia.

According to Ien Ang, the diasporic consciousness is steeped in ambivalence and characterised by a 'positive indeterminacy' (1993, 33). The diasporic identity is always caught somewhere between the myth of a homeland and the demands of the host country, between the 'where you're from?' and the 'where you're at?'. The question 'where you're from' signals the impossibility of complete integration — it is a question which foregrounds 'the bottomline of cultural identity' by equating cultural identity with national identity (Ang 1994, 10). *Charlie* problematises this equation by drawing attention to the diasporic nature of Australian history and thereby decentring the notion of a homogeneous or fixed national culture.

YOUNG ARTIST: Who are you? Where are you from?

WOMAN: I hate that question. Everyone asks me that question. You're the same as all the others.

YOUNG ARTIST: We are all the same, aren't we? I just want to know more about you.

WOMAN: If someone asks me
Who I am and where I am from
My answer is: I am one of you.
Very simple.
No one's sure when I came to this land
One thousand years, forty thousand years, perhaps a hundred thousand years
With the songs, the dances, I sing and dance every night around the fire
With the legends from the ancient time
With the Kangaroos playing in the desert
Under the flaming sun.

CHARLIE *enters.*

CHARLIE: I came here from the land of the mist
From the land where the sun never set
Where great Shakespeare was born
Struggling with questions of life and death
Like Hamlet 'to be or not to be'.

YOUNG ARTIST: I came here from every corner of the world
Europe — Asia — Africa
Bringing with me the mother's lullabies
The father's sadness
Bringing with me the unfinished love
The grief and the happiness.

WOMAN: I came here — to — live and — to share.

YOUNG ARTIST: To merge with others

CHARLIE: To sing together. (4-5)

While it is tempting for the diasporic imagination to fall into a discourse of 'planned authenticity' by valorising the lost homeland as a means of countering marginalisation in the host country, *Charlie* neither privileges the homeland nor the host country but instead maintains the tension between 'where you're from' and 'where you're at'. It is the 'multiperspectival productivity' of that position of in-between-ness which enables the Vietnamese-Australian artist to unsettle essentialist and totalising notions of cultural identity and national identity. The concept hybridity marks the emancipation of the diaspora from 'Vietnam' as the transparent master-signified of all things 'authentically Vietnamese'. Thus, the hybridised Vietnamese-Australian identity becomes the site for the productive 'construction of syncretic identities suitable for the "where you're at"' (Ang 1994, 16).

The positive indeterminacy of the hybrid Asian-Australian identity should not be confused with the postmodern concept of a nomadic identity, which celebrates the infinite and permanent flux of subject formation. The postmodernist celebration of border culture and the deterritorialised consciousness may result in an abstract, depoliticised, and ahistorical notion of 'difference'. Difference is reduced to equivalence, syncreticism and diversity whilst oppositionality is indiscriminately ascribed to all forms of cultural production. According to Krishnaswamy, 'the complex "local" histories and culture-specific knowledges inscribed in postcolonial narratives get neutralised into versions of postmodern diversity, allowing "others" to be seen, but shorn their dense specificity' (1995, 129). In order to resist this appropriation, it is vital that both the production and the reception of Asian-Australian performances focus on the historical conditions and specific trajectories from which hybrid identities are enunciated. William Yang and Mémé Thorne stress the interrelatedness of subjectivity and historicity in their very different forms of autobiographical theatre. According to Janet Gunn, autobiography is not conceived as 'the private act of a self writing' but rather 'the cultural act of a self reading' (1982, 8). Autobiographical discourse is not about the narcissistic identification of an 'authentic' subject but 'the narrative construction of a subject's social location through the active interpretation of experiences that one calls one's own' (Ang 1994, 4). The autobiographical self is a strategically fabricated performance which stages an identity that is not definitive or fully-fledged but one which uses the act of re-presentation as 'a strategy to open up avenues for new speaking trajectories, [and] the articulation of new lines of theorising' (1994, 4).

William Yang is a third-generation Australian-born Chinese who has developed a hybrid form of theatre consisting of commentary and slide show presentation. *Sadness* (1992) is the third work in an ongoing project in recovering his-story.[12] Yang is by all accounts a typical 'boy from the bush', having spent his childhood in northern Queensland. Despite a family history which spans more than a hundred years in Australia, he continues to be Othered in the national imagining. As Yang puts it, 'I *am* Australian but I *look* Chinese .... The fact that I stand up there and say I'm Asian *and* Australian, I think that helps people ... if people see you then they can change their ideas of *what a Chinese is*' (1996a). His autobiographical performances actively intervene to liberate ethnic identity from the politics of origin by juxtaposing the racially marked body of the performer/writer with the narrative of his family's integration into Australian history.

Thestereotype of 'what a Chinese is' is dismantled even further when we learn of Yang's homosexuality and of the impact of AIDS in the gay community in Sydney.

The format of the show is deliberately simple and low-key. Snapshots and studied portraits (Yang is a professional photographer) of friends, family, landscapes and architecture are projected on a screen while Yang delivers his commentary behind a microphone. Although mortality is the dominant theme in *Sadness* as Yang reflects on the deaths of friends struck by AIDS, his mother's passing and the funerals of other relatives, it is also about hope and a celebration of the human spirit in adversity. The performance consists of a complex weaving of stories about his two families, his biological Chinese-Australian family and his cultural family within the gay community. Yang is both the subject (i.e. narrator) and object of the synthesis of the two disparate worlds. There is no attempt to reconcile or neutralise the differences, antagonisms and ambivalence in the presentation of a gay Chinese-Australian identity — 'a minority of a minority', as Yang says (1996b, 14). The narration and slide projections shuttle between the two worlds creating a distinct rhythm and logic characterised by suture, gaps and silences which reflect the hybridising process. The two families and lives as lived remain separate in their differences, and yet there are also elements of resonance and irony which always refer back to the embodied presence of Yang in performance. *Sadness* as an autobiographical performance is not about revealing a fixed or authentic identity, but one which focuses on hybridity as a way of articulating a politicised and historicised identity based on difference and contingency.

Mémé Thorne's *Burying Mother* premiered at the 1996 Belvoir Street Asian Theatre Festival. It is a disturbing and evocative performance which layers movement with live and taped verbal texts. A solo piece performed by Thorne herself, *Burying Mother* deals with loss and grief, but unlike Yang's work Thorne's performance mourns an abstraction. 'Yes, I guess that's it, I mourn the absence of her, the mother I always wanted and couldn't have.'[13] The performer foregrounds the autobiographical mode in her first spoken lines: 'I am Mémé, Caroline, Veronica, Thorne. I was born in Kuala Lumpur, West Malaysia in 1953, the year of the snake' (3). Whilst demonstrating the characteristics of postmodern subjectivity in its play on self-reflexivity, multiplicity, and the problematising of authorial power, this performance of self is informed by the hybridising presence of Chinese, Catholic and Western/Australian cultures. Thorne's taped voice-over is peppered with silence and uncertainties as she tries to explain the complexities of the Chinese burial ritual to the uninitiated:

> I'd like to tell you about the ENVELOPE OF THE SOUL... It looks like one of those, er, large envelopes you use for sending official letters in China. It's a kind of paper wrapper designed to receive the soul, and it's ... it's really the first place the soul goes to when it er ... leaves the body, you know, before it's released into the spirit world...the...the...the other world. (1)

Not only is the protagonist unsure about her ability to translate for her audience, but doubts are also cast on her suitability as a source of 'native' knowledge: 'The incense is red ... the little cakes offered to the Gods are red. Cha gwoh, I think you call them ... I'm not quite sure how you say that ... Red is for birth. I think. I have a feeling but I'm not quite sure' (3). The mother in Thorne's enactment resembles Barbara Creed's category of the monstrous mother who represents all that is abject and threatening (1986). In Kristevan and post-Lacanian models, monstrosity as a category is linked to identity formation: the monster is the repository of all that is feared and rejected within the self. As such it constantly threatens to spill over its boundaries; it is excessive (Barcan 1996, 51).

This excessiveness is demonstrated at one point in the performance when the daughter transforms into her (m)Other in a terrifying moment of simultaneous identification and disavowal. The performance becomes a ritual which enables the daughter to exorcise the power of the monstrous mother and to recuperate an autonomous voice. This is not to suggest that there is an essential self to be recovered, one which is untainted by the maternal presence. Rather, the daughter is now able to construct herself as a separate identity, through the act of performance, from the parent figure. It could also be argued that the mother-daughter trope is a metonym of hybrid cultural formation. The mother figure is clearly associated with Chinese culture (signified by the huge Chinese character for 'mother' which is projected onto the backdrop in the final scene). Performance as an enunciation of self in this case functions as a 'dialogic process that attempts to track the processes of displacement and realignment that are already at work, constructing something different and hybrid from the encounter.' Hence performance creates 'a third space that does not simply revise or invert the dualities, but revalues the ideological bases of division and difference' (Bhabha 1992, 58).

The hybridisation of cultures in contemporary Australia carries with it transformed relations to tradition and the 'native homeland' which can only be experienced through the categories of the present. The experiences of Asian-Australian artists enable us to understand relations between cultures in ways which challenge orthodox notions of cross-cultural relations. As Kevin Robbins says, the crossing of boundaries brings about a complexity of vision and also a sense of the permeability and contingency of culture (Turner 1994, 77). While arguing for the concept of cultural identity as always provisional and partial *in medias res*, however, it has also become clear that unless issues of cultural difference are not linked to power inequalities and the hegemonic conditions which perpetuate these relations, then we are lost in that maze of liberal pluralism that Todd Gitlin calls 'the shopping centre of identity politics' (Gunew 1993, 60).

Notes

1 Dates given are for first performances. The following are publication dates. Jill Shearer (1989) *Shimada*; Michael Gurr (1992) *Sex Diary of an Infidel*; Anna Broinowski (1995) *The Gap*; Noëlle Janaczewska, (1995) *The History of Water*; Hilary Bell (1995) *Fortune*; and Deborah Pollard (1996)'Mother Tongue Interference'. Others mentioned are unpublished at this point.

2 Most of the analysis of Asian-Australian relations in mainstream Australian drama has to date focused on the Orientalist discourse and the creative responses to it by non-Asian Australian playwrights. See Gilbert (1994c) and (1997); Dale and Gilbert (1993); Tompkins (1994a). For analysis of colonial theatre see Kelly (1993a).

4 This is made even more difficult when prominent leaders in Asia also lay claim to 'Asian values' as a means of differentiating themselves from Western countries. Closer analysis of the use of the term however points to the mobilisation of 'Asian values' as a form of social and political control by the ruling elite. An example of this is the Singaporean government's promotion of Confucian values in the late eighties which emphasised obedience to authority and the privileging of the collective over the individual. While the 'Asian values' campaign was officially established to offset the increasing 'Westernisation' of the population, it could also be argued that the emphasis on civil obedience helped to maintain the status quo in 1990 when Prime Minister Lee Kuan Yew was succeeded by Goh Chok Tong and his promised 'relaxed style of government'.

4 According to Frost (1994), the Australia-Asia policy process is founded on the tenets of economic rationalism which has firmly linked cultural sensitivity to continued trade and investment. The elitist roots of the discourse have resulted in the construction of state-sponsored versions of Malaysian or Indonesian culture that often has little majoritarian support from the people in the countries.

5 See Broinowski (1996) for a comprehensive catalogue of Australian artistic representations of Asia.

6 While the use of the terms 'Asian' and 'Asian-Australian' is problematic since it accords with the homogenising tendencies of the dominant discourse, it should also be noted that the term 'Asian' has been recuperated and appropriated by people of diverse Asian backgrounds themselves as a counter-hegemonic strategy. There is a shift taking place in 'ethnic' cultural politics which, I would argue has been spurred by recent 'race debates' over issues such as multiculturalism, immigration and the 'Anti-Asian campaign', to claim the term 'Asian' as a way of referring to common experiences of marginalisation. 'Asian' is therefore used as an organising category amongst individuals and groups with very different histories, traditions and ethnic identities. The Asian Writers network in Sydney and the Belvoir Street Asian Theatre Festival are examples.

7 The term refers to Benedict Andersen's influential book (1983) on the construction of modern nationalism.

8 As used by Broinowski (1996); particularly pp. 216-232.

9 The stereotype of the Filipina mail-order bride, for instance, carries particular weight in Australian popular discourse, as attested by the representation of the Filipina Cynthia in the film *Priscilla - Queen of the Desert*. See Bobis, Gilbert & Lo (1994).

10 According to Roger Sworder, the *Cantata* is more than epic and more like drama. It is not truly dramatic because there is only one actor. Neither is its form lyric as the dimensions of personality explored are not personal but more archetypal. Although Magayon reveals her innermost feelings, she is not a fully realised character but an expression of the 'feminine' which is what gives the poem its 'epic spirit' (Bobis 1994, 124). For a discussion on the hybridising process of writing two versions of the epic in Filipino and English languages, see Bobis (1995).

11 Ta Duy Binh, 'Conversations with Charlie' (unpublished TS), 8. All further references in parenthesis.

12 Earlier works include: *The Face of Buddha* and *China Diary*. *The North* (1996) is the latest addition to his oeuvre.

13 Mémé Thorne, 'Burying Mother' (1996, unpublished TS), 9. All further references in parenthesis.

Reconciliation? Aboriginality and Australian theatre in the 1990s

Helen Gilbert

In the last decade, Aboriginality has become a significant force in Australian theatre, both in terms of subject matter and performative processes. Not only has there been a vast increase in the number of plays which might be termed 'Aboriginal' but also a concerted effort to put in place structures which will ensure the continued visibility of Aboriginal theatre and Aborigines *in* theatre, whether local or national. One of the most important infrastructural advances has been the proliferation of amateur and professional groups — including Kooris in Theatre (an ad-hoc collective of Sydney-based practitioners formed in the late 1980s), Ilbijeri (founded Melbourne 1991), Kooemba Jdarra (Brisbane 1993), and Yirra Yaakin Youth Theatre (Western Australia 1992) — devoted wholly or largely to the development and production of Aboriginal performance events. The work of such groups has been supported by various one-off projects and, in some instances, by the active commitment of more established companies to Aboriginal content and/or non-traditional casting choices. At the wider political level, government support in the form of policy directives and funding has also played a role in the establishment of what now seems to be a permanent Aboriginal element in the nation's theatrical culture.

The 1988 bicentennial celebration of European settlement (invasion) put Aboriginal issues on Australian theatre's agenda in an unprecedented way. As well as supporting such events as the Melbourne production of Jack Davis's *The First Born Trilogy*, itself a mammoth project involving the prior development and staging of Davis's new play *Barungin* in Perth, the Bicentennial Authority funded projects by mainstream playwrights Louis Nowra (*Capricornia*), Michael Gow (*1841*), and Stephen Sewell (*Hate*), which dealt directly or indirectly with Aboriginal issues (see Gilbert 1994b). A number of smaller local projects — notably Bob Maza's *The Keepers*, Eva Johnson's *Murras*, and Salamanca Theatre Company's *Copping it Sweet* — consolidated the Aboriginal content of bicentennial theatre in various regions.[1] In the 1990s, these achievements have been extended by numerous playwrights and practitioners whose work has found an interested audience in a society influenced by events such as the International Year of Indigenous Peoples (1993), the passing of the Commonwealth Native Title Act (1993), and, most recently, the High Court's Wik decision (1996) allowing Aboriginal title to coexist with pastoral leases. Although the early 1990s push for 'reconciliation' between Aboriginal and non-Aboriginal Australians has been somewhat diluted since the Howard government gained power in 1996, there remains in many sectors of the community a general commitment to the movement, and a groundswell of support for Aboriginal cultural production. In this respect, the political and social climate of reconciliation provides one important context within which to assess recent developments such as the diversification of Aboriginal performance styles (particularly the growth of musical theatre), the increase in plays by/about Aboriginal women, the touring of Aboriginal productions to remote communities as well as interstate and overseas, the re-staging of early Aboriginal works along with the creation of new performance pieces, and the appearance of Aboriginal actors (and less often directors) on most mainstream stages, albeit irregularly. In the latter category of developments, Black Swan Theatre Company (Perth 1991) has played a major role, regularly casting Aboriginal actors in various canonical plays as well as staging texts by and about Aborigines.

Aboriginality and cultural politics

While the recent expansion of Aboriginal theatre has not been manifest evenly across time or place, it does raise a number of important issues which are relevant to the larger performing arts industry in Australia as well as to the specific local communities involved. In particular, the current intense interest in Aboriginality raises questions of authority, ownership, and authenticity, especially when performance projects involve intensive collaboration between Aboriginal and non-Aboriginal practitioners, as is often the case. Such questions are not merely theoretical but often politically and economically crucial even if there is little consensus about what actually constitutes Aboriginality and how it functions within a settler/migrant society which is becoming increasingly multicultural.

In liberal arts circles, if not in the wider Australian community, Aboriginality is now seen variously as an energising, indigenising, and/or hybridising force. For performing arts, as for visual arts and music, Aboriginal culture is often expected to provide an archive of so-called 'traditional' forms which might extend the predictable repertoire of a transplanted Eurocentric theatre, and, at the same time, make that theatre more fully 'Australian'. Critics who regard Aboriginal performance as an energiser inevitably focus on presentational style and laud those productions which strongly convey difference, usually through dance/movement, music, costume, and scenic design. Such productions are described as 'fresh', 'new', 'exhilarating', and 'raw',[2] the latter term implying both an appealing purity of form/energy and a concomitant lack of (European) theatrical sophistication. Within this paradigm, Aboriginal performance is exoticised in much the same manner as Asian forms such as Noh and Kabuki since it is seen to offer ways of injecting life into a 'moribund' mainstream theatre (Fischer 1990, 15). This can lead to the appropriation of approved versions of Aboriginality in the service of a non-Aboriginal imperative to produce a vibrant performance culture which may not necessarily address the most urgent needs of Aborigines themselves. Collaborative projects initiated by 'whites' can be particularly tricky to orchestrate in a non-appropriative fashion because such intercultural theatre is often tacitly based on an 'hour-glass' model which posits the uncomplicated transfer of 'grains of culture' from the source group to the target audience (Pavis 1992, 4-6). One intercultural experiment based on this kind of model is the Mudrooroo/Müller project (1991), initially conceived by Gerhard Fischer as an investigation of the ways in which Aboriginal performance might re-animate a European script. In this instance, however, Fischer's Aboriginal collaborators appear to have re-appropriated the project during the rehearsal process, which culminated in a staged reading of what had been transformed into an emphatically Koori script: *The Aboriginal Protesters Confront the Proclamation of the Australian Republic on 26 January 2001 with a Production of 'The Commission' by Heiner Müller*.[3]

The indigenising functions of Aboriginality are equally important to a settler/invader society anxious to legitimise its presence in a country it has sequestered from its original inhabitants. In this formulation, Aboriginal culture, especially in its traditional guises, is now valorised as a conduit to the land and to a very ancient human history; thus the incorporation of Aboriginal elements into mainstream art forms functions to ensure the 'Australianness' of those forms. As far as theatre is concerned, this has meant that productions which exhibit approved versions of Aboriginality are quickly claimed as 'Australian', while expressly confrontational performance by/about Aborigines is relegated to alterity, tolerated out of political correctness but seldom fully engaged with. Hence, Jack Davis's *Barungin* left most reviewers disappointed because of its uncompromising treatment of Aboriginal deaths in custody — this was perceived as a departure from his earlier, 'conciliatory' works — whereas more upbeat texts such as Jimmy Chi and Kuckles' *Bran Nue Dae* (1990) and Roger Bennett's *Funerals and Circuses* (1992) have been praised for their Australianness — and less often their Aboriginality —

while being enthusiastically welcomed into our contemporary theatre canon.[4] This is not to suggest that the latter plays are inherently less political in intention or effect but to argue that their expressions of Aboriginality risk co-option by a white Australian society whose current post-colonial position as both coloniser and colonised makes the project of reconciliation particularly urgent. When Aboriginal theatre is identified as a potential export or tourist attraction, its indigenising function becomes even more prominent as discourses of nationhood come into play.[5] In such instances, internal divisions within our overall performance culture are often downplayed to allow the discursive construction of the production/play at issue as representative of the Australian nation. This situation is not necessarily detrimental to the Aboriginal agenda of decolonisation but it does pose the question, once again, of whether or not Aboriginal interests are also being served.

When it is constructed primarily as a source of energy and/or indigeneity for a broadly defined national performance culture, Aboriginal theatre circulates within an epistemological equation that maintains the centrality of the dominant group. This group is then able to influence the terms on which Aboriginality will be admitted to or excluded from Australian stages. All too often, white critics (and presumably audiences) deem Aboriginal performance to inhere in a limited range of signifiers — predominantly tribal dances, didgeridoo music, and dreaming stories — that express a commitment to 'tradition'. What has identifiable links with tradition thus becomes 'authentic' while other theatrical expressions of Aboriginality are frequently ignored, subsumed within narratives of nationhood, or, in some cases, criticised for their failure to deliver the 'real thing'. A very good example of such discursive surveillance is evident in critical responses to Bangarra Dance Theatre's recent work. Their major 1992/3 touring production *Praying Mantis Dreaming* was widely acclaimed for its exploration of traditional material derived from the culture of the Yirrkala people of Arnhem Land. Although this piece included a significant proportion of Euro-American derived movement and music, few reviewers dwelt on that aspect except to read the modern segments as appropriate to a 'tale of traditional Aboriginal *versus* urban Aboriginal values and experience' (Nemeth 1992: 64; my italics). Bangarra's 1994 dance-theatre piece *Ninni* met with a much less enthusiastic response from most critics, many of whom regretted the relative lack of traditional performance elements and claimed that the company's increased emphasis on modern dance made their work 'indistinguishable' from that of other groups (Sykes 1994; McGillick 1994). In both cases, reviewers gauged Aboriginality — or the lack of it — according to a concept of tradition that reduces Aboriginal culture to its reproducible artefacts while denying the validity of performance that reflects the lived experience of many so-called 'non-traditional' (urban) Aborigines.

As Gareth Griffiths warns, the myth of authenticity can in fact function as another form of colonialist discourse in so far as it '"speaks" the indigene within a construction whose legitimacy is grounded not in *their* practice but in *our* desire' (1994a, 83). This observation is particularly relevant to a discussion of Aboriginal theatre since it points to the gap between the processes of signification — here including both rehearsal and performance — and the processes through which an act of representation is read and understood. For better or for worse, contemporary Aboriginal performing arts have proliferated under the banner of theatre consumed primarily by non-Aboriginal audiences. Moreover, as arts which put the Aboriginal body on display, they operate within a representational system which often fetishises visible signs of racial and sexual difference. Hence, the very conditions of reception for Aboriginal theatre tend to facilitate readings which reflect the desires of the mainstream society. And yet theatre can also provide an important space for multiple and specific expressions of Aboriginality, precisely because it is a social *practice* that usually involves complex negotiations at each stage of the production process. In collaborative projects particularly, Aboriginal input into the scripting, the design, the direction, the performance, the management, and the promotion of a piece of theatre not only affects the Aboriginality of the final product but also of the theatre-making process. Similarly, negotiations of different kinds of Aboriginality occur when various indigenous groups work together or when they consult tribal experts on traditional performance styles and techniques. It follows, then, that all performative expressions of Aboriginality are mediated in some way, and that debates about authenticity (as they are currently constituted) cannot offer the most useful frameworks for engaging with Aboriginal theatre as a political and aesthetic practice.

If Aboriginal theatre must be examined in reference to a broader Australian performing arts culture — and this seems both inevitable and necessary at our current historical moment — we need analytical models that can account for the many different forms of interaction between and within the various groups involved, whether as producers or consumers. Such models will be conducive to a genuine process of reconciliation only if they allow expressions of Aboriginality to serve the strategic interests of Aboriginal peoples rather than those of the mainstream theatre and its public. At present, the concept of hybridity as it is used in post-colonial theory/criticism seems to provide the most enabling approach to the series of problems I have outlined. Homi Bhabha posits that a hybridising of cultural forms is the unavoidable outcome of any imperial project. In his particular formulation, hybridity is seen as a volatile interaction characterised by conflict between and within the constitutive cultures of colonised societies. Neither a simple fusion of differences nor 'a third term that resolves the tension between two cultures' (Bhabha 1985, 98), hybridity functions as a form of positive 'contamination' that resists the discourses of cultural purity which underpin colonialist relations. In some contexts, hybrid cultural forms circulate historically marginalised knowledges and practices as a means of destabilising the power of the dominant group. This is often the case in theatrical expressions of hybridity, where the deliberate tension between Western and indigenous theatrico-dramatic forms provides an 'in-between' space in and through which traditional narratives and performance practices can be recuperated for contemporary purposes.

For example, *Ningali* (1994), performed by Josie Ningali Lawford from a script she developed with the assistance of Robyn Archer and Angela Chaplin, uses an eclectic mix of Western and Aboriginal storytelling techniques to convey knowledges central to the protagonist's particular historical experience. In a performance that includes stand-up comedy, country and western songs, and syncretic dance sequences, Ningali confirms the continued relevance of her tribe's kinship patterns, her Wambajarri language, and the stories told by her Jabbi and Jaja (grandparents) that have guided her various journeys in Australia and abroad. Tradition functions in such texts as an inheritance through which contemporary Aboriginality can be negotiated, rather than as a form of essentialist difference that determines the status of a play and/or production *vis à vis* predetermined notions of authenticity. The performative rehearsal and re-enactment of a variety of (necessarily) hybridised signs of Aboriginality also facilitates the deconstruction of the colonialist stereotypes which have circumscribed representations of indigenous peoples on Australian stages throughout the history of white settlement. In this respect, Aboriginal theatre introduces into mainstream production and reception processes a degree of ambivalence which, in Bhabha's terms, 'ensure[s] that the meaning and symbols of culture have no primordial unity or fixity; that even the same signs can be appropriated, translated, re-historicised and read anew' (1988, 21).

Post-colonial theories of hybridity are not intended to supply a model of reconciliation which merely celebrates diversity within a multicultural society. As Sneja Gunew (1993) argues, the rhetoric of multiculturalism, in its official versions at least, may actually limit expressions of difference because it tends to homogenise minority cultural production and to proscribe certain versions of marginality. This kind of cultural pluralism also risks instituting hierarchies of difference that promote public acceptance of aestheticised cultural forms — such as the performing arts — while simultaneously disavowing aspects of Aboriginal law, land usage, and kinship systems, all of which might be legitimately regarded as 'culture'. What needs to inform the Australian multicultural formula is the recognition that markers of Aboriginality (and all other cultural affiliations) are always unstable *and* continually contested by both Aborigines and settler-migrants. According to sociologist and film critic Marcia Langton, 'Aboriginality is remade over and over again in a process of dialogue, imagination, representation and interpretation' (1993, 33). Langton identifies three broad categories of 'intersubjectivity' which constitute an 'infinite array' of Aboriginalities: the interactions of Aboriginal peoples within the contexts of their own cultures; the representations of stereotyped and/or mythologised Aborigines by white people who lack significant first-hand knowledge of their subject; and dialogue situations in which 'individuals test and adapt imagined models of each other to find satisfactory forms of mutual comprehension' (33). This explanation of Aboriginality as a process of continual becoming is particularly useful because it does not seek to locate an authentic culture but instead recognises the specificity of various representations of a cultural *construct.*

Markers of Aboriginality

If Aboriginality is both difficult to define and radically unstable, choosing criteria by which to delimit the category of Aboriginal theatre becomes an increasingly fraught task, especially given the potential variance of each enactment of a play. Most critics, reviewers, teachers and publishers assign Aboriginality according to authorship, but this itself is a problematic concept, both in terms of the diverse conceptual and technical input which goes into creating any performance text, and also in reference to Aboriginal writing as a form of cultural production. As Penny Van Toorn argues, a theory of authorship can account for Aboriginal texts only if it is 'capable of accommodating transcribed speech, translation, and other modes of collaborative and mediated writing' that point to the 'variety of institutional, cultural, social, and political contexts' in which Aboriginal people produce textual materials (1995, 9). Theatre is only rarely a site of the kind of individual writing that conventional notions of authorship validate, and it clearly involves mediation at a number of levels even when devised by a culturally homogenous group. In the case of Aboriginal theatre, these levels of mediation are precisely the points at which hybridisation can and does take place.

An instructive if perhaps controversial example is the Queensland Theatre Company's production of *One Woman's Song* (1993), a play based on the life and writings of Oodgeroo of the tribe Noonuccal. The script, written by white playwright Peta Murray, would obviously fail in most people's judgement to qualify as an Aboriginal text, and yet there is ample evidence to suggest that the *theatrical realisation* of that script was widely received as Aboriginal theatre, even though no reviewers actually describe it in exactly those terms. As well as praising the play for its timely treatment of Aboriginal issues, many commentators focus their attention on the stage presence of Aboriginal actors Lydia Miller, Deborah Mailman, and Neokigai Bonner, who played Oodgeroo at different periods in her life. The creative input of Aboriginal choreographer Michael Leslie is frequently noted as is the musical score devised by sometime composer for Yothu Yindi, Michael Havir. Several reviews also make a clear distinction between the script (regarded as competent and sincere but not inspired) and the overall theatrical event, which was widely lauded for its depictions of Aboriginal culture, and even seen as a celebration befitting the International Year of Indigenous Peoples.[6] Despite the Queensland Theatre Company's limited consultation with Aborigines in the initial stages of the project,[7] it could be argued that the various points of mediation in the production of *One Woman's Song* actually allowed Aboriginal input to suffuse a non-Aboriginal script with markers of Aboriginality, which performed (in both senses of the word) an authorial function and, in turn, *authorised* the resultant production to represent the particular Aboriginal subject at issue. The theatrical text was then given the stamp of approval by Oodgeroo herself, who appeared at the end of the play's opening night to recite one of her best-known poems. While this whole process, including Oodgeroo's own 'performance', was by no means exempt from some of the traps of collaborative cross-cultural work as I have described them above, it does locate Aboriginality at least partly in the conditions of theatrical production and reception, rather than simply viewing it as something necessarily embedded in the script.

The de-emphasising of the playwright's function as the most important locus of Aboriginality allows a wider range of texts to legitimately participate in the theatrical dialogue which seems to me essential for genuine reconciliation. This is not to suggest that the cultural positioning of the playwright is, or should be, irrelevant — indeed, authorship by Aborigines remains strategically desirable for a whole host of economic and political reasons — but to argue that we must adopt broader definitions of Aboriginal cultural production as long as there are other players in the field of 'intersubjectivity' that Langton has outlined. Production texts which might then be analysed under the rubric of Aboriginal theatre include a number of collaboratively 'authored' plays such as *Murri Love* (1995) by Cathy Craigie and Therese Collie, *Close to the Bone* (1991) scripted by Ned Manning from work done with Koori students at the EORA Centre in Redfern, and *Bidenjarreb Pinjarra* (1994), which was deliberately devised and performed by two Aboriginal and two non-Aboriginal actors to give Wetjalas and Nyoongahs equal power and ownership over the product — an account of the 1834 Battle of Pinjarra in which hundreds of Aborigines are said to have been massacred by colonial regiments.[8] Perhaps more contentiously, one could also argue that Louis Nowra's *Capricornia* and his companion plays, *Radiance* (1993) and *Crow* (1994a), along with Nicholas Parson's *Dead Heart* (1993) and Eric Earley's *The Custodians* (1993), might usefully inform a discussion of the field since these plays all foreground Aboriginal characters and have required significant professional interaction between Aborigines and whites during their production processes. There is even a good case for including 'Aboriginalised' productions of classical texts as important sites of intervention in the historical processes that have stereotyped representations of indigenous peoples or simply erased them from our stages. A recent example of such theatre is Black Swan's 1991 production of Shakespeare's *Twelfth Night*, which gave Aboriginal actors Kelton Pell, Stephen Albert, and John Moore equal billing with their non-Aboriginal counterparts.[9]

What the diversity of Aboriginal participation in Australian theatre makes clear is the necessity of examining each production in all its processual complexity. This kind of analysis demands that we focus squarely on the performance text rather than giving priority to the written script. It is then possible to delineate a number of markers of Aboriginality that are performed — rehearsed, re-enacted, and constantly reinterpreted — across many different texts and often with very different effects. Such cultural markers should not be seen as defining a fixed body of Aboriginal plays/productions but rather as indicating a politically inflected *practice* that continually (re)produces multiple and mutable instances of Aboriginal theatre.

Perhaps the most common feature across the range of recent plays by and about Aborigines is an avoidance of wholly naturalistic forms. This is manifest not only in the narrative structures and performance modes of various texts but also in the scenography, which is often stylised to convey symbolic levels of meaning. *Murri Love*, which incorporated non-naturalistic forms only in the scenography, provides an interesting variant to this general pattern. The proliferation of musical theatre, storytelling and dance theatre clearly signals this departure from naturalism, as does the growing number of plays which follow naturalistic conventions to some extent while also subverting their authority with 'wayward' signifying codes borrowed from either traditional or Western forms of representation, or both. Sally Morgan's *Sistergirl* (1992), for example, is largely styled as a naturalistic comedy but the most significant action occurs in the surrealistic dream sequences which reveal Rosy's tragic past, and in her periodic contact with the Birdman, an Aboriginal spirit who portends her imminent passage to the Dreaming. Such theatre hybridises the overdetermined spaces of naturalism to deliberately ruffle the smooth edges of the staged image, and thus challenge its presumed ideological neutrality. Expressions of Aboriginality can then be historicised — or even allegorised — within a specific representational context rather read as fixed or natural. At the same time, non-naturalistic theatre is conducive to the exploration of Aboriginal epistemologies because it welcomes experiment and delights in stylistic promiscuity.[10] This, in turn, facilitates the circulation of marginalised cultural forms, both traditional and contemporary, as well as aiding their strategic adaptations.

Whatever the choice of form, the physicalised presence of Aboriginal actors is an important marker of indigenous theatre. This is an industrial and political issue as well as a representational choice. The visible signs of Aboriginality as ascribed to the performing body will of course vary from actor to actor and according to the theatrical contexts in which that body displays itself, but, if our performing arts culture is to address the historical stereotyping of indigenous peoples, it is strategically desirable to populate Australian stages with actors who identify as Aboriginal and are recognised as such. Aboriginal theatre faces the particular problem of finding ways to emphasise racial difference as a 'scrupulously visible political interest' (Spivak 1988: 205) while at the same time refusing to endorse the concept of an essentialised racial biology which remains the cornerstone of imperialist thinking. Brechtian modes of characterisation provide one effective response to this challenge. In the recent Kooemba Jdarra production of Kevin Gilbert's 1968 play, *The Cherry Pickers*

(1994), for instance, both white and black characters were played by the all-Aboriginal cast. A similar strategy was used in SWY theatre's highly successful 1992 stage adaptation of Mudrooroo's novel *Wild Cat Falling*,[11] a play that contains few black characters aside from the Aboriginal protagonist whose impossible search for an integrated identity was highlighted by the production's multiple moments of cross-race and cross-gender representation. In both cases, Aboriginal performers commanded the stage, but the foregrounded gaps between the actor and his/her role(s) also showed the constructedness of the stage image, thereby dismantling the fixity of represented racial categories. A slightly different tactic is at work in *Bran Nue Dae* where the sheer proliferation of Aboriginal identities played out by a large multi-racial cast imbues the stage with markers of Aboriginality which nonetheless complicate notions of race based on a simple/stable and visible body-based sign system.

It is equally possible for a single performer to centralise the staged Aboriginal body while avoiding essentialist modes of representation. A number of recent monodramas provide female actors in particular with the ideal vehicle through which to play out (and play with) various Aboriginal subjectivities. Eva Johnson's *What Do They Call Me?* (1990) presents its study of marginalised women in three monologues by very different characters: an old, incarcerated Aboriginal woman who has suffered horrific physical abuse from her de facto husband; her first daughter, removed from her care as an infant and now very much part of the conservative (white) middle class; and a younger daughter, also forcefully adopted out by welfare agencies, who playfully identifies herself as a 'radical feminist, anarchist, amazon, lesbian warrior' (1991, 253). In the performance text, these three characters are held in creative tension by the solo actor, a strategy which partly reconstructs their family links and also suggests the multiple and shifting significations of the performing body. *Ningali* likewise presents a range of female Aboriginal subject positions but in this case the changes in persona — indicated by changes in gesture, language, vocal register, costume, and so forth — represent the many different roles that the one character, Ningali, has played in her 'border crossings' between cultures. The fact that productions of this text have depended on the singular talents of actor Ningali Lawford to tell stories about her life and *perform* herself — or selves — at once authenticates the play's depictions of lived Aboriginal experience and draws attention to the ways in which that experience must be artificially/artfully reconstructed for a theatre audience. In another demonstration of monodrama's versatility as a theatrical form, Kooemba

Jdarra's group-devised piece *Seven Stages of Grieving* (1995) uses the solitary Aboriginal actor, Deborah Mailman, to intensify the effect of a dramatic collage designed to convey diverse aspects of Murri experience through stories, songs, poems, documentary reports, visual images, and direct 'dialogues' with the audience.

Markers of Aboriginality ascribed to the physical body are significantly affected by how that body moves and how it is framed, especially by costume, for the spectator's consumption. A wide range of plays/productions have used dance to heighten the visibility *and* the agency of the performing body as an active subject of representation, as well as to tell stories through spatial inscription and/or to recuperate marginalised forms of cultural expression (Gilbert 1992a). Hybridised dance styles are quite common, not only in the work of specific dance theatre groups but also in plays such as *Bran Nue Dae* where these forms have the added function of mimicking[12] such conventions as the minstrel routine and the tourist version of a corroboree. Costume similarly draws attention to the performing body and has been used with great effectiveness in *Bran Nue Dae* and other plays to signal a range of Aboriginalities. Particularly important in this respect are emblematic costumes such as landrights T-shirts and other vestimentary codes which deliberately use as political signifiers red, black and gold, the colours of the pan-Aboriginal flag. In non-naturalistic forms of theatre, costume also highlights the gap between Aboriginal bodies and the roles they play. It can be utilised, then, as a form of creative mediation that furthers a text's potential for engaging in the subversive mimicry that undermines colonialist authority (Gilbert 1995).

Aboriginality also finds expression in a variety of linguistic forms that have been reinterpreted for, and through, performance. Indigenous languages increasingly mark the aural texts of very different kinds of theatre, albeit in limited amounts. Such languages are now less often employed in historical narratives to signify a loss of culture — as in Davis's epic play *Kullark* (1979) — than in depictions of contemporary Aboriginal life. *Dead Heart*, positioned emphatically in the present of a small Aboriginal community west of Alice Springs, features two characters who refuse to learn English, preferring instead to converse in their native Pintupi and often forcing a response in that language or in some form of Pidgin. In performance, unlike in the published text where the Pintupi dialogue is glossed (Parsons 1994), this articulation of linguistic autonomy confirms the agency of Aboriginal languages and their associated lore/law. An extensive use of Pidgin also abrogates the privilege of standard English by hybridising its grammatical structures and its lexicon to suit the purposes of the colonised group. Even the white 'politpalla' is induced to speak Pidgin in an effort to effectively administer his version of law and order, a situation which, paradoxically, undermines his authority in thematic terms and also in terms of the play's performed soundscape.

Hybridised linguistic codes have an especially powerful effect when they are performed as stories told directly to the audience which is then implicated in the process of intersubjectivity. For instance, when Ningali tells the story of her life using Australian English, Kriol, Wambajarri, and a parodied version of American English, each shift in register/language (re)situates viewers, depending on their racial and cultural affiliations, in a specific relation to the performer whose linguistic virtuosity enacts a fluid movement through a range of subject positions, thus preventing the audience from fixing her in any stereotyped category. Storytelling also revivifies oral traditions — themselves central to indigenous cultures not only as means of education but also as modes of entertainment — particularly via the use of verbal and visual humour which actively involves the audience (Gilbert 1994a). While many forms of Aboriginal writing use storytelling techniques, theatre provides a particularly apt medium through which to restore to traditional stories their topology as performance pieces. This restoration does not automatically lock such stories into a reified past but rather allows them to signify in multiple codes which enact cultural continuities even as they draw attention to the ways in which Aboriginal performance traditions have been ruptured by imperialism. For example, *Betrothed* (1993), devised and performed by Sydney-based group Kooris in Theatre, explores the rituals of marriage and union via three traditional stories, interwoven with a waltz and a comic sketch about gender roles, in order to historicise the overall performance. In this way, the stories of the waratah (about idealised love), the brolga (about erotic obsession), and the turtle, the oyster, and the whale (about marital squabbles) together form a cautionary tale grounded in a specific theatrical and historical tradition but reinterpreted for the modern spectator.

Contemporary expressions of Aboriginality are equally well served by modes of enactment based on storytelling, as *Ningali* and Jack Davis's *Wahngin Country* (1992) demonstrate. Whereas each of these plays is structured as a continuous narrative revealing one character's specific experience as an Aboriginal subject, *Seven Stages of Grieving* exploits the storytelling mode in order to convey a range of situations, emotions, and moral/cultural lessons which together provide a more panoramic view of Aboriginal life. In this text, grief takes many public forms, communicated variously through fables, songs, slide narratives, and, in one of the play's more chilling moments, a documentary-style account of the death in custody of Murri dancer, Daniel Yock. In addition, the performer tells a number of interlinked stories in the first person narrative voice but they are designed to weave threads of continuity rather than to build a composite image of the storyteller, who remains unnamed and somewhat elusive as a character.

The soundscapes of Aboriginal theatre are frequently characterised not only by particular uses of language but also by distinctive musical codes. The ubiquitous didgeridoo, often accompanied by clapsticks, instantly signals Aboriginality to most viewers, especially when the musical score foregrounds its more traditional resonances. It is a mistake, however, to assume that indigenous music inheres primarily in these instruments or that their effect is diluted in hybridised musical forms.[13] In fact, I would argue that the hybridising process is precisely what marks Aboriginal musicality in many 1990s plays. *Bran Nue Dae* and Chi's more recent *Corrugation Road* (1996), are, like *Funerals and Circuses*, paradigmatic examples of theatre which refuses to privilege so-called authentic or traditional music over more syncretic styles of expression.[14] As contemporary Western-style musicals, these plays participate in a tradition governed by well-defined conventions, but they are also concerned to subvert the ideological apparatus of the chosen genre by using catchy tunes and pleasant rhythms in ironic apposition to lyrics which voice less than mellow protests against European colonisation. The musical score of *Bran Nue Dae* draws rhythmic inspiration from such disparate sources as blues, country and western, calypso, reggae, gospel, and tribal chant to articulate a syncretic mixture of song/sound/music that reflects the complex genealogies of the characters portrayed. *Funerals and Circuses*, though driven more by the narrative events than by the music, also shows a range of musical influences and even gives a guest singer/musician from the audience the opportunity to perform in a staged talent quest. Through such moments of self-conscious metatheatricality, both texts point with urbane wit to the prejudices of the entertainment traditions which inform them, demonstrating, as Jacqueline Lo argues, that 'the [musical] form is not a completely closed dramaturgy whereby a single cultural discourse — that of Anglo-American Hollywood imperialism — predominates' (1994, 1-2).

Spatial markers of Aboriginality are inscribed in the scenography of a theatrical event and in its particular manipulation of proxemic codes. One of the most common design features of Aboriginal theatre is the tendency to use motifs from traditional art, either as part of a stylised set or, in dance theatre particularly, as the major element of the entire *mise en scène*. Such motifs incorporate specific Aboriginal epistemologies into the performance event as well as providing an immediate visual hook for audiences. Adapted for the stage, Aboriginal art can be deployed not only to inscribe space with markers of indigenous culture but also to denaturalise certain scenic conventions, especially those of realist theatre. In *Sistergirl*, for instance, the stage is initially set in naturalistic style to depict an austere hospital ward, but as the play begins, the entire acting space is temporarily transformed by a projected image of one of Sally Morgan's original designs. This visual layering of scenographic elements, like the kitchen set overpainted with dot designs for the Brisbane production of *Murri Love* in 1995, invests the stage with a sense of Aboriginal place/space at the same time as it creates functional interactive settings for both the present-day action and the surrealistic dream sequences. In a sense, the audience's visual field in *Sistergirl* is imprinted with the projected image whose traces continue to inform the play's spatial design even after the opening flashback scene segues into more mundane 'reality'. The recurrent usage of this same lighting effect throughout the performance contextualises the narrative action, consolidates Aboriginal inscriptions of theatrical space, and helps to position the play outside the confining parameters of naturalistic representation.

By creating specific cognitive stagescapes/landscapes, set designs influenced by Aboriginal art often stress the importance of the land, a trope which figures prominently in plays by and about indigenous peoples — and, for that matter, in much settler drama as well (Makeham 1996). This particular trope has been equally well staged in productions which use less abstract forms of scenography. A case in point is Edie Kurzer's design for the joint Black Swan/Belvoir Street production of *Dead Heart*, described by many reviewers as visually stunning (Griffiths 1994b, 39; Laud 1994, 40; Hyde 1994, 40). To dramatise tensions between various characters' relationships with the land, Kurzer constructed a massive open set within a disused warehouse, the floor of which was covered with tons of red sand to approximate an outback locale complete with a campfire, a distant waterhole, and rear-vista sand dunes.[15] Staged in this manner, the land presents as a politicised space which records inscriptions of colonialist desire — imaged, for example, by the tracks of four-wheel-drive vehicles on the dunes — *and* as a contested territory which also exerts its own palpable force on the lives of its inhabitants.

Promenade-style productions such as *Wahngin Country* and *Funerals and Circuses* spatialise their narrative concerns in a slightly different way. In performance, these plays make a symbolic claim for land rights by commandeering public spaces not normally used for theatrical purposes. *Wahngin Country*, which was specifically designed for production in the grounds of the University of Western Australia, began with a reappropriation of sorts as the storyteller urinated against a tree in what was not just a comic moment but also a deliberate claim to territorial priority over the performance venue. *Funerals and Circuses* also draws attention to contested space, in this case via a staged confrontation which occurs as audiences arrive at the theatre where an Aboriginal man (one of the actors) is debarred from entering because of his supposed disorderly behaviour. Momentarily taken in by the seeming reality of this performance, most viewers are positioned as uncomfortable witnesses to precisely the kind of racial discrimination they will witness in an overtly fictionalised form as the play progresses. Subsequent scenes staged in the foyer of theatre and in various parts of the auditorium continue to blur the usual boundaries between spectators and actors. In this kind of theatrical event, even places/spaces which are conventionally the bastion of white society lose their fixity to become possible sites of the dialogue necessary for a moral future.[16]

Reconciliation?

While I have argued that Aboriginality has been articulated in various ways in recent Australian theatre, this is not to suggest that hegemonic versions of Aboriginal culture have completely faded from our theatrical repertoire or that actual theatre practices have changed enough to allow the repositioning of Aboriginal writers, actors, directors, and designers so that they always have equal power to govern production values. But the effort to open up a productive dialogue about cultural capital, as it has been expressed in the performing arts, must be generally regarded as progressive, even in the face of specific difficulties and frustrations. If Australians on both sides of the cultural fence are committed to reconciliation, they must be prepared to negotiate the terms of each cultural encounter and each construction of cultural difference. In the theatre as in our broader socio-political practices, it remains for Aboriginal and non-Aboriginal groups to fully acknowledge their role in such constructions and to take joint responsibility for their future.[17]

Notes

1 See, for example, Milne's (1990) discussion of the relative Aboriginal and multicultural content of Melbourne theatre in the bicentennial year.

2 Among other texts, *Bran Nue Dae* and *Ningali* attracted this kind of criticism. See e.g. Evans (1991a), Radic (1991b), and Banks (1994).

3 See essays in Fischer et al. (1993) and also Dunstone (forthcoming) for a full discussion. More recently, Aboriginal ownership of this project was consolidated by the play's full production as part of the 1996 Sydney Festival.

4 See Lloyd (1990), Nugent (1990), and Koch (1990) reviewing *Bran Nue Dae*; also Harris (1993) and Scott-Norman (1993) on *Funerals and Circuses*. Stephen Gration's Foreword to the published version of the latter play invokes at length the discourses of Australianness.

5 Stephen Page's choreography for the closing ceremonies of the Atlanta Olympic Games can be examined according to this paradigm. A particularly kitsch example which also shows the harnessing of Aboriginal performing arts in the service of Australian tourism is the Dreamtime show at the Kummara Aboriginal Theatre Restaurant at the Gold Coast Arts Centre. According to Lehmann, the restaurant's appeal to international visitors rests on its combination of Queensland-inspired Australian food and a somewhat simplistic performance of Aboriginal mythology (1992, 11).

6 See, for instance, Nemeth (1993), Partridge (1993), and Sawford (1993, 91). One dissenting voice is Alison Cotes (1993b) who fixes on the fact that the play's author is not Aboriginal and proceeds to criticise the production for being patronising and not strident enough.

7 Wesley Enoch, artistic director of Kooemba Jdarra, reports that a number of Aborigines involved in the project, including choreographer Michael Leslie, were dissatisfied with the level of Aboriginal input into the actual directorial approaches to the play. Personal conversation, 8 July 1997.

8 The format of this particular work, with its emphasis on improvisation, oral histories and memories, also encouraged the audience to participate in the play writing process (see Miller 1995).

9 I would want to distinguish this kind of non-traditional casting from the more common practice of casting Aborigines in racially marked roles, as for example, in Neil Armfield's production of *The Tempest* (1995) where Kevin Smith played Caliban.

10 Such stylistic promiscuity is not always well received by reviewers. Kooemba Jdarra's 1996 production of Jack Davis's *The Dreamers*, for instance, was categorised by one reviewer as 'a curious pastiche of kitchen-sink acting and whizbangery' in which 'naturalistic and non-naturalistic production styles collided' (Lynch 1996). On the other hand, Lisa Yallamas (1996) criticised the production's naturalism as portraying

only the bleakness of Aboriginal life and ignoring the script's few transcendent moments.

11 It seems in fact that SWY's strategy of cross-race casting partly accounted for the general critical approval of this production as compared with Peter Gorman's less successful adaptation of the play for Belvoir Street Theatre in 1994 (see Turner 1992, Banks 1992, and Maher 1994).

12 Following Homi Bhabha's theories on ambivalence in colonial and post-colonial discourses (1985), such mimicry can be seen to unsettle the hegemonic status of the dominant culture's norms even while it points to certain forms of acculturation.

13 Critical response to Deck Chair's production of Eddie Bennell's *My Spiritual Dreaming* (1993) shows a marked bias against hybridised music, even though the show was expressly billed as a rock opera. One reviewer commented that there should have been many more moments when the didgeridoos were in full flight, 'yelping like feral dogs' (Neill 1993).

14 Musical syncretism is also central to Matthew Doyle and Colin Offord's *Blackman Whiteman*, which played at the 1996 Brisbane Festival, blending Celtic and Aboriginal music to produce complex hybrids.

15 In some respects, this design recalls the set of the Melbourne production of Davis's *First Born Trilogy* (1988), which used truckloads of sand to convert Fitzroy Town Hall into an appropriate playing space.

16 In his article, 'Mabo and Moral Anxiety', Tim Rowse argues that Australia can only begin to see itself as a legitimate moral community if treats issues concerning Aboriginal landrights seriously (1993).

17 Of course this might mean quite different actions depending on cultural affiliation. Critics such as Mudrooroo argue that it is the responsibility of whites to keep their hands off all forms of Aboriginal cultural production (1994, 258) but this may not be the ideal trajectory for Aboriginal theatre, which currently seems to be thriving on cross-cultural interaction.

From gay and lesbian to queer theatre

Bruce Parr

> *After almost a month of arts and festivities there is a nagging suspicion growing among us straights that you guys are having more fun than we are.*

So wrote theatre critic John McCallum (1995a), summing up his doubly satisfying and anxious response to the 1995 Sydney Gay and Lesbian Mardi Gras Festival. Earlier he had named 1995 as 'the Year of Nick Enright' (1995b), honouring the playwright whose *Good Works* (1994) had been celebrated by one critic as 'queer production of the year' (Dunne 1994). McCallum's 'nagging suspicion' betrays an anxiety which circulates around gay/lesbian/queer theatre's role, its definition and its problematic relations to the mainstream, an anxiety which reflects heterosexuality's twentieth-century dependence on and paranoia concerning its irrepressible 'other'. The 1990s proliferation of gay characters and themes in film, television and theatre — although lesbians are notably absent from mainstream theatre — begs the question of the decline of dramatic tension in conventional representations and 'tired narratives'[1] of heterosexuality, the result of its 'constitutive malaise' (Butler 1993, 314). Confronting this crisis in 'straight' sexuality, mainstream culture is gradually being 'queered' in two senses. Gay men and (to a lesser extent) lesbians seem to be 'everywhere' both as cultural producers and in representations; and seem to be unearthing the insecurities and uncertainties in heterosexuality, thereby transforming it into something strange and queer itself. Enright's *Good Works* achieves just this. Concerning much more than gay issues, it defies classification, and is open to co-option by both gays and the mainstream. It participates in the exercise of making queer all sexualities and all theatre, phenomena partly accounting for the fun from which McCallum feels somewhat excluded.

Before the attention given Nick Enright for *Good Works*, Michael Gow was queerly infiltrating mainstream theatre. Amidst the alienation and dislocation in *The Kid* (1983) is the homosexual boy, Donald, who is first seduced then cruelly (and homophobically) abused by the charming 'collector', Dean. While Gow calls the play 'quite self-declaratory' of his own sexuality (Chenery 1991), it is in *Furious* (1991) that he most forcefully critiques the dominance of heterosexuality and reveals a crumbling ruin. Heterosexuality's disarray is measured against the temporary solace the playwright Roland finds in his love for the schoolboy, Chris. Some explicit description of gay male sex in the play suggests that Gow considers a mainstream reflection on the actuality of alternative sexual practices may serve to counter the structures of masculine heterosexuality. Gay sexual explicitness is a theme that Louis Nowra takes up in *The Jungle* (1995), intertwining disturbing scenes of contemporary city life, in one part of which a man suffocates his wheelchair-confined son who is hospitalised with AIDS after he bombards his father with precise descriptions of his (homo)sexual practices. Gow is in a much lighter vein (though characteristically not without serious purpose) in *Live Acts on Stage* (1996), a pansexual romp drawing on ancient Greek myths at the centre of which are the consequences of Zeus' shenanigans with his minion Ganymede.

Concurrent with the first production of *Furious*, Nick Enright's (1994b) references a rich body of Australian playwriting replete with homosexual resonances.[2] The two competing 1970s playwrights in *Mongrels* (1994b), Edmund Burke and Vincent O'Hara, bring to mind respectively the 'prison playwright' Jim McNeil and Peter Kenna during the height of his popularity. As Veronica Kelly has shown, Enright's treatment of the sexual identities and behaviours of his 'mongrels' and their varied works has strong intertextual connections with the opportunistic homosexuality in such McNeil's plays as *The Old Familiar Juice* (1972) and *How Does Your Garden Grow?* (1974), and the 'real' homosexuality of a character like Joe Cassidy in Kenna's trilogy *The Cassidy Album* (1978).[3] According to Kelly, Enright's 'intervention in the canon of contemporary Australian drama' foregrounds the desirability of greater 'queer' analysis of a 'submerged tradition of gay playwriting traceable at least to Patrick White' (1994, 21). Since appeared, Peter Kenna's relevant 'homosexual' work has begun to receive close study and reassessment (Parr 1994, 1996a).

Although Enright's *Daylight Saving* (1989) and his plays of the 1990s, *St James' Infirmary* (1992), *A Property of the Clan* (1992) and *The Quartet from Rigoletto* (1995), all concern themselves to some marginal degree with homosexuality, it is *Mongrels* (1991) and *Good Works* (1995) which place gay men at their centre. The latter play has as one of its key settings a gay pub in a major unspecified Australian city in 1981 where the two thirty-year-old men engage in a prolonged, uneasy mating ritual. Through flashbacks we learn that they have not seen each other since when, as young schoolboys in 1962, Shane killed a Marist brother in attempting to save Tim from a vicious flogging. Tim was compelled by family pressures to betray Shane who was thenceforth projected into a life of institutionalised hardship and cruelty. In the gay bar the threat of violence is potent, as Shane carries the very knife which killed the teacher, while refusing to identify himself as Tim's former friend. The different backgrounds of the two men squarely place class and economic issues at the play's forefront. Juxtaposed with the young men's relationship is that of their mothers, which is likewise coloured by vague but discernible adolescent same-sex longings. In *Good Works* however homosexuality is but one aspect of the total sexual battleground represented. The play's queerness derives from a complexity of interrelating sexualities which Enrightshows are shaped by particular historical and social circumstances. Enright's concern for the specificity of time and place in emerging and changing subjectivities is never more apparent. His exploration of adolescent (homo)sexuality, this time in its intersections with ethnicity, continues in *Playgrounds* (1996).[4]

There is no comparable presence of lesbian characters in Australian mainstream theatre. Lesbian invisibility is reinforced by mainstream criticism which, in reviewing the theatre offerings of Sydney's Gay and Lesbian Mardi Gras Festival (SGLMG), ignores the lesbian component altogether.[5] It is ironic that often those lesbians who do appear on mainstages are conjured by male writers. Judy Connelli played a lesbian night club owner in *The Emerald Room*, a musical by Dennis Watkins and Chris Harriott staged by the State Theatre Company of South Australia in 1994. David Williamson is credited, through Katy in *Brilliant Lies* (1993), with representing 'the first self-identified lesbian character in mainstream Australian theatre' (Dunne 1993), although her sexual life is not explored in the text. It could be argued however that lesbian representation in mainstream Australian theatre began with Alison Lyssa's *Pinball* at Nimrod Downstairs in 1981. More commonly, lesbian characters created by women writers are found in mainstream subsidised theatres other than the state theatre companies, that is, in 'medium sized companies'.[6] La Boite Theatre in Brisbane, the only Australian theatre company other than STC/Playbox to have performed Gow's *Furious*, produced in 1993 Sara Hardy's *Vita! A Fantasy* (1989), which explores the relationship of Vita Sackville-West and Virginia Woolf, and premiered *No Strings Attached* (1994) by Hilary Beaton, in which Maxine's lesbianism is admittedly understated.

It is hardly surprising that lesbian voices are rare in mainstream theatre when we consider that the greater focus on contemporary Australian work by major theatre companies has not benefited women writers in general (Chesterman 1995).[7] Serious dramatic studies of women's sexuality by women themselves are relegated to the margins.

Lyssa, whose *Pinball* was staged at the Nimrod following a reading by the Women and Theatre Project (1980-81), wryly recounts the response of an agent who disapproved the subject matter of her play which deals with a lesbian custody battle: 'I don't see how anybody could put that on' (Chesterman 1995: 32). Playwright and director Alana Valentine believes that plays about issues of female (homo)sexuality have 'with some brave exceptions, been discriminated against by mainstage companies' (Chesterman 1995, 34). Sandra Shotlander whose lesbian plays, *Framework* (1983) and *Is That You Nancy*? (1991), have been performed successfully in the United States and Australia, has not yet been produced by a major theatre company. This need not suggest that there is no lesbian visibility outside subcultural theatre. In 1995 Death Defying Theatre introduced late-teenage audiences to an Australian multicultural mix in Noëlle Janaczewska's *Yungaburra Road*, including a lesbian schoolteacher's revelations of the threat of random violence to gay men and women. The professional women's theatre company in Adelaide, Vitalstatistix, has often featured issues of lesbianism in their work for general audiences, in plays by Roxxy Bent — *Waiting for Annette* (1987) and *Yellow Roses* (1992) — and in *The Gay Divorcee* (1991) by Margaret Fischer.[8]

During the 1990s divisions between gay and mainstream theatre have increasingly become blurred, such that plays and performances that direct themselves to audiences of all sexual persuasions defy simple categorisation. When one of the hits of the 1995 SGLMG Festival, Alex Harding's *Only Heaven Knows* (1988), transfers to the Opera House Playhouse and '[h]ome-grown gay theatre ... finally ascend[s] to the temple of culture on Bennelong Point' (Dunne 1995a), how 'gay' does it remain, playing to the general public? Gay and mainstream merge imperceptibly. The mainstreaming of the SGLMG is now such that the Ensemble Theatre can present Reg Livermore's *Red Riding Hood, the Speed Hump and the Wolf* (1994) in the official 1996 Mardi Gras program. The successful STC touring production of *Two Weeks with the Queen: The Play* (1992) by Mary Morris widely introduced mainstream audiences to issues of gay-bashing, discrimination, and loss and grieving through AIDS. The ubiquity of gay themes and characters in both Australian and overseas theatre works, created and produced in the knowledge that audiences share a kaleidoscope of sexual preferences, requires flexible approaches to categorisation.

In the 1995 *Companion to Theatre in Australia*, edited by Philip Parsons, gay and lesbian theatre is covered from the perspective of 'organised gay theatre' (Galbraith 1995). This term refers to gay theatre presented by gay people primarily for gay people. Larry Galbraith begins his survey with the formation of the Gay Theatre Company in Sydney in 1979, mentions the important contribution of Barry Lowe's plays and the work presented each year as part of the SGLMG Festival, includes references both to the theatre component of Melbourne's gay and lesbian Midsumma Festival and to Sydney's In The Pink Theatre Company (1990-93), and concludes with a paragraph on drag. The *Companion*'s approach — admittedly conceived before the upsurge of gay/lesbian content in mainstream media, cinema and television — serves to reinforce a restrictive notion of the overly marginalised nature of gay/lesbian lives and art forms, and fails to account for the increasing diversity of lesbian and gay cultures. Gay theatre as an academic field of study remains almost exclusively ghettoised.

The popularity of drag in Australia and its theatrical connections warrant an entry of their own in which non-text-based gay theatre is also emphasised. Neil Bartlett makes the important point that much innovative and popular gay theatre is not synonymous with 'literary theatre' (1990, 83). Gay and lesbian theatre in Australia has long encompassed other genres of performance such as cabaret, *a capella*, dance, performance art, circus and acrobatic acts, and more recently, stand-up comedy. All these forms can be found as part of hybrid queer culture performance in the popular Mardi Gras venue cLUB bENT, described as 'contemporary circus swinging above you, funky dance numbers, new form drag, anti-drag, multi-media majesty, and poets and artists in provocative modes of performance' (Decent 1996, 65). Lesbian erotic performances such as Wicked Women have also crossed over into mainstream s/m spaces. Lesbian theatre itself requires a separate category, as it sits uneasily under the banner 'gay' in the *Companion* even when the latter term is used to conflate male and female same-sex subcultural interests.[9] But more perturbing, as 'gay theatre' receives half a page in around 650 pages of entries, is the potential conclusion that the rest of Australian theatre is 'straight'. This is not the case.

Defining gay/lesbian theatre and drama, as with gay and lesbian studies in general, has always been problematical.[10] One approach, which reflects the *Companion's*, is to look at the self-proclaimed sexual identities of those involved, from writers to performers, from directors and designers to technical support personnel, and conclude that only openly gay/lesbian people, where they outnumber heterosexuals, produce gay/lesbian theatre. In 1979 William M. Hoffman defined gay theatre 'as a production that implicitly or explicitly acknowledges that there are homosexuals on both sides of the footlights' (ix). It would be far better today if all productions acknowledged that there are always potentially other sexualities besides heterosexuality at play both on stage and in the audience. Thus where Hoffman writes that '[a]bsolutely any play can be performed gay' (x), it can now be amended: any play can be performed with awareness that heterosexuality is only one of many possibilities available. All theatre has the potential to provide pleasure in varying degrees for those audiences with same-sex desires and non-heterosexual inclinations. These pleasures are not merely confined to gay communities' performance which itself may occasionally fail to offer attractions to part of its intended market audience. High standards of writing and performance are now often demanded by critics and audiences, and harsh reviews of 'gay' plays are not unusual in the gay/lesbian media. An example is Jill Jones's review in the *Sydney Star Observer* of Steven Dawson's *The Gathering of Vampires* (1995) in which she finds 'cheap shots' at lesbians and insufficient dramatic technique in confronting 'the serious political issues' such as AIDS. It also cannot be assumed that lesbians or gay men are united in viewing/reading positions (de Lauretis 1988, 170).

Following Hoffman's definition however, it becomes axiomatic that the Gay Theatre Company (1979-82) and like companies such as Witch Theatre in Sydney (active since 1987), founded by gay people for gay people, present a form of gay theatre. Of course we need to distinguish between gay men's theatre, which the Gay Theatre Company exemplified, and lesbian theatre, as the two rarely coincide. The political and social importance of this style of theatre should not be undervalued as it has provided and continues to provide a presence, a voice and representation for those marginalised and discriminated against in a homophobic society.[11] Galbraith's brief summary in the *Companion* is a valuable exercise that deserves expansion; greater attention needs to be given to recording the wealth of theatre drawing on the traditions of gay/lesbian cultures and experiences produced by openly gay/lesbian practitioners for mainly gay/lesbian audiences. Nonetheless, this definition excludes a vast range of material performed outside the gay/lesbian subcultures which features sexualities beyond the heterosexual imperative.

Basing his definition of gay/lesbian theatre on the concept of representation, Stephen Dunne would include any play containing homosexual discourse, including negative and hostile depictions. He distinguishes between plays which invite/construct a gay and/or lesbian reading position, that is, plays which are gay-affirmative, and those which contain gay, lesbian or homosexual discourse which may be interpreted as either homophobic or non-homophobic (1991, 18, 106). Dunne's definition is preferable to the 'organised gay theatre' approach as it both disregards (or places less importance on) the sexual identities of the playwrights and practitioners and widens the range of contenders for the label of gay/lesbian plays/theatre. Thus not only do mainly subcultural writers like Barry Lowe and Alex Harding feature in Dunne's listings, but also entering the spotlight are many mainstream playwrights such as Michael Gow and Peter Kenna whose works include only some, not a majority of, gay/lesbian/homosexual characters and themes. David Williamson, for example, is mentioned for *What If You Died Tomorrow* (1973) and *Celluloid Heroes* (1980) (Dunne's thesis predates *Brilliant Lies*), the latter of which is criticised for the implicit homophobia in its depiction of a stereotypical 'flabby, fragile screamer'.[12] Of value in Dunne's approach is the blurring of the clear distinction between subcultural and mainstream theatre works, given the uneasy straddling between the two by writers such as Sara Hardy and Sandra Shotlander who have constantly to confront the opposition by some program decision-makers to lesbian characters on mainstages.[13] Sara Hardy's and Adele Saleem's biographical drama, *Radclyffe* (1987), for example, skirts the periphery of the mainstream with stagings at La Mama and the Universal Theatre, Melbourne, the Performance Space, Sydney, and under Vitalstatistix's banner in Adelaide, all of which attracted reviews in the mainstream press.

Remaining problematical however is the quantity, not to mention quality, of homosexuality in any given work before it can be classified as gay/lesbian. The apparent absurdity of this quest should not obscure its strategic, pioneering importance in opening up an investigation of sexual difference in Australian drama. Dunne names Kenna's *A Hard God* (1973) as the 'first 'mainstream' Australian gay play' (1991, 77), despite Jack's and Joe's proxemic marginalisation (although not unimportance) in that play.[14] The other contender might be Kenna's *Mates* (1975) where the drag queen/homosexual Sylvia's relationship with footballer Gary is at the centre of the play. Mates fulfils Hoffman's definition of a gay play (as distinct from gay theatre) 'as one whose central figure or figures are homosexual or one in which homosexuality is a main theme' (1979, ix). But Dunne might equally argue that homosexuality is a main theme in *A Hard God. Mates* however is more 'gay' — it is set in a drag club post-Stonewall, for example — than *A Hard God* set in the pre-gay 1940s, and these debates might wish to take into account Kenna's dislike of the use of 'gay' (Wells 1978, 15).[15] In 1989, the Radikal Thesbian Theatre Company became politically divided over the comparatively small degree of lesbian content in Jennifer Rogers' *Jigsaws* (1988) which had previously played in smaller mainstream theatres (Greenaway 1990, 76).[16] Eva Johnson's *What Do They Call Me?* (1990) consists of three monologues, only one of which is delivered by a lesbian character. Does this make it a lesbian play? Whatever one's opinions, such discussions position the plays' homosexuality at the forefront of consideration. The political importance of these issues encompasses artistic relevance, including style of production. It has not been uncommon for 'gay plays' to have their homosexual component diminished in production.[17]

If the above search for definitions and labelling resembles a dog chasing its tail, it should not be forgotten that this definitional work, especially Dunne's, is important precisely because it is a reminder to those who might otherwise ignore it that Australian drama is replete with works that interrogate alternative sexualities. Gay and lesbian studies in theatre lead the way in addressing non-heterosexual possibilities, and most importantly the place of sexuality and eroticism in drama in general and that of resistant, erotically charged lesbian and gay bodies in particular. We disregard at our peril Chris Westwood's caution at the Queensland Theatre Summit in 1993 that if live theatre is to survive it has to be 'sexier' (qtd. in Waller (Waller 1993a). Scholarship which addresses the difficult questions of the nature of a gay play, and its degree of gayness/lesbianism, may have the effect of re-enlivening the reading and production of works previously considered outside the ambit of gay/lesbian categorisation. Highlighting the homosexual discourse in Clem Gorman's *A Manual of Trench Warfare* (1978), for example, may lead to productions in which the central focus becomes the homoeroticism likely to be missing when the script's sexual dynamism is downplayed.

Awareness and appreciation of gay/lesbian/homosexual energies in otherwise'straight' theatre casts a shadow over any adequate process of binary categorisation. Richard Wherrett's productions for the Sydney Theatre Company, most notably Shakespeare's *A Midsummer Night's Dream* in 1989, would sometimes attract large numbers of gay men to his style of 'high gloss, whiz-bang' theatre (Cahill 1995). While Patrick White's plays do not deal in any obvious way with same-sex passion, our appreciation of them may often be informed by White's belief that his homosexuality fuelled his inspiration for writing (Marr 1991, 581). The group of outsiders in *Netherwood* (1983) may be seen to personify non-normative sexual preferences. *Big Toys* (1977) has been described as 'White's most sustained generic exercise in the high comedic and indeed high camp genres' (Kelly 1995a, 101). In Alma De Groen's *The Rivers of China* (1987), part of which is set in a feminist dystopia, the young man, Wayne, and the Man who believes himself to be Katherine Mansfield form a gender troubling attachment, the complexities of which encompass the homoerotic. The scenes between Sally and Jill in David Williamson's *A Handful of Friends* (1976) become more engaging when they are played with heightened awareness of their former lesbian relationship. While each of these plays in no way fits the category 'gay', they all explore sexual energies beyond the narrowly heterosexual.

This short list merely scratches the surface of gay, or more specifically, non-straight, themes and energies in Australian drama and theatre. What should be apparent is that one need not necessarily visit the marginal or gay festival theatres to experience sexualities alternative to the heterosexual. Closer examination of a substantial body of Australian playwriting and theatre — indeed such canonical texts as those above — may indicate that non-straight sexuality and the perversity of desire are central to our stages, were we to open our eyes to them.[18] Tony Kushner has said that *Angels in America* makes a 'claim that the American political agenda has everything to do with groups that are considered to be minorities and marginal' (Wyndham 1993). Supposedly minority sexualities can contribute on our stages, as elsewhere, to the destabilising of the centre/margin dichotomy. Despite the crucial political importance of 'organised' gay/lesbian theatre, dividing lines between gay and mainstream are being consistently blurred. The SGLMG Festival cannot now contain the material which seeps beyond the allocated timespan. As gay/lesbian themes and issues increasingly infiltrate the mainstream, there now appears no simple distinction between gay/lesbian and other forms of artistic endeavour. It is perhaps time/ly at this historical juncture to speak and write of the circulation of 'queer' energies in the theatre.

The use of 'queer' is not intended to override or eliminate the use or importance of 'gay' or 'lesbian'.[19] It both encompasses these terms and exceeds them by emphasising the promiscuity and contradictions in all identity formations. It also invites a consideration of all forms of non-straight sexuality and eroticism and of the multiplicity of desires available to us, including those bisexual and transsexual. Queer and gay/lesbian should not be seen as conflicting, but rather as mutually dependent in their opposition to homophobia, heterosexism and the marginalisation by those in power of anyone because of his/her sexual practices. Queer also helps us to appreciate that representations involve complex intersections of identity markers like gender, race and ethnicity, class, age and ability. Importantly, queer places sexuality as a social construction at the top of the agenda in all performance analysis, not only in some avowedly non-heterosexual, gender-bending performance, and in doing so, invites constant surveillance of heterosexuality in denying it its 'naturalness'. In place of the imposition of dogmatic ideas on matters of sexual orientation, queer promotes theoretical fluidity and multiple identity positions.

Queer theories applied to theatre can enable us simultaneously to look backwards and to suggest a way forward, in both cases enriching the theatre of the present. In addition to searching the archives for references to homosexuality, we can re-read plays with supposedly heterosexual narratives to uncover queer traces and to destabilise preferred straight readings. Stage representations of gender performance, especially those in which ambiguity is at play, encourage the questioning and renegotiation of dominant meanings about the relationship of sex and gender. In this respect, if Patrick White's plays do not qualify as gay, they nevertheless provide opportunities for queer readings and stagings. Playwrights like White, who eschew naturalistic realism and create worlds of allegory and dream where power and desire are free of moral certainties, and where subjectivity is shifting and changeable, where characters take pleasure in reinventing themselves, have much in common with the queer. For example, the plays of Dorothy Hewett, Louis Nowra,[20] Janis Balodis and David Malouf at times invite queer readings.

In questioning the efficacy of heterosexuality, queer encourages us to explore male homosociality and aspects of manliness, mateship and masculinity. This is already happening on our stages in new readings which privilege the ambiguous and the complex. In reviewing the Melbourne Theatre Company's fortieth anniversary production of *Summer of the Seventeenth Doll* (1955) directed by Robyn Nevin, Jack Hibberd commented: 'For the first time, perhaps, [Roo's and Barney's] intense mateship is tinged with some homosexuality'. Such realisations spearhead the necessary re-reading of platonic same-sex relationships in canonical Australian drama for complexity and the hidden, enabling queer reworkings of much 'straight' writing. A queer reading of David Williamson's *Sanctuary* (1994), for example, might have the two men enacting a sado-masochistic dance of death. Such interpretations do not necessitate radical stagings of these plays, as that of the *Doll* in Melbourne testifies, but merely informing productions with other than surface meanings of sexualities and sexual energies.

When Jack Hibberd writes of craving an Australian theatre 'that goes the whole hog physically and evocatively' we can surmise that theatre that is queer in the current manifestation of that term might at least partially fulfil his aspirations. Hibberd's is only one of those voices calling for a reinvigorated theatre. Robyn Archer, artistic director of both the 1998 and 2000 Adelaide Festivals, has criticised the mainstream theatres for serving audiences 'a diet of innocuous, safe work' (Morgan 1994a). In asking what has happened to the audacity of Australian theatre, Bryce Hallett (1995) calls for 'the reality-distorting scenes, the extravagant gestures, the histrionic and gut-wrenching extremes; the economy and force of fantasy and invention that make all who gather know and feel the potency of theatre'. Queering the theatre of the future, even when it is engaging with the plays of the past, may provide an answer.

Playwrights were recently advised to 'focus on creating fabulous characters that actors would want to play' (Waites 1995). Queer suggests how to construct these characters and the plays to contain them. It recommends the theatre as a site for exploring both difference, especially sexual difference, and the repression of difference within oneself. Seeing culture as performative and identity as a state of 'perpetual reinvention' (Fuss 1991, 7),[21] it recommends the performance of multiple sexual identities, the exposure to which may transform a viewer's very system of identification so that conflicting viewpoints can be entertained concurrently. A queer character and performance will not reassure an audience in matters of gender or the body, but will show both to be constructed by socially regulated practices. Queer performance will critique cultural and political institutions, interpersonal relationships, and how subjectivity is given effect by the mutuality of power and desire. It will offer diverse, contradictory viewpoints, and will strive to be simultaneously dangerous, outrageous and 'fabulous'. With its enigmatic and non-naturalistic qualities, Michael Gurr's *Sex Diary of an Infidel* (1992), which uses Asian sex tours as a 'metaphor for lying, personal lying and international lying' (Gilbert & Mawson 1995, 32), invites such a queer reading. As text-based theatre, it potentially offers the qualities of queer which are more often ascribed to performance on the margins of theatre itself. Rock 'n' Roll Circus's physical theatre piece *The Dark* (1995), which includes a sexual encounter between two men performed entirely through tumbling and acrobatic skills, has been described as 'erotic, perverse, enigmatic, sadistic, sentimental, street-smart, funny, surreal and altogether terrific' (Kelly 1995b) — in other words, a queer hit, where sexuality is unconfinable. Work of Michael

Gow (*Furious*) and Nick Enright (*Good Works*) discussed above likewise provides a mix of queer possibilities. Alex Harding's *Blood and Honour* (1990) might also be similarly recognised.

Blood and Honour, recipient of a Human Rights Award, has been produced only once at the Belvoir Street Theatre during the 1990 SGLMG Festival. It therefore qualifies as a piece of 'organised' gay (male) theatre although its scope belies simple categorisation. At its core lies an uncontrollable rage against those with political and financial clout and influence in the media who respond to a virulent epidemic with apathy and inaction. The three characters carry equal weight in the drama; Colin, a newsreader with AIDS; Michael, his Asian lover, and Colin's mother, an actress and feminist deeply affected by her son's illness. Harding explores and develops a form to match the hideous irrationality of prejudice and disease, at a time when, 'One mustn't pretend, not anymore' (Harding 1996, 247). Disease is not polite, nor, Harding suggests, is the structure through which it must be presented by those who are 'living' the humiliations and powerlessness of the AIDS virus. The play is a theatrical metaphor for the virus itself, irrepressible and unpredictable. Memory, fantasy, passion, camp, and the reality of suffering coalesce in Harding's celebration of living in the shadow of death. This is not 'victim art', it is 'survivor art' in which the visceral supersedes the cerebral.[22] Harding also explores an analogous relationship between racism directed at Asians and discrimination against people with AIDS. Homophobes are predictably often racists, but *Blood and Honour* confronts gay men with the uncomfortable proposition that the oppressed may also be among the oppressors. The play's intertwining themes and discourses, such as Michael's identities as Asian in Australia and as gay, contribute to its complexity and queerness. Unusual on Australian stages is such a forceful and articulate Asian character who also happens to be proudly gay. Refusing the categorisation of 'AIDS play',[23] *Blood and Honour* provides a critique of Australian society from its colonialist past in Asia to the cultural attitudes and national traits of the late 1980s, and thus surveys many factors shaping the responses to the epidemic.

In form, structure and tone, *Blood and Honour* is dangerous; Bob Evans (1990) found it 'anarchic — its centre threatens at every moment to fly apart — so great is the rage'. In stretching the boundaries of traditional gay 'community' theatre Harding delineates a means whereby gay and queer can co-exist successfully, and a reinvigorated theatre in which difference is explored passionately can promote social change. In one of the best-selling autobiographies in Australia in 1995, *Holding the*

Man, Timothy Conigrave, the playwright and actor who died from AIDS in 1994, pays tribute to *Blood and Honour* and its theatrical verve: 'Glaringly lit moments of the human condition went whizzing past at an extraordinary speed' (202). *Blood and Honour* is also irreverent, vulgar and mischievous — it has a sense of fun, a quality integral to the concept of queer, as it has been to homosexual camp.[24] That liberating queer sense of humour accounts for the 'nagging suspicion' that something transformative is happening within and between cultures.

Notes

1 Budge & Hamer (1994, 6). They continue: 'So little is now forbidden within a heterosexual landscape that new metaphors must constantly be sought out. Homosexuality serves as a new and (still) shocking arena for the reworking of stories of sex and love, romance and desire' (6-7).

2 Remarkably, the plays were first performed on consecutive nights, *Furious* by the Sydney Theatre Company on 6 November 1991, and *Mongrels* by the Ensemble Theatre, Sydney, on 7 November 1991. *Furious* has since been seen in Melbourne, Adelaide and Brisbane, and a second production of *Mongrels* was mounted in STC's 1997 season.

3 *The Cassidy Album* comprises *A Hard God*, *Furtive Love* and *An Eager Hope*.

4 *Playgrounds* which opened at the Wharf 1 (STC) on 3 July 1996 is a double bill consisting of *The Way I Was* and *Where Are We Now? The Way I Was*, first seen in 'Sydney Stories 2' (Sydney Theatre Company, 1995), details the romance of a Greek and a Turkish boy in an outer suburban high school in the 1970s.

5 See Brian Hoad (1996). In his summary Hoad ignores two 1996 lesbian theatre pieces developed with the assistance of Mardi Gras' Development Funding, *(M)alice* and *700 Positions*, both major theatre events.

6 Chesterman (1995, 8) distinguishes between 'large mainstream', that is, state theatre companies or their commercial equivalents, and 'small mainstream', medium sized companies such as Griffin in Sydney and Brisbane's La Boite.

7 '... over the ten years [1985-1995], we have begun to see a greater focus on contemporary Australian work, but this has not benefited women writers whose work has hovered just under 20% of the seasons [of those companies brought by the Australia Council into the Major Organisations Board], although it dropped in one year to only 8%. Australian men's works have risen from 30% of the repertoire to 38%' (Chesterman 1995, 119).

8 *Wanted*, Margaret Fischer's sequel to *The Gay Divorcee*, is due to be produced by Vitalstatistix in 1997.

9 The diverse desires, histories, perspectives and experiences of lesbians and gay men are important issues which are often occluded in some uses of 'gay'. The idea of a gay or lesbian 'community' may also be illusory. Alan Sinfield recommends the use of 'subculture' because it lacks the 'cosy, togetherness connotations' of community (1994, 206).

10 See Annamarie Jagose's comments, including the use of the plague metaphor in relation to gay/lesbian definition (1993, 159).

11 For a useful account of lesbian theatre, see Greenaway (1990). An essential reference book which covers a wide range of subcultural theatre is Hurley (1996).

12 The character Gary Brady is described as such by another character in *Celluloid Heroes*. See Dunne (1991, 82-90).

13 See, for example, Playbox's rejection of Shotlander's *Is That You Nancy?* as reported in Chesterman (1995, 33).

14 Kenna's stage instructions have *A Hard God* 'performed on two stages. The larger stage represents the Cassidys' living room'. See Kenna (1992, 4).

15 Some playwrights vehemently resist categorising their plays as gay. English writer Julian Mitchell: 'I realise people will try to claim *Another Country* as gay, but I will absolutely deny it, because I want it to be seen by everybody. If it is to have any effect, it has to be seen in the straight world' (Galbraith 1985).

16 *Jigsaws* opened at the Hole in the Wall, Perth, in 1988, and played at the Q Theatre, Penrith, in 1989.

17 In terms of censorship, I relate the following overheard during the Brisbane season of Gow's *Furious* in 1993. A schoolteacher intent on including the play in a survey of Gow's work suggested that this could be done by excising the scenes between Roland and Chris. These very scenes, I would suggest, are Gow's strategy for ensuring that *Furious* is never set on high school reading lists.

18 My project is intended to address Eve Sedgwick's argument that 'virtually any aspect of modern Western culture must be, not merely incomplete, but damaged in its *central* substance to the degree that it does not incorporate a critical analysis of modern homo/heterosexual definition' (1990, 1, my emphasis).

19 Queer will always be critical of non-historicising, essentialist and anti-intellectualising gay culture. But, as Eve Sedgwick puts it: 'To begin to theorize gender and sexuality as distinct though intimately entangled axes of analysis has been, indeed, a great advance of recent lesbian and gay thought' (1993, 157). In continually stressing the 'diversity' of gay and lesbian cultures, Dennis Watkins, the artistic director (1996) of the SGLMG Festival, can be seen as implicitly supporting queer theory (qtd. in Dunne 1995b).

20 In Nowra's *The Jungle* referenced above, he tackles intercultural political and (homo)sexual issues in exploring the relationship between a gay Australian and a bisexual Romanian. *The Price of Prayer*, a short play with these two characters, which is part of *The Jungle*, was first presented as part of 'Sydney Stories, Program 1' by the Sydney Theatre Company in January 1995. Nowra also explores a homosexual relationship in his Cold War spy drama *Deceit*, first produced by Zootango Theatre Company in Hobart in 1996.

21 'Sexual identity may be less a function of knowledge than performance, or, in Foucauldian terms, less a matter of final discovery than perpetual reinvention' (1991, 6-7). For a useful discussion of the relationship between performativity and theatre, see Dolan (1993: '"Performativity"' as metaphor is used increasingly to describe the nonessentialized constructions of marginalized identities, like white and ethnic women, gays and lesbians, men and women of colour, and various conflicting combinations and intersections of these categories and positionalities' (419).

22 Marcus O'Donnell (1995) replies eloquently to critics like Arlene Croce of the *New Yorker* who refused to review Bill T. Jones's dance work *Still/Here*: 'By creating works of art about HIV, people living with the virus are refusing the option of passivity and silence which characterise a victim. They are quite actively making a statement about survival and about life in the face of death's threat'.

23 According to Stephen Dunne, an AIDS play might characteristically focus on 'death, the hospital, medical discourse and the white sheet'. He lists William M. Hoffman's *As Is* and Larry Kramer's *The Normal Heart* as typical examples (1991, 70). No AIDS death occurs in *Blood and Honour*.

24 It could be argued that Richard Wherrett was promising queer-friendly theatre in his policy statement for the Sydney Theatre Company in 1979: 'To provide first-class entertainment for the people of Sydney - theatre that is grand, vulgar, intelligent, challenging and fun' (Brisbane 1995, 573).

Recent Australian women's writing for the stage

Helen Thomson

Discussing a group of plays on the basis of the gender of their writers immediately engages us in a central ongoing debate in theatre and performance work in general. This is the argument concerning the efficacy and future direction of what Gay McAuley (1996, 140) calls 'traditional text/character/narrative', as opposed to 'theatre as a sacred space of metaphor, transformation and ritual' provocatively posited as 'true' theatre by Barrie Kosky (1996). This opposition between theatre which reflects back reality and that which transforms it, is of crucial importance to feminist writers and performers, particularly since Teresa de Lauretis (1984) revealed the connection between realist narratives and the oppression of women through their inevitable Oedipal patterning. The requirement that feminist theatre should therefore be disruptive or subversive of the phallocentric norm, recognised from the earliest second wave feminist movement which politicised the personal, has drawn many women playwrights into oppositional practices of many kinds. That they remain firmly marginalised in terms of productions in Australia may suggest a failure of their transformational aims.[1] An examination of those women writers who have achieved mainstream success, defined in terms of productions with major, usually State theatre companies, suggests that this correlates with compliance to the masculine-identified text/character/narrative, essentially realist, mode of writing. Thus a gender-based discussion of writing for performance necessarily intersects with the broader politics of theatre practice, and can be usefully analysed in the light of feminist aesthetics. This is one of the most contentiously theorised areas of feminist debate. Rita Felski (1989, 6) argues in *Beyond Feminist Aesthetics* that feminist identification with anti-realist cultural forms is only 'feminist' when addressing the political and social goals of feminism, seeking to end the subordination of women. She also points out that anti-realism has always served marginal and oppressed groups, whether that oppression is the result of race, class or gender.

Feminism in Australian theatre is quite precisely dated, a development out of the New Wave of drama which began in the late 1960s and was confirmed in 1970, in Michael Boddy and Bob Ellis's *The Legend of King O'Malley*, and that year's Festival of Perth which featured a group of plays from Melbourne's Australian Performing Group by Jack Hibberd, Alex Buzo and John Romeril. Women members of the Melbourne collective broke away from the oppressively masculine concerns of these plays and their limited range of stereotypical female roles to produce, in 1972, *Betty Can Jump*, a group-devised show exploring women's experience. Subsequently, in 1974, the Melbourne Women's Theatre Group was formed, producing 'at least twenty five original and highly innovative programmes between 1974 and 1977' (Tait 1993, 1). Peta Tait (3) points out in her history of this group that feminist theory was constructed out of theatre practice in the 1970s. What differentiated their work from similar counter-cultural feminist practices in England and the USA was its deliberate contribution to the evolution of an Australian identity. Yet there had been an earlier generation of Australian women playwrights, at least one of whom, Katharine Susannah Prichard, had her best-known play, *Brumby Innes*, winner of the Triad play competition in 1927, produced for the first time by the APG in 1972. Like Dymphna Cusack, Mona Brand, Betty Roland and Oriel Gray, Prichard's feminism was subsumed by her lifelong dedication to socialist political ideals, but it was nevertheless an important strand in all these writers' plays. If the MWTG challenged limiting female stereotypes through confronting humour, shocking transgressions of acceptable public behaviour and radical subjects, the earlier writers had, within the limitations of social realist drama, also challenged a rigidly patriarchal order with female characters who refused to conform to limiting gender roles. The newly emerging class of professional women was brought on-stage in Oriel Gray's *The Torrents* (1955) and Dymphna Cusack's *Morning Sacrifice* (1942), the former revealing the painfully difficult entrance of women into male-dominated journalism, the latter, the difficulties faced by female teachers in schools policed by male inspectors and punitive employment regulations. Significantly, in both cases the issue is that of power and the male oppression of women. Although most of these writers wrote realist drama, they also experimented with more radical theatrical modes such as agit-prop theatre, drawn primarily from Marxist theorisation. Thus a tradition of radicalism was the first distinctive marker of women's writing for the theatre in Australia.

Second wave feminism saw the development of collective groups of women who shared an awareness of sexual oppression and a concern with female identity. This was characterised by diversity from the start, embracing liberal, Marxist, material, separatist, radical, lesbian and ethnic sub-groups. The 1970s and 80s saw a number of women's theatre groups form, such as the Sydney Woman Action Theatre, Melbourne's Home Cooking Theatre Company, Adelaide's Vitalstatistix and Adelaide Women's Theatre Group, Melbourne's Flash Rat Company, and many more. Few survive into the 1990s, but many Australian women's careers in the theatre had their origins in these groups. Writer-performers such as Sue Ingleton and Robyn Archer are examples; as are administrators such as Chris Westwood, who co-ordinated the first Women Directors' Workshop in 1981 and the Women and Theatre Project in 1982, appointed in 1996 Director of the South Australian Theatre Company; and Robyn Nevin, an early actor in Sydney's Jane Street and Nimrod Theatre productions, now Director of the Queensland Theatre Company. Perhaps these administrators are the most important of players of all, because of their combination of commissioning power and feminist awareness.

The tradition of radicalism was also upheld outside women's groups by Dorothy Hewett and Alma De Groen; the former's *The Chapel Perilous* had its first Sydney production in 1972, while the latter's *The Joss Adams Show* opened in Melbourne in the same year. These are perhaps the most important women writers in Australia to date, although there are a number of significant younger women as well. Both writers exhibit what Sue-Ellen Case (1988) has identified as the defining characteristics of feminist theatre: breaking taboos on the public depiction of the female body; censuring the male gaze; and repositioning women in the subject position. These concerns clearly indicate considerable theoretical development since the early 70s consciousness-raising groups, and emphasis on disrupting gender roles. In 1993, Peta Tait considered that feminist theory in the theatre had been supplanted by theorisation of film, visual arts and performance art (9). The most significant insight from feminist cinematic theory has been Laura Mulvey's notion of 'the gaze' (1975), subsequently developed by Teresa de Lauretis (1984). In a more recent essay, Barbara Freedman (1996, 73) suggests important differences between the cinematic gaze which objectifies woman, and the performative aspect of theatre which effectively returns the gaze. Dorothy Hewett's 1972 play *Bon Bons and Roses for Dolly* remarkably prefigures these theorisations, as does her 1974 *The Tatty Hollow Story*. *Bon Bons and Roses for Dolly* actually uses the cinema as a major symbol of romantic fantasy, both the building which is constructed and the glamorous films shown in it. Dolly is one of the 'golden girl' characters found in a number of Hewett's plays, their long blonde hair and physical beauty making them the focus of male desire and the male gaze, but crucially mediated and disrupted by irony. The most disturbing aspect of these two plays is their de-construction of female glamour with culminating images, in their final acts, of female ageing and tabooed subjects such as menstruation and menopause. It was the menopausal flooding of *Bon Bons*' middle-aged and plain-spoken Ollie Pullit, dragging a flaccid, puppet husband called 'Mate' behind her, which appears to have upset its first audience. Margaret Williams records: 'During the play's premiere season at the Perth Playhouse in 1972, flowers from the foyer were stuffed into the women's toilets and anonymous letters sent to the theatre in protest at its staging' (1992, 29). Whether the result of breaking female taboos, or, conversely, of apparently reproducing glamorous sexual stereotypes, Hewett's plays have aroused emotional rather than rational responses and controversies. Williams suggests that this is partly the result of the plays' unorthodox complexity, their challenging of realistic conventions such as linear time, their mood-changing songs, mixture of dramatic modes and suggestive symbolism. Certainly the feminist criteria raised by Sue-Ellen Case are all here, the objectification of woman contested by its deliberate and self-conscious staging as Dolly repeatedly descends the cinema's grand staircase, parodying the female film-star, then subverting her image in disillusioned middle-age and suicide.

The Tatty Hollow Story, in which Tatty is on-stage in the form of a glamorous shop-window dummy propped up in a telephone booth, provides 'a literal depiction of woman as 'sexual object' (Williams 1992, 39). She is fantasised as a series of traditional sexual stereotypes — goddess, whore, bitch, witch — by her ex-lovers. Once again the impetus is strongly deconstructive: 'If *Bon Bons and Roses for Dolly* shows the femme fatale image to be a social construct, *The Tatty Hollow Story* portrays it as an explicitly male construct bearing no relation to what women know themselves to be' (Williams 1992, 42). Tatty's final manifestation is as an ageing Bea Miles figure; a dirty, crazy, ragged and irreverent street-person, finally freed from male-imposed fantasies of female glamour, having placed herself beyond the bounds of male desire. The persistence of female figures refracted in several forms (seen also in Sally Banner of *The Chapel Perilous* [1971] and Joan of Arc in *Joan* [1975]), can be read in terms of Barbara Freedman's essentially psychoanalytic analysis of the performative aspect of feminist theatre effectively returning the gaze in ways not possible in film. Margaret Williams prefigures this in her comment: 'Like the central female characters in much women's playwriting, Tatty performs herself; her enacting of successive roles is a form of self-discovery, trying on personae and images like her various costumes and discarding those she has outgrown until she finds her true self' (45). This aspect of Dorothy Hewett's rich theatricality is the most crucial source of the irony which continually subverts conventional readings of her female characters.

Dorothy Hewett's plays unsettled their audiences and thereby achieved a perverse kind of feminist success, but they are relatively rarely performed, and Hewett has returned to writing prose. Alma De Groen, eighteen years younger than Hewett, continues to write for the stage, and similarly focuses on feminist issues, employing radical and inventive theatre forms to express them. Elizabeth Perkins (1994, 142) emphasises the sense of process in De Groen's plays: 'The feminism evolving in her plays is not a system of ideas or beliefs. It is [...] an existential feminism that creates itself within the plays in the course of the action.' The most ambitious and controversial of her plays, *The Rivers of China* (1987) depicts that rare but important and revealing female figure, that of the artist, and disturbingly suggests that for the artist alienation is an unavoidable condition, inextricably linked to gender. This had also been the fate of Hewett's Sally Banner in *The Chapel Perilous*. De Groen's plays also possess a rich intertextuality that continually foregrounds art in all its forms, along with philosophy and scientific knowledge. Each play de Groen has written has created a form appropriate to its subject, some close to naturalism, such as *Going Home* (1976) and *Vocations* (1981), while *Rivers of China* challengingly interweaves not just two plots but two worlds, different in time and place, but both concerned with the writer Katherine Mansfield. De Groen's challenge to conventional feminism lies in the play's second level, that of a feminist dystopia, a world where women, through the power of the Medusa look which can turn men to stone (an ironic and vengeful returning of the male gaze) have reversed patriarchy's power relations. It is a dramatisation of the gendered binary divide, demonstrating the need to transcend the crippling dependence of each term on the other. The 1994 play *The Girl Who Saw Everything*, on the surface a naturalistic play about articulate middle-class characters, actually raises disturbing and quite profound questions such as asking whether life is possible without art. Like Dorothy Hewett's plays, *The Rivers of China* in particular is amongst the most intellectually and dramatically ambitious plays written by Australians. Both writers have broken the realist boundaries of form and content in their plays, employing a varied range of theatrical techniques, including the bold use of the poetic, the surreal, dreams, all the resources of what Brian Kiernan (1987, 479) discussing Hewett's work, calls 'total theatre', and focussing on female desire and sexuality, and the contentious, related issue of female creativity.

Three other women dramatists stand outside the 1970s and 80s collectivist feminist movement, Doreen Clarke, Therese Radic and Jill Shearer. Clarke's plays *Bleedin' Butterflies* (1980) and *Farewell Brisbane Ladies* (1981) possess many of the qualities attributed to the self-consciously nationalistic male writers of the same period: humour, often based on skilful employment of vernacular speech, working-class characters who are often 'battlers' and a stringent social commentary. Her plays' focus on women and their experience in national catastrophes such as the 1930s Depression signal the importance of the gender of their writer. Jill Shearer, who has written more than twenty plays, is another 'senior' woman playwright who appears to have no feminist agenda beyond the creating of strong female roles, such as that of the convict girl in her 1977 historical play *Catherine*. 'I've never seen myself as a predominantly feminist writer. I'm a storyteller first ... But have a good look at my women' (Gilbert 1992b, 146)). Her best-known play *Shimada* (1987), which had several major productions including a brief Broadway one, tackles the contentious issue of industrial and racial relations and foreign economic influence in Australia. The traces of Japanese theatrical forms such as Noh and Kabuki and its focus on Asian-Australian relations links this play with the earlier *The Floating World* (1974) by John Romeril, and Therese Radic's *Madame Mao* (1986) and *The Emperor Regrets* (1992). Radic's plays move beyond Shearer's heightened naturalism, incorporating Chinese acrobatics, for example, and exploring the relationship between women and power in the context of Asian society.

All of these plays refute the widely-held idea that women's playwrighting focuses on the personal and neglects public, political issues (Playworks 1995, 119). In the 1990s, the earlier urgent need to redress the gender balance, by telling women's stories in particular, has become less of an issue. There has been a cultural as well as ideological shift from the private to the public realm. However, there is disturbing evidence that women have failed to win an equal share of the growth in professional theatre over the past twenty years in Australia. This has been tellingly recorded in the survey of women playwrights conducted by Playworks for the period 1984 to 1995, published in *Playing With Time: Women Writers for Performance*, where women do less well in almost every category, from major company programming to Arts Council grants (Playworks 1995). The only areas in which they approach equal representation are marginal to the mainstream, in fringe theatre groups, Youth Theatre, Theatre in Education and Community Theatre, all of which have at best irregular project funding. Community theatre and TIE in particular are large and important sections of Australian theatre, but their status and funding are low, making professionalism difficult for their practitioners. These areas of theatre can also trap writers and facilitators in 'process', rather than 'product', with all that implies about limitations in aesthetic quality; in, for example, theatrical exercises designed to empower the participants. Many of the Melbourne Workers' Theatre productions have this aim. One which was both women-centred and enormously successful was Vicki Reynold's *Daily Grind* (1992), revealing the exploitative pressures on strippers to participate in staged sex-acts. This play quite explicitly transformed the stripper from being the object of the male gaze to the subject of her own story. Companies such as Adelaide's Vitalstatistix have been described as by Peta Tait as 'creating community-based women's theatre' including a number of original full-length plays which 'show women characters trying to reconcile the conflict between political idealism and the pragmatic circumstances of their lives in ways which fall outside the more straightforward feminist positions adopted in their issue-based productions' (Playworks 1995, 39). Another commentator has pointed out that the traditional nurturing strengths of women have been harnessed in much community theatre work, but again without the prestige and status of mainstream productions (Playworks 1995, 38). One alliance of women writers and practitioners with a specialised community theatre group has resulted in the very successful Adelaide-based Doppio Teatro, whose Italian-Australian productions tour widely. Graham Pitts' adaptation of Emma Ciccotosto's autobiography *Emma: A Translated Life* (1991) gave voice to an Italian-Australian woman's experience of migration, providing several wonderful female acting roles and incorporating a forty-voice Italian women's choir. Tes Lyssiotis has written several plays, in particular the trilogy *The Journey* (1987), *A White Sports Coat* (1988) and *The Forty Lounge Cafe* (1990), that illuminate the experience of Greek migrant women as well as their Australian-born daughters, employing multi-lingual texts that at times force the audience to experience the bewilderment of her migrant characters. The monodrama *A White Sports Coat* dramatises the particular problems of being doubly marginalised, its protagonist a pregnant writer whose ethnicity multiplies her otherness.

Women-centred theatre, like feminism itself, runs the gamut of theoretical positions from liberal to radical and lesbian. Comedy and cabaret has been the means of edging in from the fringe for performers like Robyn Archer and Sue Ingleton, whose 1989 *Near Ms's* wittily both heroicised and satirised outstanding women and provided a feminist recuperative history, as did Archer's 1980 *A Star is Torn*, *The Pack of Women* (1981) and Linn Van Hek's 1985 *Difficult Women*. Sue Ingleton's subversive comedy included the confrontational use of sanitary products as stage props, and the genuinely disturbing as well as hilarious persona of Bill Rawlings, the pregnant man. Sarah Cathcart and Andrea Lemon's *The Serpent's Fall* (1987), and their two subsequent works *Walking on Sticks* (1993) and *Tiger Country* (1995) also refute victimhood for their female protagonists, in part through the evocation of goddess myths. Cathcart's skilful and engaging portrayal of many female characters persistently presents a gendered world in the background. Nuclear war and militarism in *Tiger Country* and militaristic exploitation and torture in *Walking on Sticks* are exclusively masculinised, with the exception of one female professional soldier, in contrast to a female culture of caring and spirituality. *Tiger Country* provides a subtle feminist characterisation of Australia itself, in terms of its desert landscape, a relatively unusual gendering of the national which both feminises and spiritualises the land. All of these plays have been extremely successful, having many large-scale productions. Equally successful have been a number of female stand-up comics, such as Wendy Harmer. All of these writers and performers have been able to deliver radical and confronting feminist agendas in part at least through the medium of comedy, a useful and effective subversive tool.

Reaching beyond the limitations of the text/character/narrative forms of drama through a non-patriarchal spirituality, be that in the form of female archetypes, psychoanalytic fantasy or dream experience, is a link between writers and performers as diverse as Aboriginal Ningali Lawford, playwright and director Jenny Kemp, Andrea Lemon and Sarah Cathcart, and Sandra Shotlander, most of whose work deals with lesbianism among other issues and ideas. Even when no specific claim is being made for feminism, as in Ningali Lawford's dual-language monologue of autobiographical, traditional song, story and dance, which focuses on racially specific disjunctions of culture, it is still vocalising uniquely female experience. Her performance contests those forces which might otherwise have silenced, excluded, marginalised and made invisible such an individual and her story. Jenny Kemp's powerfully evocative plays, the 1983 *The White Hotel*, *Call of the Wild* (1989), *Remember* (1992) and *The Black Sequin Dress*, commissioned for the 1996 Adelaide Festival, draw upon the surreal paintings of Paul Delvaux, memories and dreams for their haunting imagery, and exist in the mysterious territory between inner and outer worlds. Like Dorothy Hewett ('I hate well made plays' [1996, 45]) Kemp understands the feminist necessity to create work outside male-identified realist parameters: 'I feel it is essential to build a dramatic structure which disrupts conventional time frames/patterns' (Kemp 1996, 30). Her plays deliberately disrupt the gaze with their sophisticated exploitation of performative possibilities: 'a dream has a dreamer who often watches him/herself in the dream. I find it interesting to meditate on this relationship as parallel to the audience/performer relationship. The performance becomes the audience's dream.' Peta Tait (1994, 87) sees her work as enacting feminist theory: 'Influenced by both Freud and Jung, Kemp synthesises their theories into descriptions of dream states, memories and fantasies [...] her work infers a search for a feminine unconscious, a similar purpose to that of the écriture féminine described in the work of Cixous and Irigaray.'

While Kemp's plays explore subjectivity through psychoanalytic means, many other women writers develop it through a particularly female privileging of the spiritual. This can be in goddess narratives, such as those of Lemon and Cathcart, Sandra Shotlander, and Tobsha Learner, or Alma De Groen's transcendental creativity in the female artist, and even Dorothy Hewett's heroines' search for an expression of female desire which is more than simply carnal. Rita Felski (1989, 76) describes such narratives: ' the heroine discovers her true 'feminine' self beyond male-defined roles, a subjectivity frequently described in strongly neo-Romantic terms as a form of mysticism, intuitive empathy with nature.' She then goes on to criticise such feminist works on two grounds; that of returning women to stereotypes from which they have long struggled to liberate themselves, and of re-inforcing the nature/culture binary dualism. Generally this also involves an individual's inner transformation, not a social one. Margaret Kirby's play *My Body, My Blood* (1994) is an exception, representing a political challenge to the Anglican Church and its reluctant ordination of women. Andrea Lemon and Sarah Cathcart's plays also politicise a nature-identified feminine by allying it with environmentalism and contrasting it with militarism. Felski (148) does concede a feminist efficacy for what she calls Romantic feminism, however 'the Romantic feminist vision is the product of a psychological and aesthetic (rather than political) conception of liberation, less concerned with strategic means of ending the oppression of women than with expressing a paradisal longing for harmony'. Plays written by women which express such a longing are also characterised by a sense of collective experience, even when the transformative experience is that of an individual woman.

Sandra Shotlander's plays engage with radical feminism, mostly through their lesbian content. Like Kemp, in her 1983 play *Framework* Shotlander uses paintings, in this case Picasso's portrait of Gertrude Stein and Georgia O'Keefe's 'Black Iris' to set off a series of images and associations which enrich the play's exploration of the growth of a relationship between two women. Jung is also an influence in her *Blind Salome* (1985), a play which revives the idea of the Mother Goddess, developed through a different framework in *Angels of Power* (1992) where Diana, Mary and Athena are modern-day characters as well as archetypes, involved with the issue of reproductive technology. Lesbian theatre was specifically developed by Lois Ellis and Sara Hardy in their productions of *Radclyffe* (1988) based on Radclyffe Hall's lesbian novel *The Well of Loneliness*, and Sara Hardy's *Vita: A Fantasy* (1989), about Virginia Woolf's lover Vita Sackville West, and both plays have proved to be popular. However there is an ongoing debate about the merits of historical biographies of lesbian writers versus the 'undead', sexually active, living lesbians. Peta Tait comments: 'While making lesbian artists a visible cultural presence is an important project, it still renders problematic contemporary lesbian identity as somehow risky and unacceptable' (1994, 81) and goes on to suggest that the lesbian theatre project has barely begun in Australia.

Female sexuality in heterosexual form is the subject of most of Tobsha Learner's plays, although in two of her plays *SNAG* (Sensitive New Age Guy) and *Wolf* (both 1992) the male sexual compulsive is the subject. In *The Glass Mermaid* (1994) which, like *Wolf*, received a major production with Melbourne's Playbox Theatre, an older woman rents a lover in an attempt to come to terms with the suicide of her husband. Learner's play *Mistress* (1989), like her 1987 *Witchplay*, is a monologue, the solo performer plays the roles of Aphrodite, Helen and Diana, modern-day counterparts of the goddesses. *Witchplay* has Batcha, its Auschwitz survivor, recreate twelve other characters, and explores the sexualised victimisation of women through the figure of the witch. Originally written for actor Rosalba Clemente, the play has a carnivalesque quality and a complex, dark humour. *SNAG*, which sent up the New Man with sympathy but also stripped his pretensions with corruscating humour, was popular with men as well as women in its audiences. *Wolf*, which takes us through four decades in the life of sexual predator Daniel Lupus, is a psycho-drama, a social history, and also embraces mythology and fairytale. Its realism is disrupted in many ways, from the symbolic, bleeding kitchen table with wolf paw legs to the intense, rhythmic monologue of Daniel in feral mode. Here, in these two plays in particular, is a feminist writer examining the problems of masculinity. Learner is an accomplished and interesting playwright, but the problems of securing productions, recorded in an interview at the Playing With Time Festival in Sydney in 1995 (Learner 1996, 26), notwithstanding the fact that her last play was the fringe hit *Seven Acts of Love (As Witnessed by a Cat*) (1995), seems to have led her to abandon the theatre, at least for the moment. Her most recent publication is *Quiver: A Book of Erotic Tales* (1996) and she is at present writing a novel.

Those women dramatists who are best surviving the harsh climate for writers of their sex are, unsurprisingly, those who conform most nearly to the text/character/narrative paradigm, the 'masculine' norm. However it would be simplistic to equate aesthetic formalism with conservative sexual politics, since the social and political problems of women can still be the major focus of realist plays. Hannie Rayson, Joanna Murray-Smith, Katherine Thomson and Peta Murray have all enjoyed considerable mainstream success with their realist plays. Peta Murray's *Wallflowering* (1989) has had many productions, and is one significant example where the conservative form matches its content. Its villains are a group of feminists, women who try to raise Peg's consciousness and move her out of the dull conformity of her life with Cliff, an office-worker and would-be writer. The play celebrates the ordinary, demonises difference, and employs ballroom dancing as its symbol of ideal heterosexual relationships. Its popularity with audiences is sure proof that feminism as an issue is likely to remain on the margins of drama's debates, at least in mainstream theatre. Katherine Thomson's two main plays, *Barmaids* (1991) and *Diving for Pearls* (1991), are mainly concerned with class issues. Their working-class characters are sympathetically portrayed; struggling to adjust to radical social changes, particularly the growth in unemployment, which always threatens to make victims of them.

Joanna Murray-Smith's characters are articulate and middle-class, often enacting a generational conflict with its clash of values. This underlies the tense exchange between mother and putative daughter in *Love Child* (1993), in which the mother Anna's second-wave feminism and ecologically sound employment is derided by soap-star Billie. The abandoned child exacts a savage revenge on a mother whose youthful conformity to respectability sacrificed the maternal bond the child craves. Yet the play gives the older woman little chance to criticise the values of the younger. In this play, as in her earlier *Atlanta* (1990), Murray-Smith is very much the spokesperson of her own generation. Her 1995 play *Honour*, which won the 1996 Victorian Premier's Literature Award for drama, charts the breakdown of a middle-aged marriage when a younger woman becomes the husband's lover, and is a moving and sympathetic depiction of female 'honour', the play's highest value, possessed by the discarded wife Honor. The play's sympathies are mature, and seem to have swung away from the younger generation towards a re-valuing of the older woman, and it captures the minutiae of relationships with an appealing veracity.

Hannie Rayson's *Hotel Sorrento* (1990), made into a film after a successful theatre debut, like the subsequent *Falling From Grace* (1994), provides a set of strong female roles. Beginning in community theatre, Rayson has achieved considerable mainstream success with her comedies; her witty one-liners and shrewd analysis of middle-class Australia have led to comparisons with David Williamson. A self-confessed feminist, Rayson's particular strength lies in her sympathetic portrayal of the bonds between women; three very different sisters in *Hotel Sorrento*, and three close friends in *Falling From Grace*. She also provides strong portrayals of working women and their struggle to balance personal and professional lives; an important contemporary feminist issue. *Falling From Grace* is a play about the ethics of feminism itself, setting up a plot where the professional commitment to help other women is in conflict with the affectionate duty of care between female friends. Her most recent play, *Competitive Tenderness* (1996) is a farce set in the offices of local government, satirically tackling the economic rationalist agenda for so-called reform, but the theatrical form of the farce ultimately works against the satirical intentions behind it.

These younger playwrights, and their success, throw into question the gendered binary of realist versus transformative or transgressive theatre on which this discussion has rested. The realist writers cannot be written out of the feminist project, indeed feminism is a concern in everything they write. In fact it justifies a gendered discussion, for every woman writer speaks differently to her male counterparts, even if she does not fulfil every aim of feminist theatre. Political aims other than feminist ones can still embrace the radicalism of projecting women as subjects, for example. Sandra Shotlander identifies perhaps the simplest form of disruption in plays written by women, even among those who might not call themselves feminist: 'I believe that a playwright writing with a feminist consciousness without being didactic still can very easily disrupt the theatrical space, simply through portraying strong female protagonists, who propel the action rather than being acted upon' (Sturak 1990). The disruptiveness of female sexuality, pioneered on the Australian stage by Dorothy Hewett, now finds new form in the challenging eroticism of Tobsha Learner's plays. 1970s Australian feminists spoke to their own constituency in the first instance, which confined them to the fringe. 1990s women playwrights now battle for fair representation in mainstream theatre productions. There is no longer an agreed feminist agenda, but rather many of them, taking a variety of forms. There are a number of fronts. Still on the fringe and in community theatre there are groups of women aiming for empowerment — Melbourne Women's Circus is one example — and therefore concentrating on the process of making performances rather than the product itself. However, when a script is submitted to Playbox Theatre, or any of the State Theatre Companies, it must have at least the promise of the kind of quality such companies require. That 'quality' may involve some compromise; the liberal feminist aims of equal opportunity may find more favour than radical ones which seek to change the patriarchal structures, including theatre managements, which impede women's progress. The price of a presence in mainstream theatre productions would seem to be the loss of the radicalism which was posited as a marker of feminist theatre. Yet a writer like Alma De Groen has demonstrated that this is not inevitable. But it may also mean that women writers for the stage will increasingly focus on the issue of power itself, and therefore the need to depict a world where men as well as women interact.

Notes

1 Playworks, the national organisation committed to nurturing new women writers for the stage, published a survey of the progress made in grants, funding, productions and the entrance by women into the creative and decision-making positions in Australian theatre companies between 1985 and 1995 and reported very little advancement over that period. See *Playing With Time: Women Writing for Performance*.

Inter-referentiality: interrogating multicultural Australian drama

Joanne Tompkins

> *Thou shalt be ethnic, our legislators say; thou shalt honour thy mother tongue; thou shalt celebrate thy difference in folk festivals; and thou shalt receive monies to write about thy difference (providing thou art a member of an ethnic organization that sponsors thy application). And we have responded to that call, ethnics and non-ethnics alike; we have responded by discovering that difference is sexy.* (Kamboureli, 146)

The rhetoric that surrounds multiculturalism has, as Kamboureli's satirical epigraph suggests, attempted to introduce an air of authenticity that can, by definition, never be achieved. While multiculturalism appears to design a cultural unity for the country, the most striking resistance to authenticity in Australian theatre is a highly interrogative approach to representations of Australia. This paper locates the operation of multicultural discourses in contemporary Australian theatre between the context of the sexiness of difference[1] and the unattainable authenticity that multiculturalism seems to still require.

First, however, a brief history of multiculturalism in Australia and in Australian theatre will help contextualise this study. The national identity that has generally been used to define Australians for most of the twentieth century suggests that Australians share an Anglo-Celtic ethnicity almost exclusively, a heritage which conveniently forgets that Australia has never been just an Anglo-Celtic nation. In fact, there were West Indians transported to Australia as convicts as early as the 1790s (via convictions of theft while being servants in England), while as many as four hundred South African blacks were transported from Cape Town to Australia between 1828 and 1838 (Hughes 196). Many Australians assume that it is only after World War II that migrants arrived from southern Europe and that immigration from 'Asia' is mostly confined to the more recent and now stereotypical Vietnamese 'boat people'. The country has, of course, been composed of a much more diverse population for virtually all its post-settlement history, including the Aboriginal inhabitants and the Kanaka labourers who were brought from the Torres Strait Islands to work in Australia. Many of the Chinese goldminers who came to Australia in the 1850s (Rolls 74) with the intention of returning to China remained in Australia, and Chinese sailors had long since traded with Aborigines in Australia. Italians, Greeks, Lebanese, Scandinavians, and Germans were established in Australia by the 1880s (Castles et al, 19).

The Federation of Australia in 1901 was based on an assimilationist union of the various colonies: the Immigration Restriction Act, more commonly and colloquially known as the White Australia policy, was passed very early in the life of the new nation to restrict immigration from Asia whereas immigration from Europe was deemed reasonable and even desirable. As late as 1969 Billy Snedden, Minister for Immigration in the Liberal Gorton government, maintained,

> We must have a single culture — if immigration implied multi-culture activities within Australian society, then it was not the type Australia wanted. I am quite determined we should have a monoculture, with everyone living in the same way, understanding each other, and sharing the same aspirations. We don't want pluralism. (Wilton & Bosworth, 17)

While the official White Australia Policy was abandoned by this point, the unofficial assimilationist practice prevailed. By this time, the ethnic mix in Australia had continued to grow: more European migrants arrived in Australia, as did many Turks in 1968 (Castles et al, 53).

Multiculturalism was first mooted as a potential policy in 1973 by Senator Al Grassby, the Minister for Immigration in Gough Whitlam's government, and taken up by the tabling in Parliament of the Galbally Report during Malcolm Fraser's government. Judge Frank Galbally's 1978 report, the *Review of Post-Arrival Programmes and Services to Migrants*, marks the institution of multicultural policies in Australia. Multiculturalism purported to make a place in Australia for all cultures, in the hope of developing greater and plural Australian culture (to replace the assimilationist model that had been fostered) but its genesis is more in fears of economic hardship — even isolation — as a result of discrimination claims by 'Asian' trading neighbours. Successive governments have continued to promote multiculturalism but the form that they choose to acknowledge is more often than not merely ornamental or token. Often reduced to reduced to folk-dancing, 'ethnic' food, and photo opportunities for electioneering politicians, multiculturalism as policy is also regularly cited as the basis for economic and/or social problems, most recently in 1996 by Pauline Hanson's racist misperceptions of Aboriginal land rights, economics, employment, migration, and privilege.

Regardless of Hanson's ignorance, two decades after the tabling of the Galbally Report multiculturalism has stalled. There are numerous problems with the parameters of multiculturalism: while it generally embraces all cultures in a location against the Anglo-Celtic majority — and usually also against Aboriginality — it tends to misleadingly erase the differences within and between cultures. The case of Aboriginality in the context of multiculturalism is confusing and complex. In some versions of multiculturalism Aborigines are welcome, whereas in others they are not. Further, Jon Stratton and Ien Ang point out that attempting to contain Aborigines within the false unity that some versions of multiculturalism try to embrace 'eras[es] the memory of colonial dispossession, genocide and cultural loss and its continued impact on Aboriginal life' (155). They detail further Australia's difficulty with locating Asian multiculturalism in a theory that is primarily designed for European immigration (155). None of the cultures that generally comprise multiculturalism (usually Mediterranean European countries, and increasingly Asian migrant cultures) can boast a unified history or culture in their own right, so the supposition that a unified multiculturalism in the context of living in the diversity of Australia must remain a fiction. Inevitably, the concerns voiced and literary tropes chosen by these disparate writers differ, even among writers who share a history and/or geography. While most multicultural theorists today recognise these differences, a great deal of the assumptions regarding contemporary multiculturalism rely on the early theory and social policy concerned with this material, most of which account only for a one-unity-per-culture model.[2] Stratton and Ang explain:

> The problem with official multiculturalism is that it tends precisely to freeze the fluidity of identity by the very fact that it is concerned with the synthesising of unruly and unpredictable cultural identities and differences into a harmonious unity-in-diversity. So the metaphor of the mosaic, of unity-in-diversity, is based on another kind of disavowal, on a suppression of the potential incommensurability of juxtaposed cultural differences. (Stratton & Ang 152-3)

But if the politics of multiculturalism attempt to smooth over the differences of race, history, culture, the theatrical practice of multiculturalism cannot: the relationships between and across cultures in the arts and in human interactions are complexly intertwined.

Given the confusions that continue to be generated or uncovered around the concept/location of multiculturalism, it is not surprising that the relationship between multicultural theory and the practice of Australian playwrights is unsatisfactory. Throughout its history from colonial times, Australian theatre has also been neither purely Anglo-Celtic nor Anglophone. Various twentieth-century immigrant communities have, of course, set up theatre companies in Australia employing languages other than English. The use of English — or English interspersed with other languages — for such theatre was popularised in the 1970s when plays employing themes relating to migrancy also emerged.[3]

The representation of migrants has a much longer theatrical history in Australia: for instance, the 'stage Chinaman', used for comic purposes in nineteenth-century Australian theatre, is well-documented by Margaret Williams (1983, 153). More recently than the stage Chinaman, the stage Greek became popular on television in the 1980s through the character of Con the Fruiterer and the sitcom *Acropolis Now*, among other representations. Mary Dimech notes that the highly popular play *Wogs out of Work* — begun as a comedy sketch at the Melbourne Comedy Festival in 1987 (Milne 1994, 497) and launched to several successful seasons on its own — sparked an important recognition among many of its audiences: 'For thousands of NESB [non-English speaking background] people, *Wogs out of Work* (whatever one's ideas about its aesthetic values) demonstrated a hunger to see themselves represented in the public domain' (172). Frequently, however, the 'stage' version of many racial groups becomes limited to the stereotypical comic type to the exclusion of all other possible representations. More 'serious' representations of non-Anglo-Celtic Australians are found as early as the young French woman in Betty Roland's 1928 *A Touch of Silk*, and comprehensively in Richard Beynon's Italian family in *The Shifting Heart* in 1959. Contemporary theatre in Australia tends to explore multiculturalism in more complex ways. One of the most important achievements of multiculturalism is normalising the representation of the 'ethnic' even to the point of replacing the more stereotypical 'bronzed Aussie' images of Australians.

Contemporary multicultural plays in Australia demonstrate a much higher degree of playful ambivalence with identity politics and identity tropes than the theory generally acknowledges. This paper examines two highly interrogative plays by writers who, on the basis of their surnames and/or 'ethnic' associations, are considered multicultural: Noëlle Janaczewska's *Cold Harvest* and Dina Panozzo's *Varda che Bruta* (Look How Ugly She is ... Poor Thing). The writers share a non-Anglo-Celtic background and their plays, to some extent at least, discuss this positioning as 'other' Australians. I intend firstly to analyse (to varying degrees) these 'multicultural' plays according to the signifiers that are generally assumed to be part of multiculturalism: storytelling; the use of English and at least one other language; and representation of 'home'. From there, I will consider the gaps that such a reading reveals, and offer an alternative model for the possible analysis of these plays. The model I am using here, rather than just the examples that the plays provide, will be useful in analysing a broad range of play texts. My intention is both to encourage the analysis of their works in the larger context of so-called 'mainstream' Australian writers, and to incorporate into the theory of multicultural writing the differing senses of Australian identities that the plays clearly demonstrate. My method takes a lead from Michael Fischer's concept of 'inter-reference' which he explains thus: 'It is the inter-references, the interweaving of cultural threads from different arenas, that give ethnicity its phoenix-like capacities for reinvigoration and reinspiration. To kill this play between cultures, between realities, is to kill a reservoir that sustains and renews humane attitudes' (1986, 230). This inter-referentiality does, I suggest, contribute to a sort of meta-discourse on cultural levels, particularly surrounding Australian identities in plays by 'multicultural writers'.

First performed at Sydney's Stables Theatre in 1992,[4] *Varda che Bruta...Poretta* chronicles the experiences of a young woman whose family emigrated to Australia when she was a child. Later in life she returns to the family village determined to claim what is rightfully hers, while also attempting to come to terms with her own identity. The one actor in this play is accompanied on stage by a video camera on a movable pod: the camera, which reproduces the action on the 'stage' as well as playing pre-recorded tapes, acts as an alter ego, in many respects, for Dina, the actor, who tries to resolve her fragmented sense of self.

Noëlle Janaczewska's *Cold Harvest*[5] combines two migrant cultures, Polish and Korean, to explore their relationship to Australia through the eyes of two women who are classified as 'second-generation migrants'. Kasia's parents, Tadeusz and Franciszka, approach living in Australia differently to Mi-Kyoung's Korean father, Yongsu (Tony), and Australian mother, Janice. In both cases, the parents' memories of pre-Australian life are circumscribed by war. In this play, Kasia and Mi-Kyoung try to resolve their confusions surrounding their parents' birth cultures, and both women return to their parents' country of birth. Each actor takes on several multi-racial roles, while language and food frame the play. More specifically, each woman's off-stage brother is getting married and the structuring device for the play is the baking of three wedding cakes according to 'Australian', Korean, and Polish recipes.

Both plays employ story-telling in a self-conscious way: the characters weave one story into another and the texts discuss the convoluted nature of story-telling; its veracity, its association with reality, and its inter-reference with other commodities such as language, home, and identity. *Varda che Bruta* tells a variety of 'tales' in a non-linear manner. Dina has several structuring narratives: the story of her family's claim on the mountain which is their family's ancestral land and the reason for her visit to Italy, and more generally her attempts to decipher her own identity, or, as she puts it, to 'work this stuff out' (1994a,1). In telling these stories she finds that she must tell several others: some are required in order to make the mountain story clear to her audience, while others are revealed to her as she progresses through the tale; including how her parents met, how they came to leave Italy, and how people live in the village. Still others are retained for her to deliberately deploy when she deems it necessary. The several layers of subjective authoring in this play remind the audience that while Dina appears to be unsure of herself, she ultimately oversees the direction of the play. All the stories are told fragmentarily, so that it is only at the end of the play that the audience can apprehend all the layers of all the narratives: for instance, not until the end of the play does she reveal the circumstances of her father's death and his relationship with the dominating family mountain, both of which have precipitated Dina's trip to Italy. The play exploits several story-telling devices including the fairy-tale format, and the enticing dramatisation of the stories from several perspectives — all, of course, performed by Dina Panozzo, the actor and 'subject' of the play.

As in *Varda che Bruta*, the story-telling techniques of *Cold Harvest* serve several purposes. Firstly, and most comically, Janice Kim and Mi-Kyoung know Yongsu's stories well enough to recite them; they tease Yongsu by supplying the punchline before he can. The main story of *Cold Harvest* is, like *Varda che Bruta*, a story of discovery: he audience — like Kasia — wants to learn what mysterious events happened in Poland before the emigration, and who was Konrad? Finally, story-telling is the means by which the young women locate a clearer sense of identity and home. All these forms of story-telling are associated with migration but none is simply containable in a fairy-tale format:

FRANCISZKA: Once there was poverty, adversity and struggle,
YONGSU KIM: Then there was a long journey to a new place

TADEUSZ: Where we worked hard to earn money and be successful,
JANICE KIM/TADEUSZ: And look at us now!
YONGSU KIM: A big house,
TADEUSZ: Children at university
FRANCISZKA: Enough money to help the family back home
KASIA: But there's more to the story than happy endings.... But sometimes the storylines falter,
MI-KYOUNG: Don't quite fit the new country. (47-48)

The round-singing quality to this passage suggests its infinite repetition, but Kasia and Mi-Kyoung provide a sense that the story cannot remain one of 'just' migration: the stories must also interact with the new country.

Language is a second means by which the plays operate inter-referentially. This is not surprising, given Brian Castro's comments regarding the multi-dimensional ways in which language itself communicates:

> Language learning has been reserved for academic or economic pursuits, overlooking entirely the notion that to translate between languages is a border crossing not only between the purely intellectual, but, more importantly, between the artistic elements within our being. When we translate from one language to another we not only reinvent ourselves but we free up the sclerotic restrictions of our own language. We feel freer to read between the lines. (1996, 70-71)

Both plays mix a myriad of languages, although most of the non-English passages are decipherable by means of the context, scripted actions, or repetition in English. Inevitably, translation becomes more than merely a function of communication as the characters explore the difficulty of operating in (at least) two languages. In *Varda che Bruta* several forms of Italian compete with English; complications with language arise when Dina assumes that the Italian that she grew up speaking in Australia will be the same as in Italy. When she returns to the Veneto she finds to her surprise that her Italian is different to even those who speak the Venetian dialect that she was taught. It's not even a question of different regional dialects; she finds that the language has changed during her family's absence, resulting in desk clerks exclaiming about her: 'Heeeyy, she speaks like an old man' (35).[6] Despite her acting experience in Australia, she learns that 'I can't get any acting work in Italy. I don't speak the language. Anyway, I'm too loud for this place' (47). Even conversations with her relatives prove difficult:

literal translations are meaningless in the context of local idioms that are beyond her grasp of the 'language' and its 'meaning'. As if to emphasise that translation is always more complicated than can be solved by phrase books, the volume at which Dina speaks (in either language) also proves to be all wrong for Italy. Her search for herself in what is ostensibly her home constantly leads back to language: at one point, the short-hand stage directions read, 'hard to speak, the need to find the words, searching for them' (33). The complications of language in *Varda che Bruta* mirror the complicated nature of the story-telling and, like stories, the self-conscious ways in which language can be manipulated.

It is language in particular that enables the multiple descriptions of 'home', memory, and even story in *Cold Harvest*. On the level of naming, both young women attempt to translate themselves into more acceptably Australian personas via language when, as teenagers, they temporarily swap their first names for 'Kathy'. While this is intended to be a permanent Australianising move, both eventually return to the names that mark them with a sign of cultural difference: these two young women translate their names — and what they represent — into English in an effort to 'de-ethnify' themselves, only to later 're-ethnify' themselves by returning to their birth names. The translation eventually works in both directions as the young women learn the possibilities associated with inter-referentiality.

The language of the 'non-Australian' also works inter-referentially in this play. With the exception of words associated with food, Kasia has not learned Polish as a child, an act of conscious Australianisation on her parents' part that she regrets in adulthood when she travels to Poland. Kasia's inability to interpret the events around her means that she, like Dina, has to 'improvise meanings all the time' (39). While Kasia's mother acts as a translator in Europe, her father explains the calculated way in which he sometimes speaks English incorrectly:

> TADEUSZ: Frania [his pet name for his wife, Franciszka]! Our neighbours have fallen in!
>
> KASIA: Dropped in.
>
> TADEUSZ: I know! I make deliberate mistakes with my English. Australians like that; it makes them feel comfortable. (13)

Tadeusz recognises that language is more complex than this attempt to tease his Australianised daughter. The convoluted relationship that the Polish and Korean characters have with their new home and the traditional culture begins to become clear here. Australia is not a promised land:

YONGSU KIM: We chose Australia because—

TADEUSZ: Everyone thinks we'll go to America. (17-18)

It becomes the country in which they have made do and adapted several traditions.

Language in both plays inevitably overlaps with representations of home, where fixing 'a' location becomes, not surprisingly, impossible. Language underscores Dina's confused relationship with 'home': the place she expected to call home is a place where she cannot even make herself understood. Home is always a vexed place in multicultural writing: it is both the new, if uncomfortable, unforgiving Australia, and the old familiar home of the country which one (or one's parents) left. Dina and her relatives in *Varda che Bruta* are able to return 'home' to Italy with relative frequency and ease. It is, nevertheless, risky to go back. Indeed, Dina's relatives from Chicago returned there fifteen years ago and have been 'trapped' there ever since. The response of those in the village is also not always welcoming: Dina's aunt exclaims that she is 'sick of you all coming back here "dying", wanting money, causing "Disgracie!!"' (50).

Dina's own response to Italy surprises her. At one point, she tells her Italian lover Ugo, 'I miss my family, home, Australia. Did I say that??' (49). Her program notes to the play draw attention to the possible reconciliation of her two 'homes':

> This journey home [...] sharpened my perceptions about living in Australia. Instead of returning me safely to my roots, it drew out ambiguities, confusions and frustrations. It made conscious feelings that I had grappled with all my life. At difficult times I've often resorted to seeing myself as coming from somewhere else, seeing Italy as my real home. [...] And when I returned to Australia from this trip I felt home for possibly the first time. Even so, the search for clarity of race and culture was not simple. I belong here and there. (1994b)

Cold Harvest complicates 'home' further. It chronicles attempts by first-generation migrants to create homes exclusively in Australia, particularly in the case of Kasia's family, but the second generation finds that the 'other' home is too significant to forget. For Kasia's parents Australia is the place that both allows them to leave behind their Polish existence and paradoxically forces them to abandon their Polish identities. Kasia's mother Frania tries to explain to her sister the difficult but welcome process of immigration:

> I left it all behind me when I stepped onto the boat and began that long shedding process of emigration. Somewhere over the

> sea I lost my history, my family, my language, until all I had left was an empty biography and a name, and I lost even that when I arrived in Australia and the immigration officer, too busy or too lazy to tackle Polish consonants assigned me a brand new one. He looked out of the window, and there was the name 'Coles New World' above a shop. So I became an Australian shop. There were a lot of Coles and Bushells and Arnotts who got off that boat. And at that point, I started to forget that I'd ever been anyone in particular, and began to re-draw my vacant biography. Filling the great empty space of Australia with my new life. And Franie Coles gradually took up more and more space, and Franciszka Barszczewska less, until I got to where I am now: all Australian. (24)

Frania's sister retorts, 'You sound like a tin of peaches' (24). Home represents a complicated memory of the past, most of which they attempt to forget; it is often not a defined geographical place. Generally, in this family, this 'memory' home is confined to the time when Kasia was little, when the family was well-ensconced in Australia. This ambivalent location is confusing for the young Kasia who reads the differences between Poland and Australia as the differences between home-made goods and food bought in a box from Coles, in accordance with the way she sees her Australian friends living. For the family generally the cold food-storage room replaces a homeland: it is the place of memory — both good and bad memories. Perhaps this is why food becomes so central as a structuring device in the play. It is from this location of a substitute homeland within the house that Kasia tries to recreate her multiply-situated home. My-Kyoung's father, on the other hand, tries to 'create a little Korea inside the Australian brick veneer' (26). Her family is determined to 'have the best of both worlds: How to have our cake and eat it' (26), until their daughter's ambitions threaten that dream: 'I didn't leave Korea for you to become a hairdresser!' (40).

It is not difficult to recognise that the three stereotypical signifiers of multicultural writing — story-telling, the use of multiple languages, and various representations of home — are more complexly represented in *Varda che Bruta* and *Cold Harvest* than one might first imagine. Indeed, *Cold Harvest* accurately depicts one of the problems that Stratton and Ang find with multicultural theory in its customary form: the Polish experiences in themselves disavow a fluidity of identity or a unity-in-diversity model, and when compared to the equally complicated circumstances of Mi-Kyoung's Korean family, any sense of unity disappears. The plays demonstrate the ways in which a variety of multicultural tropes operate, and more importantly, the way they operate differently in each play. The Polish parents of *Cold Harvest* make a conscious decision not to teach their children Polish and to try to cut their ties with the past, while Dina Panozzo can only sever her ties with very limited success. In other words, the significant lies in the various ways in which these plays do not maintain the multicultural commodities that the theory leads one to expect. Indeed, if one were to limit an analysis of these plays to just the commodities that are customarily assumed to be the multicultural signifiers in literature, one would neglect a variety of other factors central to these plays, including their transformational acting styles and the crucial concern with body image in *Varda che Bruta*, factors which deserve substantial analysis in themselves.

More crucial is the way that these two plays provide a playful inter-reference with the stereotypes of Australian identity. Neither play merely 'represents' home, storytelling, or language without also situating such tropes clearly in Australia, among signifiers of a white, Anglo-Saxon (or at least non-specific) Australian identity that are not normally considered part of 'the multicultural experience'. The ways in which 'Australia' is interwoven with (an)other cultural tradition alter the reference points for both cultures. This inter-reference denies the opportunity for any assertions of an impossible (and spurious) multicultural 'authenticity' because an authentic Italian-Australian or Korean-Australian is an undefinable entity. Inter-reference encourages a substantial alteration to the way that drama regarding/by 'multicultural Australians' is categorised and analysed.

The inter-reference in *Varda che Bruta* revolves around Dina's confusion between her home in Italy and her home in Australia: deciding which location is really her home is central to the sense of self that is emerging from what she perceives to be an unwieldy, ugly body. This awkward positioning in both countries initially represents for her a loss rather than a gain of an additional facet to her identity. The play concludes with Dina deciding whether or not to make a life in Italy, but the play that results from this experience is presented in Australia and uses Australian references to explain the peculiarities of regional Italy to Australians. For instance, she relies on Australian regional jokes: 'My mother's maiden name is Panozzo just like Papa's. [The village of Tesche Conca is] the Tasmania of Italy really' (16). 'Kangaru' is the name that Dina's Italian aunt uses to refer in disgust to Dina's father and to all of the Australian Panozzos. Dina's tanned father finds that on his return to Italy, he is the 'wild man... the black man' (22) who is now a disgrace to the family. Italians she meets, however, tell her to say 'hi' to cousins in Melbourne even though she lives in Sydney.

Stereotypes operate similarly in reverse in Australia: at the beginning of her acting career, her Italian name is deemed inappropriate for the stage or television and she is encouraged to drop Panozzo for 'James' (24). She is led to believe that she is being treated highly favourably by being allowed to 'play a real Australian' in a television soap opera (30). She is able to speak positively about the options that the 'new world' offers at the same time as complain about Australia being a 'youth culture' (49), while recognising overtly the irony in repeating such clichés. Again, the ambivalent locations of Australia and Italy that continually emerge for Dina at what she perceives to be the wrong moment create an inter-referential position that appears to resolve none of her problems. In fact it seems to create for her more problems than those presented by her own identity crisis. The playful inter-referentiality regarding Italy and Australia mimics Dina's equally playful relationship with the video camera, a relationship that alternates between comic, parodic, and anxious reactions: these dynamic relationships refuse to be limited to stereotypical representations of either Italy or Australia, theatre actor or movie screen representation of actor; even though they all frequently make use of stereotypes in order to deconstruct the fixity of such representations.

Cold Harvest also plays with Australian stereotypes. Kasia recalls her invention of Harry and June to replace the parents who embarrass her; her invented 'parents':

KASIA: (*Singing*) Harry and June never shout
Laugh too loudly, lose their tempers,
And never, ever cry.
Harry and June eat shepherds pie
Have never heard of kopytka (dumplings),
Kwasne mleko (sour milk), makowiec (poppy seed cake)
.... (*Speaking*) On Sundays Harry and June and the
family go for a drive, taking a picnic of
KASIA/MI-KYOUNG: (*Singing*) White, pre-sliced bread
And shop-bought cakes
With pale pink icing. (19)

As she later recognises, the overtly stereotyping of this 'quintessential Australian couple' is exactly what she required as a child, but it is a construction which the adult Kasia can see through. That is, as a child, she can pretend to traverse quite effortlessly and fluidly the social and national boundaries between her second-rate Polish parents and the ideal

Australian Harry and June. When she is ready to embrace her parents' Polishness, that existing inter-referentiality between a stereotypical Australian couple and a typical (if not stereotypical) Polish family refracts in a manner that is at first distressing for Kasia, who is forced to realise that her parents are no longer the Polish parents that she, in adulthood, wishes to reclaim. The exasperated parents explain:

FRANIA: When you were a child, you spent all your time wanting to be Australian ... like Tom and Peggy Liles

TADEUSZ: Do you remember?

YONGSU KIM: Wanting to be different from me

FRANCISZKA: Then, suddenly, when you're grown up you decide you want to be Polish

YONGSU KIM: Pretending to be Japanese of all things

TADEUSZ: And you want us to embrace our Polish daughter into some fiction you've created;

YONGSU KIM: Do you remember?

FRANCISZKA: Some imaginary place that exists only in your head!

YONGSU KIM/FRANCISZKA: But we've changed too! (38)

The metaphor which communicates the highly syncretic versions of being an 'Australian' is the three wedding cakes. Mi-Kyoung, Kasia, Janice Kim, and Franciszka chant or sing about the decorations covering, in particular, the Polish kolacz:

MI-KYOUNG: Chicken/chestnuts/fruits/traditional/Korean

KASIA: Kolacz/chooks/pigs/leaves/birds/kangaroos

JANICE/KIM: Candles/red/blue/threads/wooden/ducks

FRANCISZKA: dough/figures/bride/groom/branches/ribbons /nuts/paper/flowers. (56)

Yet this Australianising of the wedding cake — adding chooks, pigs, birds and kangaroos — does not represent an easy hybridity of Polish and Australian: like everything else in the play, the complicated negotiations that are required to build this wedding cake rely on an inter-reference with Australian (and, here, Korean) signifiers as much as Polish ones. This alteration to Kasia's perception of her parents and her own place in Australia extends the inter-referential mapping of her world, if perhaps not in the direction that she anticipated.

Approaching these plays through a frame of inter-referentiality broadens the ways to read and to compare them to other Australian theatre. The ambivalence of the Australian identity is, of course, a topic of some prominence in much 'mainstream' Australian theatre. The work of Louis Nowra, for instance, is based partly on an exploration of otherness. *The Golden Age* (1985) in particular refuses to specify definitively which 'marginalised' group its lost family from the forest represents. Other plays such as *Summer of the Aliens* (1992) and *Radiance* (1993) — frequently imbricate 'new' Australian with Anglo-Saxon and Aboriginal Australians. Andrea Lemon and Sarah Cathcart stage a cultural history for various Australian women in *The Serpent's Fall* (1987) including a Greek migrant and a young Aboriginal woman; the collective experiences represent a range of Australian portraits that do not necessarily confirm any Australian stereotypes. Janis Balodis's Latvian heritage is frequently a subject of his plays but his success frequently tends to preclude him from the multicultural 'ghetto' (Kelly 1992). In his Latvian trilogy, *Too Young for Ghosts* (1985), *No Going Back* (1992) and *My Father's Father* (1996) the contemporary Latvian characters merge with representations of Leichhardt and Aborigines in the nineteenth century to alter the cultural face of Australia today. Michael Gurr turns to Asia in *Sex Diary of an Infidel* (1992) to consider Australia's relationship with its neighbours and to unsettle Australia's composure on various fronts. These are just a few examples of plays that take very seriously how one constitutes and stages Australia and an Australian persona/character: the very tropes of multiculturalism and the playful inter-referentiality are frequently the subject of contemporary Australian playwrights' work in the exploration of multiple subject positions; the addressing of a variety of cultural contexts, backgrounds, and locations; the play with the limits of the English language; and the questioning of the attempts to determine 'an' Australian identity.

The disjunctions between multicultural theory, the practice of multicultural plays, and the frames of reference in these plays that exist outside the limited multicultural framework reinforce the problems that classifications such as Australian 'multicultural' drama versus 'mainstream' drama generate. The tropes that describe multicultural theatre, after all, are equally relevant to 'mainstream' Australian drama. Ethnicity will of course continue to be deployed ambivalently on the various Australian stages to reinforce the transitional nature of identities that can be taken up or hidden depending on situation. This inter-referential play seems determined to resist any appeal to authenticity regarding both Australian and multicultural identities. Annette Blonski's comment that multiculturalism 'requires constant vigilance and continual negotiation and debate' (1994, 206) is certainly true; what is also required now is the resituation of debates and negotiation regarding multiculturalism to the centre-stage of Australian cultural and critical practice.[7]

Notes

1 While some might read difference as sexy or exotic, the actual experience of multicultural writers has often been one of ghettoisation. In 1992, Rosa Safransky explained that 'Multicultural has become synonymous with Martian. The term denotes a literary kiss of death... Ethnic or multicultural writers are little green men and women from Mars landing on Anglo-Celtic Australian soil with their foreign-sounding names and ray-gun typewriters' (204). Expressing a similar opinion, Tes Lyssiotis (1997) has commented that she feels compelled to remain just a 'Greek writer' and that to write about other than 'Greek' topics would be unacceptable.

2 See work by, among others, Sneja Gunew (1987, 1988, 1992), Manfred Jurgensen (1986), Con Castan (1988), George Shaw (1986), and Castles, Kalantzis, Cope & Morrissey (1992).

3 There are exceptions, including Vasso Kalamaras's *The Bread Trap*, written in Perth in 1960 but not performed until 1980. See also *Love* (1985) on theatre by Chinese goldfield labourers from 1858-1870, and Pavlyshyn (1992) on Ukrainian theatre in Australia from 1948-1989. Castan (1988) lists dramatic work by Greek Australians 1917-1988.

4 *Varda che Bruta* was performed again at the Stables in 1993 as part of Carnivale, at the Universal Theatre in Melbourne in 1994, and at the State Theatre Company of South Australia for the International Women Playwrights' Conference in Adelaide, later the same year.

5 *Cold Harvest* is likely to premiere in Sydney in 1997 or 1998.

6 The 1993 movie *Le Gioie delle Donne* makes the point that those who leave Italy for countries like Australia tend to retain a version of Italian that is outmoded to those who remained in Italy. For Italians in Italy the language changes, whereas those who leave retain a static form of the language. The same has been noted of Greeks who leave Greece to live permanently in other, non-Greek-speaking countries.

7 There is reason to believe that as a term, 'multiculturalism' may need to be replaced. I propose 'polynationalism' which would highlight the intersection of the competing forces of nationality, nationalism, ethnicity, identity and subjectivity more accurately addressing the interdependent relationship of theories such as post-colonialism and feminism with multiculturalism. This would also rectify the frequent placement of multiculturalism in isolation or in opposition to a mainstream national paradigm. Poly-nationalism would not pretend to unite disparate groups that have hitherto resisted nationalist stereotypes; instead it would reconsider relationships in contested space, as well as reconsidering the ways in which literatures are categorised, funded, distributed, and marketed in national and specific communities.

I would like to thank Tseen Khoo for her constructive comments on this paper.

Maintaining cultural integrity: Teresa Crea, Doppio Teatro, Italo-Australian theatre and critical multiculturalism

Tony Mitchell

Since the 1996 election of a Liberal-National Coalition government in Australia the policy and doctrine of multiculturalism — always a vexed and contested notion at the best of times — has begun to be dismantled in the context of a series of rabid funding cuts in favour of what increasingly seems like a throwback to the 'white Australia' immigration policies of the 1950s. As a result, the reality of multiculturalism in Australia has become increasingly fragile and fractious, a mood reflected by the diminishing number of artists and theatre groups working in the area of bilingual, bicultural or multicultural theatre.

While multiculturalism as an Anglo-Australian government policy was designed to group a colourful array of 'marginal' non-Anglo communities, customs and cultures around an Anglo-Australian mainstream, and frequently took on tokenistic and cosmetic aspects related to the consumption or toleration of exotic ethnic food, folklore and traditions (Hage 1991), it also provided a valuable conduit for the artistic expression of artists and performance groups from ethnic minorities. This outpouring of expression from artists from Non-English-Speaking Backgrounds (NESB) reached its peak in the late 1980s before going into a decline in the 1990s. The sometimes aggressive and self-congratulatory expressions of a rather homogenised and 'othered' form of multicultural community theatre by Sydney-based Sidetrack Theatre were abandoned for explorations of postmodern notions of performance in the early 1990s; the Sydney-based Italian FILEF (Federation of Migrant Workers and their Families) Community Theatre group had disbanded after half a dozen productions; the Melbourne-based Italo-Australian Theatre Company had ceased to perform the Italian language plays of Nino Randazzo, which it had done regularly each year at the Melbourne Italian Arts Festival from 1980 to 1990 (Schiavoni 1983); the Greek and Italian-Australian *Wogs Out of Work* troupe dispersed after two series of the formulaic 'ethnic' TV situation comedy *Acropolis Now*; and Tes Lyssiotis, Greek-Australian playwright, director and founder of the Melbourne-based Filiki Players, moved further into the theatrical mainstream as a playwright (Mitchell 1987a, 1987b, 1988, 1992b). While community-based theatre groups in Sydney like

Death Defying Theatre, Pact Theatre and other members of the Multicultural Theatre Alliance continue to present multicultural works and projects on a limited scale, the official acknowledgment which the Labour Government's 1989 'Arts for a Multicultural Australia' policy attempted to give to multicultural artists and performers came too late (Gauntlett 1993).

Doppio Teatro — 'Double Theatre' — is one of the few professional Italo-Australian, bilingual, non-Anglo or 'multicultural' theatre groups which has managed to survive into the 1990s. It was formed in Adelaide in 1983 by Teresa Crea and Christopher Bell, graduates in Italian and Theatre Studies from Flinders University. Crea, who also studied at the Silvio D'Amico Accademia Nazionale dell'Arte Drammatica in Rome, and was strongly affected by visiting her parents' birthplace in Calabria, has described the rationale of the group, which was encouraged by the emerging government policies of Community Arts and Multicultural Arts in the early 1980s, as follows:

> The idea behind Doppio Teatro is to underline the duality that exists here in Australia for many people who have two cultures within them — or rather, who have one culture of origin, plus their confrontation with the dominant culture, which is the common code we live by, the Anglo-Australian culture. (Mitchell 1992a)

Maria Shevtsova has identified the principal themes of Doppio Teatro's work as re-inscribing the importance of past history for Italian immigrants to Australia, representing the struggles of the children of Italian migrants to assert their social, cultural and psychological independence, asserting the strength of Italian social and cultural traditions, especially southern rural traditions, on the alien environment of contemporary Australia, and dealing with the cultural stagnation resulting from 'freezing' life in the past and with the difficulties of integrating into the Australian way of life without losing Italian cultural identity (1993, 162). To this could be added an exploration of Italian traditions of performance, such as the masks and the physical and vocal performance techniques of the commedia dell'arte re-interpreted in an Australian context. In a 1994 brochure, the company expressed its aims more broadly as 'celebrating tradition and change through Italian and Australian cultures'.

Doppio Teatro began performing plays such as Pirandello's *Cece* in Italian, Carlo Maria Pensa's *L'innocente* in English and Vincenzo Franceschi's *Qui tutto bene* (Everything's Fine Here), a play about Italian migrants in Germany, to supplement the Italian syllabus in South

Australian schools in 1984 and 1985. But, as Crea later commented, they soon became aware that they were operating within academic and 'high' cultural confines which had little connection with most Italo-Australians, who responded more to popular cultural forms: 'We realised [...] that Italian culture was a different Italian culture to the one we were living here' (Sutton 1989b, 5). Establishing what has become an ongoing polemic with some representatives of Italian culture in Adelaide, Crea began to explore popular cultural forms such as story-telling, songs and masks, particularly those of the peasant traditions of southern Italy.

After performing the Franceschi play at the 1984 Adelaide Fringe Festival, Doppio decided to deal directly with the experiences of Italo-Australians, devising a bilingual touring show for Italian social clubs in South Australia from improvisations they conducted with Italo-Australian actors about their parents' and relatives' experiences of migration. *Il cabaret dell'emigrante* (The Migrant Cabaret) premiered at the Juventus Sports and Social Club in November 1984, and combined historical scenes of migration from Italy to Australia (at one point the stage becomes a ship) with Italian popular songs from the 1950s and 1960s in a cabaret format. As Crea commented in an introductory note to the published version of the play's text:

> Our intention was to explore the experience of migration from the migrant's pint of view. Many of the actors drew upon their own personal history and that of their extended family as source material. We chose also to place the work in a historical context (1950-84), thus reflecting the experiences of both the first and second generation Italians in Australia. A major recurring theme was the impact of Australia's 'assimilationist' policy on the migrant's self-concept (Doppio Teatro, 1988, 11).

One of the effects of assimilation was the development of an Italo-Australian dialect which Italianised English words for Australian phenomena which had no exact equivalent in Italian; words such as *iarda* (yard), *fensa* (fence), even *carro* (car) and *marchetta* (market). Doppio Teatro began to refer to this migrant dialect as *emigrante*, and it became part of the four-tiered bilingual texture of the group's shows which switched from Italian to Sicilian, Veneto or Calabrese dialects and from English to *emigrante*, sometimes within the same scene. As Crea has explained, this was a natural occurrence in bringing together an Italian *nonna* (grandmother) who spoke only a regional dialect, her daughter who might speak standard Italian if she had had some education, as well as a mixture of dialect and English, and her grandchildren, who would speak

English with a bit of *emigrante* thrown in (Mitchell 1992a). *Il cabaret dell'emigrante* contrasted the mores of customs officers and the Anglophone education system with the dilemmas of Italian migrants, culminating in the celebration of an Italian wedding at the Veneto Club. It was so successful among the Italian community of South Australia that it was given a return season in 1995, and the following year Doppio Teatro devised and performed another cabaret show along similar lines, *Un pugno di terra* (A Fistful of Earth). Using regional Italian work songs, a mock family soap opera, and comic sketches such as an ethnic 'New Faces' talent contest, the show, like its predecessor, alternated scenes in English with scenes played almost entirely in Italian or dialect. It explored the often traumatic and disorienting experiences of Italo-Australians visiting their country of origin. Based on interviews within the Italian community of South Australia, it dealt with migration in terms of love, work, isolation and alienation. By the end of its run, Crea estimated, the show had been enthusiastically received by more than three thousand people of a variety of ages and cultural backgrounds, illustrating an evident need for re-evaluation by both adults and young people of the whole concept of migration (Doppio Teatro 1988, 39). In 1985 Doppio also contributed to a retrospective of Fifty Years of Migration to Australia held at the Alabarda Club in South Australia.

Doppio then devised a play to tour schools, using the workshopping process which had become their stock in trade. *Just Call Me Jo* was a theatre-in-education piece about the stigmas of 'otherness' and 'difference' experienced by NESB children in Australian schools, and featured two actresses, Antonietta Morgillo and Lucia Mastrantone, who were to become key figures in the group's subsequent work. The play, which featured in Adelaide's 1987 Come Out youth theatre festival, presented the problems of a fifteen-year-old Italian girl, Josie, and her seventeen-year-old brother Gino, in coping with school life alongside the difficulties they and their parents have in understanding one another's problems. In the final scene, as the cast write anti-racist graffiti in the schoolyard, Josie and Gino express their difficulties in coming to terms with their mixed identities, but finally assert their dual identities as both Italian and Australian. After the play, audience discussions were held.

Doppio Teatro then returned to the Italian community in November 1987 with *La Madonna emigrante* (The Migration of the Madonna), which took the form of an outdoor procession transporting a patron saint through the streets of an Italian village, performed in the Norwood Oval in Adelaide. The play dealt with the chain migration of entire villages in

Italy to America, as a miracle play in which each scene was performed on a different stage along the procession route. The protagonist Tonino, a young Calabrese who emigrates to the USA, is given a plaster statue of the Madonna by his local parish priest. Amidst the consumerism, materialism and negation of other ethnicities in the USA, he finds this religious icon the only thing of spiritual substance he has left, and it becomes the symbol of the spirituality lacking in the world around him. This story-line has a striking resemblance to that of Nino Randazzo's first and most successful bilingual play *Il pane e le rose* (Bread and Roses), first performed by the Italo-Australian Theatre Company in 1980, where the protagonist Cirino Pignataro brings back to Melbourne a wooden station of his Sicilian village's patron saint San Nunziante, who has recently been abolished by the Vatican. In establishing a San Nunziante cult in Melbourne, he asserts the importance of spiritual values in a culture dominated by 'Saint Dollar and Johnny Walker' (the latter of which is associated with an Irish catholic priest, Father Callaghan). Cirino sums up the play's ethos as follows:

> We, simple migrants [...] are not going to accept that saints no longer exist. For us saints [...] are a good thing, they keep us company, they tell us that we are not alone in a foreign land. We have come to seek bread, but we also want roses. Otherwise, ours would be a dog's life! (Schiavoni 1983, 113)

La Madonna emigrante similarly does not question the repressiveness of traditional Italian religious practices, but it does represent alternative manifestations of popular pagan folk culture in the form of a witch chorus figure, played by Antonietta Morgillo, which recur in subsequent Doppio Teatro productions. As Crea has stated:

> The play was saying that migrants used religion in a functional way — it's a folk approach, not an institutional one — so the saint becomes almost a pagan idol. And the psychological power of that icon had a purpose. When the migrants here lost touch with that function, it was replaced with other things. [...] What I was trying to explore were the icons of popular culture, which used to be religious but have now been replaced by the icons of money and the car and the two-storeyed house. (Mitchell 1992a)

A radio version of *La Madonna emigrante* was broadcast by the ABC's Radio National in 1993, and was a finalist in the 1993 New York International Radio Festival. This broadcast was repeated in April 1996 as a representation of multicultural Australian drama in the 1990s in the ABC's celebration of sixty years of radio drama. With its predominance of Italian and Calabrese dialect, often with little English explanation or framing dialogue, and its strong use of accordion-based folk music and chants incorporating Calabrese tarantellas, it made for a highly distinctive radio event which made few concessions to the Anglophone listener in conveying a striking sonic impression of the experiences of Italian migration. Doppio Teatro had earlier experimented with radio plays for the Italian community in 1988, when they also performed *Presepio Vivente* (Living Crib), a live nativity play in Italian, and *Caffè Teatro*, a cabaret show.

Ricordi (Memories), which premiered at the Adelaide Festival Fringe in March 1989, was the play which finally brought Doppio's work to audiences beyond the confines of the Adelaide Italian community (and some non-Italian spectators). The play toured to Victoria, New South Wales and Queensland, and was widely acclaimed by mainstream Australian audiences, selling out its season at Sydney's Wharf Theatre. In 1990 the company took it to the international Mayhem Youth Theatre festival in Leeds, where it was also enthusiastically received. *Ricordi* was a relatively small-scale work, devised and directed by Crea with Antonietta Morgillo, Josie Composto-Eberhard and Lucia Mastrantone. All are from southern Italian backgrounds, with which they maintain strong links, but were educated and studied drama in Australia. They set out to explore the processes of cultural transmission and change which have taken place through three generations of migrant Italian women in Australia, with the three actresses playing nine characters, ranging from a Sicilian grandmother to a teenage 'wog girl', Viviana, born in Australia of Italo-Australian parents, who frequents the Rio Discotheque in Adelaide and speaks broad 'strine' (her favourite word is 'freaky').

The character of Viviana invited comparison with the highly successful Melbourne-based second-generation migrant satire of the comedy show *Wogs Out of Work*, and in particular Mary Coustas's Greek-Australian character Effie in the television series *Acropolis Now* which developed out of that show. But Crea was quick to point out that Doppio's work had a wider scope than *Wogs Out of Work*, as it also 'deals directly with the experiences of a first generation, drawing upon the stories of the community elders to record and give expression to traditions fast disappearing both in Australia and Italy' (Crea 1992, 3). With a strong emphasis on physical gesture and choreography , rituals of birth, marriage and death as well as domestic rituals like washing, cooking, ironing and cleaning were represented on a largely bare stage and the performers drew on the experiences of their own grandmothers, mothers and younger sisters to build up a powerful mosaic of scenes which combined biting irony and humour with powerful emotion. The open-throated Mediterranean singing known as 'belting', which the performers developed with musician Linsey Pollack, a specialist in Macedonian bagpipe music and Mediterranean singing, added extra power to the play in songs which ranged from an old woman's comic song about her husband's inability to get an erection ('*Se il marito non ce l'ha*') to a tragic song of domestic violence ('*Guarda quanto para bella*'). Much of the play was in Sicilian and Campanian dialect, reflecting the dilemma of older migrant women who never had the opportunity to learn English, and who share a nostalgia for rural Italian life. Despite the substantial Italian and dialect content, the play was praised by mainstream Australian theatre critics who saw affinities with both European and African-American drama: Leigh Sutton (1989a) invoked Arrabal, the film directors Cacoyannis, Rossellini and Whoopi Goldberg, while Peter Goers saw the play as an Italian version of Ntozake Shange's 'choreopoem' *For Coloured Girls Who Have Considered Suicide When the Rainbow is Enuf.*

Ricordi represents a peak of public acceptance in Doppio Teatro's work, coming after the extensive tour around Australia of *Wogs Out of Work,* which since its runaway success in Melbourne in 1987 became the most successful non-Anglo comedy show in Australian history, and *The Journey*, a compendium of works by Melbourne-based Greek-Australian playwright and director Tes Lyssiotis and her group the Filiki Players, which had been acclaimed in New South Wales, the ACT and Queensland, also in 1987. Multicultural theatre had 'come of age' as an expression of the identity politics of NESB communities, and community groups like Sidetrack and FILEF in Sydney, the Melbourne Workers' Theatre, and the numerous groups contributing to the Multicultural Theatre Alliance's annual festivals in Sydney were increasing the profile of non-Anglo theatre. But looking back on the success of *Ricordi* ten years after workshops for the play began, Crea sees the acclaim for its expression of identity politics as rather hollow:

> In the Australian theatre scene its success corresponds to a historical moment, as an emerging group we gave voice to ideas that were in the air. [...] But ten years later [...] it is no longer a question of Italian-Australians in terms of the expression of identities — it is much more complex. I got to a position where I hated *Ricordi*, because everybody wanted to see us doing that sort of theatre and when we wanted to shift and do something else they just left. (Fensham 1996, 1, 4)

After *Ricordi* Doppio delved further into the complexities of Italo-Australian culture, devising a puppet theatre piece for five to ten-year-olds called *Peppino*, loosely adapted from the Pinocchio story, and Antonietta Morgillo wrote and co-directed the group's next major play *The Olive Tree*, developed through workshops and discussions with the three cast members of *Ricordi* and others. Like *La Madonna emigrante* it was an open-air piece, and was first performed during the 1990 Adelaide Festival in the courtyard of the Adelaide Migration and Settlement Museum (which was at the time running an exhibition on Italian migration to Australia, *Il cammino continua*). The title of *The Olive Tree* derives from a folk tale which the mother of the play's protagonist relates in a mixture of English and Italian, about three witches who create an olive tree in Sicily for Michelina, a peasant woman whose husband has raped a fourteen-year-old girl — an act which causes the olive oil crop to spoil, but which she refuses to report.

Like *Ricordi*, which ends with a song about Italian women 'finding a voice', *The Olive Tree* is about the denial of migrant women's self-expression by dominant patriarchal and Anglocentric cultures. It begins with the suicide of Belinda, a 37-year-old woman born in Australia, who has lived in Italy and then returned to Australia. The events leading up to her suicide are reconstructed in a series of flashbacks which show her return to Italy, her mental disintegration in Australia, her daughter Francesca's problems in adjusting to school, alongside monologues by Belinda expressing her oppression in both the worlds she has lived in. Belinda's disturbed dreams are paralleled by Francesca's expressions of frustration at the traditional straitjacketed Italian values imposed on her by her family. It is revealed that Belinda's mother, Rosa, unable to cope with life in Australia, left her husband and family and subsequently returned to Italy. This emerges during Belinda's funeral service, and at the end of the play three witches appear and exhort Rosa to 'use this experience to give wisdom to your offspring [...] If you don't acknowledge and give wisdom to your grand daughter, she will come to the same end as your daughter' (Morgillo 1990, 154). As in *Ricordi*, the experiences of three generations of migrant women are compared and contrasted in order to illuminate one another. As Crea has stated, the group's tendency to focus on women characters reflects the fact that 'Traditionally, in the Italian culture women have been the custodians of life rituals and customs. Significantly, in these works, they have come forward with the strongest voice' (Crea 1992, 3).

With their next play, Doppio's focus shifted from the feminist concerns of *The Olive Tree* to an exploration of local Italo-Australian political history. With a cast of six men and one woman (Lucia Mastrantone) *Tinto di rosso* (Red Like the Devil, 1991) dealt with the life and confinement of Francesco Fantin, an Italian anarchist who emigrated to Australia in 1924 from the Veneto region in order to escape fascist reprisals in Italy. Fantin's story had previously been presented as a photographic exhibition and musical performance entitled *Francesco Fantin: Myth and Reality* in 1990 by the Adelaide FILEF and the Italian Folk Ensemble. Like many other Italian migrants at that time Fantin worked as a cane-cutter in Queensland where he continued his anti-fascist activities. But in 1942 he was interned along with 2,200 Italian and 3,000 other migrants in the Loveday Camp in South Australia, where the play was first performed. Described by the Australian authorities as a 'fascist communist enemy alien', Fantin was in danger of reprisals from the fascist sympathisers who were among his fellow-internees, and his name appeared on a hit-list when he gave his support to an appeal for sheepskins for Russian soldiers fighting on the European front. In November 1942 he died in one of the compound hospitals after what was officially described as an 'accident'. Crea encountered difficulties in researching the play, as many camp survivors were embarrassed at being labelled fascists as well as having been interned. The bilingual play which resulted had an all-male cast (with the exception of Lucia Mastrantone), led by Nicholas Papademetriou as Fantin and former FILEF and Sidetrack Theatre actor Silvio Ofria. It took an expressionistic approach to its subject, recreating the gloomy expanse of the camp, using flashbacks to recreate Fantin's biography, and interspersing these with scenes from camp life and Italian songs of the period sung by Mastrantone. After a season in Adelaide, which Shevstova (1993) shows was attended by a significant majority of non-Italian Australians (a sample of a quarter of the audience found that 59% were Anglo-Australian and 18% of Italian background) the play was chosen for the annual Australian Theatre Festival in Canberra in 1991. Samela Harris described it as 'an austere and compelling piece of theatre [...] serious and impressionistic. It also melds well-choreographed aesthetics with moving drama' (1991). The play toured to North Queensland in 1994 and a radio version was broadcast by ABC's Radio National in September 1996.

After touring a bilingual production for primary schools, *Naso Bello Naso Brutto* (Pretty Nose Ugly Nose), Doppio presented another outdoor show for the 1992 Adelaide Festival, *Una festa di nozze* (A Wedding Feast) in the Armoury Courtyard of the University of Adelaide. Taking the form of an Italo-Australian wedding reception in which part of the audience sits at tables around a circular stage and is served a 'wickedly delicious wedding feast prepared by prominent Adelaide cook Rosa Matto and served by some of this city's best-loved and notorious waiters, superb Italian wines and liqueurs, traditional and contemporary songs' (Doppio Teatro 1992), the play took the form of a series of comic anecdotes taken from local oral history about experiences of love and marriage. Employing an exaggerated *buffo* comic style with stylised white makeup, the bride dressed in leopardskin tights and an enormous billowing veil, and the groom in a white tuxedo with huge gold lamé lapels, with Mastrantone playing a grotesquely over-solicitous Italian *mamma*, the production was greatly enjoyed by local Italian audiences. Nonetheless *Sydney Morning Herald* critic Bob Evans complained at being alienated both by not being part of the catered audience, and by the large proportion of the songs and recollections which were in Italian. Comparing the play unfavourably to *Ricordi* and Jack Hibberd's Anglo-Australian wedding-play *Dimboola*, Evans described *A Wedding Feast* as 'a scrappy antipasto offering few comic morsels that the audience can get its teeth into' (Evans 1992). While a knowledge of Italian and first-hand acquaintance with the rituals and customs of Italo-Australian weddings no doubt enhance an appreciation of what Crea has acknowledged as a rather rough and 'underdeveloped' production (Crea 1996), Evans' complaints reflect an incomprehension of the more extreme and culturally-specific aspects of Doppio Teatro's work, illustrating the cultural barriers they were encountering within Australian mainstream theatre. As Crea has commented, 'because we make a statement about our theatre being in another language we still get hostile reviews. It is foreign-language theatre but too close to home' (Fensham 1996, 4). In 1996 Doppio re-mounted *Una festa di nozze*, making it more polished and cohesive, and touring it to Canberra, Newcastle and Lismore, performing it on the site of the historic Italian settlement Nuova Italia in the New South Wales town of Griffith, noted for its large Italian population, and at the Singapore Arts Festival. Reviews of the new production were positive but still reflected a stigmatising of the play's perceived exoticism. Samela Harris concluded her review, for example, with a summation of the play's 'Italianness':

> *Una Festa Di Nozze* has grown in both fun and style from its original production. With its universal theme and the loving embellishments of the hospitality industry, it is an experience very heartily Italian. As a dividend of the new sense of cultural diversity from today's proud-again Australian Italians, it should raise a bright flag for Australia in Singapore. (1996, 27)

This response reflects what Crea has perceived as a tendency of reviewers to 'focus on the work as *Italian* (rather than accept it as an expression of the contemporary, albeit culturally diverse *Australian* theatre scene) and thereby constantly view/position us as the "other"' (Crea 1996). Doppio's successive show, *Le voci del silenzio* (*Filling the Silence*), was commissioned by the 1993 Brisbane Biennial International Music Festival, and also performed in Adelaide, Wollongong, Mullimbimby and Lismore. Written and directed by Crea as more of an experimental music theatre performance than a play, it consisted of a musical duologue between Linsey Pollack and Lucia Mastrantone. The former was attached to a sound booth and played flutes, trumpets and Macedonian bagpipes, and the latter sang and vocalised in a series of characterisations ranging from an Italian peasant woman washing sheets and herding farm animals to a disco dancer. In Evans' view, the non-verbal allusiveness of the duo's performances made excessive demands on the spectator in forestalling normal avenues of critical interpretation: 'It is possible to read into the juxtapositions of score and action thematic concern about generational change, women and men, the natural (analogue) and the artificial (digital), village and metropolis. But the dialogue between the two is fairly limited, in both languages and, theatrically, the production takes it no further' (Evans 1993). This contrasted with other reviews of the production in Brisbane, which responded to the play as an experimental, predominantly sensory amalgamation of sound and image, rather than a play about Italian migrants. Veronica Kelly, for example, praised its 'resonant collage of mime, spectacle, vocalising and instrumentation ... an integrated spectacle where music, mime and image collaborate in a dialogue between contemporary civilisation and its fractured, mechanised soundscapes' (1993b). Richard Waller found Mastrantone's 'transition from an Italian peasant unearthing the music and magic in the somewhat mundane routine of clothes washing, to a high-tech post-Metropolis acid-house dance floor diva [...] at once frightening, amusing, thrilling and touching' (1993b); sentiments echoed by David O'Brien in the youth-oriented street magazine *DB*, who found 'an emotional power and range which keeps the modern and old world in perspective' (1994). Alison Cotes suggested that attempting to interpret the piece in terms of representations of reality or rational explanation was futile: 'If you give yourself over, as the peasant woman does, to the power of the music and the effect of the lighting, then you may just find it one of the most stimulating experiences you've had for a long time' (1993b).

In 1991 Crea was invited by Belvoir Street Theatre to direct *Mad Forest*, Caryl Churchill's play about the revolution in Romania, for Sydney Carnivale. Instead she chose to direct a relatively obscure 1970 play by the controversial Italian film director Lina Wertmuller about the 1940s Neapolitan murderess Leonarda Cianciulli, *Love and Magic in Mamma's Kitchen.* Crea regards Wertmuller's films as an important influence on Doppio Teatro's work, particularly in her often unpopular and contentious use of Southern Italian stereotypes which nonetheless manage to express a sense of poignancy and political resonance. A cast of six Italo-Australian actresses from Sydney, Melbourne and Adelaide, including Doppio members Antonietta Morgillo and Eva di Cesare, Melbourne Workers' Theatre performer Laura Lattuada, Rose Clemente, Dina Panozzo and film and TV star Peta Toppano, impersonated a range of eccentric and volatile Felliniesque Neapolitan characters. Toppano, who had done little exploration into her Italian background before, found it 'one of the greatest experiences of my life' (Shevtsova 1993, 192), while it provided an impetus for Panozzo to develop her own bilingual one-woman show about her return to her family's town in the Veneto, *Varda che Bruta ... Poretta* (Look How Ugly She is ... Poor Thing) in Sydney in 1993.

Incorporating snippets of Italian into Wertmuller's wild, aria-like long speeches, and using Italian songs, the production and the lurid aspects of *Love and Magic* in which Leonarda, who has lost twelve children, believes she can save her thirteenth by murdering three of her friends, dismembering them, and melting them down into soap, seemed to confuse doctrinaire feminist Belvoir Street audiences, and was seen by relatively few Italians. Shevtsova (1993, 168-172), finds only 10% of her audience sample to be of Italian origin. It also received negative and uncomprehending reviews. Typical was Bob Evans' response, again resorting to culinary (and mixed) metaphors: 'It's quite a stew to cook up in any mamma's kitchen and Doppio Teatro's Teresa Crea does well to keep it simmering as imaginatively as she does even if it isn't quite al dente' (Evans 1991). Nonetheless from a production and performance perspective *Love and Magic* stands as something of an unheralded triumph in Italo-Australian theatre, and proved that Crea had emerged from the 'ghetto' of migrant and multicultural community theatre to join the front ranks of Australian directors. It also showed that her work had diversified into freelance directing as well as pursuing the tripartite terrain explored by Doppio Teatro — multicultural theatre-in-education, community-theatre based in the Italian clubs of South Australia, and the historical representation of Italian migration to Australia — work that was beginning to shift from 'ethnic theatre' territory into the theatrical mainstream.

Crea had worked on projects outside of Doppio Teatro as early as 1989, when she collaborated with Margaret Fischer on *Home Sweet Home*, a play about domestic violence which was performed by the women's theatre company Vitalstatistix in Adelaide and Tasmania. She also acted as a facilitator of theatre skills workshops for Italo-Australian performers (together with Doppio member Max Lorenzin) on *Water from the Well*, a theatre-in-education play written by Darrelyn Gunzburg and directed by Venetia Gillot which explored Italo-Australian identity among young people and was commissioned by the Campbelltown Youth Action Group and the Co-Ordinating Italian Committee in Adelaide in 1990. In 1994 she wrote and directed *Windows*, a half-hour play for television which was broadcast as part of SBS Television's multicultural drama series *Under the Skin*. *Windows* deals with the relationship between two middle-aged cleaning women: Pasqualina, an Italian-Australian, and her supervisor Silvia Popov who is of unspecified Eastern European origin. Pasqualina is new to the job which involves cleaning a large office building throughout the night. Interspersed with her attempts to come to terms with the job in voice-overs (in both Italian and English at different times), and her conversations with Silvia about sex, their daughters and husbands, are brief flashbacks of Pasqualina's first communion, wedding night and arrival in Australia. A bond develops between Pasqualina and Silvia as '*femmine di una certa eta*' (women of a certain age), and the two women enact a series of male and female roles, dancing together and eventually making love.

In 1995 Crea was invited by Chris Westwood, artistic director of the State Theatre Company of South Australia, to direct Pirandello's *Six Characters in Search of an Author* at the Playhouse in the Adelaide Festival Centre. Apart from representing something of a full circle back to Pirandello, this also marked her progression to one of the country's main stages. Vastly reduced in scale from Pirandello's original array of characters, and with a cast of predominantly Italo-Australian actors (including Mastrantone as the Daughter), her production of her own translation of Pirandello incorporated cinematic devices and projected film clips along with local theatrical references. Crea described her approach to the project in terms of preserving an Italian cultural perspective with actors she did not normally collaborate with, and who tended to be products of a 'monocultural perspective, monocultural training [...] which is very Anglocentric': 'The State Company wants an Italian perspective but in these circumstances I have to work with people from a different cultural framework, so part of my job is how to maintain my cultural perspective — I have to brief these artists culturally so I can give another reading of the work' (Gallasch 1995). According to Peter Ward (1995), the acting in *Six Characters* was uneven, and the production was 'an ingenious reading and ingeniously done, though in the final analysis it really doesn't take the play much further than a conventional one' (Ward 1995). As with *Love and Magic*, some of the conflicts and difficulties of working outside Doppio Teatro with trained professional actors from mainstream theatre appeared to be reflected in the production.

The less than satisfying experience of *Six Characters* contrasts with the insights Crea gave into her approach to collective bilingual Doppio projects such as *Pane e cipolla* (Bread and Onions), which was being developed at the same time, where an essentially visual, elliptic and poetic theatrical language is developed :

> We'll play in the clubs — Sicilian, Veneto with their very different languages. So we start the piece, get the bi-lingual writer in; then we have to work out the different characters from different regions and translate each part into a different language. Then we have to find the actors fluent in the dialect, let alone the Italian, change cultural perspectives of the characters, not just the language, according to who we are playing to. And we have a stage manager without the language trying to follow a script that changes in these different version of the show. All I can say to the stage manager is, 'Think of it as dance. Go with visuals.' (Gallasch 1995)

Pane e Cipolla was followed by *Eremophilia: Pulcinella*, which was performed at the Space Theatre and the Norwood Concert Hall in Adelaide in 1995, and drew on commedia dell'arte mask and physical movement workshops which the company had done with Paolo Consiglio and Valeria Campo in 1993. Transposing the masks and *lazzi* of the commedia into the Australian outback, the play, scripted by Italo-Australian writer and academic Elio Gatti, combines the Neapolitan mask of Pulcinella, (Adelaide singer Guido Coppola), and traditional Neapolitan song with characters, images and sounds of the Australian outback. This cultural fusion, in which an encounter between the Neapolitan Fiammetta (Cinzia Coassin) and the Australian archetype Bruce (Phil Spruce) is acted out, is symbolised by the chorus-like figure of a Hermaphrodite (Laura Lattuada). Reviewing the production in the Adelaide *Advertiser*, Tim Lloyd found

> the sets, masks and costumes [...] are the highlights of the show. Along with the Italian songs and music, and the traditionally inspired dance, they speak volumes more than the dialogue [...] which is less well defined. Where Doppio Teatro's bilingualism has been one of the trademarks of this company, Gatti has written a more cumbersome text, where the play seems to continually pause for translation rather than constantly evolve in two languages. In addition, the development of plot and setting are poorly expressed, and the play diverts to explore some pointless side issues. (1995)

After more than a decade Crea and Doppio Teatro's work has proved to be highly durable, and has established itself as the most significant body of work by a non-Anglo theatre group in Australia. That they are one of the only survivors has caused Crea to comment: 'I cannot understand why after all these years of advocacy, funding and policy etc., there are not more companies like us in existence. Could it be when work is produced in different communities and different languages/cultures it cannot be adequately critically reviewed [and] thereby given opportunity for exposure and growth?' (1996). Doppio Teatro's stature as an Australian performance group was officially acknowledged by its sharing with the Aboriginal Bangarra Dance Theatre the Sydney Myer Foundation Group Award in 1993 for their 'distinctive contribution to the Australian Performing Arts'. In Shevstova's view, Doppio remains

> the most important example of a theatre that grows out of a specific ethnic community and aims to return, to that community, the history, cultural particularities, immigrant experiences and present state of affairs which define the community and distinguish it from any other. [...] [A]lthough functioning on a shoe-string within the economic as well as ideological confines suffered by all community theatre groups, [it] has succeeded in creating works having the strength, polish and finish normally expected of professional, 'high' art and/or mainstream companies. Extremely sophisticated from both a conceptual and artistic point of view, Doppio belied the idea in vogue during the eighties that community theatre was a people's theatre of some sort and, therefore, by definition could not aspire to 'real' art. [...] How it extends audiences for both community and mainstream theatre, merging the boundaries between them, is a measure of Doppio's public importance and success. (1993, 160-161)

While *Ricordi* may represent the group's high point in terms of audience and critical acclaim, all aspects of Crea's and Doppio Teatro's work, from one-off mainstream productions and independent projects to work in social clubs and schools, from mime and mask workshops to outdoor festivals, music theatre and plays, continue to explore and interrogate the social and cultural dilemmas of being an Australian of Italian origin, and to preserve strongly-held notions of 'cultural integrity'. In 1996 Crea summed up Doppio Teatro's continuing marginal position in Australian theatre, and their refusal to succumb to the representations of Italian cultural identity as folksy exotica which continue to be perpetrated by the Australian theatrical mainstream:

> Any work that happens on the margins, the mainstream eventually picks up, the centre needs to continually feed itself with new ideas. But often it incorporates them and sanitises them. With work that springs from an Italian background, you show it can happen and the excitement somehow penetrates the veneer of the mainstream [...] But difference is then invested with cuteness [...] It is a constant challenge, but you have to continue to believe in the integrity of your work. I hope it comes from the process, values, the dialogue you have with a particular cultural background, your approach. I hope. I have started to use this term cultural integrity because we began to be overwhelmed by the diffusion of Italianness. There are moments when we have been picked up for the cute value, but how do you maintain the core beliefs about your work when everyone else is wanting you to be something else? (Fensham 1996, 1)

This statement was made in the context of the widespread success in the mid-1990s of *Emma*, an adaptation by former Sidetrack Theatre founder Graham Pitts of *Emma: A Translated Life*, an autobiography of West Australian-based migrant Emma Ciccatosto as told to Michael Bosworth (Ciccatosto & Bosworth 1995), one of the most moving and powerful accounts of migration to Australia ever published. Essentially a piece of transcribed oral history, the book lets the events recounted by Emma speak for themselves in an unfussy, unadorned and transparent prose style. Bosworth translates Emma's oral account of her life story into a sequence of episodes in which the social, historical, political and cultural aspects of the migrant experience in Australia since the 1930s are reflected, along with a vibrant and unsentimental account of the peasant lifestyle in the Abruzzi region of Italy which Emma left behind as a child for Waroona and later Fremantle.

Originally performed to much acclaim by Deck Chair Theatre in Fremantle in 1993 with Rosemary Lenza as Emma and music by the Italo-Australian women's song group Le Gioie delle Donne (The Joys of the Women, of which Emma Ciccatosto is a member), Pitts' play had a sellout season in the 1993 Festival of Australian Theatre in Canberra, was broadcast in a radio version in 1994, and was subsequently given separate productions directed by Rosalba Clemente at the Belvoir Street Theatre in Sydney in November 1995; at Playbox Theatre in Melbourne in March 1996; and at La Boite, Brisbane in 1997 (revived 1998). An example of the play's exaggerated dramatic methodology is the account of Emma's first meeting with her husband Peter, a 'naturalised' Australian who helps Emma's family out on their farm when her father is interned during the war. In the book, this event is narrated briefly in broad strokes almost as an incidental detail. In the play, Peter appears with a piano accordion and recounts how he marched down the main street of Waroona playing it and protesting that he had not been interned with the other Italians, finally confronting police and internees and throwing the accordion on the floor. As played by Nicholas Papademetriou in the Belvoir Street production, as a 'barbershop' Italian prone to sinking to his knees, waving his arms about and speaking English with an exaggerated Italian accent, Peter immediately becomes a caricature in the style of 1950s Anglo-Australian portrayals of Italo-Australian .

The role of Emma is padded out with a series of sentimental homilies (e.g. 'You can always get what you want if you have love ... and a brain') and dialogues with characters from Emma's life who are conjured up gratuitously from her stream of reminiscences. Emma herself works at a gas stove for most of the play's duration, preparing *pasta con melanzane* for a few fortunate members of the audience in the first act, and catering for her granddaughter's wedding reception in the second. 'If you have an eggplant, you have a meal. If you have a meal, you have a home with a contented husband and children. All because of the infallible eggplant' (Pitts 1994, 111). The Belvoir Street production took this culinary characterisation as a keynote, subtitling the play 'Amore e melanzane' (Love and eggplants) and covering the posters and publicity material with tomatoes, while in the program all the cast and crew, Anglos included, provide their favourite recipes. After the success of the play, the book was re-issued in a new, glossier edition augmented with some of Emma's favourite recipes (Pitts, 1996).

In a program note to his adaptation of *Emma*, Pitts rejects multiculturalism for a vaguely-defined and essentialist notion of universalism: 'I did not write this play because I wanted to do something "multicultural" or bash up Anglo-Australian attitudes. The time for such art has departed (and in any case I had been there and done that already). I wrote it because I sense that her story was the essence of a migration which must happen to us all' (Pitts 1995). Nonetheless Robyn Archer states in her introduction to the playtext in *Australasian Drama Studies* that *Emma* 'had all the right credentials. It was not bred of Sydney or Melbourne [...] It was Italian Australian. What's more it was the very population responsible for one of the most touted tourist spots in the continent — the pasta, pizza and espresso of Fremantle's Italian strip were already legendary' (1994, 99). This suggests a conflation of *Emma* with Anglo-Australian perceptions of the culinary, exotic and politically correct aspects of multiculturalism which were echoed in some reviews of the production, such as James Waites who found 'the evening overflows with the joy of life' (1996). But the most alarming implication of Pitts' statement is that his version of Emma's story demonstrates that a rejection of multicultural polemic has simply re-inscribed antiquated, pre-multiculturalist ethnic stereotypes. Crea has commented on this kind of rejection of multiculturalism:

> The problem is people say we've done multiculturalism and forget that rather than looking at it as a political theory it's a description of the complex and vibrant society we live in [...] it just remains on the level of an issue, rather than exploring the very tricky but fascinating territory of different perceptual frameworks and cultural aesthetics. (Gallasch 1995)

It is this perceptual and aesthetic territory that *Emma* singularly fails to explore, resulting in the perpetuation of stereotypical perceptions of Italians in Australia so entrenched they cannot be reversed even by the involvement of Italian actors and directors in the play's various manifestations. The mainstream acceptance of spurious token representations of Italians which *Emma* celebrates serves to make the continually careful, self-analytical and interrogating work of Doppio Teatro appear even more isolated and difficult. Rather than rejecting and reinforcing multiculturalism as a superficial, cosmetic and culinary concept, Doppio Teatro's work perpetuates the notion of critical multiculturalism, accepting it as an inevitable reality and exploring rhetorical strategies and cultural critiques which rescue it from tokenism. In doing so, it reinforces Homi Bhabha's conceptualisation of the mainstream or centre of a culture being constructed by the conflictual interventions of its 'ethnic' margins:

> the marginal or 'minority' is not the space of a celebratory, or utopian, self-marginalisation. It is a much more substantial intervention into those justifications of modernity — progress, homogeneity, cultural organicism, the deep nation, the long past — that rationalise the authoritarian, 'normalising' tendencies within cultures in the name of the national interest or the ethnic prerogative. (Bhabha 1991, 4)

In 1996 Doppio returned to themes of migration with *Preludes to an Exile*, performed as part of the Adelaide Festival. Dealing with the theme of migrant women who work from home, the production took the form of a hybrid visual arts/performance installation mounted at a second-hand furniture store in suburban Adelaide. Working within a huge loom-like structure, three performers acted out through a combination of movement, stories and dialogue their characters' relationship to the cluttered space they both live and work in. The result was a fragmentary, expressionistic piece which had little in common with any conventional dramatic structure or characterisation, and where, as Noëlle Janaczewska commented:

> amid the drone of machinery, memories, hopes, humour and fragments of stories that hint at whole histories of war and loss bubble to the surface in words, gesture and movement — just momentarily — before sinking back into the landscape of repetition. And in their wake, they leave tantalising glimpses, unanswered questions and a powerful mosaic of exile — not only exile from a homeland but also various states of internal and internalised exile. (1996)

Moving out from the specificities of Italian-Australian culture, *Preludes to an Exile* took as its starting point the 1994 United Nations statistic that 125 million people, the equivalent of the population of France and Italy combined, are migrants from their countries of origin. Along with its aesthetic concerns with continuing the exploration of an experimental audio-visual form of theatre begun with *Filling the Silence*, it continued to explore the issues defined by Crea in 1991:

> After ten years of work we can [...] openly state that we are no closer to a definition of Italian-Australian culture than when we first started. What we do know is that we must continually question the relevance of our work. Is the culture of today the same as it was some years ago? What has changed? What has stood still? Why? When will it be no longer necessary to say what we have been saying? (Crea 1992, 3)

In their acknowledgment of the constantly shifting and complex nature of reality and identity for Australians of Italian extraction, Teresa Crea and Doppio Teatro have continued to pose difficult self-critical and self-analytical questions about Italo-Australian identity within increasingly experimental theatrical forms. Through the continuing efforts of Crea as artistic director and Peter Heydrich as company and operations manager, they have also established a strong collaborative base which has provided a working space and training ground for many performers, writers, visual artists, composers, production artists and administrative staff. Shevtsova sums up the political, social and cultural imperatives the company continues to take on board in its bilingual productions:

> [to] tackle material of relevance to immigrant communities but which mainstream theatre still ignores; show that the issues raised concern the whole of Australian society and not merely its ethnic enclaves; validate the history of immigrants, Italian immigrants in particular, by bringing to light the role they have played in the history of Australia; make theatre accessible to the Italian-born who for economic, linguistic and related sociocultural reasons not only do not go to mainstream or even 'alternative' theatre, but have been marginalised in other respects as well; reach their children, namely the second and third generation of Italo-Australians who may have been more or less assimilated into the dominant Anglo/Celtic culture but who, on the other hand, are losing or have lost touch with their language and culture of origin; evaluate positively a cultural legacy that had been virtually driven underground by the immigrants in question and derided by their adoptive country. The purpose, then, of working in two languages, was to foreground all these difficulties and help alleviate them. (1993, 17)

In the process they have shown that the cultural, theatrical and social statements their work presents, and their declared mission to contribute to 'the development of bicultural theatre practice of popular appeal through working and linking across cultures, generations, artforms' have continued to be vital and necessary ones within the context of contested, and often contentious, notions of a multicultural Australia.

Acknowledgment: parts of this study originally appeared in *New Theatre Quarterly* 8:29 (1992), 70-80. Thanks to Teresa Crea and Rachel Fensham for additional material.

Theatre in education: dead or alive?

Geoffrey Milne

One of the most vigorous growth areas in Australian theatre during the 1980s appeared to be Theatre for Young People (TYP). In 1978/79, some twenty-seven young people's theatre companies received grants from the Theatre Board of the Australia Council, the Australian Commonwealth Government's national arts funding and advisory body. A handful of puppet companies, which performed mostly for young audiences in those days, also received grants. Young people's theatre accounted for about 10.34% of the Theatre Board's grants in that financial year. Ten years later, eight full-time professional puppet companies and another thirty-seven young people's theatre organisations won grants amounting to 28.94% of total theatre funding. It should be added that there were a number of other young people's theatre companies which did not receive Commonwealth Government funding but which nevertheless operated on a full-time professional basis, generally with support from the state and territory Arts ministries (and, in some cases, from their Education ministries and departments) [1]. Growth in the art of puppetry was pronounced during the 1980s. Unfortunately, space constraints do not permit a detailed discussion of puppetry, although some of Handspan's work in particular will be mentioned later on; puppetry is a subject deserving its own chapter and interested readers are advised to track down *Theatre of the Impossible*, an excellent study of puppetry in Australia (Vella & Rickards 1989).

By 1989 there were in fact nearly three dozen professional Theatre in Education (TIE) companies in Australia, including the puppetry companies, receiving funding from the Commonwealth and/or the State and Territory Governments. By 'Theatre in Education' I mean professional theatre companies dedicated principally to the performance of purpose-made productions in schools (and occasionally in theatres), on themes relating directly to school syllabuses or to wider social issues. At the same time, there were a further eighteen Youth Theatre companies (meaning theatre companies with fully-professional infrastructures to facilitate public performance by young people aged, generally, from six to twenty-five years of age) in all states and territories, especially in New South Wales and South Australia. In addition to the specialist Young People's Theatre companies, there were a number of other companies which made a particular commitment to performance for young people in addition to their principal adult stock-in-trade. There were also major youth arts infrastructural organisations in South Australia (the South Australian Youth Arts Board and its excellent centre at Carclew in North Adelaide); Western Australia with the short-lived Performing Arts Services Centre at the Subiaco Theatre Centre in Perth; and Victoria, through the St Martin's Youth Arts Centre in South Yarra; and major biennial youth arts festivals with important and very vibrant theatre components; in Adelaide with the Come Out Festival beginning in 1975, and Melbourne with a Next Wave Festival inaugurated in 1985. Further Young People's Theatre activity was entrepreneured on a massive scale throughout the country areas in their respective states by the Queensland and Victorian divisions of the Arts Council of Australia, and highly-organised young people's theatre programs had emerged in the Adelaide Festival Centre and the Victorian Arts Centre, the latter known as the Art-Ed Program.

By 1994 support for young people's theatre was still generally strong: the Australia Council's Performing Arts Board that year provided funding worth more than $2,456,300 (or 21.5% of all theatre grants) for fifty-four young people's theatre organisations (not counting puppetry). However, the composition of the field had changed markedly during the first half of the 1990s. In 1988/89, the so-called TIE companies such as Toe Truck Theatre, Freewheels Theatre in Education, Sidetrack Theatre and the Theatre of the Deaf in NSW; Magpie and Patch Theatre in SA; Arena Theatre, the Woolly Jumpers, FM Live and Barnstorm Theatre in Victoria; Salamanca Theatre in Tasmania; Jigsaw Theatre in the ACT and Acting Out in WA; among many others, accounted for just on 75% of the Australia Council's total young people's theatre funding, whereas Youth Theatres, among whose leading members were the Flying Fruit Fly Circus in Albury-Wodonga, Canberra Youth Theatre, 2 Til 5 Youth Theatre in Newcastle, La Boite's Youth Theatre in Brisbane and Unley Youth Theatre in Adelaide, received barely 22% of the young people's theatre quantum. Infrastructural organisations like South Australia's Carclew Youth Arts Centre,[2] the Salamanca National Script Centre[3] and a national Youth Performing Arts Association received the remaining 3% of grants.

In 1993/94, infrastructure organisations (now including ASSITEJ — the Australian branch of the Association Internationale de Théâtre pour Enfants et Jeunesse, based at Carclew in Adelaide — along with others previously funded) enjoyed an increase in funding to about 5% of all young people's grants. Youth Theatre had grown massively over the past five years: thirty-nine organisations (twice the number funded in 1989) now received more than 38% of the total, while the erstwhile TIE companies — now reduced to only twelve receiving funding from the Australia Council — got only 57% of its young people's theatre grants. Two of those twelve companies went out of business in 1995 and at least one other (not directly funded by the Australia Council) was also wound up in the same year. So at the time of writing late in 1996 there is clear evidence to suggest that what we knew as 'theatre in education' in the 1970s and 1980s is now on the wane in the 1990s. Whether 'TIE is dead', as David Carlin proclaimed in the 1994 Arena season brochure, when he was artistic director of Arena Theatre Company in Melbourne, is a question to which we shall return. But first we should briefly sketch the history of young people's theatre in Australia prior to the 1990s.

Children's theatre

Professionally produced theatre for the entertainment of children of various ages, but principally for younger children, has been with us for many generations. Commercial theatre entrepreneurs and amateur companies alike, alert to the audience potential of a youthful population, frequently produced pantomimes and other theatrical entertainments for children, especially during periods of school holidays. One of the first organisations to specialise in theatre for children was the Australian Children's Theatre (Clarke 1972), a national touring company formed in Melbourne by Joan and Betty Rayner in 1948, although puppeteers, whether working alone or in companies, also practised their art principally for the delight and entertainment of young children. With the growth and diversity of subsidised theatre in the 1970s and 80s, including the burgeoning of Theatre in Education, and with the concomitant decline of the older commercial theatre networks, children's theatre as such became somewhat less fashionable for a time. However the subsidised Nimrod Theatre regularly added children's holiday productions (especially those on Clarke Island in Sydney Harbour) to their annual adult seasons through the late 1970s and early 80s, and Melbourne's Playbox Theatre Company during the mid 1980s, when James McCaughey was artistic director, also made a feature of productions for children in January.

However over the past decade there has been a revival of interest in children's theatre outside the subsidised theatre network, and it is not uncommon to see as many as fifteen commercial Christmas holiday shows for children every year in the larger cities, many of them in open-air locations in parks and gardens. These range from interpretations of traditional northern hemisphere children's stories (*Pinocchio* is always popular, as are *Cinderella*, *Robin Hood* and some of the tales from the *Arabian Nights*) to adaptations of stories by Frances Hodgson Burnett and Roald Dahl and — occasionally — versions of Australian tales like

Norman Lindsay's *The Magic Pudding* and May Gibbs' *Snugglepot and Cuddlepie*. Among the most popular attractions in Melbourne are the annual Glenn Elston production in the Royal Botanic Gardens of Kenneth Grahame's *The Wind in the Willows* (which celebrated its tenth birthday in the miserably wet summer of 1995/96) and Garry Ginivan's very elaborate annual productions of stylish and sophisticated children's musicals, usually at the Alexander Theatre at Monash University in the eastern suburbs; these have included Enid Blyton's *Noddy in Toyland* stories, the ubiquitous *Pinocchio* and, in 1996, Blyton's *The Magic Faraway Tree*. In addition, the amateur suburban Oxford Children's Theatre has packed in appreciative audiences for children's fairy-tale adaptations for many years. As can be seen, children's theatre is designed solely to entertain, although some managements still perceive the Christmas-treat theatre visit as a useful means of cultivating the adult audience of the future as well. Elements of fantasy and romance tend to predominate in a milieu where the theatrical experience is very much an end in itself for the child spectator. Children's theatre has never been subsidised in Australia and it has remained very much a commercial activity, operating at the 'safest' end of the repertoire spectrum.

Youth theatre

Professionally organised youth theatre is a more recent phenomenon in Australia; the oldest still extant organisation of this kind, the Australian Theatre for Young People, began life in 1964 in Sydney. While the ATYP was created primarily as a professional children's theatre it had diversified its functions by 1967 to include leisure-time instruction in the theatre arts for young people. Youth theatre of the kind I am talking about here is, on the whole, extra-curricular and is practised outside the education system as such, including the professional vocational drama schools.[4] One of the vogues sweeping both alternative theatre and educational drama in the late 1960s was improvisation: books extolling the educational, vocational and theatrical benefits of improvisation by English educationists like John Hodgson and Ernest Richards (1966) and theatre practitioners like the American Viola Spolin (1963) were widely read and applied, as were the writings on new experimental theatre in Europe and America to be found in the pages of *Tulane Drama Review* (later *The Drama Review* or *TDR*). Improvisation — of a wide variety of kinds and with a wide variety of aims — was certainly taught in the participatory workshops of youth theatres like ATYP, along with more orthodox skills in dramatic art. Consequently, when ATYP first began presenting work emanating from its youth theatre workshop stream in 1970, its first two productions were of Anne Jellicoe's extant script *The Rising Generation* and of the group-devised *Yukkety Yuk*, developed through improvisation by the performing group under director Richard Wherrett. This duality in Australian youth theatre has prevailed since the early 1970s: some companies specialise entirely in group-devising or 'play-building' original work through participatory workshops, sometimes with writers-in-residence engaged as part of their professional infrastructure, while others tend to prefer extant works or plays specially commissioned from professional playwrights. A third camp within the youth theatre movement blends the two approaches in interesting ways, with playwrights employed as dramaturgs to facilitate the creative writing of the groups' young members, as well as (or instead of) writing commissioned original material for the companies' young actors to perform.

Erroll Bray has been one of the principal influences in youth theatre in New South Wales and a great devotee of the play-building process (Bray 1976, 1991). He was involved with ATYP early in his career before founding another of Sydney's longest-serving youth theatres, the Shopfront Theatre for Young People, established in 1975 in that city's southern suburbs. Bray and his successors at Shopfront have developed practically all of their work through improvisatory workshops, the theory behind the work being that young people will thus be empowered to find their own voice and to express their own views of the world in which they live to audiences of their own peer groups in their own communities. The Shopfront approach has been emulated — consciously or coincidentally — by a large number of others throughout Australia. Barney Langford, for example, has successfully pursued a similar agenda at 2 Til 5 Youth Theatre in Newcastle for many years, as have most of the directors of well-established companies like the Canberra Youth Theatre; Contact Youth Theatre and La Boite Youth Theatre in Brisbane; Corrugated Iron Youth Theatre in Darwin; Port Youth Theatre Workshop in Adelaide; Coco Youth Theatre in Albany, Western Australia, and many of the other Sydney youth theatres like Powerhouse, Warringah and PACT. Much of the work of newer organisations like Gambit Youth Theatre and Theatre Now! in Tasmania, Slice of Ice in outer suburban Brisbane, and the Southwest Arts Project in the New South Wales country town of Hay, has also tended to be developed along group-creative lines.

Two further companies whose work is always original should be mentioned here, both youth circuses. One is Bowden Brompton Youth Circus, better known as Cirkidz, a smallish-scale organisation catering for young people in Adelaide's inner northern suburbs; Cirkidz's performance work emanates more or less directly from its circus training programme. The other is the Flying Fruit Fly Circus,which grew out of a special International Year of the Child project created in 1979/80 by the regional community theatre company at Albury-Wodonga, the Murray River Performing Group. The Fruit Flies are probably Australia's best-known Youth Theatre company, and they have toured widely in Australia and overseas with great success in addition to hosting a number of influential national and international circus training programmes. They have had professional performing and training contacts with the Nanjing Acrobatic Troupe and the Guangzhou Acrobatic Company, and members performed with the Great Moscow Circus during its 1990 Australian tour. As well as being a fully-fledged performing circus, the FFFC is also the national centre for circus training through its educational arm, the Victorian education system-accredited Acrobatic Arts Community School, which teaches a complete academic curriculum — plus circus skills — to an enrolment of upwards of sixty kids; it is said to be unique in the western world. While the productions of companies like these could hardly be said to be 'play-built' in the Errol Bray tradition, they are nevertheless devised on the spot and with the performers, by professional directors, designers, musicians and writer/researchers.

Having successfully pioneered a considerable variety of approaches to youth theatre in its earliest days, the Australian Theatre for Young People is better known nowadays as a presenting company rather than a creating company. Its productions by Mark Gaal of Frank Wedekind's *Spring Awakening* (1989) and Shakespeare's *Romeo and Juliet* (1990) are typical of one aspect of its more recent work, while commissioned plays like *Burger Brain: The Fast Food Musical* (1988) by Dennis Watkins and Chris Harriott (Watkins 1990), *Grommitts* (1987) by Kathy Lette (Lette 1988), or *All Stops Out* (1989) by Michael Gow (Gow 1991), represented another side of this company's commitment to providing well-written, high-powered and relevant scripts for its youthful companies to perform to a wide audience. Such was the profile of this company in those days that some of these plays, published by Currency Press, were subsequently taken up by other youth companies and the latter two productions toured to Melbourne. Unley Youth Theatre and St Martin's are other companies which occasionally produce plays from the national and international repertoire.

Some of the most interesting work in Australian youth theatre however, from the point of view of the public spectator, at any rate, is that written for specific groups by professional writers on a commission basis, the 'rock' musical in various guises providing much of the staple diet. St Martin's in Melbourne has been prominent in this regard; one of its first productions in its new South Yarra venue in 1982 was a large-scale show about Melbourne teenage life called *Brunswick: the Musical* by Geoffrey O'Connell, whose theatrical bravado and local topicality were such that it ran for six weeks. A musical of a different kind was *Cosmé* by Peter Charlton and Bill Just in 1987; a quasi-documentary show about the tensions that developed among the group of idealistic Australians who migrated to Paraguay at the turn of this century to found a new Utopian colony. Yet another large-scale St Martin's musical was an *a capella* opera about the life of Vincent van Gogh; written by Anthony Crowley and Luke Devenish, *Vincent* enjoyed a successful public season in 1991. Even more ambitious was Leeming Youth Theatre's huge 1995 Festival of Perth production, *Here! Now!*, an amalgamation of Greek mythology and the teen nightclub and drug subcultures, in which Graham Pitts' script was backed by music by Pat Crichton and Mike Kingham with the WA Youth Jazz Orchestra and augmented by the Steps Youth Dance Company. While Youth Theatre productions certainly are of interest to general public audiences, as well as to the performers' peers and families, the principal value of the theatrical experience is to young people as participants.

Theatre in Education

Theatre in Education is a form of performance activity that came to Australia late in the 1960s from England, in the wake of progressive developments in educational theory concerned with the notion of learning through experience. As the British commentator Pam Schweitzer put it, the theatrical experience in TIE is 'a means not an end. TIE companies are not in the business of converting young people to the theatre experience per se and [in TIE programmes] theatre is essentially a vehicle rather than an end in itself. It is a means of communication with a group of youngsters, and the content of the communication is of prime importance' (1980, 9). Another British expert in the field, John O'Toole, concurs: TIE 'was conceived as an attempt to bring the techniques of theatre into the classroom, in the service of specific educational objectives [...] perhaps to teach something as specific as road safety or languages, more often to kindle the imagination and awake understanding of important issues' (1976, vii-viii). He stresses that 'the distinguishing feature of TIE is that *its overall primary aim is always educational'* (16) and that it was 'designed to operate within the school system' (13). Some of the leading Theatre in Education companies in England whose work was largely emulated during the late 1960s and throughout the 1970s in Australia were the Theatre Centre, Cockpit TIE and Greenwich Bowsprit TIE (all in London); Bolton Octagon TIE; Belgrade Coventry TIE; Leeds Playhouse TIE; and the Oxford Playhouse Team.

Some of the more specific characteristics of TIE work prior to the 1980s in Australia as well as in the UK included the following. Virtually all work was devised by the presenting company (TIE companies being known as 'teams', comprising 'actor-teachers', directors and 'writer/researchers') even if the final performance script might have been completed by a writer as such; all work was done in schools, whether in the classroom or the school hall, for very small groups, often just a single class; 'programmes' were composed of several elements, the theatre performance as such usually being preceded by some sort of preliminary session and 'followed up' by a participatory 'workshop', and they often took a half or even a whole day. Sometimes the separate elements were spread over a three-week period to enable the classroom teacher to build upon previous elements and to prepare the children for the next visit. Even the performance element was usually participatory in nature, especially in primary school programmes, to increase the potential for 'learning through experience'. The follow-up workshops typically re-exposed the pupils to the programme's material in ways that were designed to shed alternative light on the content, the educational issue or the characters, or to enable them to make connections between the specifics of the performance and the 'universals' of the theme. As can be seen, British-style TIE when pursued to its fullest extent was exceptionally labour-intensive and time-consuming; it need hardly be added that it was also extremely expensive, or 'cost-inefficient' in the economically rational sense.

One of the first organisations to pursue a form of TIE in Australia was Children's Arena Theatre, founded in Melbourne in the late 1960s. While its first productions were done in suburban halls in holiday time — largely in the more orthodox Children's Theatre mode — it is interesting that the first works chosen were by Brian Way, a prominent figure in British educational drama circles. One of these was Way's 1951 adaptation with Warren Jenkins for the Arena Theatre Company of Llandudno of the familiar old Collodi story *Pinocchio*; this was a very flexible adaptation which involved a lot of audience participation, enhanced by its deliberately chosen arena setting. It is interesting that O'Toole and others claim the mid-1960s as the time when the term 'TIE' was coined (O'Toole 13; Wyatt & Steed 7),[5] whereas Way's *Pinocchio* was published by Dennis Dobson in 1954 as part of an already extensive

'Theatre in Education' series (Way & Jenkins, 1954). In due course, Children's Arena Theatre of Melbourne went on to become one of the leading TIE companies in Australia, changing its name during the 1980s to Arena Theatre Company.

Other TIE companies which sprang to life in Australia in the 1970s with all the educational zeal of their UK models were Tasmanian TIE, founded in Hobart in 1972 by Englishwoman Barbara Manning but known since 1976 as Salamanca Theatre Company; TIE/DIE (Theatre in Education/Drama in Education) in Darwin; Toe Truck Theatre Company in Sydney (which took its name from 'theatre of education'); and a breakaway group in Newcastle called Freewheels TIE; as well as Magpie Theatre, formed in Adelaide in 1977 by another British pioneer of the form, Roger Chapman. As in England, some of the state theatre companies established TIE offshoots, though not all based exactly on the same relentlessly educational models; these included Magpie (still a part of the State Theatre Company of South Australia), Roadworks (attached to the Queensland Theatre Company but known after 1988 as Brolgas), and Acting Out (formed by the National Theatre in Perth, later known as the Western Australian Theatre Company) which is now an independent company called Barking Gekko. Other companies were set up by, or with major support from, state education departments: among these were TIE/DIE in Darwin; Bouverie St TIE, Crosswinds Theatre in the Community and Four's Company (later Barnstorm Theatre) in Victoria; Troika in South Australia and Kite in Brisbane. Even the independent Salamanca Theatre Company in Tasmania and Jigsaw Theatre Company in the Australian Capital Territory were principally funded by their respective education departments for many years (Jigsaw still is), while Magpie and others had the benefit of seconded teachers on their singularly capacious staffs.

At its peak in the early 1980s Magpie had a full-time staff of eleven (an artistic director, a writer/researcher, a stage manager and eight actors, including the seconded teacher), plus a part-time administrative officer, two trucks filled with free diesel fuel courtesy of the state government, and access to the State Company's designers, wardrobe and scenery construction departments. The company was often split into two teams to enable it to cover the primary and secondary sectors simultaneously, and the company as a whole usually had up to five shows in its repertoire at any one time, all devised by the company. At the other end of the scale companies like Four's Company and Crosswinds,which toured out of bases in regional education offices in Ballarat and Benalla respectively, were made up of just four people — with some administrative backup from the education office, admittedly — and still somehow managed to cover primary and secondary schools throughout their regions with purpose-made shows of their own devising and production.

The content of the programmes developed by Australian TIE companies during the 1970s and early 80s, which can be reckoned to be the heyday of the form in this country, ranged from specific curriculum subject-matter to more general social and developmental issues. The broad curriculum field of social studies provided the material for many productions focusing on environmental and conservation issues, health education, especially sex and drug education of various kinds, and Australian history. Programmes on road safety, political awareness and questions of industrial relations, peer-group pressure, family and personal relationships, the clash between city and country life and so on, were also prominent in many companies' work; there were even shows about mathematics!

Almost as soon as it had begun, however, Australian Theatre in Education began to shed the trappings of its British models and to develop a style of its own. I don't believe the passion of British TIE teams for total child participation and multiple-part programming was ever pursued with as much vigour in Australia, where the notion of an in-school, stand-alone dramatic performance of excellent communication in its own right was cultivated. Whereas the Belgrade Coventry TIE team made a three-visit saga out of *Rare Earth*, a primary school programme about pollution and environmental politics generally, Australian companies preferred to perform *Drink the Mercury*, the one genuinely dramatic performance piece from that programme, as a single stand-alone play, or to devise their own shows with specific reference to Australian conditions. Likewise the early preference of groups to devise all their own work gave way, during the early to middle 1980s, to a trend towards commissioning plays on specific topics from a growing pool of specialist professional playwrights (often playwrights in residence), although some of the education department-sponsored companies (like TIE/DIE, Troika and Bouverie St TIE) continued with devised pieces of a highly participatory kind until they died. Australian TIE thus became one of the consistent money-earners for a number of Australian playwrights and gave its school audiences an almost entirely purpose-made, original Australian repertoire, even if some of it was second-hand in the sense that companies began to put on plays commissioned and first performed by interstate colleagues. In a parallel development, Australian companies of the 1980s increasingly tended to employ professional performers engaged almost solely to act in plays, rather than the all-purpose actor-teachers (again, with the general exception of the education department companies). The actors were nonetheless supplemented in many cases by one teacher-trained staff-member responsible for such things as schools liaison, the increasingly rare follow-up workshops, and the often highly detailed and very valuable teachers' resource kits with suggestions for follow-up classroom work.

During the late 1980s extra funding for Theatre in Education became available in some states, thanks to money raised from tobacco taxes and distributed through organisations like the Victorian Health Promotion Foundation, Foundation South Australia and Healthway in Western Australia. Health issues suddenly became all the rage, with splendid productions from Handspan Theatre about sex education (*We Repeat Ourselves*) and drug abuse (*Lunatic Soup*); and from FM Live, whose *On the Rocks* was a very stylish piece about alcohol abuse. At about the same time TIE plays about gender issues also enjoyed a spirited vogue; Arena Theatre's *Fix It Alice!*, an exemplary tale about a female apprentice in the Ford car factory, was one that played high schools with much success for several terms.

By the late 1980s and early 1990s, however, most of the diminishing band of TIE companies had done away with the term 'Theatre in Education' in their titles and mission statements, opting for more generic terms like 'Theatre in Schools' or the even blander 'Theatre for Young People',[6] and were employing all artists on play-by-play (or term-to-term) contracts, like their colleagues in adult theatre. One of the factors which brought about a decline in the number of TIE companies was the gradual withdrawal of state Education Departments from the field; by end of the 1980s Bouverie St TIE and Crosswinds in Victoria had been wound up, Troika had ceased to exist in Adelaide and TIE/DIE had ended its vigorous career in the Northern Territory. Barnstorm Theatre in regional Ballarat was one of very few companies that had any Education Department involvement at all, its two seconded teachers (crucially, the artistic director and playwright in residence) still faithfully funded by the Victorian Ministry of School Education. It was the decision of that ministry (rather than of Arts Victoria, the state's arts funding body) to pull the plug on the long-standing teacher secondment that led to Barnstorm's lamentable demise in 1995. This left the Australian Capital Territory as the only state or territory whose education department directly funded theatre in schools.[7] Government campaigns in New South Wales, the ACT and Victoria during the 1990s to close and/or amalgamate large numbers of schools — and substantially to reduce teacher numbers and schools' discretionary budgets — and the increasing emphasis in all states and territories on school education purely as a job ticket or University entrance prerequisite, have also made it more difficult for the erstwhile TIE companies to 'sell' such extra-curricular luxury items as visiting theatre performances to increasingly harassed and overworked teachers, particularly in increasingly impoverished state schools.

Under these circumstances one might have expected schools-touring theatre companies during the 1990s to increase their focus on curriculum-based educational programming, but this has — perhaps paradoxically — not always been the case. Increasingly, the old TIE companies are now seemingly more inclined to prefer performing in theatres than in schools, and providing a broadly entertaining repertoire than an educational one. If David Holman (arguably the English-speaking world's most prolific and effective writer for young people's theatre) could say at a conference in 1983 that TIE generally offered a social experience first and an aesthetic experience as a secondary consideration, then Barbara Ciszewska, director of Arena Theatre from 1989 to 1993, echoed the sentiments of many practitioners in 1990 when she affirmed (in private interview) that the primary consideration now is to provide a stimulating theatrical and aesthetic experience to children of all ages. 'We're not teachers, we're actors; teachers teach and actors act. Why should we pretend to take over the teachers' role in the classroom?' seemed to be a common response to questions about why 'theatre' had parted company from 'education' in the original theatre in education formula. It was not a long journey from there to the position claimed by her successor at Arena, David Carlin, that in the 1990s 'TIE is dead'.

I suspect that one of the reasons for this recent change of attitude is that practitioners of schools-touring theatre have grown tired of what the experienced TIE designer Trina Parker has privately called the 'four people and a floor-mat' syndrome; there is not a lot of joy in the daily grind of setting-up and performing in draughty, often sub-standard halls, with poor acoustics and the sounds of the school canteen and the headmaster's amplified announcements constantly undermining the performance. Likewise, parents of school-aged kids, and many school-kids themselves for that matter, have increasingly grown accustomed since 1985 to theatre as a highly technologically advanced phenomenon, thanks to a commercial theatre dominated by sophisticated (if vapid) musicals by Sir Andrew Lloyd-Webber et al., so why should kids put up with low-tech, issues-based tub-thumping — however earnest and educationally well-motivated — outside the real theatre? I believe, too, that the introduction during the late 1980s and 1990s of Drama and Theatre Studies subjects as legitimised fields of study in higher school curricula will also have immunised students against anything less than full-scale theatrical product and encouraged teachers, especially in high schools, to opt to take students to neatly packaged in-theatre productions rather than to bring into their schools scaled-down versions of the real thing. Finally, the killing-off of teacher-training in this country since 1987 in the wake of the wholesale 'amalgamation' of the former Advanced Education and Teacher Training colleges into the national unified university system, has also cut off the supply of graduates trained in both education and drama. What we're left with now is actors who don't teach, and are no longer interested in what TIE used to be about. Thus companies like Arena and Magpie, to name but two of the original pioneers of Australian theatre in education, are now unlikely to spend more than one-third of their time in schools and hardly any of it outside the metropolitan area; the same could be said of most of the puppetry companies that used to work in TIE.

That said, it should be added that Arena's tendency under Carlin's direction to do commercial children's theatre, like *The Emperor's New Clothes* and Red Shed remounts like *In Cahoots*, is not entirely typical of 1990s YPT. Jigsaw and Skylark in Canberra, Barking Gekko and Spare Parts in Perth, Patch and Carouselle in Adelaide, Self-Raising Theatre and Freewheels in regional New South Wales, Polyglot Puppet Theatre (for pre-school and primary children) in Melbourne, and Salamanca in Tasmania do spend a lot of their time in schools, mostly balanced with in-theatre productions, including some for adults. And, of course, the drift into theatres is neither entirely new nor restricted to Australia; companies like Magpie, Arena and others have been doing festival productions in theatres since the late 1970s. Some of Magpie's in-house productions were the brace of Dorothy Hewett commissions in 1981 and 1983: *Golden Valley* and *Song of the Seals* (Hewett 1985); and Holman's *No Worries* (1984), *The Small Poppies* (1986) and *Beauty and the Beast* (1988) (Holman 1989). British companies like Cockpit also ran in-house programmes with great success during the 1970s.

Thus, on the one hand, we have in the mid-1990s pieces of supremely entertaining and moving in-house theatre for adults and older youth alike such as Magpie's *Verona*, directed by Neill Gladwin, formerly of the comedy duo Los Trios Ringbarkus. This is an innovative performance piece which reduces Shakespeare's *Romeo and Juliet* to a seven-handed eighty-minute mime show, crossing Buster Keaton-style silent film comedy with new circus in a brilliant hybrid which nonetheless retains the most gut-wrenchingly poignant tragedy of the original in a context of anarchic comedy. Brilliant though it is, *Verona* is a far cry from TIE as Magpie practised it back in the days of Roger Chapman. At another end of the spectrum, Freewheels TIE commissioned Nicholas Enright to write *A Property of the Clan* (1994a), a seeringly authentic reconstruction of a much-publicised gang-rape and murder that took place in Newcastle a few years before the play's première in 1992. This was issues-based, open-ended, brilliantly-written, schools-touring TIE of a kind that Cockpit or Belgrade Coventry would have envied two decades earlier (Enright 1994a). In between, the touring Zeal Theatre (also from Newcastle) produced a three-handed mini rock musical called *Joyride*, a very stylish piece for upper secondary students about the joys and dangers of car-theft and high-speed police pursuit with their predictably tragic aftermath for the families concerned. *Joyride* is no-holds-barred TIE, as tough as it comes; yet it has played in schools and town halls all over eastern Australia for four years and is one of the most-performed young people's shows in Australian history.

I shall finish with a few more words about the dynamic growth of Youth Theatre in recent years. Faced with daunting problems of youth unemployment, homelessness, drug abuse, violence and crime, governments throughout Australia have devoted a lot of rhetoric, and considerable sums of money, to youth policies. One of the outcomes is clearly a prioritisation of participatory rather than sedentary youth leisure-time activity, resulting in a preference for funding youth theatre rather than TIE. And in an ironic twist in the tale of young people's theatre, youth companies are increasingly turning to issues-based and often didactic works on youth unemployment and homelessness, sex and drug abuse, and all the other hot TIE topics of the late 1980s and early 90s! I cite Corrugated Iron's *Branded*, 2 Til 5's *Rubber, Steel and Confidence* and St Martin's *Skids*, all in 1995, as recent examples of this trend. *Branded* was a lively large-scale rock musical about a debutant Darwin rock band experiencing all sorts of difficulties rehearsing for its first gig; band members on their way to rehearsal keep getting waylaid at the pub, another has unsafe sex with a rival singer, and so on. The piece written by Maggie Miles, the company's Artistic Director, took a strongly didactic line on drinking, screwing and peer group pressure, but it was nonetheless richly enjoyable and very successful at the box office. Mark Readman's *Rubber, Steel and Confidence* for 2 Til 5 Youth Theatre in Newcastle was an orthodox didactic piece of safe-sex education, with a simple set and a cast of six which made it eminently suitable for touring in schools, youth festivals and conferences; it was quite a hit with youthful audiences at Canberra's Festival of Contemporary Arts at Gorman House in 1995. The third piece, *Skids*, devised by a group of street kids for St Martin's in Melbourne, didn't set out to be a didactic TIE-style piece, but its honest, up-front illustration of teenage street life was nonetheless highly instructive in an authentic kind of way.

Theatre in education is clearly not yet dead, although it has changed considerably over the last two decades and has certainly got a good deal more theatrical and sophisticated. Despite sometimes draconian changes in government social policy and funding priorities there is obviously still room for a young people's theatre that is challenging, original and topical, but still leaving space for the skilled classroom teacher to use the performance as a base for further educative work.

Notes

1 Statistics drawn from Australia Council, *Annual Reports* (1978/79-1993/94).

2 As well as servicing a wide variety of youth performing arts activity in South Australia, including a statewide schools touring service, an artists in schools programme, a sound recording studio and publicity services, plus creative workshops for young people of all ages, Carclew also publishes the national youth arts magazine *Lowdown.*

3 Now known as the Australian Script Centre, the invaluable organisation in Hobart houses a massive collection of plays for young people and publishes an annually updated catalogue for its subscribers in schools, theatre companies and so on throughout Australia.

4 There were some exceptions: Midnight and John Curtin Youth Theatres in WA are based in high schools, while LYT Company (Leeming Youth Theatre, Perth) was begun in the suburban Leeming High School before becoming independent during the 1990s. The Flying Fruit Fly Circus in Albury-Wodonga is actually an accredited school in its own right, of which the circus training is but a component of the whole curriculum.

5 O'Toole attributes the coining of the term to the Belgrade Coventry civic theatre; Stephen Wyatt and Maggie Steed (1976) agree in their Introduction and cite 1965 as the year of the birth of TIE.

6 As always there were exceptions. Newcastle's Freewheels is still (proudly against the trend) known as Freewheels TIE, and companies like Threadbare Theatre and Suitcase Theatre in Perth are still totally in favour of the devised, participatory child experience taking place over a (usually) day-long period: the former offers fascinating insights into foreign cultures, e.g. through experiential participation in locations like a reproduction African village; while the latter spends the morning in a school training up selected kids to participate in a circus performance for a wider audience the same afternoon.

7 This in itself remains a rather bizarre arrangement. The ACT Education Department presently invites companies to tender competitively to supply 'Theatre in Education' to Canberra schools. Only if a the long-term resident company, Jigsaw Theatre, offers the most competitive tender will it continue to win the contract. If not, someone else from somewhere else will get the gig ... which rather belittles the value of local knowledge and purpose-built product which TIE originally claimed as its strengths.

Community stories: 'Aftershocks' and verbatim theatre

Paul Makeham

At 10.27 a.m. on 28 December 1989, an earthquake measuring 5.5 on the Richter scale struck the New South Wales city of Newcastle. Thirteen people were killed in the quake, and large sections of the city were extensively damaged. One of the worst affected sites was the Newcastle Workers' Club, a large building in which nine people died and which was all but completely destroyed. About one year later, a group of community cultural development workers from Newcastle Trades Hall Council decided to produce a documentary play about the collapse of the Workers' Club. *Aftershocks*, the play which resulted, is Verbatim Theatre. That is, it consists entirely of stories gathered in interviews from real people who were directly affected by the destruction of the Club: members, staff, patrons and friends. Although mediated by a complex process of recording, transcription, editing and performance, the authenticity of these accounts remains relatively uncompromised.

The play's shared storytelling form, and the simple presentational mode of performance it compels, reflect a commitment to collaborative cultural production and to the expression of voices normally marginalised by dominant processes of historiography. Moreover, the telling of real stories directly to the audience serves always to remind that the play is not merely an artefact, produced by a group of professional specialists to be passively consumed as 'Art'. Rather, performance of the text directly engages and includes its audience as participants in an exchange, thereby enhancing the play's potential for social effect. It must be recognised, though, that the degree of such potential is directly conditioned by the physical and cultural context of performance, since, as Baz Kershaw has argued, 'the context of [any] performance directly affects its perceived ideological meaning' (1992, 33). This point will be elaborated later in this discussion, with particular reference to critical responses to a production of the play staged outside its immediate community context.

This discussion is especially concerned with the ways in which the construction of urban space in *Aftershocks* reflects and reinforces the play's status as a piece of community theatre. For while the text makes many references to Newcastle as a complex of autonomous built structures (albeit many of them in ruin), the city itself emerges as more than the sum of its physical parts. Both as a location and as an idea, it becomes closely aligned and in some senses inseparable from the individuals who live in it. Despite the manifestly physical — the geological — character of its crisis, the city here is understood in its most important aspects to be a socio-political structure constituted of people in community. Notions of Newcastle as a physical location are thus subordinated to notions of the city as a discursive construction, a set of sites brought into being and textualised by a community of voices speaking collaboratively. It is this complex social formation to which the play is responsive.

In any performance of *Aftershocks*, the spoken word is foregrounded. Language, to a far greater extent than visual images or other signifying media, does the work of the drama. Through the interweaving of a variety of spoken perspectives, the city is communicated to audiences members who, serving in a sense as interlocutors, also become participants in the performance; they are 'detectives for whom fragments of story become variously signposts, echoes, hard evidence or confirmation of theories' (Brown 1994). The actors' dialogue keeps intact the original storytellers' authentic and characteristic speech patterns, including pauses, repetitions and *non sequiturs* — the hallmarks of conversational speech. A certain 'unwriterly' and spontaneous quality is thus generated, and the dialogue consistently signals to audiences the process by which the stories were originally told and recorded. This becomes 'a way, a Brechtian way, of actually revealing to the audience the way in which you got the material' (Paget 1987, 333),[1] as a result, it is the source material which 'becomes the *true* protagonist in the drama' (Paget (318). A distinctive feature of *Aftershocks*, then, is that the spoken text itself rather than the characters or actors who speak it becomes the principal focus in performance.

Given the particular nature of *Aftershocks* as a community theatre project using Verbatim Theatre techniques, critical analysis of the play demands some consideration of the process which generated the written text, because the text itself is deeply inscribed with and continually foregrounds this process. Verbatim Theatre is a specialised form of theatrical production and performance belonging to the larger tradition of documentary theatre.[2] As defined by Derek Paget, it is 'a form of theatre firmly predicated on the taping and subsequent transcription of interviews with "ordinary" people, done in the context of research into a particular region, subject area, issue, event, or combination of these things'. It has frequently been the case that plays produced by this method are '*fed back* into the communities (which have, in a real sense, created them), via performance *in* those communities' (Paget 1987, 317).

Aftershocks fits squarely into Paget's definition. As an initiative of the Workers' Cultural Action Committee (WCAC) — a sub-committee of Newcastle Trades Hall Council, whose premises were (and are again) part of the Newcastle Workers' Club — the project was always firmly grounded in the community whose physical and symbolic locus was the Workers' Club. Writer in Residence Paul Brown and a team of eight researchers working under the auspices of the WCAC tape-recorded twenty-three separate interviews with staff and patrons of the Club in December 1990; these supplemented some existing interviews which had been taped by various parties in the days immediately following the earthquake. The recordings were transcribed by the interviewers, producing an initial document of some two hundred and fifty pages. There followed an extensive process of editing by Paul Brown, public readings of early drafts to interested audiences, and detailed consultation with the Workers' Club community until the final shape of the performance script was arrived at. Stories had been closely edited and arranged to create an overall dramatic structure, but no dialogue was invented by the writer. Open auditions were held by the (then) Artistic Director of the Hunter Valley Theatre Company Brent McGregor, himself a member of the WCAC, and a company of six local performers was formed. The play premiered at the Civic Playhouse in Newcastle on 12 November, 1991. Paul Brown's introduction to the published text provides a more detailed account of the process which led to the final draft of the script (Brown et al. 1993, vi-xx).[3]

This type of work entails a fundamental obligation on the parts of the research team and the performance company to the people who give their stories. It is imperative, both in ethical and practical terms, that storytellers are confident their personal experiences will not be exploited, distorted or disparaged in the process of being theatricalised. The integrity and authenticity of the *Aftershocks* project was ensured by the formation of an extensive consultative network, both formal and informal, within the Workers' Club community. This mechanism gave the research team, most of whom were personally acquainted with the individuals they interviewed, continuing access not only to the storytellers but also to a steering committee made up of trade unionists and club staff. Formed specifically for the project, the steering committee provided information, criticism and advice throughout the development phase of the project. The public readings of early drafts allowed this consultative network to hear the text, and to gain a sense of the ways in which their friends and colleagues — and in some cases they themselves — would eventually be represented onstage as theatrical characters (albeit 'characters' in an unconventional sense).

Even from this brief account of its key developmental stages, it will be clear that *Aftershocks* was informed by a model markedly different from that which characterises most theatrical production. The modes of production and presentation, for instance, insisted upon the authenticity of the dialogue. More than this, the emphasis on collaboration and consultation, the factual nature of the play's subject matter, the direct audience address, as well as other aspects, all distinguish the project from the more familiar paradigm which sees plays written by individual playwrights, often on fictional subjects and almost exclusively with invented dialogue, presented for commercial consumption by audiences largely unconcerned with the process by which the work came before them. In terms of its methodology, then, *Aftershocks* serves as a useful illustration of documentary theatre techniques. Of more importance, however, is that the entire project was also energised by the same kinds of ideological concerns which have been central to the documentary theatre tradition. Many participants were alert to the project's political dimension, and specifically to the key position occupied by documentary theatre in the 'arsenal of oppositional theatrical techniques' (Paget 1987, 335).

In the days and months after it occurred, the 'Newcastle Earthquake' was recorded and contained as public or official 'History' — by the media, by local authorities, and by a Coronial Inquiry. Yet it is likely that the myriad psychological, social and political consequences for those 'ordinary' people most affected by the loss of the Workers' Club would have remained unrecorded and largely unheard. It is this imbalance between 'official' and 'unofficial' histories which *Aftershocks* seeks to redress. The decision to focus the play on the Workers' Club — a site inherently inscribed with the leftist collectivist ideologies of labour and unionism — reflects a commitment to a politics of cultural intervention. The text's concentration on the Club provides a platform for a community of workers whose experiences had become the *object* of international media attention, but from external, imposed and often voyeuristic perspectives. Few mechanisms existed for members of the Club community formally to represent their own experiences, amongst themselves and to others, in terms of their own language and subjectivities; accordingly, as the play makes clear, the community's experiences were largely misrepresented in the public media.[4] This is characteristic of a public culture, and certainly of an 'Art' culture, in which working class voices are rarely heard except when invented or exploited by middle-class producers as the objects of pity or derision. *Aftershocks* might thus be understood as a history written 'from below'.

Documentary theatre projects of this type 'move beyond the determinist fallacy of seeing people *solely* as the products of a given, and pre-existing, culture, and take into account their role as co-authors of that culture' (Kelly 1984, 51). Community artists in particular have been drawn to the documentary theatre mode, which is unsurprising given its capacity to facilitate community self-expression. For central to community arts theory and practice is an understanding of 'community' as an active and self-conscious process, a protean 'event' rather than a fixed and stable grouping. Owen Kelly, emphasising the consensual and dynamic nature of community, considers it necessary that:

> the members of a community acknowledge their membership, and that this acknowledgment plays a recognised part in shaping their actions. [...] Community then is not an entity, nor even an abstraction, but a set of shared social meanings which are constantly created and mutated through the actions and interactions of its members, and through their interaction with wider society.

Kelly goes on to argue that communities thus conceived have a potential for social agency, and that the dynamic view of community becomes an oppositional tool against the pressures exerted by the 'centralised and centralising state' (1984, 49-51). David Watt suggests that dynamic notions of community 'allow the creation of purposive communities of interest which, by the process of self-definition, resist being [...] subsumed and can retain an oppositional integrity' (1991a, 64).

These theoretical observations on the nature of 'community' provide the basis for a closer analysis of the play, and particularly of its discursive construction of space. It has already been indicated that the play's rendering of space takes the form of a series of shared stories. Many of these are short-lived within individual scenes; others, most notably John's and Lyn's, are revisited and elaborated as the show progresses, and constitute 'throughlines' in the play's structure. Yet while John's and Lyn's stories have an important organising function within the text, no single story or character takes narrative precedence over another. The play's sixteen voices are individuated, but can also be understood collectively to stand for the Workers' Club community from which the stories were gathered. Characters' feelings and experiences are spoken to the audience simply and directly, relatively unmediated by the theatrical conventions of naturalistic playing and fourth wall illusionism. Members of the audience are thus reminded that the material is authentic, and that it was produced in much the same way as it is being performed: by storytellers talking to interested listeners.

The idea of the Club as a community, as a dynamic 'event', is reflected in the collaborative nature of the play's representations of the city and the earthquake. The modes of speaking and listening, upon which community proceeds, are emphasised in performance; non-verbal signifying codes more familiar in other theatrical forms, while still important in *Aftershocks*, are subordinated always to words. The published text specifies that the setting in performance should be the simplest possible, and it is certainly possible — perhaps preferable — to perform the play with no set at all. No need exists for elaborate 'atmospherics' or technical effects, since the felt authenticity of the piece is in no way dependent upon an illusionistic representation of the Club or the city. Indeed, a complex staging would very likely detract from the raw immediacy and authenticity of the material, which is compelling enough to stand on its own simply through storytelling. Minimalist staging enables rapid transformations in time and space, and engages the audience more fully in a willing imaginative collusion than would be the case with naturalistic scenic detail.

Together, but from a variety of perspectives, characters use language to create the city, evoking images of entire buildings in ruin, of people dead or injured lying in rubble, on streets, under cars. Their speeches range from intricately detailed descriptions of single moments and tiny spaces — 'I only had about a ten inch square to breathe in' (Brown et al. 1993, 16) — to sweeping, sometimes surrealistic views across newly exposed city blocks — 'I can see as far as Hamilton....And up to Bull Street...There's just nothing' (11). In broad structural terms, the play traces a movement from interior, detailed views of the Club to more generalised, exterior perspectives on the surrounding city. This constitutes a narrative progression of sorts. It is a form of journey from inside to outside, paralleled by the play's shift in focus from the physical damage and chaos of the early scenes, to more overtly politicised and historicised thematics in Act Two. Stefo's speech, half way through the first act, provides the first exterior perspective on the Club and various other locations around the city; the series of speeches at the beginning of Act Two (23-25) signals the enlargement of the play's thematic scope throughout the second act. Such structural patterns in the text are evidence of Paul Brown's efforts in organising the raw material, but as he makes clear in his introduction, 'the selection [also] reflects the central concerns and the mood of individual interviews'. Many of the storytellers felt that the events of the year following the earthquake amounted 'to a protracted aftermath ... more full of crisis than the day the earthquake struck' (xiii, vii). The geological phenomena indicated by the play's title thus accrue a metaphorical significance as the play proceeds.

Importantly, the play's community centres specifically on the Club, as distinct from Newcastle generally. Certainly there is a level at which the sixteen characters can be understood to speak on behalf of all Novocastrians, and many locals identify strongly with the events depicted. But the play's people and events do not stand for Newcastle as a whole, and the text resists any simplistic reduction of the city to the Workers' Club community. Aspects of the city and its administration are shown in an unfavourable light, and elements of conflict and controversy — relating to certain rescue personnel for example[5] — are important features of the text's 'negotiation' of the city and the construction of its particular community.

Thus the city becomes identifiable with the characters who describe it, and whose points of view are always resonant with personal experience. Their descriptions of the (altered) cityscape proceed in direct relation to remembered and habituated patterns of living, of physically being, in the Club and in the city. John Constable's first speech conveys this sense of lived space as he describes his work routine: 'The place [Club] was amazing. Just every nook and cranny. I've been in the roof, on the roof, underneath stages, above stages, up where the chandeliers are in the big auditorium' (2). In thus describing where he worked, John helps to establish who he is. And in a sense, the character Stan is made knowable as much by his references to locations around Newcastle as by his and others' descriptions of himself:

> I was ... I'm a fisherman, mate. And a surfer. A surfer and a bloody fisherman. I love me old beach fishing and that sort of stuff. I do a lot of beach fishin' at Dixon Park, and Bar Beach ... I go on holidays up Stockton Beach for about three weeks every year ... Me mate's got a hut up there, a shack. We have a lovely week's seven or eight days holiday on Stocko Beach. (21)

Similarly, Eddie's and Julie's speeches in the 'Barriers' scene (25-27) convey the deep sense of distress prompted by being physically separated from familiar parts of the city:

> I heard on the radio that you weren't allowed to enter the city ... [I]t's like being cut off from someone who's ill .... It was like having a wide shot of something, and what you really want is a close up, you know. And all I could really think of was little bits of buildings in my head visually, like corners of windows,

> and I just wanted to be closer .... There was this ... yeah just a constant thing of no go areas, which to me reminds me of childhood things a lot. (27)

For this storyteller, the inability to interact physically with the city as usual alters her entire conception of it; it also engenders a deep anxiety. In the larger context of the play, the barriers become signifiers of social conflict between 'Authority' and the Club community.

While multiple perspectives are given on what was obviously a protracted and chaotic situation, the textual arrangement of voices is such that the individual stories bring a kind of order to the chaos, while simultaneously conveying its full extent. This is achieved in large part by the intersection and overlapping of separate narrative lines at key points. Paul Brown refers to such intersections as 'nodes' in the drama: 'Wherever multiple perspectives on the same incident are available, such an incident becomes a "node" within the play, a point in time to which the narrative may return before branching along a new path' (xiv). Brown uses the phrase 'a point in time' here, but in fact these nodes occur very often in relation to physical locations — that is, as points in space. One of the best illustrations of such a 'spatial node' occurs when Howard, describing his separation from Stan as the earthquake struck, says that 'just by sheer luck, he went west, and I went east'. In the scene immediately following, Stan's account of the same moment corroborates Howard's version to the extent that he adopts the same spatial terms: 'Yeah, Howard went east, and I went west.' (8) These separate voices, using the same spatial 'currency', negotiate the collapse of a particular structure (the main auditorium). Yet it is only when received by a third party — the audience — that the exchange is complete and becomes meaningful. Indeed at one point in his first speech, Stan actually makes a direct appeal to the audience to confirm their role as participants in the storytelling: '[E]verything just come down. You got this massive ... you been to the main ... you been up in the main auditorium? ... Well that dance floor's still there' (9).[6]

One of the most engaging features of verbatim dialogue is its quality of idiosyncrasy, a kind of natural spontaneity that Rony Robinson describes as 'the strength, the boniness, the quirkiness, the oddity of the words' (Paget 1987, 333). Such language manifests itself in many striking ways throughout *Aftershocks*, sometimes with poetic effect — Bob describes the Club's collapse as the 'death of a building' (7) — and occasionally in a way which produces surrealistic imagery. In fact a surreal quality pervades many of the stories, some of which convey the storytellers' subjective impressions of the Club and the city as being strangely and shockingly altered. For Elaine Gibson, encountering a covered corpse lying in the street was like 'stepping into your TV ... to see something in Beirut or somewhere. It was just unrealistic' (20). Similarly, while Club Secretary Manager Wayne Dean's first speech is characterised by its tone of careful officialese, it also includes details which have a strange dreamlike quality:

> And I recall that falling like confetti were the aluminium slats off the ceiling. Ten metre long slats floating down like confetti, hundreds of them. Then it struck me that those slats belonged on the ceiling of the auditorium, the level above. They'd fallen through two floors (28).

The play's long closing speech, spoken by John Constable, intertwines the personal with the political; the entire speech acquires a quality of poetic surreality, including references to a dream prompted by the earthquake:

> And I dreamt that I'd found the core of the earthquake. It was in the basement of the Workers' Club. What it was, was just this deep hole. I'd got all the bosses together and I said, 'Listen, this is where the earthquake comes' .... They've gone, 'John, John, we want you to prove it' .... And that was it ... I'd found the core of the quake ... And I'd just left all the bosses in the middle of the club and I'd escaped my own way. (45)

Here the Club — but specifically the basement, an occluded space associated with John's identity as a rank-and-file worker — is simultaneously poeticised and politicised. The 'deep hole' symbolises both the cause of physical disorder and an escape from the political disharmony prompted by such disorder.

Thus the play's many voices function collaboratively to create the city. The depiction of Newcastle, and specifically the Workers' Club, is enabled through what Owen Kelly calls 'a set of shared social meanings'. In these terms, the city is conceivable as a type of textual formation, a system of topographical signs (streets, buildings, signal locations) which becomes culturally encoded in performance as it is evoked. It is established by a polyphony of voices whose common symbolic relation to the city helps to constitute them as a community. Kelly argues that:

> to establish the boundaries that provide the basis of a sense of community, any particular community's members must ... agree to use the same symbols. [...] [T]he continual and collective making of meanings through the use of common symbols constructs the boundaries of particular communities

> and gives them their specific ideological complexion. (Kershaw 1992, 30)

It is in the context of these remarks that the play's potential for cultural intervention can begin to be gauged, and it is instructive here to consider some of the problematics inherent in the performance-audience relations established within different performance contexts. This is important because *Aftershocks*, like any play, is subject to different readings by different audiences; it will mean differently depending upon who reads or decodes it. But with *Aftershocks*, variations in audience response are especially problematic, because the play makes a special appeal to local knowledge of Newcastle on the part of its audience. The characters' textual encoding of Newcastle in the play operates in specific ways, and generates particular meanings for local audiences who have themselves a similarly local, lived, and textualised conception of the city. This is not to suggest that for audiences outside Newcastle the experience of watching the play is somehow diminished or less authentic; it is to suggest, though, that responses to the play by non-local audiences must differ from those of local audiences, and that substantial dangers inhere in some of these different responses.

For the purposes of this discussion, it might be said that there are many 'Newcastles': one is that city which is textually encoded by the play's characters; another is the 'city-text' of Newcastle as conceived and inhabited by Novocastrians; yet another is the idea of the city as it is perceived by others. The relationship between the first two of these 'Newcastles' — the city created in the play, and that inhabited, and hence textualised, by its residents — is understandable as an intertextual one. Intertextuality refers here to 'the ways in which a performance text gains meaning for an audience through its relationships to other texts, including non-theatrical texts which communities produce' (Kershaw 1992, 33). In this formulation specific types of relations are established between particular audiences and performances. This is a key consideration here, because the ways in which *Aftershocks* inscribes Newcastle with a particular community's ways of seeing — that is, in which the play's city is invested with ideological meaning — are subject to re-inscription when the play is performed outside the context of its community:

> To say this is simply to stress the *ideological relativity* of performance, to make the fairly obvious point that the same performance may meet with vastly different reactions in different ideological contexts.[...] However, the point also underlies a crucial notion [...] namely, that *the context of performance*

> *directly affects its perceived ideological meaning* [...] [Furthermore], the socio-cultural complexion of the audience, its sense of community (or lack of it) is the most crucial factor in evoking the contextuality of a text. (Kershaw 1992, 33)

So it is important to consider the *types* of reading which occur when the play is performed outside Newcastle. If the ideological transaction between performance and audience is conditioned by the context of performance, then this play's construction of Newcastle as a type of 'city-text' must work differently for audiences outside the city. More specifically, audience members unfamiliar with the old Workers' Club — including (perhaps most) residents of Newcastle — will attach meanings to images of the Club which differ from those attached by members of the Club community.

It must be stressed that such variations in perceived ideological meaning are not necessarily 'wrong' or 'bad'; virtually all texts circulate beyond the time and place (the socio-cultural context) of their production, and so are continually subject to re-inscription by new audiences. The presentational nature of performance, governed by the text's verbatim dialogue, engages all audiences as participants in the performance event to a similar extent, and there is a level at which virtually all audiences can empathise with the drama of the play's events. Further, audiences outside Newcastle can imaginatively create their own localised dramatic world through what is said onstage. But on the evidence of several newspaper reviews it would seem that some audiences at the second production of *Aftershocks* staged by Sydney's Belvoir Street Theatre in 1993, tended to make sense of the play — to gain access to it — by reading beyond the surface level of the text and the particular events described there. The play's 'meaning' was inferred through reference to a humanist/universalist paradigm in which the characters were understood not as particular individuals, but as emblematic 'human-in-crisis' figures. 'Ordinary people in extraordinary circumstances'[7] appears to have been a standard reading of the events depicted. This represents a fairly substantial compromise of the play's specificity, and hence, of its political potential. For where the play's complexities are in fact at the surface level of the text, the universalist response finds some apparently deeper, but actually more reductive, meaning behind the surface.

This present discussion is not concerned with the Belvoir Street production *per se*, but with responses to it. Moreover, reactions by newspaper reviewers to that production cannot be used to gauge the perceived ideological meaning of the play for Sydney audiences generally, whose readings were no more monolithic or unitary than those in

Newcastle. These reviews do indicate nonetheless how different reading formations — metropolitan as opposed to local/regional, for example — produce different, and in some cases politically disabling, readings of texts. The special relation of this play to a particular group of people, its status as a piece of theatre produced by a particular community, ultimately had little bearing on responses by most newspaper reviewers to the Belvoir Street production of *Aftershocks*. Staged outside the immediate context in which the play was written, and in a state capital city, the specificity of the characters' experiences became subject to a set of readings which universalised them as 'human experience'. The play's discourse of localism was refigured in different ideological terms, such that the events depicted became 'as eloquent and moving a portrait of humanity laid bare as anything in Shakespeare'.[8] In particular, two reviewers' readings of the Belvoir Street production's 'Clubscape' are used in the service of broader universalist readings of the play. Describing the set design at Belvoir Street, Angela Bennie remarks that the stage, 'like the story and the people it is complementing, is dressed in the vernacular: heavily figured carpet, veneer-coated table, plastic chairs, a very ordinary room to be found in any and every leagues/RSL club across Australia' (1993). Bennie here makes the Club knowable by containing it within a stereotype; her implication is that the Workers' Club was identifiable as an Australian 'Everyclub'. She goes on to conclude that the play 'becomes a communal experience: Newcastle's story becomes our story, everyone's story'.

Frank Gauntlett, writing for the *Telegraph Mirror*, insinuates a personal connection to the play by beginning his review with a nostalgic evocation of Saturday nights at Grove House, the Trades And Institutes Union in London's East End of which his 'Dad is a life member'. It becomes clear that Gauntlett's response is underpinned by assumptions similar to those of Angela Bennie. He reduces the characters, events and spaces of *Aftershocks* to an overarching 'working class, working club' apparently applicable to all such institutions, even when his model is on the other side of the world and distanced by perhaps thirty or forty years. Again, Gauntlett's is a strategic stereotypification, a simplistic homogenisation of 'working class experience':

> The punters at Grove House would understand *Aftershocks* which, through its sharpness of focus on the devastating events of December 28, 1989, becomes a universal celebration of the courage, community, vitality, depth and subtlety of the extraordinary people we call ordinary people. If this gripping liberation of neglected richness was plucked from our Belvoir

> Street Theatre and plonked down at The Grove, those good people would understand this superb quasi-documentary perfectly .... *Aftershocks* is important — it's about us.... (1993b).

Aftershocks is not in fact about 'us', whoever that might be, but about a group of individuals who experienced and responded to something in very particular ways.

Once again, the contention here is not that *Aftershocks* can be authentic only within its original context. Clearly, the play was well received in Sydney where the text was given an entirely new style of production in which audiences found new meanings. But it does not automatically follow that the play has always to be inscribed with, or read in, humanist/universalist terms when produced outside Newcastle. No implicit quality in the text exhorts audiences to efface those *differences* — of locale, class, experience and so on — which necessarily exist between them and the community of voices which creates the play's dramatic world. For to understand the play in terms of a dehistoricised, unlocalised 'universal human spirit' is ultimately to negate its power as a history written by a particular group of people in unique circumstances. To reduce the play's collectively negotiated, inhabited cityscape to a kind of generalised backdrop against which the 'real' human drama is played out is to undermine the unique spatiality of the events depicted. It is to abrogate the complexity and specificity of the relationship between these individuals and the (radically changed) landscape which forms part of their communal identity. And ultimately, the universalist response is one of appropriation, a falsely inclusive reading which serves the purposes of the dominant 'Art' culture and nullifies the play's potential to make, 'from below', a contribution to the politics of cultural intervention. Such appropriation has the effect of a form of censorship — a censorship of inclusion rather than exclusion — but serving nonetheless to repress the voices of a particular socio-political formation.

Notes

1 Rony Robinson, cited in Derek Paget (1987). Robinson also states: 'There is, I would contend, a direct connection between the collecting of the material and the successful performing of it' (327).

2 Documentary theatre techniques have been widely employed internationally throughout this century. Some of the examples best-known to English-speaking audiences have been the Federal Theatre and Living Newspaper projects in the USA in the 1930s; and in Britain, Joan Littlewood and Ewan McColl's Theatre Workshop (both pre- and post-

war), whose methods directly informed Peter Cheeseman's work at the Victoria Theatre, Stoke-on-Trent, in the 1970s and 1980s.

3 This account first appeared in 1991 as '*Aftershocks*: Verbatim Theatre about the 1989 Newcastle Earthquake: A Work in Progress' in *Oral History Association of Australia Journal*, 13, 49-55. The article includes as an appendix a copy of the 'Letter of agreement about a taped interview' which all interviewees and researchers signed.

4 As one of the play's characters, John Constable, remarks: 'They had a radio goin' and one of them said, "Fifty dead at the Workers' Club" ... and I thought, "how do they know that", y'know? It was the Sydney media that said that, it wasn't the local media....' (Brown et al. 1993, 34).

5 John Constable remarks that some members of the rescue services must have stolen money which had spilled onto the Club floor from broken tills and poker machines: 'I thought it just goes to show there's some people got just enough time to fill their pockets while they go help someone' (33-34).

6 There are many other examples of such exchanges in which individual accounts function co-operatively to create detailed, collaborated images of the city. See in particular 'Poker Machine Room' (13-16); 'Barriers' (25-27); and 'Homes' (33-36).

7 For example: '[T]he way in which ordinary people confront disaster', (Payne 1993a); and '[T]he extraordinary people we call ordinary people', (Gauntlett 1993b). Both reproduced in *Australian and New Zealand Theatre Record* 7:7 (July 1993), 10-11.

8 This phrase appears in the promotional statement on the back cover of the Currency Press program/playtext. Notions of 'timeless' and 'universal' human truths are, of course, commonly invoked in reference to Shakespeare's works.

Sidetrack Performance Group and the post-modern turn

Tom Burvill

Early in 1994 Sidetrack Theatre Company, which had operated in Marrickville, a inner western suburb of Sydney under that name since its establishment in 1979, changed its name to Sidetrack Performance Group. This was done to signal a change in the nature of their work which can be dated from 1990 when co-founder Don Mamouney rejoined the company as Artistic Director, or more accurately from 1988/1989 and the production of *Whispers In the Heart* with Mamouney as director. It might appear that Sidetrack's trajectory from 'community theatre' through the 1980s to 'performance' in the 1990s exemplifies a paradigm movement from a modernist to a post-modernist aesthetic. While the widespread cultural and artistic tendency Ihab Hassan (1987) calls the 'postmodern turn' is implicated in this story, a periodisation suggesting a total break with the earlier work would sell short the company's complex history and obscure the continuities which are also crucial.

I wish to indicate some of the ways the changes in the work are part of a continuing experimental project informed by cultural theory and responsive to contemporary definitions of the political. Although there will not be space to fully develop this point, I believe that the continuities between Sidetrack's current work and their work in the 1980s with multicultural issues (Burvill 1988) indicate that the idea of 'community theatre' in the Australian context should not be allowed to become retrospectively over-homogenised. Australian community theatre of the 1970s and 1980s was a diverse field of practices with strong common political aims which non-prescriptively embraced a range of forms and styles. The name was a tactical definition in a particular cultural context. The term 'community' itself was always a paradoxical label for a movement which actually foregrounded the contradictions and exclusions of the mainstream society, telling the stories of those politically marginalised and positioned as Other by 'the community' at large, and which sought artistic alternatives to mainstream theatre's practices, forms and audiences. The term suggests consensus when the work was energetically seeking to further diversity. In any case, the loose but persistent definition of Sidetrack as community theatre seemed to the company by 1994 to be increasingly at odds with the current phase of what I see as a continuing cultural-political project for the group.

Sidetrack's official 'Objectives', as stated in its 1990 funding application to the Australia Council, included:

> 1. To create performance works which will contribute to the development of a truly contemporary Australian theatre through valuing and affirming the diverse cultural experience of the Marrickville and more generally the Australian population, and the conscious utilisation of the range of performance languages available in contemporary theatre practice.
> 2. To provide a low cost, high quality theatre service to Marrickille and other communities especially in Western Sydney and communities which have substantial populations of people from non English-speaking backgrounds. (Sidetrack Theatre Company, 1990).

The statement of 'Company Objectives' in the company's early 1995 artistic report on the 1994 (Fifteenth Anniversary) Program began:

> To contribute to the development of a contemporary Australian theatre and performance culture;
> To critically explore the specificity of contemporary being and its implications for theatre and performance. (Sidetrack Performance Group, 1995)

A continuing and tenaciously pursued objective — under constant threat by the funding policies of the major granting bodies — is to pursue these aims through working as an ensemble: to 'develop and sustain a performance group made up of artists from diverse cultural and performance backgrounds and through this experiment with and develop methods of collaborative performance making' (Sidetrack Performance Group, 1995).[1]

A continual process of conscious development of their overall project (indicated by the changes in emphasis even in these formalised 'Company Objectives') is an essential part of the working practice of this company. It is worth emphasising that this involves both relatively autonomous developments in the work itself and an informed response to changes in the intellectual, social and cultural environment. In the period in question these involve both the development of autonomous 'ethnic' theatre, particularly the Sydney Multicultural Theatre Festival's annual increase in confidence and visibility, and quite different developments including the success of Sydney Front and its consolidation of an audience for avant-garde (postmodernist) performance. Sydney Front became, from soon after its inception in 1986 to its voluntary self-liquidation at the beginning of 1995, the most continuously well-known group and, especially in its close identification with the Performance Space as a performance and visual arts venue, crucial in consolidating the level of audience support — small but influential as it is — which currently exists in Sydney for avant-garde performance.[2] But there recently exists also a broader philosophical shift away from both the humanist/reform and subversion/resistance paradigms which underpinned much community theatre work towards modes of thought which can be seen as more thorough-going, and ultimately more deconstructive of established and oppressive concepts, but which also involve far more self-consciousness on the part of artists and other intellectuals about the power-relations of the discourses they work in and with. To what extent this can be understood in terms of a turn to postmodernism requires first some definition of the 'postmodern turn' in contemporary culture in general. In particular, it involves treating post-modernism philosophically, as more than a set of stylistic devices.

Postmodernism is at times presented as a state of radical disenchantment which practices nostalgia or pastiche; devices apparently of the 'surface', because 'depth' social analysis involving models emphasising structure has been shown to be either dangerous or naive. At the same time, post-modernism can be the name for an ensemble of sophisticated and powerful positions about, for example, subjectivity (rather than individuality); language (as signifying practice rather than referential system); and representation generally (as intertextuality and play rather than as mimeticism) — a set of poststructuralist concepts which are crucial to the understanding of contemporary culture, and arguably, contemporary being.

The concept of post-modernism is perhaps systematically ambiguous.[3] It names both a recognisable set of styles, like playful allusion in architectural decoration; the foregrounding of inter-textuality and play with genres in advanced performance, dance etc; and (in another inflection), a celebration of popular culture — 'Learning from Las Vegas' (Venturi & Scott-Brown, 1972). In this version commercial or 'mass' culture is positioned as a source for non-commercial, non-mass culture, and rhetorically all cultural signs are put on the same level of significance, or in the words of the late Ron Vawter of the Wooster Group in New York — 'We're just sellin' sex like everybody else'[4]. At another level, there is an important strand of critique which refers to the emergence of a post-industrial economy and society. The cultural phenomena we call postmodernism are, in Frederick Jameson's canonical formulation, signs displaying the 'cultural logic of late capitalism' (Jameson 1991). The move to culture without depth, where all is spectacle, 'icons, mirrors, surfaces' (Hebdige 1986, 85) is the cultural correlate of an altered economic reality, a development within capitalism as a social system, and not 'simply' a phase or fashion in the arts, popular culture, communications or architecture. If it is the case that, as Jameson puts it, post-modernism is the 'cultural dominant' of our times, then it is appropriate to see in what ways we can see alignments with this dominant in the work of politically-aware and theoretically-reflective cultural practitioners .

Before exploring further some of the features of postmodernism and relating these to Sidetrack's post-1990 work, I wish to describe a major pre-1990 show in order to clarify the nature of the experimental and political theatre which was being produced in their 'pre-postmodernist' period. This is important to my contention that the company's continuing political project carries on through different phases of style or forms of theatre. It is also important to my theme of the company's apparent change of approach being typical of its continuing commitment to formal experiment. There is a danger that at the moment, when the company is receiving regular reviews for work recognised as experimental or avante-garde, that the earlier work may be retrospectively assigned a place as formally unsophisticated, naturalistically documentary and un-exploratory.

As I have indicated, *Whispers in the Heart* (1988/89) clearly shows the formal break towards the new style. I will however discuss *Adios Cha-Cha* (1986) as the example here, since it is possible to read it as crystallising some key problems of political theatre. This narrative about an exploited third-world society, which functioned at one level as an allegory aimed at an Australian (first-world) audience, raised issues which relate to the postmodern critique of 'representation'.

Adios Cha-Cha concerned the coming to political awareness of a fictional third-world community in an imaginary composite village combining features from the Philippines, El Salvador, East Timor, Nicaragua, and other imperialised world-debtor third-world countries. The village of St Alyossa was peopled with representative characters including Father Pablo (the liberation theology priest), Snake (peasant teenage boy attracted to the military), Old One-Eye (canny village elder woman), Cha-Cha (village teenage girl who eventually decides to take up arms with the liberation guerillas), and Cruz (questioning village woman, mother of Cha-Cha). Other characters represented the social forces oppressing the villagers. These included the Patrone, the local capitalist owner and monopolistic employer, owner of the mine where most of the people of the village work for starvation wages, and who also now grows carnations for export in fields which once grew staple food. Other characters include the Army Sergeant and his raw recruit, stationed in the area to crack down on dissent whose every appearance is violent and threatening, representing repressive forces of the state directly supporting the Patrone's exploitation.

The show set up right on the floor of the performing space a large thrust playing-space with a band platform upstage on which there was always at least one musician, and sometimes the whole company as a band. The all-live music was lead by Chilean guitarist and singer Hernan Flores from the group Papalote. Three of the female performers became a trombone trio to introduce the Patrone's Ball — where the cast danced with grotesque life-size fabric dummies of members of the local ruling classes — tittering in chorus to the Patrone's witticisms as he was confronted by Father Pablo. The instruments included guitar, trombones, keyboard, trumpets, and percussion of various kinds including maracas and hand-drums.[5] Original compositions drew on the music of Spain, Macedonia, South Africa, Chile and Timor. Some existing songs and poems were used including a song version of the East Timorese 'Kolele Mia' ('What is the Reason?') sung in Tetum and English.

Adios Cha Cha had an epic episodic structure beginning with the farewell of the old establishment priest and a sermon from him on how godliness requires obedience and docility to authority, and a Felliniesque farewell procession involving the offering of simple gifts: vegetables, a single bottle of coke, an umbrella. This scene opened with a processional entry of the people as mute suppliants, conveying the emotional power of a faith involving humility and resignation for people taught to have no expectations of change in this existence or of anything other than struggles for survival. This was conveyed both in ritualised group movement across the playing space in extreme gestures of supplication; bent over, holding the most precious idea close to their bodily centres, and the singing by Hernan of the 'Sanctus' from the *Carmina Burana*. Other music throughout was played live by cast members from the band-stage at the head of the thrust playing-space. This was lead by one musician who had only that role, but joined by other cast members as musicians changing functions from time to time. Some cast members doubled and trebled parts. Adam Hatzimanolis played the ancien-regime priest, the Patron and the Sergeant. Stefo Nantsou played a peasant in the opening and from then on Father Pablo. Gabriela Cabral played second guitar, peasant woman, the old priest's wife, and a 'fashionable' village girl terrorised by the soldiers while returning home at night.

Scenes in *Adios Cha Cha* progress from the Farewell to the old priest; the Work; the Pay; the Arrival and Challenge to the New Priest (he arrives on a bicycle — 'you can't be a real priest — priests wear clean clothes, and ride in cars!' says Snake); the liberation literacy scene the Naming; the Patrone's Ball; the Soldiers' Training; the Tortured Crucifixion of Father Pablo; the Decision and Farewell of Cha Cha going into the hills; and the People's Resistance to the guns. These performance segments were not named to the audience, but their arrangement into emblematic epitomising scenes is crucial to understanding the form of this show. In Brechtian terms each scene existed 'for itself', and the scenes are 'representative' or 'socially typical' of the underlying structure of the situation being presented. Each scene was the product of specific research: into the language of liberation theology and the situation of socially progressive priests in Nicaragua, Chile, the Philippines, etc; into the World Bank and International Monetary Fund and their impact on the social fabric of debtor nations in Latin America. There was also research into training of soldiers and torturers, and the differential effects of state-sponsored violence on men and on women and girls. The iconography of revolution, particularly photographs from Nicaragua and photographic evidence of brutality, notably in El Salvador, were drawn upon.

Performing these characters as passionately embodied representative figures drew on political analysis as much as on the actor's resources in observation, physical 'reporting' and emotional re-creation. Personal crisis, like that of Cha-Cha when she resolves to take up arms, is seen as not purely personal but rather as structured by and revealing the historical character of the situation. Social processes are the subject matter, not the individual nuances of the imaginable reactions to them. The choice of characters to be represented was based on the emotional, ideological and economic forces which might typically be at work in an illiterate group of villagers coming to a class analysis of their situation and making decisions around this. The idealism of Cha Cha in deciding that she must take up arms is inspired by the teaching of Father Pablo about equality — 'Equality is not the same, it is being treated the same' — but causes a crisis for his pacifism which cannot sanction the use of arms against arms. The decisive individual choices in a moment of historical crisis gave rise to a moving scene when the young girl tells the Priest what she has decided, and he is horrified. The words Cha Cha is given to say here include a quotation from Father Dan Brennan, speaking in the late 1960s to American Vietnam War draft resisters. The scene I've called the 'liberation literacy scene' involved the company analysing the basic structure of Paolo Friere's methods of teaching literacy and supposing a completely fictional but parallel process, starting with commonsense ideas of social dependence and getting to the point where people saw exploitation structurally.

In many ways this piece — the whole show — was of course framed to give allegorical messages to its late-1980s Australian audiences. These were messages about taking political responsibility resisting cynicism or despair, and of seeing world political issues structurally rather than in terms of fatalistic cliches. The terrifying machismo of Adam Hatzimanolis's Sergeant spoke to many not just of some exotic and possibly racist Latin stereotype-Other, but as an embodiment of a persistent tendency of masculinity to harden its outer boundaries, evacuate its affective centres, and carry out brutality instrumentally and within deliberate gender-specific terms, including rape as political weapon. The seduction of the younger soldier by the temptations of sadistic violence, when Father Pablo is presented as political enemy and licensed victim, was also part of this gendered analysis.

Adios Cha-Cha was aware of itself as a construction, as not a simple reflection, foregrounding its own theatricality through the doubling and tripling of roles, actors who became musicians and ritualised movement and staging in key scenes. It was certainly not naturalism. But it did make claims to show the real underlying state of things 'over there', in a society not our own but connected to use by trade, investment and other global economic systems. It also operated emblematically, as I've emphasised, and offered to epitomise the essential features of a number of structurally similar situations. It was performatively self-reflexive and 'theatrical', played in an open non-illusionistic stage, and clearly indicated it was not attempting a documentary reconstruction of any particular society. But it did make claims which could be differed with about real conditions, real processes. Some local left activists from the Italian community thought it overplayed the progressive role of the Church, and was especially dangerous in making the Priest a martyr. Another political critique was that the villagers were portrayed as being unable to analyse and organise without outside help. My point is that the show made claims about the causes and origins, and indeed the remedies, of real-world social conditions and made them in away that provoked a strong emotional identification, if not with individual characters in an Aristotelian sense, then with their situation as portrayed and with the show's point of view about that.

Post-modernism as epistemology (or anti-epistemology), as a theory about what and how we can know the world, has been described as both radically relativist and in a paradoxical sense as a return to empiricism. Ihab Hassan in *The Postmodern Turn* (1987, 43) cites the 'evolution of a radical empiricism in art as in politics or morality' as part of Post-modernism's Anti-Antinomianism. This refers to a preference for the collection or collation of fragments as a principle of composition, a composition not aimed at a formal unity (Hassan also notes the anti-formalism of the post-modern) but at a sense of a discontinuous field, one 'composed', if at all, by the assembling gaze (perhaps dis-composed or decomposed would be better); a collection of intertextually linked moments without the oedipally-anxious compositional tensions of narrative exemplified for instance in the naturalist drama. I see this as a characteristic of experimental postmodernism, but not of postmodern popular culture narratives such as Hollywood film genres: disaster films, science fiction adventure and the action genre.

Hence in experimental postmodernist performance, instead of the tension of narrative with its withheld information, its enigmas and discoveries and eventual resolution and closure, we may have arbitrary and purely phenomenal climaxes; rhythms of advance and retreat; movement between moments not organised in a coercive logic towards a revelation. Also, since there is no plot to be driven by character choices there perhaps are no characters; and indeed, since this is process and not progress, also no struggle of wills or of inner moral conflicts. Don Mamouney has noted in interview (1995) that in preparing the production of *Heaven*, for instance, he worked with his performers to 'shed subjectivity'. I take this to mean avoiding the construction in performance of anything like a 'character' with the appearance of unity, 'roundedness' and centred individuality.

Hassan's paradoxical formulation 'radical empiricism' suggests techniques for dwelling on the phenomenal rather than the explanatory, on the intensity of moments rather than the elaboration of explanatory structures, whether in narrative (e.g. plot) or in discourse (e.g. symbolic patterns). The post-modern performance may for instance use repetition, taken to extremes by Robert Wilson and John Cage in *Einstein on the Beach*. Repetitions of sets of actions, movements, sounds in that work — the playing over and again without pause of the same musical phrases in the same order by a suite of violinists all bowing together — produced the sensation of an almost indefinitely extended moment, inducing in turn a state of meditation rather than anything like a revelation of a moment's 'deeper' meaning as a clue to a pattern enigmatically hidden in the work. It also allowed audience members to leave the auditorium for a while and not 'miss' anything.

An example of ritualised repetition in the recent Sidetrack repertoire is *The Measure* (1994), an outdoor work of flexible duration made for public spaces. Three performers repeat each other visually, all being dressed in white stretch cotton overalls with white solar topees and white shoes; androgynous outfits somewhere between sporting uniforms, sterile laboratory coveralls and spacesuits. They perform repeated series of related actions, apparently taking their cue from a soundtrack consisting of sampled snatches of martial music, radio cricket commentary, outdoor sounds, other voices etc., on a twenty-five by fifty metre 'pitch' laid with bright orange traffic cones forming a symmetrical grid. As time elapses the sound loop gradually moves out of synch with the action loop, as they are of different durations. The apparently precise but obscure cueing between the action and the sound 'tracks' proves to be illusory. Many spectators would not be present long enough to notice this combination of randomness and repetition, as the piece is designed to be happened upon by passers-by who are given no incentive to think that the thing is 'going anywhere'.

The Measure aims to suggest connections between the scientific discourse of measurement, the mathematical grids of cities, and the imposing of patterns on experience by the objective gaze which is also the symbolic violence of colonialism and of anthropology. It cites the repetition of sports — the measured run of the bowler to the crease, the semaphore of the Aussie Rules goal umpire — alongside the formal gestures of the gavotte and the quadrille, the precise 'look' of the surveyor, and the repeated brushing aside of a fly, all ritualised to hermetic and inscrutable signals. In dealing with the second category of negation, the opposition to teleology or the scepticism of Post-modernism to the idea of decidable causes and origins, Hebdige (1986, 85) summarises the rhetorical tropes which form the literary-artistic-critical means for effacing the traces of teleology as 'parody, simulation, pastiche and allegory'. All of these, he notes, 'deny the primacy of the "author" as sole source of meaning', remove the injunction to be 'original', and instead 'confine the critic/artist to an endless "reworking of the antecedent" in such a way that the purity of the text gives way to the promiscuity of the inter-text'.

Another form of 'repetition' in performance emphasises the pervasive intertextuality of contemporary culture. Sometimes this involves what Jameson (1991) also calls pastiche, but distinguishes from parody. Pastiche is composition by incorporating cut-up portions of prior texts taken as it were at their face value (taking their face or appearance as their value or meaning) into a new textual ensemble, a repetition in another dimension, but as it were without irony, without criticism. In Sidetrack's *Drunken Boat* we see the quotation of both deep and banal moments of earlier performance texts; moments like the moment of applause or the moment of entrance are recalled as generic to the phenomenon of performance in Western culture, but there is also reference to deep formal moments characterising other charismatic or canonical texts. One sequence cites the now-canonised primitivism and mysticism of Brook's *Mahabharata.* The repertoire of grand operatic gestures creating tragedy around the death of 'heroes' makes available but does not insist on thematic associations between Columbus, colonialism, Brook, voyeurism and heroic and romantic 'tragedy'. *Drunken Boat* stages European myths of discovery and adventure as inscriptions of desire and as myths of spiritual transcendence. This is written across with references to the material violence of imperialism and the sense in which exploration was both product and displacement of European conflicts. Usually the access to these deep cultural myths is through their previous, sometimes unconscious, textualisations; in opera, in Baudelaire. Characteristically for Sidetrack, these jostle with comic routines about domination involving a famous Italian anarchist women's song. This mixing of registers through quotation is also characteristic of current Sidetrack work.

It is important to recall that works like *Drunken Boat* are in Barthes' terms open or readerly texts; they require the readers, the audience, to actively work with the materials of the performance to make meanings. This also implies that the interpretations, or rather re-combinations of materials, made by the audience are not controlled or limited. Don Mamouney regards this inciting of the audience to be active, to take pleasure in and responsibility for meaning-making, as essential to the politics of the work.[6] For this audience member some of *Drunken Boat*'s 'quotation' worked in Jameson's terms as parody rather than as pastiche — there was a meta-textual commentary or framing of the primitivism of the battle scene recalling Brook's *Mahabharata.* In a performance citing cultural aspects of colonialism (the myth of the discovery, the exotic Other of Orientalism), the references I saw to Brook took on a critical resonance, as did the gestures taken from grand opera in a work partly reflective on performance, grandeur and spectacle itself.

Dick Hebdige includes the interrogation of the unitary subject and the crisis of representation amongst the 'negations' of postmodernism. The idea of the crisis of representation brings the cultural and the political senses of the word together, so that the aesthetic claim of 'realism' to re-present a pre-existent real is regarded as problematic, as are the claims (in 'representative democracy' for instance) to 'speak for' the other. The artist, intellectual or political party speaking on behalf of a minority group, seeking to re-present their reality, is seen as usurping that other voice. Simultaneously therefore, it is asserted that no representation, 'no image or utterance, [not only] political speeches [but also] narrative films ... news broadcasts ... advertisements ... [could] be regarded as innocent.' Hebdige quotes Jean-Luc Godard: 'In every image we must ask who speaks. These two senses of representation were 'run together around and through the notion of discourse and language as *in themselves* productive of social relations, social and sexual inequalities, through the operations of identification, differentiation and subject positioning' (1986, 83). At the same time there is a parallel assault on the classical idea of the subject as a unitary 'I', the self-present, self-conscious self 'capable of intentional transparent communication and unmediated action on the world. On the other hand, there is the 'subjected subject', subject to authority, the Law, etc. 'The project of freeing the subject from subjection to the subject was interpreted after '68 ... [as involving the direction of activism towards] ... particular, localised struggles ... directing attention to the play of power on the ground as it were in particular discursive formations' (Hebdige 1986, 85).

Sidetrack has a history of 'representation', in both senses, of socially dispossessed groups. As Mamouney often stated in the years 1983-1986, it sought to provide an affirmative picture of themselves in all the otherness of their lives for working-class migrant families, alienated kids, workers organising to deal with change, political minorities, women and girls in patriarchal structures. For Sidetrack then the post-modernist critique that this 'representation' was replacing, rather than amplifying, people's own voices, or more radically that 'speaking for' anyone — perhaps even one's de-centred self — was illusory, has been felt strongly as an intellectual challenge to respond to. Alongside its aesthetic experimentation discussed, the company continues as an enabling centre for others and continues its tradition of broad contacts in working and migrant communities.

The Sidetrack performing company continues to be deliberately multi-ethnic in its composition. Through the annual Contemporary Performance Week organisation of workshops and master-classes, and hosting of a festival of contemporary performance, the Company also welcomes and showcases a range of other artists, with an emphasis again on experiment and cultural diversity. In 1994 the Company worked with the Builders Labourers branch of the Construction Workers Union to make an AIDS/HIV education show *No Condom, No Start* which played to thousands of mostly male workers of all backgrounds on construction sites in Sydney, Newcastle and Wollongong. In 1995 Sidetrack produced *Fright*, with Nigel Kellaway of Sydney Front as director, a recently-arrived senior Peking Opera singer, and performers from the Sydney drag scene. *Future Tense*, made in collaboration with the Wollongong Trades Hall Council and Newcastle Workers' Cultural Action Committee, set up performance installations in five suburban shopping malls in May-June 1995 exploring women's time and women's work. In September 1996 the company staged a return season of *sit.com,* a play in three acts with dialogue and video projections about the comedy of banality in the lives of a group of friends and set in part in an RSL club, made with and directed by Derek Kreckler, which appeared at the Perth Festival in February 1997. At the same time, autonomous groups based in particular communities have emerged and are developing in their own ways. Sidetrack has provided a training-ground, sometimes formally by attachments of artists with development grants, sometimes by providing advice, a venue, office facilities, and more generally by example and by personal support for these autonomous developments. Some of these groups have begun theatre practice with sophisticated techniques encouraged by the Sidetrack example of making contemporary performance while still firmly based directly under the main Kingsford Smith Airport North-South flight path in Marrickville. A work by Don Mamouney with seventeen young performers graduating from a training program in new performance methods run by Sidetrack from November 1995 to March 1996 was called *Plane Truth — A Show About an Airport and Other Low Flying Acts.*

At the end of 1996 Don Mamouney as Artistic Director of Sidetrack took the decision to discontinue the project of working with an ongoing ensemble of performers, which in any case had been severely compromised by a change since 1994 in the Australia Council funding regime. This change from an operating grant to a project grant system had coincided with a reduction in overall company funding which had made continuous employment of the ensemble impossible. At the same time Mamouney has signalled another turn in the development of Sidetrack; a turn towards a more popular and accessible style. The turning point may well turn out to be the deceptively enjoyable *Frontier* Stories, made in collaboration with the Aboriginal and Islander Dance Theatre and co-directed by the AIDT's artistic director Raymond Blanco, a show he refers to an 'a risqué approach to indigenous issues' (Blanco 1996).

Notes

1 Gareth Griffiths (1996) has recently highlighted the advantages of a properly-funded ensemble company in developing advanced performance work, comparing Sidetrack to overseas companies including the London company Theatre de Complicité and Canada's Robert Lepage company, and drawn attention to the difficulties of doing this in Sidetrack's case, given current Australian funding policies.

2 Sydney Front has its precursors, without which it is unlikely to have taken the form or to have had the success it did. This pre-history cannot be covered here, but includes the ground-breaking work of Nicholas Tsoutas and his All Out Ensemble, of Mike Parr and others. This history needs to be written.

3 Dick Hebdige (1986, 78-98) suggests that the success of the term post-modernism had (already by 1986) generated its own problems. 'It becomes more and more difficult to specify exactly what it is that "post-modernism" is supposed to refer to as the term gets stretched in all directions across different debates, different disciplinary and discursive boundaries, as different factions seek to make it their own, using it to designate a plethora of incommensurable objects, tendencies, emergencies.' Hebdige does not take this to indicate that the term is meaningless, but that, taking a cue from Raymond Williams in *Keywords*, we should proceed as if the more complexly nuanced a word is, 'the more likely it is to have formed the focus for historically significant debates'.

4 Verbal comment in response to a question at an open forum on the work of the Wooster Group, and *The Temptation of St Anthony* in particular, during a residency by the company at Smith College (Northampton, Massachusetts), June 1986. From personal notes in possession of the author.

5 In addition to Hernan Flores, the company was joined for the show by Robyn Laurie from Circus Oz, and eighteen-year-old Greek-Australian classical dance-trained Helen Dallas joined the company to play Cha-Cha. Other cast members were Uruguayan-born singer and actor Gabriela Cabral and longer-term company members Stefo Nantsou, Tom Lycos, Adam Hatzimanolis, Jai McHenry and Silvio Ofria.

5 Experiment with the audience — not only in playing space/audience configurations but with inter-activity, is a feature of recent work by several companies. Different approaches to the aesthetics and ethics of inter-activity might be one mark of difference between Sidetrack and Sydney Front. Sydney Front, in such pieces as *First and Last Warning* (1992) and most radically in their last work, *Passion* (1992) forced the audience to confront the ambiguity of even passive (voyeuristic) participation in variously 'transgressive' activities.

Melbourne's Women's Circus: theatre, feminism, community

Alison Richards

The Women's Circus, operating out of the Footscray Community Arts Centre (FCAC) in Melbourne's western suburbs, is one of the few good news stories to emerge in Victoria's 'other theatres' in the 1990s (Richards 1992, 1994, Women's Circus 1997). I will identify factors which have contributed to the Circus's success as a theatre-making organisation and its effectiveness as a feminist community theatre project. I will also analyse the cultural, organisational and funding base of the Circus, and point to some tentative conclusions as to the survival of community theatre in the context of increasingly complex political and cultural policy formations.

Background

The Women's Circus was founded in 1991 by Donna Jackson, then Theatre Co-Ordinator for FCAC. One of its main goals was to encourage women, including survivors of sexual abuse, to develop means of physical expression through theatre in a safe and supportive environment. Each year since then, up to eighty women have attended weekly training sessions culminating, except for 1996, in an annual performance season. Groups representing the Circus have also performed at community and city festivals and are in demand for promotional events and public celebrations.

The cheery athleticism of Women's Circus participants and the striking theatricality of its performances have now attracted national and international attention, with tours in 1995 to Sydney and Beijing. While its performance style includes the demonstration of some traditional acrobatic skills, it is better described as being strongly physical within a tradition of popular theatre. The Circus's performance style is accessible, it aims to entertain as well as to embody and promote feminist values 'The Women's Circus is not in the business of preaching to the converted ... we want to reach as many different people in the wider community as we can' (Donna Jackson, qtd. in Fitzgerald et al 1996). However, the Circus is not simply a successful producer of popular theatre. Integral to its existence is the fact that it is *not* a professional theatre company. Apart from a small core of paid staff, its participants are amateurs who pay for their training and volunteer their time for rehearsal and performance work. The Circus is a contemporary product of the women's movement and of the Australian Community

Arts and community theatre movements of the 1970s. Each of these influences must be given equal consideration in describing its history and assessing its importance.

The Circus as effective theatre

Academic analysis of performance generally concentrates on the performance text, the time and space of presentation, or the significatory structure of the theatre event. While a consideration of the social context of performance and/or its processes of realisation will tend to raise different issues, attention to the *habitus*[1] of those who shape the moment of performance is essential for a fuller understanding of theatre-making as social activity. Such a focus is especially important in discussing community theatre. Where and when the activity takes place, the people and resources involved, the ideologies negotiated by and through it, and the other social activities with which it intersects, have meanings for the participants and potential social outcomes which are at least as important (and in some cases more important) than the aesthetics of the theatre event itself.

In *The Politics of Performance: Radical Theatre as Cultural Intervention* Baz Kershaw (1992) raises the issue of the efficacy of recent political theatre in the United Kingdom in terms of its usefulness to particular communities. Kershaw confronts the relation between desire and outcome, between theatre that articulates the need for social change and the events which bring it about. He asks a question that is not only very difficult to prove, but is the constant anxious companion of the practitioner of political theatre — did it make any difference, did I make any difference, did anything happen or was it all just piss and wind?

In asserting the power of performance while confronting its ephemerality, Kershaw makes a strong claim for the primacy of the theatre event. His picture of community theatre is largely one in which a dedicated group of fulltime theatre workers creates performances for and on behalf of — even at times in deliberate confrontation with — the cities and regions in which they locate themselves. 'Community' thereby becomes a synonym for audience, or in a wider sense the hoped-for community of language and understanding between the theatre-maker and the audience. He also describes an extended community of theatre workers which includes other theatre companies in networking contact, and the wider social movements or projects of social change they both embody and represent. In his final chapters, Kershaw considers the community plays of Ann Jellicoe (see also Jellicoe 1987). Jellicoe's work has been viewed from the Left as an ambiguous model of participatory cultural democracy, in which celebration of community tends to reinforce the status quo. Kershaw's final judgement, however, is reasonably favourable. His point is that by collaborating with radical or otherwise oppositional writers and play creators, the conservatism of Jellicoe's work is balanced by the reinvention of a sense of community with an openness to change. This allows for the possibility of subversive readings, and the airing of themes that could begin what Augusto Boal (1985) describes as a poetics of liberation.

Radical theatre in Australia in the past quarter century has presented us with a variety of models of community, through the images it presents and in the practices undertaken by both full time and part time theatre creators (Hibberd *et al.* 1984; Fotheringham 1987). Given that there are parallels between the situation of Australian community theatre and the difficulties faced by political theatre in Britain as Kershaw describes them, it is interesting that the participatory model of the Women's Circus comes close to the direction in community practice Kershaw tentatively points to as a fruitful way forward.

Any assessment of the Circus's effectiveness must begin with its performance style, which has without doubt been a major component of its success. This style relies primarily on the striking visual effect created by multiple female bodies in unorthodox costume, massed in highly theatrical stage images. The Women's Circus has done more than replicate the forms and conventions either of the traditional circus or of its Australian predecessors in the 'new circus' movement such as Circus Oz, the Flying Fruit Fly Circus or Rock 'n' Roll Circus. The Women's Circus style has been built on a base of acrobatic and manipulative skills, combined with styles of composition and presentation drawn from European alternative and visual theatre (with a dash of Polynesian and Chinese techniques) to create an abstract, allegorical and image-based performance language that, while it changes and develops from season to season, is instantly recognisable.

Donna Jackson's dominance as leader and chief performance-maker within the Circus, her skill as a director of spectacle and her own theatrical and political background and preferences, have undoubtedly contributed to the development of a 'house style' for the Circus. Its constant is a basic acrobatic vocabulary which includes balances and their enlargement into group formations such as pyramids, together with other selected skills such as trapeze, fire-juggling and other object manipulation, bicycle work and so on. Music, an 'industrial' style with simple melodic patterns over dominant rhythms marked on grouped forty-four-gallon drums, has been a feature during the Circus's performing life, despite changes in the Musical Director and other personnel. Another performance feature has been the use of non-traditional spaces. While these have changed from year to year, the Circus's response to the scenic opportunities offered by outdoor venues and disused industrial buildings has become an important element of its performing tradition. There is no dialogue. Performances in the first three years were entirely non-vocal, and the introduction of choral work in 1994 and 'voice-over' style narrative links in the 1995 season have not so far fundamentally altered the emphasis on physical image over verbal communication. The signature black on white makeup devised by each woman individually within a common convention, and the white bathing caps worn during performance, combine in a mythic de-individuation and magnification of the sign 'woman' which forms the basis for the Circus's stage identity.

The vocabulary of images in the performance text reveals a familiarity with the history as well as the politics of spectacle. Costume has played a major part in the meanings layered within the stage images from year to year. Very often the costumes have de-feminised the performer's bodies through the use of androgynous coveralls, ironically created 'male' uniforms and even 'muscles' made of juggling balls stuffed into stockings! Signs of femininity are subverted through decontextualisation and satire, such as the use of ancient underwear dyed bright red and worn in odd combinations in the 1991 show; or magnification, such as the exaggerated blond rope wigs worn by the 'heroines' of *Death: The Musical*. On the other hand the Circus has also produced idealised, if recontextualised, images of the essential feminine such as the Great Goddess, and does not shy away from borrowing traditional and even romantic images where they will be effective. The vaguely Breughelian women with calico skirts and headscarves sweeping and scrubbing, airing and folding sheets, who first appeared in the 1992 season, have become something of a staple of Circus' performances, as the effectiveness of the full circle skirt has been exploited in massed cartwheels and trapeze routines in subsequent seasons. The visual language of European Expressionism and Futurism has been mined on a number of occasions, such as in the enormous machines and outsize styrofoam numerals used in the 'eight-hour-day' sequence constructed for the river pageants in Melbourne's Labour Day Moomba Festival; a Brechtian influence is evident in the placards that have been used in most seasons to identify particular locations or to give a title to particular sequences.

The specificity of style or reference of any single image is however subsumed within a larrikin eclecticism, 'postmodern' in its effect but fuelled more by a combination of thrift and imaginative freedom than by undue concern for the history of theatre or visual art. The Circus is just as happy to borrow from itself, and successful images have been recycled and recontextualised from river barge to theatre show, and from one year to another. Apart from the circle skirts, one of the most resilient sequences has been the scary 'Bitches from Hell' — performers with stilts on both arms and legs and clad in vinyl dog heads with bright lamp eyes — who first appeared in the 1994 Moomba river pageant, but who were equally at home as servants of the Goddess in *Death: The Musical* and have even appeared at the football.

Closer examination however reveals considerable variation in the processes of theatre-making, and shifts in the composition, message and meaning of the theatre image over the five years of the Circus's performing life. In each year the major performances have followed a theme. In 1991 the theme was 'Women and Institutions'. The theme for the 1992 season was 'Women and Work', the 1993 theme 'Women and Sport'. 1994 saw a departure from the 'Women and ...' series with the production of *Death: The Musical*, followed in 1995 by *Leaping The Wire*, a co-operative venture with Amnesty International. This show featured the stories of women political prisoners and other victims of violence and oppression, and was the basis of the small-group tour to Beijing as well as the 'end of year show' with the whole Circus.

There has been a loose narrative structure in each show, and it has been possible to identify associative and occasionally denotative meanings in particular image constructions. An overall ideology has been clearly evident in a celebration of women's bodies, history and power, and an iconic mythology of the resistance of the many to oppression by the few. However until 1995 there was no attempt to articulate or define particular political positions or interpretations for the audience, and the abstract and non-verbal nature of the style generally militated against the directly pedagogical or dialectical efficacy Kershaw almost automatically associates with the political theatre message and image. Donna Jackson consistently refused mimetic representation and referential closure in either the larger themes or the constructed images in the performances. I will expand below on the playing out of the 'Sport' theme in 1993, which was deliberately allegorical and depicted none of the immediately obvious issues such as anorexia, the restriction of women to particular types of sporting activity or the relative undervaluing of women's sport. Donna's argument was that the Circus reserved the right to comment on universal issues in a universal way, and was not restricted to a 'woman's issue' perspective (Jackson 1993).

If the Circus does not conform to the didacticism expected of Left-wing political theatre, neither is this the absorption with formal intertextuality, risk, and the unconscious evident in the 'performance' avant-garde. Despite ambiguities in meaning within the stage composition there is little doubt about the core coding of the event. This is simply the Circus's existence as 'show'; at once the metaphor and bodily manifestation of women's strength and capacity. For contemporary Australian women, whether or not they have been the victims of sexual and physical abuse, the public presentation of the female body is still not generally an occasion for celebration and a feeling of shared power. Recognition of the Circus's part in changing that has been a feature of audience and critical response. Reviewing the 1995 season, Helen Thomson (1995) writes 'This show is not simply an expression of victim feminism. The sheer joy of performance, of each individual woman being her personal best at a variety of circus skills, underpins the celebration of women who are defeated by force, but morally triumphant.' This joyful display of strength is spontaneously brought up by participants as a major reason for joining and a major incentive to continue. As well as being entertaining in their own right, mass acrobatic, trapeze and juggling routines show off a wide and wonderful array of female body types and shapes, all in the act of demonstrating fitness, flexibility and sheer active enjoyment of the exercise.

The 1993 season: artistic and community crisis

The core message of the Circus as spectacle might then be identified as a species of optimistic essentialism, the instantiation and hypostatisation of the performer's bodies as Women/Now/In Charge. However, the Circus's ambitions as a feminist theatre company extend beyond simple celebration. Given the inclusion of any member who volunteers to participate in a given performance[2], variations in image construction and reference may be read as responses to the nexus of personnel, choice and circumstance in each show's processes. It is however interesting to trace links between shifts in style and focus in the annual performance season, and internal developments in the Circus's political self-consciousness, organisation and decision-making structure. The 1993 season deserves attention from this point of view as an instance of a crisis in both the artistic and organisational development of the Circus.

It should be remembered that the 1991 season was the result of a single year's work on the part of a group of women, many of whom had very little performance experience and whose level of physical fitness and confidence was often not high, at least at the start of training. Donna Jackson as director and Sally Forth as chief trainer were responsible for all major decisions about skill acquisition, artistic direction and the ethics, morale and internal culture of the Circus. Participants were left free to concentrate on their own development, but were encouraged to support fellow performers and to participate in a group ethic of respect for individual differences in background, political and sexual orientation and personal goals. In the first two seasons spectacular individual moments and sequences were certainly possible, but the overall effect relied on layering and interweaving a number of less cohesively worked-through contributing elements.

In subsequent years the skill level of individual participants, and the evenness of technique in basic skills across the whole group noticeably increased. Despite the need to induct new members each year, as original members consolidated their skills and women with substantial previous performance experience joined the group as performers and/or trainers, the segmented nature of the performances allowed for the exhibition of special skills as well as the construction of effective mass routines. Donna Jackson and the other professional trainers and directors involved with the Circus became able to construct co-ordinated images and routines that relied on symmetry and synchronisation to a far greater extent than was previously possible. Donna remained the chief artistic 'eye', and continued to take primary responsibility for shaping the show as well as for drilling individual routines within it.

This trajectory reached its peak in the 1993 season. Despite the announced choice of 'Women and Sport' as the year's theme, there was no reference at all to the theme of the show in the printed program. Amongst the show's dramatis personae were a queen in skirt and crown of black and white vinyl like an animated chess figurine, together with figures (designated verbally as referees) who carried sticks, organised the women into two groups and got them to compete against one another. Eventually the women took off their identifying 'team' costumes, approached the queen and drove her off to the accompaniment of a fire sequence which incorporated a flaming Women's Circus symbol — a voluptuous leaping female figure whose incandescent hair streamed behind her. The choreographic language was strongly reminiscent of rhythmic gymnastics, and particularly the acrobatic and theatrical spectaculars of the 1930s and 1940s in Germany and Russia. One might identify a Bauhaus influence, a nod to Meyerhold, the stirring of a reference to the ballets of the Chinese cultural revolution — an overall

Expressionism which called up images of Mary Wigman's displays for the 1936 Berlin Olympics.

In the absence of an overt political message, the compositional style itself became the main vehicle (apart from the body/bodies of the performers), from which audience members might attempt to draw meaning. This style more than ever before subsumed particular bodies into the dominance of line. With its emphasis on abstracted shapes and exactly repeated gesture, this was very much a poetics of mass physical display rather than an exposition of feminism. One older male left-wing audience member near me became quite agitated at what he read as a depiction of a repressive society, and, what's worse, one run by women. Despite the eventual triumph of 'the people', and while it was clearly not Donna's intention to valorise repression, the performance as a celebration of the Circus's capacity for disciplined, uniform movement carried more than a whiff of authoritarianism — a problem very much at the core of a political theatrical dialectic.

Whatever the interpretive hesitations of the audience, the participants at the time appeared to be uniformly enthusiastic, describing the show as their best and elaborating on their enjoyment of the Circus's ability to deliver a 'together' show. Far from sparking a palace coup, the immediate response was one of pride in the quality of the performance discipline they had achieved. Nevertheless there was a recognition that something significant had changed. 'It was as if we all suddenly realised this was *our* group, *our* performance .... It was an enormous realisation for me, a moment when I understood what it meant to make a commitment to the future and well-being of this community. It felt like growing up, or like watching a flower open' (Rad, *Newsletter* [Summer 1994], 3). Rumblings of disquiet were also in evidence. Not only was there now a significant group of women ready and willing to take on greater responsibility for training others, and several interested in directing, but an increasing number of continuing participants wanted a say in the policies and future direction of the Circus. The lack of internal democratic processes had become an obstacle to development. Donna realised that, should things continue as they were, she herself would be locked into her invested position. It is to her credit that she recognised the artistic and organisational dead-end looming behind the success of the 1993 season and responded quickly by facilitating the changes required for the Circus to continue and to grow.

In late 1993 and on into 1994 a review of the Circus's processes began. The future contribution of the larger group of Circus women and, in particular, the future of the Circus's reliance on Jackson as sole artistic decision-maker and charismatic authority figure, was thoroughly reassessed. A policy group was formed to discuss the formulation of a three year plan, leading to recommendations for an organisational restructuring, and another group led by Adrienne Liebmann began work on a book by and about the Circus (Women's Circus 1997). Sally Forth, who worked only during the middle workshop period, was joined by other specialist trainers including experienced Circus women. Clowning workshops taken by visiting Brazilian performer Angela de Castro were the inspiration for a research group led by member Karen Martin, who developed a storyline for a black comedy about Death for the end of year performance. Donna also held directing workshops. The 1994 season featured the work of several other directors from within the group, and an exploration of vaudeville and sideshow techniques which marked a return to a much looser, if equally spectacular, popular performance style.

Subsequent developments support my contention that the dynamics of the Circus *as* a community must be read in parallel with the content and form of its performances in any consideration of its theatrical effectiveness. During 1995 a formal representative structure was developed. FCAC's Board of Management retains final responsiblity, however in day-to-day matters the Circus now exercises effective internal control. The new structure provides for quarterly meetings of the whole Circus membership as well as regular meetings of the administrative staff with sub-group representatives. At the same time, the Circus appears to be heading in new directions artistically. The more directly articulated stories of political oppression in *Leaping the Wire* were well received critically; Helen Thomson (1995) concluded 'there are serious ideas [...] that have pushed both director and performers into more creative uses of their skills.'

A renewed openness to other theatrical influences is also likely to affect the Circus's future work. Collaboration with guest director Meme McDonald during the 1995 performance season was followed in 1996 by workshops with well-known women theatre makers Andrea Lemon, Sarah Cathcart, Robyn Laurie, Jenny Kemp and Robyn Archer. The most significant change however was the appointment of Sarah Cathcart as Artistic Director to succeed Donna Jackson, who announced her resignation in October 1996. While it is too early to make predictions as to the directions it may take, it is clear that 1997 marks a new phase both organisationally and artistically for the Women's Circus.

The Circus as feminist community

We should now leave the presented image, and turn to the effectiveness of the community-building process. I will concentrate on the ways in which these aims have been articulated and negotiated through the priorities and actions of the Circus's participants as revealed in the communal journal kept in the rehearsal room, quotes and reports in the Circus *Newsletter*, and conversations with members of the Circus including a round of formal interviews I conducted in late 1993. A self-consciousness about articulating and recording participants' feelings and responses has been a feature of Circus culture since its inception. The quarterly *Newsletter*, run as part of the Labour Exchange program, regularly carries profiles of members and trainers, anecdotes from training and performance, and extracts from the open Circus journal to which women contribute whenever they feel so inclined. The desire to produce the Circus's own record, preserving the voices and personalities of the community, culminated in the long-awaited 'Women's Circus Book' published in 1997.

Unlike the women's theatre companies of the 1970s, the Circus was not established as a collective. Its goals and values as a self-consciously feminist enterprise, and the relationships between workshop and performance activity, were put in place prior to the initial intake.

- To reaffirm women's control over their bodies.
- To build self-esteem through physical and performance work.
- To allow women to set their own personal goals for development.
- To create a safe, non-competitive environment for women to work in.
- To enable women of different ages, abilities, shapes and sizes to come together to create a theatre event which is of a very high standard.
- To communicate feminist ideas in an entertaining and challenging fashion.
- to establish a women's circus/theatre company which will be on-going at the Footscray Community Arts Centre. (Women's Circus 1997, xvii)

The Circus's aims are upbeat but far from simple; if the points are read as an order of priority, to be effective in its own terms, the Circus must act as an environment in which the acquisition of a set of physical and theatrical skills becomes the means as well as the metaphor for personal growth and social change. It must also stage works of theatre which are entertaining, communicate to an audience and presumably manifest high production values.

The list of aims is replete with probable tensions and contradictions. The drive to create 'a *very* (my italics) high standard of theatre event' could well clash with the setting of personal goals for development, let alone the creation of a safe non-competitive environment for women. Conflicts experienced in other woman-centred communities, for example between lesbian and straight women, between adherents of different feminist positions, or between the pull towards separatism and the drive for a public profile, are not addressed. Neither is the Circus's public commitment to survivors of incest mentioned, apart from the initial statement about 'women's control over their bodies', familiar as a slogan of second-wave feminism referring to contraception and abortion rights as well as domestic violence, incest and other matters. How this commitment will actually be negotiated within the day to day interactions of the Circus community remains unspecified. Nevertheless, these principles establish a strong emphasis on individual self-development, trust and mutual support. Despite the initial lack of a formal participatory structure, an emphasis on internal communication, forward planning and solid practical organisational skills create the context for a participatory culture. Participants sign a contract on entry, which contains a job description in which they undertake to recognise and value each others' differences, to commit to training however difficult the circumstances, and to engage in assertive conflict resolution procedures in order to resolve disputes as quickly as possible.

Read together, these documents reveal a strong subtext of pragmatism, a wily and determined bid to outrun the factionalism that has dogged the women's movement. Donna Jackson's refusal to specify sources of conflict, emphasising the positives of women getting together while making sure that conflict resolution procedures were firmly in place, made getting on with it, and being seen to get on with it, the unstated top priorities of the Circus culture. It is noteworthy that the closest thing to a definition of feminism comes as an item in the Job Description, rather than the Aims, and contains both a principle and an imperative for action. Working with other women 'in a feminist way' is elaborated as 'to recognise all women are different — support, encourage other women'. This is a square shot for the feminist middle ground, 'leaping off the edge' in more ways than one.

Although the original training project was extensively advertised through networks of women's services in the Western suburbs, the community of origin the Circus draws on is not a geographically based one but has a 'movement' flavour — a community of interest. It appears to have a similar profile to that of the active women's movement in general. Circus participants come from a variety of ethnic backgrounds and a broad age range; policies have been developed to give priority to incest survivors, women over forty, and women from non-English-speaking backgrounds. However, a high proportion of women are aged in their mid-twenties to mid-thirties, middle-class, and of Anglo-Irish origin. Inner-city feminist and friendship networks have been instrumental in either recruiting women or in bringing them to the performances as audience members, who then often become involved as participants or supporters.

Many of the women involved devote large amounts to time to the Circus in addition to the weekly training sessions. Women who cannot pay for training volunteer their time in a labour exchange program; others are involved in regular support group and task group meetings. The Circus's structure thus provides a network of relationships within which a sense of community can develop. For the new member, the emphasis on trust is crucial. Many women find the physical work confronting, and survivors of incest may encounter particular difficulties. Helen describes her reaction on such an occasion 'We were just doing balances, which I knew I was physically capable of, but there was an occasion where I just felt paralysed. It's something I've become aware of through the Circus, my body just numbs at times. I see that as a direct consequence of being raped when I was four. [...] But what was really good about the Circus was that I could say "Look, I know I can do this physically but I'm just not able to lift my leg up there. Could you lift my leg?" And they did it, and I managed to do a balance [...] to leave thinking "I can do this with support" [...] it's a really good way of letting go of some of the responsibility for the effects of child sexual assault' (*Newsletter* 1992, 10-12).

My interviews with participants produced a remarkable unanimity of response on the issue of feminist principles and policies; they emphasised their lack of interest in discussing the theoretical implications of feminism. Rad, a continuing member of the Circus since 1991, went so far as to say that it was precisely the priority of activity over analysis that attracted her and kept her involved: 'the fact that it's noncompetitive, it's co-operative, it's supportive, it's fun. It's not, you know, ultra serious and political and it's not sitting around talking all the time about feminism. I mean instead of talking about feminism it's actually living it. ... I'd rather act.' Nevertheless the

Circus was 'a really good model for feminism; for modern feminism' (Smith 1993).

All, however, acknowledged the existence of conflicts and the effort required to deal with them. Andrea, who joined in 1992, had criticisms to make of the internal organisation of the Circus, and of Donna's perceived autocratic style. She nevertheless emphasised the trust that members of the Circus had for Donna, and expressed confidence in her judgement overall (Ousley 1993). Dealing with dissatisfaction may have been more difficult for women who came to the Circus with particular expectations of action or support. Helen was already active in incest survivors' groups before she joined the Circus. She grew increasingly frustrated, not only with a perceived discrepancy between the rhetoric of process and the reality of skill-building and performance pressure, but with the way in which she felt that particular survivors were being left to take responsibility for keeping the issue alive, both publicly and within the Circus itself (North 1992). Typically, there have been efforts to resolve issues in ways that stop short of bitter splits. While Helen eventually decided to leave the Circus, she was careful to acknowledge the personal benefit she had gained from the chance to grow in physical confidence, and underlined her appreciation of the clarity with which the goals and power structures of the Circus had been established. She remains a supporter. Jean Taylor, an experienced feminist activist, responded to concerns about the profile of older women and lesbians by starting POW — Performing Older Women — in 1995, as well as continuing her involvement with the Circus proper.

It is clear that over the seven years of its existence the Circus community has grown and changed. It has dealt with arrivals, departures, and the illness and death of valued members. It has gone through a yearly cycle of adaptation and incorporation, preparation for performance and its aftermath, and has also developed an increasingly participatory system of self-government. Throughout, it has maintained a very strong sense of itself *as* a community. 'It's funny, people come and go but it's still the same Women's Circus' (Lim 1994). Writing in the *Newsletter* of September 1994, Rad acknowledges the organisational achievements behind the success: 'It might seem strange to those of us who joined the Circus as "a short term bit of fun" [...] but we are rapidly becoming one of the older and more successful community circus organisations in Australia. [...] No matter how glamorous the concept of performance, it won't get anywhere without good organisation, direction and commitment. I realise now how incredibly important it was to work out aims, objectives, political message and money before we even started'.

The Circus as community theatre

A third significant factor in the Circus's development has been its status as a community theatre activity, and as a potential model for future community arts and community theatre projects.

The interdependence of arts activity and government policy in Australia has been pointed out by a number of commentators. Tony Bennett, in his introduction to Gay Hawkins' *From Nimbin to Mardi Gras*, argues that community arts in particular may be viewed 'as an administrative field — that is, as a set of policy objects and targets brought into being by and through the activities of government arts and cultural policy bodies, agencies and programs' (Hawkins 1993, x). This formulation, while acknowledging the critical role government bodies (in particular the Community Arts Board/Community Cultural Development Unit of the Australia Council) have played in advocacy and support for the development of arts practice at a community level, significantly understates the contribution of arts practitioners and participants in establishing networks of creative activity with strong links to other, broadly left-leaning, political and social movements.

There are few cultural activities and institutions in Australia which have not attempted to bring the lobbying power of associated interest groups and social formations to bear in the formation of government arts policy, affecting choices of support for the arts in specific instances. Bennett's implied conclusion that 'community arts' is a creature of the State denies the considerable effort that has gone into securing government resources for otherwise marginalised cultural and artistic endeavours. Australian community arts, and especially community theatre, cannot be adequately understood without reference to its history of cultural, artistic and political activism (see e.g. Watt 1990, 1991b, 1992; Watt & Pitts 1991; Milne 1992, 1993, 1994).

It is certainly true that the community arts movement, lacking the support of established institutions and patrons of the arts, has relied heavily on support from government in both policy and financial terms. The institution of significant and continuing government funding of the arts by the Whitlam Labor government after 1972 was accompanied in the community arts field by the rise of a new class of professional 'arts worker'. The strategy of Ros Bower, founding Director of the Community Arts Board, was to entrench community arts activities within a service framework at local government level, rather than attempt to battle for resources contested by 'high art' practitioners and institutions. Community arts workers, either employed directly by local government, by the union movement, or located at Community Arts

Centres, operate on the 'animateur' principle. They seek support from a variety of government, charitable and private sources, offer professional support to existing local groups, act to initiate and administer projects and, in many cases, lead non-professional participants in a range of artform activities. Despite restructuring and retrenchments in local government employment, this strategy appears to have secured a reasonably resilient base for community arts/community development activities in most states including Victoria.

Most of the community theatre companies founded after 1975 followed the model established by British community theatre and theatre in education companies. 'Teams' of professionally paid actors were established, based in, but touring within and around, a working-class suburb or regional centre. They relied on a mix of funding from Australia Council and State government sources, including support from the Theatre Board in competition with other mainstream and alternative theatre organisations. As competition became more intense, drama companies catering to a middle-class urban audience were able to consolidate their position at the expense of community theatre, theatre in education and theatre companies with a radical political profile.

The troubles of the British alternative and political theatres have generally been laid at the door of Thatcherism. However, despite there having been a Labor government in power federally for much of the same period, the funding climate in the decade since the mid-eighties has been a distinctly unfriendly one for the once burgeoning Australian community theatre movement, at least as far as professionally performed activity goes (Milne 1993). As Gay Hawkins pointed out, 'While the concept of disadvantage was central to Whitlam's social democratic reforms its political effects within the field of arts policy were fundamentally conservative' (1993, 156); as the battle for funds became more intense, elite companies catering for an established middle-class audience were the major beneficiaries at the expense of increasingly marginalised 'community' theatre.

In Victoria, the number of continuing companies, and one-off community performance projects supported by funding at a State and Federal level, has drastically declined since its peak in the previous decade. The current situation appears to reflect a 'one of each' approach on the part of the funding bodies. Companies such as the Mushroom Troupe and West in Melbourne, and the Mill Theatre in Geelong, had disappeared by the mid-eighties. Recently Barnstorm in Ballarat and the Woolly Jumpers in Geelong have seen their funding cut to the point where continuing activity has become impossible. Those alternative 'art theatre' companies who, like Danceworks and Anthill, sought to include a community component in their general performance program, encountered a negative response from the funding bodies which may well have hastened their demise. In 1996 Arena Theatre, the Theatre in Education company first established in Melbourne in 1966, the Murray River Performing Group and its now independent offshoot the Flying Fruit Fly Circus in Albury-Wodonga, Geelong's Back to Back Company of actors with intellectual disabilities, the Melbourne Workers' Theatre and Theatreworks in St Kilda are the survivors. Most rely heavily on a range of non-arts support including funding from education and health sources. Only the internationally successful Circus Oz, having managed to consolidate its status as a national organisation in its artform area, has managed to retain anything like significant funding.

Theatre activity associated with the women's movement never attained either the level of sustained support or the organisational infrastructure enjoyed between 1974 and 1984 by the professional community theatre companies. Apart from the Melbourne Women's Theatre Group, which established itself with the help of International Women's Year funding and maintained continuous production from 1974-77, and the Women and Theatre Project at Sydney's Nimrod Theatre in 1981-82 (Westwood 1982), women's and feminist theatre has been sustained on the rhizome principle, with different initiating individuals and groups of women coming together to engage in more or less short-term projects manifesting a wide variety of processes and performance styles, feminist discourses, and intents with regard to political content, aesthetic standards and company structure (Tait 1993, 1994). Despite a strong series of sympathetic networks, feminist theatre has remained a fringe activity in terms of funding, organisational location and level of production output.

Under these circumstances, it is significant that the organisational and artistic continuity of the Women's Circus has emerged from the community arts rather than the community theatre trajectory. The Footscray Community Arts Centre (FCAC), founded in 1974, was part of the community arts/arts worker infrastructure described above. While it has certainly benefited from its status as a 'model organisation' in its relations with government funding bodies, FCAC's success rests not only on support from the kaleidoscopic ethnic, political and artistic communities of Melbourne's West, but on its decidedly entrepreneurial approach to the business of community arts and community development. Its activities have a multi-arts and multi-cultural focus, and its ability to service a wide variety of arts projects (and a large number of people) with a small professional and administrative staff makes it an attractive and economical option for government arts and further education, as well as corporate and private, support. FCAC's Theatre Department focuses on youth and multicultural theatre, and continues to support considerable workshop and production activity in addition to the Women's Circus, including a successful Vietnamese youth theatre group.

FCAC's support was vital in establishing the Circus; its further expansion however has depended on successfully identifying additional sources of income. The decision to send Circus representatives to Beijing in 1995 entailed a massive fundraising effort over nine months. Performances, dinners, auctions and dances as well as individual donations raised over $40,000 — enough to send thirteen women overseas. Welcome recognition of the Circus's achievements and reputation has come in the form of Australia Council funding for particular activities. However, as government funding for the arts continues to decline, Circus administrators are aware that sophisticated development and marketing strategies are required if the Circus is to retain the loyalty of its existing following, as well as attract public and corporate support for future activities (Fitzgerald et al. 1996). The Circus continues to diversify its sources of support. Considerable press coverage in the daily papers and in magazines such as *Woman's Day*, *She* and *Who* has helped build a public profile. The commitment of its participants, its popular appeal and the strength of its networks, give it significant political muscle. When combined with organisational flexibility and continued artistic innovation, this suggests that a base in community participation with arts worker leadership may well prove a more fruitful model for effective Australian community theatre than the over-reliance on government funding which, when withdrawn, has proved so calamitous for professional community theatre companies in the past decade.

Conclusion

Despite the Circus's growing reputation as a performing company, it continues to rely for its survival on the strength of the community it creates, the continued loyalty of its supporters, and its ability to attract new audiences and allies. The fact that this support is forthcoming is evidence that the Circus has tapped into a seam of popular feeling, as well as being attractive to the patrons of cultural policy. Rather than debate and division amongst feminist positions, the discourse of participants in the Circus culture is overwhelmingly inclusive, to do with the generation of trust and the value of women giving to one another and acting together. Critics such as Stephanie Bunbury (1994) acknowledge the Circus's performance as worthy in an unstuffy and enjoyable way. Audiences continue to respond to the excitement of the spectacle, and funding bodies to the perceived excellence of the product. Public and political support is gathered by the appeal of the causes of women's health, and action against incest and other forms of violence against women.

Has the Circus established itself with its participants, audiences and other supporters sufficiently well to survive? The next few years will demonstrate whether its internal structure is now appropriate to support a continuing organisation, and whether it can continue to accommodate the desires, and acknowledge the contributions, of its members in a way meaningful to them. More change is probable; the Circus cannot remain static as an organisation if it is to function effectively in terms of the goals it has set itself as a women's performance company developing and manifesting a feminist way of working. A simultaneous appeal to aesthetics, community and the feminist middle ground is indeed a balancing act; the Circus's ethic holds differences in suspension even while valorising difference. However, the contradictions inherent in its charter also give it the flexibility to move, creating a field of potential action and the chance to capitalise on difference in building support from the various constituencies to which it appeals.

Whatever the difficulties that may yet face the Circus in the course of its next phase of development, it is clear that the skilled, joyful bodies of the Circus women stand for a tangible expression of a feminism with a broad appeal, beyond the limits of the theatre image and apart from the strictures of any one articulated feminist position. Those of us overly preoccupied with language and textuality — feminists, critics and policy-makers alike — could well take notice.

Notes

1 As most recently developed by Pierre Bourdieu (1990) the notion of habitus is a productive way of considering both the conscious and unconscious elements in the behaviours people produce in response to the conditions under which they live.

2 Financial restrictions on the tour in 1995 to the Non-government Organisation Forum associated with the Fourth United Nations Conference on Women in Beijing meant that for the first time this rule was superseded in favour of a selection process. This caused a great deal of discussion and heart-searching. When at the last minute it appeared that one of the selected group might miss out due to a funding shortfall, the other women volunteered to 'chip in' the extra money.

Performing sexed bodies in physical theatre

Peta Tait

A man jumps into a woman's arms and she carries him across the performance space. Is this the staging of an act of social subversion or a comic parody of heterosexual romance? This action is a recurring motif in recent performances by Australian physical theatre groups.[1] It may range in tone from playful comic clowning to grotesque Gothic spectacle but, as a physical embrace, it indicates how the languages of physical theatre utilise the bodies of the performers to establish cultural meanings rather than the spoken language of more conventional theatre. If this is an embrace between two lovers it may be a sexual act, but it defies the cultural conventions of traditional romance where the man takes the woman into his arms.[2] In this instance, the woman would seem to initiate the embrace and the man surrenders to her.

Acts of strong bodies

This chapter will discuss how some of the recent developments in physical theatre which reconfigure acts from circus in postmodern performance, redefine the cultural meanings of 'sexed' bodies (Grosz 1994) performing in social spaces. The example of a female performer catching a male performer is taken from an acrobatic style of physical theatre which is part of a larger movement developing innovative visual texts over the past twenty years of Australia theatre.[3] This broad category of theatre work ranges from, for example, Handspan which enlarges the miniaturised worlds of puppet theatre for the spectator, to the radical experimental performances of Sydney Front where the spectator moves through large spaces.[4] Most theatre and performance involves the viewing of bodies located in different kinds of spaces, albeit fictionalised contexts, where each performer creates a 'body-text' (Fischer-Lichter 1992). Physical theatre, however, adds an extra language of bodily skills with the adaptation of circus routines which extend the interpretative social meanings of performing bodies. The skills and techniques of athletic bodies doing extraordinary feats in unexpected spaces suggests the additional pleasures of viewing the visual texts of physical theatre.

Although his comments are not specific to theatre, Maurice Merleau-Ponty explains that the body 'transforms ideas into things' without the specificity of words and 'can symbolize existence because it realises it' (1981, 164). Physical theatre deliberately physicalises ideas with bodies. But the language of physical theatre confirms what

Merleau-Ponty discerns as the relationship of the sign to meaning which cannot be one-way with bodies (166). The body is an object in the text of physical theatre as well as representing its subject positions. The performer's body sets up a spectatorial economy which is perceived through the spectator's experience of what Merleau-Ponty discerns is the lived presence of bodies. The spectator views the actions and movements of other bodies in physical theatre performance with the understandings acquired through the experiences of his or her own body.

It is assumed that the spectator will assign significance to the materiality of bodily display in physical theatre. Firstly, there is the explicit context of the theatre text's narrative and presentation of social personae, and secondly there is an implicit mode involving skilled physical bodies doing tricks. Returning to the action of a female body carrying a male body, among the possible meanings of its implicit text is a reversal of the gendered polarisation of bodies as either that of masculine strength or feminine weakness. Regardless of the narrative context, the trick of carrying the weight of the male body reveals the female body as physically strong. Because the physical body is socially intelligible as 'sexed', bodies in physical theatre produce and are produced within a field of cultural meanings.

While the explicit narrative links in physical theatre can be straightforward, the visual text of bodily interactions suggests layered and complex meanings. Theatre Physical's show *Miss Haversham's Dream* (1995) framed a postmodern reference to Dickens' *Great Expectations* by evoking one of its minor characters; the waiting, jilted bride frozen in time at the moment of her betrayal, seeking revenge. When the male persona (Lee Wilson) jumped into the arms of the female persona (Beth Keyes) the action oscillated between sexual passion and an underlying violent combat. The bride is both the victim and the perpetrator of bodily aggression in a text of Gothic intensity. This presented a wild demonic bride who moved in and out of confinement within a large metal cage shaped like the skeleton of a dress who at the end of the show ascends to the roof in this frame. The performer's athletic physicality, her muscular prowess, supplant cultural images of the bride as emblematic of soft, compliant femininity. The failure of the heterosexual union in the Dickens story is suffused with a mutual suspicion and hostility between the lovers as they join together in this text. As a concession to the wide cross-section of spectators who might encounter this performance in the vestibules of public spaces such as shopping centres, a narrator bridged the nonverbal physical theatre briefly with a more conventional telling of a story. But it is the striking action of a muscular female body literally rising in the air at the end of the show which subverts the aura of social submissiveness associated with the feminine persona of a bride.

When Legs on the Wall abseilled down the side of Sydney's high-rise Australia Square building in their show *Exbendable* (1996) and performed in the courtyard below, they expand the vertical spaces of physical theatre into high-rise city scapes.[5] As Thor Blomfield, Bernadette Regan and Gavin Robins descended they swung out on their wires from the walls of the building in slow-motion balletic poses, so that their bodies became silhouetted against the sky in tantalising, gravity-defying images of unrestricted physical freedom. In contrast, once the performers were on the ground, they became interchangeable personae engaged in acrobatic struggles with each other as they emerged out of confined worlds (boxes). The group's suspension of bodies between sky and ground in *Exbendable* revoked not only the social convention which allocates bodies to the inside rather than the outside of walled structures, but it expands theatre into the spaces produced by aerial apparatus.

The members of Stalker Stilt Theatre transform the shape of the body using stilts so its appearance is elongated, almost ethereal, navigating the ground on spidery, thin legs.[6] In public spaces this group create images of dream-like surreality, climbing ropes and moving along metal frames, so that the physical body becomes almost insect-like transversing even the limits of its species. Described as beautiful but 'somehow animal rather than human' (Maclean 1995), this work expands the visual possibilities of a physicality of ideas. The body is viewed as an object in the text, as a subject in the context, but it is deployed in action so that bodily movement is the central device for creating meaning in physical theatre.

Importantly though, apparatus and inanimate objects or props are used freely, rather than mime which is considered peripheral to physical theatre. Instead, the performer's capacity to use the body to stage 'presence' is an important element of this work. The group Etcetera developed a reputation in the 1980s for staging to comic perfection a tableau of grey-suited, urban personae carrying briefcases in numerous outdoor, city-scapes throughout Australia. In addition, the group's indoor theatre productions utilised illusions derived from circus and magic shows to create beautiful texts of visual trickery. *In Which Case* (1993) suitcases vanished into other suitcases and similarly performers disappeared and reappeared undertaking a journey through a maze of grey office cabinets.[7] In their use of illusion, Etcetera's work suggests how the visual perception of physicality may be deceptive because it is also a function of the imagination.

The language of physical theatre sets up tensions around bodies in union and separation; attraction and rejection; fusion and dispersal; encounter and collision. The actions and movements of bodies delineate rhythms, grammar and rules in the languages of physicality. The performers train in disciplines to stretch the body's athleticism, and adapt this to imaginative conceptual and social spaces in performance. This is not the theatrical reproduction of a specific identity, but a particular body which is constituted in a visual text of movement and action. The cultural meanings of a language of physical theatre, however, are established in the acts between bodies.

Circus origins

When Becky Ashton performs her beautifully executed triple somersault from trapeze bar to her catcher Pepe's hands, she is demonstrating the pinnacle of achievement in aerial performance and circus skills.[8] This is a significant and breathtaking feat, and as the first Australian-born aerial flier to complete this trick Becky joins half-a-dozen women internationally who have done so since 1897 (Tait 1996). But as a third-generation aerialist in Ashton's Circus, Becky is firmly located in a mainstream tradition of the family circus performing to a large number of Australians who might not otherwise attend live performance. The skills of members of the family circuses ensure that they continue to be a significant part of Australian culture. In 1997 circus celebrates one hundred and fifty years in Australia and for its first seventy years it was most popular form of Australian entertainment; it is important to recognise this long-standing record of achievement because the origins of physical theatre are found in traditional circus.

The current practice of reinterpreting traditional circus acts such as aerial performance in physical theatre follows on from earlier precedents when, for example, circus performers often worked in vaudeville theatre in the 1920s,[9] or circus routines were adapted to touring side-shows in the 1950s. The recent expansion of acrobatic display, clowning and aerial routines into imaginative theatrical contexts derives from the adaptation of circus skills to Australian political theatre in the mid-1970s. This had evolved out of an amalgam of street theatre delivering a strong message at political rallies, and the efforts of groups like Melbourne's Australian Performing Group at the Pram Factory who sought to take popular theatre forms to audiences outside conventional theatre spaces (Radic 1991a, 158). If this ad hoc political circus of the 1970s was initially meant to be confrontational and educational, physical theatre in outdoor spaces is now a distinct genre which is expected to happen during Australian festivals.

The formation of Circus Oz in 1978 and its continuous history of national and international touring has been a formative influence on the notion of presenting circus with a political message.[10] Described as a 'national treasure' (Gauntlett 1993) and 'a larrikin's delight' despite its uneven levels of circus skills (Musa 1993), this circus without animals seems emblematic of a unique Australian brand of comic larrikinism with an eclectic combination of popular entertainment styles. As Louise Nunn points out, a performer with Circus Oz must be able to sing, dance, and play more than one musical instrument as well as perform circus tricks. She writes: 'Bursting with energy and vitality, rarely has a line between breathtaking and batty been so finely drawn' (Nunn 1995). As an example of a continuity of political intention behind the work of Circus Oz, an alignment of circus forms and the politics of representing cultural diversity was evident in the 1993 production under Sue Broadway's artistic direction which utilised the skills of Lu Guang Rong, an ex-member of the Nanjing Acrobatic Troupe, to recount the little-known story of Sam Poo, a Chinese bushranger in the 1860s based around Mudgee.

This tradition of new circus in Australia has evolved its own practice of distinctive ventures including nearly two decades of feminist projects in circus (Tait 1994, 111-120), including the performances of both professional groups (see below) and community arts projects.[11] Two recent examples of community-based women's projects are the annual productions of the Melbourne-based Women's Circus founded in 1991 and directed by Donna Jackson, which has also run year-round workshops; and the Brisbane-based Vulcana Women's Circus which evolved from circus workshops run in 1994 by Antonella Casella and Kareena Oates, members of Rock 'n' Roll Circus (Postle 1996). These women's circuses seek to physically empower women through the mastery of physical skills and acts of strength. New South Wales now has a regional touring physical theatre group with the Bathurst-based Precarious. But probably the foremost community arts project in this field is the Flying Fruit Fly Circus, established in 1979 in Wagga Wagga, which has been training hundreds of young people in circus skills in the same way that family circuses encourage members to perform from a young age. Fruit Flies' slogan of 'ordinary kids doing extraordinary things' encapsulates its remarkable achievements. This organisation has become a training school for a new generation of performers now working in both new and family circuses.[12]

While performers in new circus and physical theatre might not match the mastery of skills still evident in traditional circus, the intention to utilise circus skills to challenge cultural categories of the physical body creates new modes of performance. This is particularly apparent in relation to the staging of gender identity. Certainly, even in traditional circus, bodies move across categories of gender identity: the circus trick is more effective as a spectacle of daring when it exploits social beliefs about the weakness of the female body by contravening these in the performance. In traditional circus the codes of a feminine body are transgressed by a female body engaged in an act of masculine strength and daring, and the male body contravenes social perceptions in acts of feminine lightness and grace. But in new circus and physical theatre, the female aerialists and acrobats initially rejected the traditional circus practice of wearing sequined leotards with high-cut thighs and low-cut tops together with high-heeled shoes, and discarded the sexual differentiation of sets of physical gestures which open and close each trick. Where these have been reinstated for theatrical effect, they often suggest a deliberate parody of gender identity in the use of form. Physical theatre challenges the performance of cultural identity as part of the circus act. If the female aerialist in traditional circus signs a feminine body before and after executing an act of masculine strength, the physical theatre performer rearranges the inscription of gender codes as part of the performed text so that the feminine body is not reinstated in the visual text. Instead, the acts of new circus open up the cultural spaces for a different physicality of sexed bodies in action.

Sexual bodies

Individual performers from Australian groups using circus skills to redefine images of the female body have influenced comparable groups in England.[13] Club Swing's aerial show *Appetite* (1993) exemplifies how the professional work by women performers in Australia has progressively moved from redefining the gestures of a gendered body in physical theatre to representing sexualised bodies in aerial performance. But when it toured to the Edinburgh Festival in 1995 it became highly controversial because an Edinburgh city councillor, Moira Knox, tried to have it banned. She called the show a 'dirty-minded disgrace' in the *News of the World.*[14] *Appetite* is directed by Gail Kelly, initially in collaboration with Robyn Laurie, and it is performed by Celia White, Anni Davey, Simone O'Brien and Kathryn Niesche. The physical action suggested that the four bodies come together as lovers in various combinations amidst a profusion of foods, fruit and flowers. The performers worked above the stage on trapezes, a catch frame, a web (hanging single rope) and a cloud swing (a large rope swing). Moving between the stage and space above it, the performance interchanged the pleasures derived from food, sex and the mastery of aerial tricks against a sound-track which includes M People's 'Heaven', Ella Fitzgerald's 'I Love Paris', and an aria from *La Wally*.

The extensive media coverage of the sell-out show in Edinburgh highlighted the show's use of food as a perversity, particulaly focussing on Anni Davey's opening ploy of inviting the audience members to eat strawberries from parts of her body. The sexualised behaviours around food generated as much, if not more, interest than the viewing of aerial routines by female bodies in close proximity suggesting sexual acts. The representations of desiring female bodies in the text can be interpreted as acts of fetishised desire displaced onto food, or into aerial tricks which can also be read as lesbian. The controversy surrounding this show would seem to arise from the representation of female bodies desiring not just other female bodies but engaged in acts of fetishised consumption. This contravenes the heterosexual norm of a desiring male subject and the female body as object of desire. Instead, the text represented the female body in the action of consuming what it desires, and this can be perceived as perverse and threatening. But *Appetite* sets out to comically invert the form of aerial work whereby aerialists work in close contact while denying the sexual implications of body-to-body contacts, so that the doing of sexualised actions between female bodies becomes a comic parody of lesbian acts as well as circus. In this show, the dangers and risky thrills of aerial tricks signified lesbian.

Some of the most intriguing and innovative postmodern physical theatre in Australia has developed around the concept of physicalising contacts between circus bodies as sexual. Male and/or female bodies engaged in prolonged close contact, balanced off, or climbing over each other suggest erotic foreplay and completely subvert the traditional circus display of skills as wholesome family entertainment. The sexual possibilities of bodies in aerial and acrobatic routines is exploited rather than denied. But this is not a literal enactment of scenes of simulated sex. The nonverbal style of performance encompasses how the ambiguous meanings of performing sexual bodies sets up what Merleau-Ponty refers to as 'the phenomenon of eroticism' (1981, 167). The eroticism of bodies working together which is evident in the implicit meaning of the physical theatre text is deliberately exploited in its explicit interactions. Moreover, the actions of sexual bodies in this type of work can be read across categories of heterosexual and homosexual behaviours.[15] This style of physical theatre stages the erotic acts of body-to-body routines as sexual circus.

Rock 'n' Roll Circus, based in Brisbane, has a ten-year history of imaginative productions. *Body Slam* (1992) directed by David Bell, marked a shift in the group's work towards an aesthetic reminiscent of the famed Circus Archaos, as weird acts offset each other in bizarre incongruity. Alison Cotes describes how 'young lovers in Karma Sutra ecstasies came hot on the heels of a mad juggler carelessly tossing three bullock hearts in the air' (1992). Wrestlers in body suits featuring oversized genitalia were juxtaposed with an irreverent presentation of the overweight bodies of two lovers, alongside a half-naked female wire walker. As part of their acrobatic act for their next show, *Circus Under the Tin Top* (1993), Kareena Oates reversed the trick of sexed bodies in circus by lifting Rudi Mineur into the air and holding him there.

The Rock 'n' Roll Circus' production of *The Dark* (1995), directed by Gail Kelly, won the 1995 Brisbane critics' Matilda award for innovative work.[16] The show frames circus tricks; aerial routines, extraordinary head balances, and bicycle balances, with discordant images of psychic disturbance reflecting the imperatives of perverse desires and murderous urges. As an adults-only circus parody of horror thrillers, *The Dark* ironically framed perceptions of circus as fun entertainment with skeletons doing acrobatic routines and body parts in jars tended by a psychotic nurse — the nurse continued to pursue live specimens with a meat cleaver and ate a man's brains like a bowl of spaghetti as his head disappeared and reappeared in a magic box. A caress signalled death; a gun kept appearing; the image of a sad clown became one of repeated attempts to commit suicide, and the aerial body broke into song during its act. Circus as a place of heightened bodily risk and fear translates into a site for an exposure of the images conjured up by the dark recesses of the psyche. Throughout these acts bodies are engaged in highly sexualised encounters; for example, in an explicit heterosexual aerial duet two veiled women dressed in mourning lifted their dresses to display their naked bodies underneath and two men kiss. Veronica Kelly writes : 'As befits a circus, the energy and physical skills make one gasp while serving to build images of breathtaking surreal eroticism' (1995b).

As a specialist director of new circus and physical theatre, Gail Kelly has been exploring the possibilities of performing sexual bodies in physical theatre in a number of productions since 1990. In her direction of groups such as Legs on the Wall, Club Swing, The Party Line and Rock 'n' Roll Circus, Kelly develops a postmodern physical theatre which parodies the actions of circus bodies in its form, while retaining recognisable elements from circus such as its continuous sound track, its clowning intention and the execution of aerial and acrobatic tricks. The cultural meanings of bodies are displayed across the surface of Kelly's texts by using a visual language of incongruity and absurdity reminiscent of rock music videos. Her work uses the demonstration of circus skills as its starting point rather than as the focus of the final spectacle so that the performed text is invigorated by a highly theatrical aesthetic of images and ideas. Her productions involve specialist designs for costumes, often in collaboration with Angus Strathie, and a set which facilitates the performing body's trajectory through imaginative spaces. If the routines come from circus, the artistic concepts draw on cultural mediums from the visual arts to cinema, and Kelly's work is informed by feminist and performance theory. Working in collaboration with a writer and/or visual artist and the performers, she has been developing new languages for the body in physical theatre.

The performance of sexualised routines in postmodern physical theatre both resists and confirms the cultural meanings of bodies. Because the female body is not necessarily signed as feminine in this work, it brings to the fore social contradictions related to the visual identity of performing bodies as sexed. For example, the performance of a desiring female body in *Appetite* might be read as the sexualised behaviours of a neutral rather than a sexed body, or it can be looked at in conjunction with the body which it is desiring as an act of lesbian desire. Likewise the interactions between male bodies kissing in *The Dark* can be sexual or specifically homosexual. Regardless of whether physical theatre intends the body to be a neutral instrument, it would seem to be perceived in the visual texts of physical theatre as sexed. Therefore the larger question of whether the physical body can be viewed as neutral, that is, as existing outside cultural categories at least in the athletic execution of the aerial or acrobatic tricks, is particularly relevant to a consideration of how the body is represented in physical theatre texts. Judith Butler (1990) would argue that this is an impossible question to answer since social identity arises from the repetition of performative acts which implicates the gendered body. As Grosz explains, it is problematic to see the body as neutral in a text since its materiality is culturally determined (1994, 156). The action of a female body carrying a male body across the space cannot be interpreted as an act of neutral bodies when its cultural significance is apparent as the action of sexed bodies inverting social routines. Therefore the act of a female body carrying a female body becomes socially transgressive because it mimics social perceptions of how this act takes place between a male and female body, and is implicitly understood to have sexual significance.

These sexualised behaviours in physical theatre do not suggest that bodies are neutral so much as suggesting that they perform a text of circulating energies between bodies. Bodies in acrobatic and aerial tricks are constantly in motion in this form. If physical theatre work transgresses normative standards of traditional circus when it highlights sexual bodies in its routines, it retains the fundamental premise of circus that the spectacle of the movements and actions of the body and between bodies constitutes a performed text. This work remains orientated to the spectator's viewing of an interactive display between bodies. The interactions between performing bodies in physical theatre suggest what Grosz identifies as alternative notions of corporeality and materiality (1994, 165) by bodily tracing flows and energies within a plane or visible text (1994, 170).

Restaging body forms

An underlying premise of physical theatre is that the physicality of executing actions — balances, leaps, jumps, and swinging high — is contrary to notions of a compliant docile body which sustains conformity to social categories of identity. The expressive physicality of the body in this work becomes a political act. In reconfiguring the aesthetics of body forms, it suggests radical possibilities for representing difference in theatre.

While it is not strictly part of a category of physical theatre, the one-woman show *The Seven Stages of Grieving* (1995) written for Kooemba Jdarra by Deborah Mailman and Wesley Enoch and performed by Mailman is nonetheless an example of a visual text in which the political meanings of viewing the actions of the physical body are explicitly foregrounded in ways which also restage body forms in theatre. The text charts the legacy of grief experienced by Aboriginal people as a consequence of colonisation, and captures intimate personal voices as well as the widespread devastating impact of violent deaths on Aboriginal communities. In production, a visual text with slide images and a slow-dripping block of ice ran across the spoken text delivered by Mailman. But in addition Mailman created a physical body text by sitting, then rolling on a blackened area of the stage so that her body became blacker as the performance progressed. These physical actions contain a potent political message about the indivisible relationship of the lived experience of the body and racial oppression. In *The Seven Stages of Grieving* the black body becomes visible, and in this instance, it is performed as a racially marked female body.

The representation of different bodies in physical texts challenges cultural and theatrical preconceptions about body forms.[17] Alternatively, the disjuncture produced by bodies working across movement forms revokes the discrete separations established by artistic norms and, by inference, its cultural structures. In the most obvious examples, as dance comes to dominate performance work in the 1990s, dance and physical theatre intersect in a number of recent works including Meryl Tankard's Australian Dance Theatre's *Furioso* and *Possessed. Furioso* encapsulates the sexual difference in domestic worlds as a state of exaggerated movement. Jill Sykes (1995) describes how the choreographer Tankard has the ten dancers 'flying' through the air 'harnessed to ropes'. She continues 'They hurl themselves about the stage [...] If it were no more than an aerial circus and a sense of violence — aspects that dominate its initial impact — it would be memorable only for its acrobatics'. The social meaning of violence in these bodily contacts becomes more pronounced with this adaptation of harness work from physical theatre into dance. In contrast, Teresa Blake and Dan Whitton of the group Desoxy has established a reputation for integrating dance and acrobatics in their routines, which range between playful, comic teasing to threatening confrontation. The repetitions of action in their work imply the compulsion in the orchestrated momentum of the body's movement. But interestingly, Blake and Whitton minimise the gender specificity of their bodies as if to suggest that bodies are interchangeably sexed. In *A Vulgar Ear* (vulgar because the ear cannot be closed), moments of simple calm are offset by the dancer's bodies contorted into extreme positions in a text, wherein women toss men into the air in what Robin Grove (1994) describes as reinventing dance.[18] The different acts of bodies can realign forms in the performance of physicality.

Leaking bodies in 'uneven joins'

Social identity is represented in physical theatre and circus by the acts of a physical body. It is a material condition of bodily display, gesture and action. This depiction of identity sets physical theatre apart from preceding theatrical experiments with visual texts which in the 1960s and 1970s sought to represent the innate essential self of the performer (Auslander 1992) or in the 1980s and 1990s, either signify fragmented states of subjectivity or reveal the inner self as a socially performative condition; such as in the conversation texts of Open City by Keith Gallasch and Virginia Baxter.[19] The outer surfaces of bodies in physical theatre indicate presence so that there is no pretext of performing inner states. While it is exhilarating and exciting for the spectator to watch a skilful execution of tricks in physical theatre, the performed text deliberately obscures the performer's experience of the body. The traditional circus practice of championing the dangerous feat while making the execution of the trick appear effortless is also indicative of physical theatre. This maintains a separation between the performed text perceived by the spectator and the performer's experience of the body during performance. In physical theatre, the performing body masks its physical exertion, its pain; the bruises and other markings across its surface.

But the spectatorial appeal of physical theatre and circus is, in part, its contestation of socially delineated limits to the body's movement. It confounds social beliefs about the boundaries of bodies as natural by expanding the movement of what is perceived as physically feasible. In addition, in circus, physical bodies are located in acts of illusion and magic which frame concepts of the natural body in illusion, at least in its performance. If Merleau-Ponty suggests how a phenomenology of bodily self-knowledge is related to the viewing of other bodies, then physical theatre suggests one of the social spaces for the heightened viewing of the acts of other bodies. But Grosz's contention that bodies are irreducibly sexually-divided has implications for the spectator's viewing of physical theatre. If understandings of the performing body in physical theatre arise from the spectator's experience of sexually-differentiated bodies, regardless of the text's intentions, then the actions of bodies in physical theatre are interpreted as sexed. Therefore a female body performing acts of strength is viewed by a female spectator as expanding the possibilities of what have been socially designated as the natural limits of the acts of female bodies.

The cultural significance of body surfaces in physical theatre is evident in the changing shapes of muscular bodies in acts of exertion which confuse sexual differentiation. In the execution of dangerous and risky tricks, the body sweats across the skin's surface as if it is leaking. Grosz writes that 'Body fluids flow, they seep, they infiltrate; their control is a matter of vigilance, never guaranteed' (1994, 194). While she argues that the female body is conceived to be in a state of uncontrollable corporeal flow as 'seepage' (203), it would seem that such 'seepage' is especially socially regulated. Yet the surface leaks in physical theatre are emblematic of the body's risky actions rather than fixed states of its interiority. The social display of bodily fluids is gendered so that sweating is an act of social power for a male body and becomes one of social transgression for a female body. Undoubtedly, the social risks for a leaking female body are far greater. When the female physical theatre performer undertakes an act of strength in which her body sweats, she contravenes not only the social demarcation of behaviours and identity, but also notions of how the surfaces of bodies are sexed through the display and containment of fluids.

In her explanation of how bodies are intelligible as symptoms of something else, Peggy Phelan (1997) describes how they also elude conscious narration and by implication, ideas. Phelan argues that perceptions of the body do not conform to the narrative order established by consciousness and, instead, the body exists in what she terms an 'uneven join' in time. Therefore the viewing of bodies in performance confounds the social contract which arranges bodies as ideas in a temporal sequence of past and present. The peculiarities of watching performing sexed bodies in physical theatre reflects Phelan's schema, because acts of watching do not smoothly dovetail into cultural concepts of what the body might be. Bodies produced in physical theatre can be located in the spaces of Phelan's uneven joins because the performed text implicitly conjures up a continuous present related to the spectator's bodily experience. The immediacy of viewing the performing body defies its location in the separations established by cultural language and narrative order. Bodily display in physical theatre disturbs temporal spaces and this is particularly evident in the viewing of acts of sexed bodies. The female body sets up an 'uneven join' in its performance of a strong body which carries a male body because it disrupts the preceding hierarchical order of previously sexed relationships and the cultural narrative of the female body as weak.

A female body lifts and carries the male body across the performance space repeatedly in physical theatre productions by Rock 'n' Roll Circus, Legs on the Wall, Desoxy, Theatre Physical and numerous other Australian groups. The appearance of sweat on the skin of the female body in this strong act is not only transgressive of its socially prescriptive actions but the surface materialities of its cultural identity. The repetition of such bodily acts throws off the accumulated weight of belief from the past about gendered bodies. Performing in a continuous present of strong bodies, the female body in Australian physical theatre navigates the spaces surrounding the polarisation of sexed bodies, in the fluid, mobile energies of physicalised ideas.

Notes

1 Legs on the Wall have used this action in a number of their productions since 1990. For example, in *All of Me* by Mary Morris (directed by Nigel Jamieson, performed at the Performance Space, Sydney 7-26

September 1993). Pamela Payne writes: 'But the basic language of this production is visual: the language of bodies flung from ladders, spun head high and at arm's length, clambering and clinging, balanced on shoulders, feet or thighs, bodies hurled and hurling themselves at other bodies' (1993b). In the Magpie Theatre production *Verona* which tells the story of Romeo and Juliet using a vaudeville style of slapstick physical theatre, Romeo jumps into Juliet's arms. Directed by Neill Gladwin in conjunction with Desoxy, this production was first staged in Adelaide at the Norwood Concert Hall, 5-8 April 1995, and performed in Sydney at the Glen Street Theatre in January 1996. Samela Harris writes: 'Throughout, there is tumbling and acrobatics of superb precision and glorious wit and whimsy' (1995).

2 The identity of one performer jumping into the arms of another may vary according to the context so it could also indicate other types of relationships; for example, a mother and a child, or even two children.

3 Some of the groups who have worked in this form since the early 1980s are as follows: Acrobat, Actrobaticus, Antematter, Bent Legs, Bizicircus, Brink, Circus Oz, Club Swing, Crome, Desoxy, Earth, Etcetera, Frumpus, Harpies Bizarre, Hunting Party, Icarus, Knee-High, Legs on the Wall, Post Arrivalists, Rebound Acrobat, Rock 'n' Roll Circus, Sista-web, Splatto, Splinter, Stalker Stilt Theatre, Strange Fruit, Stretchmark 2, Sweet FA, The Flying Fruit Flies, The Leapers, The Leaping Loonies, The Naturals, The Party Line, Theatre Physical, Vertigo, Vulcana Women's Circus, Wimmin's Circus, Women's Circus. This list is compiled from conversations with Celia White, 28 April 1996 and David Clarkson, 3 June 1996.

4 Handspan Theatre Company are a Melbourne based group specialising in puppetry which have created over thirty productions since 1977. The artistic directors of Handspan have been Ken Evans, Trina Parker and Peter Wilson, and puppeteers include Michelle Spooner and Maeve Vella. Sydney Front, a Sydney-based ensemble of Andrea Aloise, John Baylis, Clare Grant, Nigel Kellaway and Chris Ryan worked from 1987-1993 developing performance spectacles to redefine the rituals of performing. Their performances include: *Waltz* (1987), *Pornography of Performance* (1988), *The Burnt Wedding* (1989), *Don Juan* (1992), *Passion* (1993). In their performance *First and Final Warning* (1992) at the Performance Space (November 1992), the audience were either initially separated by sex with both men and women asked to undress and put on knee-length black petticoats in which to watch the show, or they could pay double the admission price and watch a different performance from the stage.

5 Legs on the Wall descended the lower third of Australia Square in performances for the 1996 Sydney Festival.

6 Current members of Stalker are: Rachael Swain, David Clarkson, Emily McCormick, Brett Nancarrow and recent productions have included Catia Malino, and Sophia Gibson.

7 Directed by Julia Cotton and performed by Russell Garbutt, Katrina Sedgwick, Carlos Russell, Celia White and Edwina Entwistle with music by Ian Farr and Wayne Freer and design by Stephen Curtis. This was first

performed at the Performance Space, Sydney, January 1993. Members of Etcetera included Julia Cotton, Wayne Freer, Russell Garbutt, Carlos Russell and Katrina Sedgwick.

8 The current Flying Ashtons team are Becky, her brother Pepe, and Michelle.

9 Meyerhold (1969), who developed a physical form of training for the actor's body in the 1920s refers to the circus in his discussion of the theatricality of popular theatre forms.

10 Circus Oz first performed at the 1978 Adelaide Festival. See Radic for a description of the use of Circus Oz in Robert Draffin's direction of Therese Radic's *Madame Mao* in 1986 (1991a, 235).

11 Recent examples of community-based projects using circus are Bizicircus from Western Australia, and the collaboration between the Melbourne-based Back to Back Company, whose members have a physical or mental disability, with Circus Oz in a celebratory reinvention of the freak show, and *Cabaret Erratica*, a show with similar conception performed in Brisbane in 1994. Also New South Wales has a regional touring physical theatre group with the Bathurst-based Precarious.

12 The graduates of Flying Fruit Fly can be found working in Circus Oz, Ashton's Circus, Silver's Circus and other performance and dance groups, as well as a wide range of unexpected fields such as Guy Newman in water polo and Emma George, current holder of the World Record for Women's Pole Vault.

13 Sue Broadway and Sally Forth influenced the training of female performers in the aerial work of new circus in London in the early 1980s (Tait 1994, 119). In support of this claim, Deborah Pope, trapeze and corde lisse performer with the English group RaRazoo, recounted to Celia White in 1996 how, in the early 1980s, Sue Broadway taught aerial skills to a generation of female performers in comparable groups in England. Also Sophie Griffiths, the co-founder of the London-based aerial dance group High Vaultage, trained and worked as an acrobat in Australia.

14 One of her fellow councillors, Mike Pringle, called it 'degrading to women' (*Sunday Mail*, 5 August 1995) supported by a third councillor, George Hunter.

15 The physical theatre performance *700 Positions* directed by Gail Kelly and performed by Celia White, with writer Peta Tait, visual artist Jane Becker and video artist Maria Barbagallo, co-won the 1996 Award for Outstanding Performing Arts Event at the Gay and Lesbian Mardi Gras Festival.

16 Members of Rock 'n' Roll Circus for this production were Derek Ives, Kareena Oates, Rudi Mineur and Matt Wilson, with dramaturg Hilary Beaton and composer Brett Parker.

17 In 1996 Stalker Stilt Theatre, in collaboration with the traditional owners of the Aboriginal stories and Aboriginal dancers, produced *Mimi*

which represented the shadow world of mimi spirits using dancers on stilts. Directed by Rachael Swain and performed at the Boya quarry in Perth with the members of Stalker, and the dancers Richard Talonga, Stephen Oliver, Darlisa Pigarm and Lorrae Coffin. This integration of movement traditions from Aboriginal storytelling and the physical theatre suggests new body forms.

18 *A Vulgar Ear* was performed by Xenia Hanusiak, Teresa Blake, Belinda Lloyd, Ruth Bauer, Jill Pearce, Dan Whitton, Adam Broinoswki and the opening season was at the Napier Street Theatre, Melbourne, August 1994.

19 Open City's productions include *Tokyo/Now/Thriller* (1987), *Photo Play* (1988), *The Girl with a Stone in Her Shoe* (1989), *All That Flows: Out There* (ABCFM, 1990), *The Museum of Accidents* (1991), *Tokyo Two* (1992), *Sense* (1993), *Shop and The Necessary Orgy* (1995), *Promiscuous Spaces: Mondo Lingo* (1996).

Works Cited

[*ATR* =*Australasian Theatre Record*; later ANZTR = *Australalian and New Zealand Theatre Record.*
ADS = *Australasian Drama Studies*]

Akerholt, M. (1988) *Patrick White*. Amsterdam: Rodopi.
Alter, N. M. (1996) *Vietnam Protest Theatre. The Television War on Stage*. Bloomington & Indianapolis: Indiana UP.
Andersen, B. (1983) *Imagined Communities: Reflections on the Origins and Spread of Nationalism*. London: Verso.
Ang, I. (1993) 'Migrations of Chineseness: Ethnicity in the Postmodern World'. In D. Bennett, ed. (1993), 32-44.
— (1994) 'On Not Speaking Chinese: Postmodern Ethnicity and the Politics of Diaspora', *New Formations* 24, 1-18.
Anon (1996) 'Hybrid Fellowships', *Artforce* 92, 11.
— (1991) 'Crossing Cultures in Dance', *Artlink* 11:1&2, 102-103.
Archer, R. (1994) 'Introduction to *Emma*', *ADS* 24, 99-100.
Auslander, P. (1992) *Presence and Resistance*. Ann Arbor: U of Michigan P.
Balodis, J. (1991) *Too Young for Ghosts*. Sydney: Currency.
— (1992) 'No Going Back'. Unpub. TS.
— (1996) 'My Father's Father'. Unpub. TS.
Banks, R. (1992) Review of *Wild Cat Falling* adapt. Alan Becher, *ANZTR* (July), 32.
— (1994) Review of *Ningali*, by Josie Ningali Lawford, Robyn Archer and Angela Chaplin. *ANZTR* (August), 53.
Barcan, R. (1996) 'Bad Mothers on TV; TV as Bad Mother: The Case of "Noeline"'. In S. Holt & M. Lynch, ed., *Motherlode*. Melbourne: Sybylla Feminist P. 1996, 45-59.
Bartlett, N. (1990) 'Preface', *A Vision of Love Revealed in Sleep (Part Three)*. In M. Wilcox, ed., *Gay Plays: Four*. London: Methuen, 82-84.
Baxter, V., ed. (1996) *Telling Time: Celebrating Ten Years of Women Writing for Performance*. Sydney: Playworks.
Beaton, H. (1994) *No Strings Attached*. Brisbane: Playlab.
Bell, H. (1995) *Fortune*. Sydney: Currency.
Bennett, D., ed. (1993) *Cultural Studies: Pluralism and Theory*. Melbourne: Melbourne U. English Department.
Bennett, R. (1995) *Funerals and Circuses*. Sydney: Currency.
Bennie, A. (1993) [Review of *Aftershocks*, *Sydney Morning Herald*. (15 July).
Bent, R. (1992a) *Waiting for Annette*. In Bent et al. (1992b).
— et al. (1992b) *Around the Edge: Women's Plays*. South Australia: Tantrum Press.
Bhabha, H. (1985) 'Signs Taken for Wonders: Questions of Ambivalence and Authority Under a Tree Outside Delhi, May 1817.' In Barker, F. et al, *Europe and Its Others: Proceedings of the Essex Conference on the Sociology of Literature, July 1984, Vol. 1*. Colchester: U of Essex P, 89-106.
— (1988) 'The Commitment to Theory', *New Formations* 5, 5-23.
— (1991) 'Introduction: Narrating the Nation'. In Bhabha, *Nation and Narration*. London: Routledge, 1-8.
— (1992) 'Postcolonial Authority and Postmodern Guilt'. In L. Grossberg et al. ed. *Cultural Studies*. NY: Routledge, 56-68.
Binns, V. (1991) *Community and the Arts: History/Theory*/Practice: *Australian Perspectives*. Leichhardt [NSW]: Pluto Press.
Blanco, R. (1996) Program note, *Frontier Stories* by Sidetrack Performance Group and Aboriginal and Islander Dance Theatre, Sidetrack Studio Theatre, Marrickville [Sydney] (November-December).
Blonski, A. (1994) 'Persistent Encounters: The Australia Council and Multiculturalism'. In Gunew & Rizvi (1994), 192-206.
Boal, A. (1995) *Theatre of the Oppressed*. Trans. C. A. & M.-O. Leal McBride. New York: Theatre Communications Group.
Bobis, M. (1993) *Cantata of the Warrior Woman Daragang Magayon/Kantada ng Babaing Mandirigma*. Manila: Babaylan Women's Publishing Collective.
— (1994) 'Re-inventing the Epic: Notes on Adapting a Traditional Genre', *ADS* 24, 117-129.

—— (1995) 'Redreaming the Voice: From Translation to Bilingualism', *Rubicon* 1:2, 24-36.
Bobis, M., Gilbert, H. & Lo, J. (1994) 'What *Priscilla* Said', *Real Time* 4, 4-5.
Bourdieu, P. (1990) *The Logic of Practice*. Trans. R. Nice. Oxford: Polity Press/Blackwell.
—— (1993) *The Field of Cultural Production: Essays on Art and Literature*. Ed. R. Johnson. Cambridge: Polity.
Bray, E. (1976) *Are We Heroes...? Experiences in Educational Drama*. Sydney: New South Wales UP.
—— (1991) *Playbuilding*. Sydney, Currency.
Brisbane, K., ed. (1989) *Plays from Black Australia*. Sydney: Currency.
—— (1995a) 'Playwriting'. In Parsons & Chance. (1995), 446-457.
—— (1995b) 'Sydney Theatre Company'. In Parsons & Chance (1995), 573.
Broinowski, A. (1995) *The Gap*. Sydney: Currency.
—— (1996) *The Yellow Lady: Australian Impressions of Asia*. Melbourne: Oxford UP.
Brown, P. (1994) '*Aftershocks* Film Treatment'. Unpub. TS.
Brown, P. & Workers' Cultural Action Committee (1993) *Aftershocks*. Sydney: Currency.
Budge, B. & D. Hamer (1994) 'Introduction'. In Hamer, D. & Budge, B. ed., *The Good, the Bad and the Gorgeous: Popular Culture's Romance with Lesbianism*. London: Pandora, 1-14.
Bunbury, S. (1994) 'Female Circus Brims with Worthiness, Vigor and Vulgarity', *Age* (22 November), 19.
Burvill, T. (1983) 'The Politics of the Popular', *ADS* 1:2, 19-32.
—— (1988) 'Sidetrack's *Kin*: Intervening in Multiculturalism', *ADS* 12/13, 59-71.
Butler, J. (1990) *Gender Trouble*. London: Routledge.
—— (1993) 'Imitation and Gender Insubordination'. In Abelove, H., Aina Barale, M. & Halperin, D. M., ed., *The Lesbian and Gay Studies Reader*. New York: Routledge, 307-320.
Cahill, P. (1995) 'Ringmaster Wherrett,' *Sydney Star Observer* (24 August), 23.
Capelin, S., ed. (1995) *Challenging the Centre: Two Decades of Political Theatre*. Brisbane: Playlab.
Carroll, D. (1994) *Australian Contemporary Drama* (Sydney: Currency). Rev. ed.
Case, S. (1988) *Feminism and Theatre*. New York: Methuen.
Castan, C. (1986) 'Ethnic Australian Writing: Is it Really Australian Literature?' *Outrider* 3:2, 64-79.
—— (1988) 'Greek-Australian Plays', *ADS* 12/13, 17-33.
Castles, S., Kalantzis, M., Cope, B. & Morrissey M. (1992) *Mistaken Identity: Multiculturalism and the Demise of Nationalism in Australia*. Sydney: Pluto.
Castro, B. (1996) 'Masked Balls: Or, All Translators are Faithless', *Heat* 1, 69-73.
Cathcart, S. & A. Lemon (1988) *The Serpent's Fall*. Sydney: Currency.
Chenery, S. (1991) 'Brief Respite for Gow's Tormented Soul,' *Australian* (19 November), 12.
Chesterman, C., ed. (1995) *Playing with Time: Women Writers for Performance*. Glebe [NSW]: Fast Books.
Chi, Jimmy, & Kuckles (1991). *Bran Nue Dae*. Sydney: Currency.
Chow, R. (1993) *Writing Diaspora: Tactics of Intervention in Contemporary Cultural Studies*. Bloomington & Indianapolis: Indiana UP.
Ciccatosto, E. & Bosworth, M. (1995) *Emma: A Translated Life*.. Fremantle: Fremantle Arts Centre Press. Rev. ed.
Clarke, M. T. (1972) *Joan and Betty Raynor, Strolling Players*. Melbourne: Lansdowne.
Clifford, J. & Marcus G., ed. (1986) *Writing Culture: The Poetics and Politics of Ethnography*. Berkeley: U of California P.
Conigrave, T. (1995) *Holding the Man*. Ringwood, [Vic]: McPhee.
Copeman, P. (1994) 'The *Hearts and Minds* Project: Towards an Austral/Asian Theatre', *ADS* 25, 166-176.
Cotes, A. (1992) Review of *Body Slam*, *Review Independent Monthly* (September 1992), 81.
—— (1993a) 'It's the Experience That Matters' [Review of *Filling the Silence*], *Brisbane Review* (3 June).
—— (1993b) Review of *One Woman's Song* by Peta Murray, *ATR* (June), 92.
Crea, T. (1992) 'Doppio Teatro - Towards a Bicultural Theatre Practice'. In Bent et al (1992b).
—— (1996) Letter to Tony Mitchell, 28 June.

Creed, B. (1986) 'Horror and the Monstrous Feminine: An Imaginary Abjection', *Screen* 27:1, 44-70.
Curtis, P. (1969) *A Time to Kill. Quadrant* 13:57, 10-20.
Dale, L. & Gilbert, H. (1993) 'Looking the Same? A Preliminary (Post-colonial) Discussion of Orientalism and Occidentalism in Australia and Japan', *Yearbook of Comparative and General Literature* 41, 35-50.
Darwin Theatre Group (1988) *Dust Off Vietnam.* Darwin: Darwin Theatre Group Inc.
Davis, J. (1982) *Kullark/The Dreamers.* Sydney: Currency.
— (1989) *Barungin.* Sydney: Currency.
De Bono, E. (1996) *Edward De Bono's Textbook of Wisdom.* Harmondsworth: Penguin Viking.
De Groen, A. (1988) *The Rivers of China.* Sydney: Currency.
de Lauretis, T. (1984) *Alice Doesn't: Feminism, Semiotics, Cinema.* Bloomington: Indiana UP.
— (1988) 'Sexual Indifference and Lesbian Representation',*Theatre Journal* 40, 155-77.
Decent, C., ed. (1996) *Sydney Gay and Lesbian Mardi Gras* [Guide]. Newtown, NSW: Sydney Gay & Lesbian Mardi Gras Ltd.
Dimech, M. (1994) 'Consultation and Ethnic Communities'. In Gunew & Rizvi (1994), 165-79.
Dolan, J. (1993) 'Geographies of Learning: Theatre Studies, Performance, and the "Performative"', *Theatre Journal* 45, 417-41.
Doppio Teatro (1988), *Working Scripts,* Vol. 1. Adelaide: Doppio Teatro. [Vol. 1 contains scripts of *Cabaret dell'emigrante* and *Un pugno di terra*, Vol. 2 contains *Just Call Me Jo* and *La Madonna emigrante*.)
— (1992), Press Release for *Una festa di nozze.*
Dunne, S. (1991) '"As Many Pearls As Possible": Gay Theatre in Sydney'. BA Hons Thesis. U of Technology, NSW.
— (1993) 'Exuent [sic], Pursued by Realism', *Sydney Star Observer* (22 December), 37.
— (1994) 'So That's That Then', *Sydney Star Observer* (28 December), 27.
— (1995a) 'Quirky Charmer Still Joy to Watch', *Sydney Morning Herald* (13 April), 23.
— (1995b) 'Festival Director Wants to Avoid Mardi-ocrity', *Sydney Morning Herald* (15 May), 19.
Dunstone, B. 'Mudrooroo: The Politics of Aboriginal Performance and Aboriginal Sovereignty'. In Gilbert, H. ed., *Performing Postcoloniality : Critical and Creative Views* (forthcoming).
Earley, E. (1993) *The Custodians.* Sydney: Currency.
Eccles, J. (1993) 'June is Bursting out all Asian', *Sydney Review* (June), 6.
Enoch, W., & Mailman D. (1996). *The Seven Stages of Grieving.* Brisbane: Playlab.
Enright, N. (1990) *Daylight Saving.* Sydney: Currency.
— (1993) *St James' Infirmary.* Sydney: Currency.
— (1994a) *A Property of the Clan.* Sydney: Currency.
— (1994b) *Mongrels.* Sydney: Currency.
— (1995) *Good Works.* Sydney: Currency.
Evans, B. (1990) 'Eloquence Fashioned From Anarchy', *Sydney Morning Herald* (12 February), 12.
— (1991a) Review of *Bran Nue Dae* by Jimmy Chi & Kuckles, *ANZTR* (January), 8-9.
— (1991b) 'Simmering, Not Quite al Dente', *Sydney Morning Herald* (7 October).
— (1992) 'A Nuptial Feast More Like Scrappy Titbits of Antipasto', *Sydney Morning Herald* (3 March).
— (1993) 'A Dialogue That Goes Nowhere', *Sydney Morning Herald* (28 June).
Felski, R. (1989) *Beyond Feminist Aesthetics: Feminist Literature and Social Change.* Cambridge, Mass: Harvard UP.
Fensham, R. (1996) Interview with Teresa Crea, Adelaide 15 March. Unpublished MS.
Ferrier, C., ed. (1992) *Gender, Politics and Fiction: Twentieth Century Australian Women's Novels.* 2nd ed. St. Lucia: U of Queensland P.
Fischer, G. (1993) 'Genesis of a Theatre Project'. In Fischer, Behrendt & Syron, ed. (1993), 3-17.
Fischer, G., Behrendt P. & Syron, B., ed. (1993) *The Mudrooroo Müller Project: A Theatrical Casebook.* Kensington: New South Wales UP.
Fischer, M. (1996) *The Gay Divorcee.* In Parr, ed. (1996b), 277-308.
Fischer, M. M. J. (1986) 'Ethnicity and the Post-Modern Arts of Memory'. In Clifford & Marcus (1986), 194-233.

Fischer-Lichte, E. (1992) *The Semiotics of Theater.* Trans. J. Gaines & D. L. Jones. Bloomington: Indiana University Press.
Fisher, R. ed. (1983) *Seven One-Act Plays.* Sydney: Currency.
Fitzgerald, B., Grinblat, A., & Trevaskis, J. (1996) 'Women's Circus Marketing Plan 1996'. Melbourne: unpub. document.
Fitzpatrick, P. (1979) *After the 'Doll': Australian Drama Since 1955.* Melbourne: Edward Arnold.
— (1985) 'Asian Stereotypes in Recent Australian Plays', *Australian Literary Studies* 12:1, 35-46.
— (1987) *Williamson.* Sydney: Methuen.
— (1991) *Stephen Sewell: The Playwright as Revolutionary.* Sydney: Currency.
Footscray Community Arts Centre (1995) 'Women's Circus Business Plan 1995-97'. Melbourne: unpub. document.
Forth, S. (1992) Sally Forth interviewed by Alison Richards (16 June).
Fotheringham, R., ed. (1987) *Community Theatre in Australia.* North Ryde, NSW: Methuen Australia. See also Rev. ed. (Sydney: Currency 1992).
— (1992) 'The Politics of Theatre and Political Theatre in Australia,' in Holderness (1992), 66-83.
— (1993) 'Performing Arts Policy in Queensland in the 1990s,' *Culture and Policy* 5, 45-66.
— (1995) 'Research and Scholarship', in Parsons & Chance (1995), 495-497.
— (1997) 'Cultural Policy and Regional Theatre'. In Webb (1997), 36-53.
Freedman, B. (1996) 'Frame-up: Feminism, Psychoanalysis, Theatre'. In Case, S., ed. *Performing Feminisms: Feminist Critical Theory and Theatre.* Baltimore & London: Johns Hopkins UP, 54-76.
Frost, S. (1994) 'Broinowski Versus Passmore: A Dialogue of our Times', *Continuum* 8:2, 20-48.
Fuss, D. (1991) 'Inside/Out'. In Fuss D. ed., *Inside/Out: Lesbian Theories, Gay Theories.* New York: Routledge, 1-10.
Galbraith, L. (1985) 'Julian Mitchell', *Campaign* (March), 40.
— (1995) 'Gay Theatre'. In Parsons & Chance (1995), 242.
Gallasch, K. (1995) 'Border Difficulties: Teresa Crea on a Significant Gap in Arts Training in Australia', *Real Time* 7 (June-July), 5.
Garnaut, R. (1989) *Australia and the Northeast Ascendancy.* Canberra: AGPS.
Gauntlett, F. (1993a) Review of Circus Oz. *Telegraph-Mirror* (25 February 1993), *Australasian Theatre Record* (February), 29. Circus Oz
— (1993b) [Review of *Aftershocks*], *Telegraph-Mirror* (17 July).
Gauntlett, M. (1993) 'Funding "Australia"', *Canadian Theatre Review* 74, 12-17.
George, R. (1983) *Sandy Lee Live at Nui Dat.* Sydney: Currency.
Gerster, R. (1992) *Big-Noting: The Heroic Theme in Australian War Writing.* Melbourne: Melbourne UP.
Gilbert, H. (1992a) 'The Dance as Text in Contemporary Australian Drama: Movement and Resistance Politics', *ARIEL* 23:1, 133-147.
— (1992b) 'Telling It in Multiple Layers: An Interview with Jill Shearer', *ADS* 21, 138-153.
— (1994a) 'De-scribing Orality: Performance and the Recuperation of Indigenous Voices.' In Tiffin & Lawson (1994), 98-111.
— (1994b) 'Monumental Moments: Michael Gow's *1841*, Stephen Sewell's *Hate*, Louis Nowra's *Capricornia*, and Australia's Bicentenary', *ADS* 24, 29-45.
— (1994c) 'Occidental (Sex) Tourists: Michael Gurr's Sex Diary of an Infidel', *ADS* 25, 177-88.
— (1995) 'Dressed to Kill: A Post-colonial Reading of Costume and the Body in Contemporary Australian Theatre.' In Gainor, J. E., ed. *Imperialism and Theatre: Essays on World Theatre.* London: Routledge, 1995, 104-31.
— (1997) 'GI Joe Versus Digger Dave: Contemporary Australian Drama and the Vietnam War'. In Rutherford A. & Wieland J., ed. (1997) *War: Australia's Creative Response.* Sydney: Allen & Unwin, 305-19.
Gilbert, H. & Mawson, M. (1995) '"Pulling The Rug Out From Under Your Feet": An Interview with Michael Gurr', *ADS* 26, 22-35.
Gilbert, H. & Tompkins, J. (1996) *Post-Colonial Drama: Theory, Practice, Politics* (London & NY: Routledge)
Gilbert, K. (1988) *The Cherry Pickers.* Canberra: Burrambinga Books.
Giles, M. (1983) *Rest and Recreation.* In Fisher, R. (1983), 41- 64.
Gorman, C. (1996) *A Manual of Trench Warfare.* In Parr, ed. (1996b), 71-139.

Gow, M. (1983) *The Kid*. Sydney: Currency.
— (1986) *Away*. Sydney: Currency & Playbox Theatre Company.
— (1988) *1841*. Sydney: Currency.
— (1991) *All Stops Out*. Sydney: Currency.
— (1996) *Furious*. In Parr, ed. (1996b), 341-384.
Gration, S. (1995) 'Unapologetically Australian'. In Bennett (1995), vii-x.
Greenaway, J. (1990) *Political Acts: Lesbian Theatre in Sydney*. Sydney: Amazon Desktop Publishing.
Griffiths, G, ed., (1993) *John Romeril* (Amsterdam: Rodopi)
— (1994a) 'The Myth of Authenticity: Representation, Discourse and Social Practice.' In Tiffin & Lawson (1994), 70-85.
— (1994b) Review of *Dead Heart*, by Nicholas Parsons, *ANZTR* (February), 39.
— (1996) 'Work in Progress Report', *Australian* 'Weekend Review' (13-14 January), Arts 13.
Grosz, E. (1994) *Volatile Bodies*. Sydney: Allen & Unwin.
Grove, R. (1994) Review of *A Vulgar Ear* by Chronochromia and Desoxy. *Australasian Theatre Record* (July), 3.
Gunew, S. (1984) 'Migrant Writing: Promising Territory', *Kunapipi* 6:1, 12-19.
— (1987) 'Multicultural? Ethnic? Towards a New Australian Writing?' *Outrider* 4:1, 50-4.
— (1988) 'Multicultural Literature: Towards a New Australian Literary History', *Antipodes* 2 (1), 75-8.
— (1992) 'Migrant Women Writers: Who's on Whose Margins?' In Ferrier (1992), 163-78.
— (1993) 'Multicultural Multiplicities: US, Canada, Australia'. In Bennett, D., ed. *Cultural Studies: Pluralism and Theory*. Melbourne: Melbourne U. English Department, 51-65.
— (1994) 'Arts for a Multicultural Australia: Redefining the Culture', in Gunew & Rizvi (1994), 1-12.
Gunew S. & Longley K. O., ed. (1992) *Striking Chords: Multicultural Literary Interpretations*. Sydney: Allen & Unwin.
Gunew S. & Rizvi F., ed. (1994) *Culture, Difference and the Arts*. Sydney: Allen & Unwin.
Gunew S. & Yeatman A., ed. (1993) *Feminism and the Politics of Difference*. Boulder: Westview.
Gunn, J. V. (1982) *Autobiography: Towards a Poetics of Experience*. Philadelphia: U Pennsylvania P.
Gurr, M. (1992) *Sex Diary of an Infidel*. Sydney: Currency.
Hage, G. (1991) 'Racism, Multiculturalism and the Gulf War', *Arena* 96, 8-13.
Hainsworth, J. (1987) *Hibberd*. Melbourne: Methuen.
Hallett, B. (1995) 'Can Theatre Stage a Comeback?' *Australian* 'Weekend Review' (25-26 November), 10.
Harding, A. (1996) *Blood and Honour*. In Parr, ed. (1996b), 237-276.
— (1997) *Only Heaven Knows*. Sydney: Currency.
Hardy, S. (1991) *Vita! A Fantasy*. In Spender D., ed. *Heroines: A Contemporary Anthology of Australian Women Writers*. Ringwood: Penguin, 421-61.
Harris, S. (1991) 'Message of a Martyr Whose Days ended in the Riverland', *Advertiser* (18 April).
— (1993) Review of *Funerals and Circuses* by Roger Bennett, *ANZTR* (September), 24-25.
— (1995) Review of*Verona* by Magpie. *Australasian Theatre Record* (March), 40.
— (1996) 'Feast Spreads Joy' [Review of *Una Festa Di Nozze*], *Advertiser* (20 April).
Hassan, I. (1987) *The Postmodern Turn: Essays in Postmodern Theory and Culture*. Ohio: Ohio State University Press.
Hawkins, G. (1993) *From Nimbin To Mardi Gras: Constructing Community Arts*. Sydney: Allen & Unwin.
Hawthorne, S. & Klein, R., ed. *Australia for Women: Travel and Culture*. Melbourne: Spinifex Press.
Hay, T. (1996) 'Yellow Lady Meets Black Stump: An Obscene Postmodern Heroine in Australia'. *Real Time* 10, 12-13.
Hebdige, D. (1986) 'Post-modernism and "The Other Side"', *Journal of Communication Enquiry* 10, 78-98.
Hewett, D. (1985) *The Golden Valley* and *Song of the Seals*. Sydney: Currency.

—— (1996) 'It Doesn't Have to be a Blood Sport' [Interview with Margaret Williams]. In Baxter, ed. (1996), 43-47.
Hibberd, J. (1984a) *Asian Oranges.* In *Squibs: A Collection of Short Plays by Jack Hibberd.* Brisbane: Phoenix, 103-121.
—— (1984b) *Commitment.* In *Squibs: A Collection of Short Plays by Jack Hibberd.* Brisbane: Phoenix, 123-153.
—— (1995a) [Review of *Summer of the Seventeenth Doll* by Ray Lawler], *Australian* (28 April), 8.
—— (1995b) [Review of Honour by Joanna Murray-Smith and *Scenes from a Separation* by Andrew Bovell and Hannie Rayson], *Australian* (17 November 1995, *ANZTR* (November 1995), 18.
Hibberd, J., Harper, K., Kendall, D., ed. (1984) 'Performing Arts in Australia' *Meanjin* 43:1.
Hoad, B. (1996) 'Love's Labours Not Lost, But Missed', *Bulletin* (12 March), 76.
Hodgson, J. & Richards, E. (1966) *Improvision: Discovery and Creativity in Drama.* London: Methuen.
Hoffman, W. M. (1979) 'Introduction', in. Hoffman, W. M., ed. *Gay Plays: The First Collection.* New York: Avon, vii-xxxix.
Holderness, G. ed. (1992) *The Politics of Theatre and Drama.* London: Macmillan.
Holloway, P., ed. (1981) *Contemporary Australian Drama* . Sydney: Currency.
—— (1987) *Contemporary Australian Drama* . Sydney: Currency. Rev. ed.
Holman, D. (1989) *No Worries, Small Poppies* and *Beauty and the Beast.* Sydney: Currency.
Hopgood, A. (1966) *Private Yuk Objects (A Comment on Vietnam).* Unpub. TS. Fryer Library, University of Queensland.
—— (1995) Letter to Elizabeth Perkins (12 October).
Hughes, R. (1986) *The Fatal Shore: The Epic of Australia's Founding.* New York: Vintage.
Hunter, M. A. & Fotheringham R. (1993) *Community Cultural Development in the Tertiary Sector: A Report.* Sydney: Australia Council.
Hurley, M. (1996) *A Guide to Gay and Lesbian Writing in Australia.* Sydney: Allen & Unwin.
Hyde, J. (1994) Review of *Dead Heart* by Nicholas Parsons, *ANZTR* (February), 40.
Jackson, D. (1990) Donna Jackson interviewed by Alison Richards (7 November).
—— (1933) Donna Jackson interviewd by Alison Richards (24 September).
Jagose, A. (1993) 'Homosexual Writing in Australia', *Meridian* 12, 159-64.
Jameson, F. (1991) *Postmodernism, or the Cultural Logic of Late Capitalism.* London: Verso.
Janaczewska, N. (1993) *Blood Orange. ADS* 22, 79-108.
—— (1994a) 'Cold Harvest'. Unpub. TS.
—— (1994b) 'In the Winter Garden'. Unpub. TS.
—— (1995) *The History of Water/Huyen Thoai Mot Giong Nuoc.* Sydney: Currency.
—— (1996) [Review of *Preludes to an Exile*], *Real Time*, 12 (April-May), 12.
Jellicoe, A. (1987) *Community Plays: How To Put Them On.* London: Methuen.
John, R. (1986) *Luck of the Draw.* Sydney: Currency.
Johnson, E. (1989) *Murras.* In Brisbane, ed. (1989), 79-107.
—— (1991) *What Do They Call Me?* In Spender. D., ed. *Heroines* Ringwood: Penguin, 237-55.
—— (1996) *What Do They Call Me?* In Parr, ed. (1996b), 213-236.
Jones, J. (1995) 'The Mad, Bad and Bitchy!' *Sydney Star Observer* (21 September), 56.
Jones, R. (1989) 'Donna Spits! Rai Jones talks to Donna Jackson about Women, Theatre and Music', *Community Arts Network News* 3 (October), 9-11.
Jurgensen, M. (1986) 'Multicultural Literature', *Outrider* 3:2, 80-90.
Kamboureli, S. (1993) 'Of Black Angels and Melancholy Lovers: Ethnicity and Writing in Canada'. In Gunew & Yeatman (1993), 143-56.
Kelly, O. (1984) *Community, Art and the State: Storming the Citadels.* London: Comedia.
Kelly, V. (1987a) 'Apocalypse and After: Historical Visions in Some Recent Australian Drama', *Kunapipi* 9: 3, 68-78.
—— ed. (1987b) *Louis Nowra* Amsterdam: Rodopi.
—— (1992) 'Falling Between Stools: The Theatre of Janis Balodis', *ARIEL* 23:1, 115-32.
—— (1993a) 'Orientalism in Early Australian Theatre', *New Literatures Review* 26, 32-45
—— (1993b) Review of *Filling the Silence*, *Australian* (28 May).

—— (1994) 'Enright's *Mongrels* as Intervention in the Canon of Contemporary Australian Drama', *Southerly* 54:2, 5-22.
—— (1995a) 'Smashing Temples: Cultural Symptoms of the 1980s in Australian Mainstage Comedy and Farce', *Modern Drama* 38:1, 97-108.
—— (1995b) Review of *The Dark* by Rock'n'Roll Circus. *ANZTR* (November), 32.
Kemp, J. (1996) 'A Dialogue With Disjunction'. In Baxter, ed. (1996), 29-31.
Kenna, P. (1980) *Furtive Love*. Sydney: Currency.
—— (1992) *A Hard God*. Sydney: Currency.
—— (1996) *Mates*. In Parr (ed.) (1996b), 41-70.
Keneally, T. (1968) *Childermas*. Unpub. TS. Fryer Library, University of Queensland.
Kershaw, B. (1992) *The Politics of Performance: Radical Theatre as Cultural Intervention*. London & New York: Routledge.
Kiernan, B. (1987) 'Seeing her Own Mischance'. In Holloway, ed. (1987), 476-485.
—— (1990) *David Williamson: A Writer's Career*. Melbourne: Heinemann. [Rev. ed. (1996) Sydney: Currency.]
Koch, P. (1990) Review of *Bran Nue Dae*, by Jimmy Chi & Kuckles, *ANZTR* (December), 35.
Kosky, B. (1996), 'I See What's Wrong: Kosky's View', *Age* (11 November), B7.
Krishnaswamy, R. (1995) 'Mythologies of Migrancy: Postcolonialism, Postmodernism and the Politics of (Dis)location', *ARIEL* 26 (1), 125-146.
Langer, B. (1996) 'From Contested History to Cultural Unity: Refugees and Multiculturalism'. In Bennett, D., ed. *Multicultural States: Rethinking Difference and Identity*. London: Routledge (forthcoming).
Langton, M. (1993) *Well I Heard it on the Radio and I Saw it on the Television...* Sydney: Australian Film Commission.
Laud, P. (1994) Review of *Dead Heart* by Nicholas Parsons, *ANZTR* (February), 40.
Lawler, R. (1978) *Summer of the Seventeenth Doll. The Doll Trilogy*. Sydney: Currency.
Le Gioie della Donne (The Joys of the Women) (1993). Film. Dir. Franco Di Chiera.
Learner, T. (1996) 'Survival'. In Baxter, ed. (1996), 25-27.
Lehmann, J. (1992) [Comment on Kummara Aboriginal Theatre Restaurant]. *ANZTR* (May), 11.
Lette, K. (1988) Grommits. Sydney: Currency.
Light, N. (1965) 'Alan Seymour's new play.' [Review of *The Gaiety of Nations* by Alan Seymour]. *Canberra Times* (9 December), 31.
Lim, S. L. (1994) Swee Leng Lim interviewed by Alison Richards (15 January).
Litson, J. (1996) 'Tour for the Show'. *Australian* 'Weekend Review' (15-16 June), 12.
—— (1997a) 'Queer Art with Mainstream Appeal', *Australian* (24 January), 9.
—— (1997b) 'For Love, Not Money', *Australian* 'Weekend Review' (29-30 March), 10.
Lloyd, T. (1990) Review of *Bran Nue Dae*, by Jimmy Chi & Kuckles. *The Advertiser*, (12 October), 12.
—— (1995) 'Culture in the Outback' [Review of *Eremophilia: Pulcinella*], *Advertiser* (28 August).
Lo, J. (1994) 'Tropes of Ambivalence in *Bran Nue Dae*'. Unpublished paper.
Love, H. (1985) 'Chinese Theatre on the Victorian Goldfields 1858-1870', *ADS* 3:2, 47-86.
—— ed. (1984) *The Australian Stage: A Documentary History*. Sydney: New South Wales UP.
Lynch, M. (1996) Review of *The Dreamers*, by Jack Davis, *Real Time* (October-November), 12.
Lyssa, A. (1996) *Pinball*. In Parr, ed. (1996b), 141-211
Lyssiotis, T. (1997) 'Pigeon-holed in an Ethnic Box' [Interview with Carolyn Pickett]. In Tompkins & Holledge, ed. (1997), 150-152.
Maclean, A. (1995) Review of *Angels Ex Machina* by Stalker. *Australasian Theatre Record* (October), 38.
Maher, S. (1994) Review of *Wild Cat Falling*, adapted by Peter Gorman. *Theatre Australasia* (July), 10.
Makeham, P. (1996) '"Across the Long, Dry Stage": Discourses of Landscape in Australian Drama'. Ph D Thesis, University of Newcastle.
Mamouney, D. (1995). Interview with Tom Burvill (May).
Manning, N. (1994) *Close to the Bone*. Sydney: Currency.
Marr, D. (1991) *Patrick White: A Life*. Sydney: Random House.
Maza, B. (1989) *The Keepers*. In Brisbane, ed. (1989), 167-229.
McAuley, G. (1996) 'Theatre Practice and Critical Theory', *ADS* 28, 140-145.
MCallum, J. (1987) *Buzo*. Melbourne: Methuen.

—— (1995a) 'Outrageous Comedy Festival', *Australian* (3 March), 10.
—— (1995b) 'Not Drowning, Diversifying', *Australian Magazine* (7-8 January), 10-11.
—— (1996) 'Theatre's Form Guide', *Australian* 'Weekend Review' (9-10 March), 8.
McCulloch, S. (1996) 'The Oriental Express'. *Australian* 'Weekend Review' (20-21 April), 1-2.
McGillick, P. (1987) 'Jack Hibberd's Naturalism' [1979]. In Holloway, ed. (1987), 370-382.
—— (1988) *Jack Hibberd* . Amsterdam: Rodopi.
—— (1994) Review of *Ninni* by Bangarra Dance Theatre, *ANZTR* (May), 11.
McNeil, J. (1987a) *The Old Familiar Juice. Collected Plays*. Sydney: Currency, 37-92.
—— (1987b) *How Does Your Garden Grow?* In *Collected Plays*. Sydney: Currency, 95-188.
McQueen, H. (1997) *Suspect History: Manning Clarke and the Future of Australia's Past*. Adelaide: Wakefield.
Merleau-Ponty, M. (1981) *Phenomenology of Perception*. Trans. C. Smith. London: Routledge & Kegan Paul.
Meyerhold, V. (1969) *Meyerhold on Theatre*. Trans. E. Braun. London: Methuen.
Miller, S. (1995) Review of *Bidenjarreb Pinjarra* by Geoff Kelso, Trevor Parfitt, Kelton Pell & Phil Thomson,*ANZTR* (July), 73-74.
Milne, G. (1990) 'Black and White in Australian Drama: Melbourne 1988', *Meridian* 9:1, 33-43.
—— (1992) 'Community Theatre in Melbourne: *The Bridge'*, *ADS* 20, 70-72.
—— (1993) 'Wanted (Presumed Dead): Community Theatre in Victoria', *ADS* 23, 147-160.
—— (1994) 'The Other Side of the Story: Multicultural Drama in Australia', *Meanjin* 53:3, 495-503.
Milner, A. & Quilty, M. (1996) *Communities of Thought*. Melbourne: Oxford UP.
Mitchell, T. (1987a) 'Italo-Australian Theatre: Multi-culturalism and Neo-colonialism' Part One, *ADS* 10, 31-48.
—— (1987b) 'Italo-Australian Theatre: Multi-culturalism and Neo-colonialism' Part Two, *ADS* 11, 37-46.
—— (1988) '"Going to the Source": Tes Lyssiotis Talks to Tony Mitchell', *ADS* 12/13, 5-15.
—— (1992a) 'New Forms, New relationships: An Interview with Teresa Crea', *New Theatre Quarterly* 8:29, 75-80.
—— (1992b) 'Wogs Still Out of Work: Australian Television Comedy as Colonial Discourse', *ADS* 20, 119-133.
Morgan, J. (1994a) 'Aussie Art Plays Safe for Sore Bums', *Australian* (24 June), 5.
—— (1994b) 'Talent Waits in the Wings', *Australian* 'Weekend Review' (20-21 August), 12.
—— (1996) 'The Art of Staying Afloat', *Weekend Australian* (21-22 December), 26.
Morgillo, A. (1990) *The Olive Tree*, *ADS* 17, 117-155.
Morris, M. (1993) *Two Weeks with the Queen: The Play*. Sydney: Currency.
Mudrooroo (1993) *The Aboriginal Protesters Confront the Proclamation of the Australian Republic on 26 January 2001 with a Production of 'The Commission' by Heiner Müller*. In Fischer, Behrendt & Syron, ed. (1993), 75-121.
—— (1994) 'Passing for White Passing for Black: An Ideological Con-pro-testation'. *Continuum* 8:2, 258-69.
Mulvey, L. (1975) 'Visual Pleasure and Narrative Cinema', *Screen* 16:3, 6-18.
Musa, H. (1993) Review of Circus Oz. *Australasian Theatre Record* (March 1993), 22.
Neill, R. (1993) Review of *My Spiritual Dreaming* by Eddie Bennell & Mike Burns. *ANZTR* (February), 41.
Nemeth, M. (1992) Review of *Praying Mantis Dreaming* by Bangarra Dance Theatre. *ANZTR* (October), 63-64.
——. (1993) Review of *One Woman's Song*, by Peta Murray. *Time Off* (2 June), 29.
North, H. (1992) Helen North interviewed by Alison Richards (17 April).
Nowra, L. (1983) *Sunrise*. Sydney: Currency.
—— (1988) *Capricornia*. Sydney: Currency.
—— (1989a) *The Golden Age*. Sydney: Currency.
—— (1989b) 'The Shrinking Vision'. *Island Magazine* 11:39, 11-13.
——L. (1992) *Summer of the Aliens*. Sydney: Currency.
—— (1993) *Radiance*. Sydney: Currency.
—— (1994a) *Crow*. Sydney: Currency.
—— (1994b) *Così*. Sydney: Currency. Rev. ed.

Nugent, A. (1990) Review of *Bran Nue Dae* by Jimmy Chi and Kuckles, *ANZTR* (October), 75-76.
Nunn, L. (1995) *The Advertiser* (22 April 1995), *Australasian Theatre Record* (April 1995), 54.
O'Brien, D. (1994) [Review of *Filling the Silence*] *DB* 62, 2-15 March.
O'Donnell, M. (1995) 'The Politics of Art', *Outrage* 148 (September), 62.
O'Regan, T., ed. (1994) *Critical Multiculturalism*. Sp. Issue of *Continuum* 8 (2).
O'Toole, J. (1976) *Theatre in Education: New Objectives for Theatre – New Techniques in Education*. London: Hodder & Stoughton.
Ousley, A. (1993) Andrea Ousley interviewed by Alison Richards (22 November).
Paget, D. (1987) '"Verbatim Theatre": Oral History and Documentary Theatre Techniques', *New Theatre Quarterly* 3:12, 317-336.
Panozzo, D. (1994a) 'Varda che Bruta ... Poretta' (Look How Ugly She is ... Poor Thing). Unpub. TS.
—— (1994b) Program Note. *Varda che Bruta ... Poretta*. Universal Theatre, Melbourne.
Parr, B. (1994) 'Peter Kenna's The Cassidy Album: A Call for Re-Viewing', *ADS* 24, 77-98.
—— (1996a) 'Peter Kenna's Mates: Camping It Up'. In Wotherspoon, G., ed. *Gay and Lesbian Perspectives 111: Essays in Australian Culture*. Sydney: Department of Economic History, 71-94.
—— ed. (1996b) *Australian Gay and Lesbian Plays*. Sydney: Currency.
Parsons, N. (1994) *Dead Heart*. Sydney: Currency.
Parsons, P. & Chance, V., ed. (1995) *Companion to Theatre in Australia*. Sydney: Currency.
Partridge, D. (1993) Review of *One Woman's Song*, by Peta Murray. *ANZTR* (May), 89-90.
Pavis, P. (1992) *Theatre at the Crossroads of Culture*. Trans. Loren Kruger. London: Routledge.
Pavlyshyn, M. (1992) 'Culture and Emigré Consciousness: Ukrainian Theatre in Australia 1948-1989', *ADS* 20, 54-69.
Payne, P. (1993a) [Review of *Aftershocks*], *Sun-Herald* (25 July).
—— (1993b) Review of *All of Me* by Legs on the Wall. *Australasian Theatre Record* (September 1993), 44.
Perkins, E. (1970) *Squeaking of Rats: 6 One-Act Plays*. St Lucia: Queensland UP, 99-124.
—— (1994) *The Plays of Alma de Groen*. Amsterdam: Rodopi.
Phelan, P. [1997] *Mourning Sex*. London: Routledge (forthcoming).
Pierce, P. (1987) 'Revaluing Australian Legends' [1978]. In Holloway, ed. (1987), 358-369.
Pitts, G. (1994) *Emma*, *ADS* 24, 102-144.
—— (1995) 'From the Writer', Program of *Emma* (Sydney, Belvoir Street Theatre, 1995).
——. (1996) *Emma. Celebrazione!* Sydney: Currency.
Playworks (1995) *Playing With Time: Women Writing for Performance*. Sydney: Playworks.
Pollard, D. (1996) 'Mother Tongue Interference'. In Baxter, ed. (1996), 93.
Portus, A. (1988) 'Vietnam Turns into a Musical.' [Review of *Pearls Before Swine* by Dennis Watkins and Chris Harrison], *Sydney Morning Herald* (6 June), 16.
Postle, J. (1996) 'Accessing the Performing Body', *Real Time* 12. (April-May), 33.
Price, C. (1975) 'Introduction'. In Price, C., ed., *Greeks in Australia*. Canberra: Australian National UP, 1-17.
Radic, L. (1987a) *Sideshow*. Montmorency, Vic: Yackandandah.
—— (1987b) *The General*. In Radic, L., ed. *Short Plays for the Australian Stage* Vol. 2. Montmorency, Vic: Yackandandah, 97-125.
—— (1991a) *The State of Play*. Melbourne: Penguin.
—— (1991b) Review of *Bran Nue Dae* by Jimmy Chi and Kuckles, *ANZTR* (January), 9.
Reade, H. (1982) *The Naked Gun*. Montmorency, Vic: Yackandandah.
Reinberg, L. (1991) *In the Field: The Language of the Vietnam War*. New York: Facts on File.
Richards, A. (1992) 'Women's Circus ... Leaping Off The Edge', *Meanjin* 51:1. Photographs by Vivienne Méhes facing p. 96.
—— (1994) 'Women's Circus ... Leaping Off the Edge'. In Hawthorne, S. & Klein, R., ed.(1994) 151-157.
Rogers, J. (1988) *Jigsaws*. Sydney: Currency.
Rolls, E. (1992) *Sojourners: Flowers and the Wide Sea*. St. Lucia: U of Queensland P.

Romeril, J. (1970) *Chicago, Chicago.* In *Plays: Buzo, Hibberd, Romeril.* Harmondworth: Penguin, 231-320.
Rowse, T. (1993) 'Mabo and Moral Anxiety', *Meanjin* 52 (2), 229-52.
Safransky, R. (1992) 'The Goulash Archipelago'. In Gunew & Longley (1992), 202-5.
Sawada, K. (1996) 'The Japanese Version of *The Floating World*: A Cross-Cultural Event Between Japan and Australia', *ADS* 28, 4-19.
Sawford, G. (1993) Review of *One Woman's Song*, by Peta Murray, *ANZTR* (June), 91-92. *Rave* 9 June 1993
Schiavoni, F. (1983) 'The Theatre of Nino Randazzo', *Meanjin* 42:1, 110-117.
Schweitzer, P. ed. (1980) *Theatre-in-Education: Four Secondary Programmes.* London: Methuen Young Drama.
Scott-Norman, F. (1993) Review of *Funerals and Circuses* by Roger Bennett. *ANZTR* (September), 22. *In Press* 15 September 1993
Sedgwick, E. K. (1990) *Epistemology of the Closet.* Berkeley: U of California P.
—— (1993) *Tendencies.* Durham, NC: Duke UP.
Sewell, S. (1983) *The Blind Giant is Dancing.* Sydney: Currency.
—— (1988) *Hate.* Sydney: Currency.
Shaw, G. (1986) 'Memory and the Making of Australian Literature', *Outrider* 3:2, 60-3.
Shaw, G. B. (1932) *Our Theatres in the Nineties.* 3 vols. London: Constable.
Shearer, J. (1989) *Shimada.* Sydney: Currency.
Shevtsova, M. (1993) *Theatre and Cultural Interaction.* U of Sydney: Sydney Association for Studies in Society and Culture.
Shotlander, S. (1987) *Framework.* Montmorency: Yackandandah.
—— (1996) *Is That You Nancy?* in Parr, ed. (1996b), 309-339.
Sidetrack Performance Group (1995) 'Company Objectives', Report to the Performing Arts Board of the Australia Council (February).
Sidetrack Theatre Company (1990) 'Chairperson's Letter', Application for Assistance by an Arts Company to the Australia Council (August).
Sinfield, A. (1994) *The Wilde Century: Effeminacy, Oscar Wilde and the Queer Moment.* London: Cassell.
Smith, L.R. (1993) Louise Radcliffe Smith interviewed by Alison Richards (4 November).
—— (1994) In Women's Circus, *Newslatter* (Summer), 3.
Spivak, G. (1988) *In Other Worlds: Essays in Cultural Politics.* New York: Methuen.
Stewart, K. (1996) 'Introduction'. In Stewart, K., ed. *The 1890s: Australian Literature and Literary Culture.* St Lucia: U of Queensland P, 1-26.
Stratton, J. & Ang I. (1994) 'Multicultural Imagined Communities: Cultural Difference and National Identity in Australia and the USA'. In O'Regan (1994), 124-58.
Sturak, K. (1996) 'An Interview with Sandra Shotlander', *Ant News* 29 (November), 6.
Summons, J. (1979) *Lamb of God.* Sydney: Currency.
Sutton, L. (1989a) [Review of *Ricordi*], *New Theatre Australia* 10, 36.
—— (1989b) 'Culture Within a Culture', *New Theatre Australia* 12 (September-October), 5-8.
Sykes, J. (1994) Review of *Ninni* by Bangarra Dance Theatre. *ANZTR* (May), 10-11.
—— (1995) Review of *Furioso* by the Australian Dance Theatre. *Australasian Theatre Record* (October 1995), 38.
Ta, D. B. (1996) 'Conversations with Charlie'. Unpub. TS.
Tait, P. (1993) *Original Women's Theatre: The Melbourne Women's Theatre Group 1974-77.* Melbourne: Artmoves.
—— (1994) *Converging Realities: Feminism in Australian Theatre.* Sydney & Melbourne: Currency/Artmoves.
——. (1996) 'Feminine Free Fall: A Fantasy of Freedom', *Theatre Journal* 48:1, 27-34.
Terracini, L. (1996) 'In the Star Court' (Interview by Keith Gallasch), *Real Time* 14, 36.
Thomson, H. (1995) 'Circus of Joy and Politics', *Age* (27 November 1995), 15.
Thorne, M. (1996) 'Burying Mother'. Unpub. TS.
Tiffin, C. & Lawson, A., ed. (1994) *De-scribing Empire: Colonialism and Textuality.* London: Routledge.
Tompkins, J. (1994a) 'Re-Orienting Australasian Drama: Staging Theatrical Irony', *ARIEL* 25:4, 117-33.
—— (1994b) 'Celebrate 1988? Australian Drama in the Bicentennial Year', *Australian and New Zealand Studies in Canada* 11, 103-112.
Tompkins J. & Holledge J., ed. (1997) *Performing Women/Performing Feminisms: Interviews with International Women Playwrights.* Brisbane: ADSA.
Travers, M. (1997) 'The Arts Crunch is Coming', *Republican* (11 April), 17.

Trinh, T. M. (1991) *When the Moon Waxes Red: Representation, Gender and Cultural Politics*. NY: Routledge.
Turcotte, G. ed. (1994) *Jack Davis: The Maker of History*. Sydney, Angus & Robertson.
Turner, G. (1994) *Making it National: Nationalism and Australian Popular Culture*. Sydney: Allen & Unwin.
Turner, J. (1992) Review of *Wild Cat Falling* adapted by Alan Becher. *ANZTR* (August), 86.
Van Toorn, P. (1995) 'Re-mediating Silence: Aboriginal Writing 1976-1963.' Paper delivered at the 'Writing Postcolonial Literary History' Conference, Deakin University, 12-14 July 1995.
Vella, M. & Richards, H. (1989) *Theatre of the Impossible: Puppet Theatre in Australia*. Sydney: Craftsman House.
Venturi, R. & Scott-Brown, D. (1972) *Learning from Las Vegas*. Cambridge, Mass: MIT Press.
Waites, J. (1995) 'Travails at the Steelworks', *Sydney Morning Herald* (28 August), 15.
Waller, R. (1993) 'Sexy is the Word', *Courier-Mail* (5 July), 7.
—— (1993) [Review of *Filling the Silence*], *Courier Mail* (27 May).
Ward, P. (1995) [Review of *Six Characters in Search of an Author*], *Australian* (3 November).
—— (1997) 'Dodging Slings and Arrows', *Australian* (22-23 March), Arts 11.
Watt, D. (1990) '"Art and Working Life": Australian Trade Unions and the Theatre', *New Theatre Quarterly* 22, 162-173.
—— (1991a) 'Interrogating "Community": Social Welfare Versus Cultural Democracy', in Binns (1991), 55-66.
—— (1991b) 'Mainstreet: Making Theatre in the Country', *Meanjin* 2/3, 219-30.
—— (1992) 'Community Theatre: A Progress Report', *ADS* 20, 3-15.
Watt, D. & Pitts, G. (1991) 'Community Theatre as Political Activism: Some Thoughts on Practice in the Australian Context', in Binns, ed. (1991), 119-133.
Way, B. & Jenkins, W. (1954) *Pinocchio*. London: Dobson.
Webb, J. ed. (1997) *Re-Siting Theatre: Approaches to Regional Theatre Development*. Rockhampton: Central Queensland UP.
Webby, E. (1990) *Modern Australian Plays*. South Melbourne: Sydney UP.
Webby, E., Love, H., Fotheringham, R. & Radic, L. (1995) 'Repertoire' in Parsons & Chance (1995), 487-494.
Wells, F. (1978) 'The Drama of Peter Kenna', *Campaign* 32 (May), 15-16, 58.
Westwood, C. (1982) 'The Women and Theatre Project 1980-81', *ADS* 1:1, 39-63.
—— (1995) 'Getting in on the Act', *Australian* 'Weekend Review' (23-24-December).
White, P. (1978) *Big Toys*. Sydney: Currency.
—— (1994) *Netherwood. Collected Plays* Vol. 2. Sydney: Currency.
Wilkie, A. (1984) 'Allan Wilkie Assembles a Shakespeare Company'. In Love (1984), 166-168.
Williams, M. (1983) *Australia on the Popular Stage 1829-1929: An Historical Entertainment in Six Acts*. Melbourne: Oxford UP.
—— (1992) *Dorothy Hewett: The Feminine as Subversion*. Sydney: Currency.
Williamson, D. (1974) *Jugglers Three*. In *Three Plays by David Williamson*. Sydney & London: Currency & Eyre Methuen, 64-135.
—— (1986) *What If You Died Tomorrow? Collected Plays* Vol. 1. Sydney: Currency.
—— (1993a) *A Handful of Friends. Collected Plays* Vol.II. Sydney: Currency.
——. (1993b) *Brilliant Lies*. Sydney: Currency.
—— (1994) *Sanctuary*. Sydney: Currency.
—— (1997) *Third World Blues*. Sydney: Currency.
Wilton, J. & Bosworth, R. (1984) *Old Worlds and New Australia: The Post-war Migrant Experience*. Ringwood, Vic.: Penguin.
Winning, F. (1993) 'Cultural Policy and Community Theatre', *ADS* 22, 73-78.
Women's Circus (1991-). *Newsletter*. Melbourne: Footscray Community Arts Centre
—— (1997) *Women's Circus: Leaping Off the Edge*. Melbourne: Spinifex.
Wyatt, S. & Steed, M. (1976) *Rare Earth: A Programme About Pollution*. London: Methuen Young Drama.
Wyndham, S. (1993) 'Angels, AIDS and an American Epic', *Weekend Australian Review* (20-21 February), 10.
Wynhausen, E. & Scott, J. (1996) 'Eye of the Storm', *Weekend Australian* (16-17 November), 27.
Yallamas, L. (1996) Review of *The Dreamers*, by Jack Davis, *Courier Mail* (3 September), 21.

Works Cited

Yang, W. (1996a) Interview on *Review* program. Australian Broadcasting Corporation Television (November).
— (1996b) *Sadness*. Sydney: Allen & Unwin.
Young, R. J. C. (1995) *Colonial Desire: Hybridity in Theory, Culture and Race*. NY: Routledge.
Zuber-Skerrit, O. ed. (1988) *David Williamson*. Amsterdam: Rodopi.

Index of proper names

1841. *See* Gow, Michael
2 Til 5 Youth Theatre 153, 156: *Rubber, Steel and Confidence* 165-166
700 Positions 101, 227

ABC. See Australian Broadcasting Commission
Aboriginal and Islander Dance Theatre 193
Aboriginal Protesters Confront the Proclamation of the Australian Republic on 26 January 2001 with a Production of 'The Commission'. *See* Mudrooroo
Acrobat 226
Acrobatic Arts Community School 157
Acropolis Now 120, 132, 137
Acting Out (TIE) 153, 160. *See also* Barking Gekko
Actrobaticus 226
Acworth, Elaine 4. *Solitary Animals* 14
Adelaide Festival 53, 99, 111, 134, 137, 139, 140, 150, 227
Adelaide Festival Centre 32, 144, 153
Adelaide Women's Theatre Group 106
Adios Cha-Cha. *See* Sidetrack
ADSA. *See* Australasian Drama Studies Association
Aftershocks. *See* Brown, Paul & WCAC
Ah Q Goes West. *See* One Extra Dance Company
Albert, Stephen 79
Albert Hall (Brisbane) 37
Alexander Theatre 155. *See also* Monash University
All of Me. *See* Legs on the Wall
All Out Ensemble 194
All Stops Out. *See* Gow, Michael
All That Flows: Out There. *See* Open City
Allan Wilkie Shakespeare Company 20
Aloise, Andrea 226
Amnesty International 199
Angels in America. *See* Kushner, Tony
Angels of Power. *See* Shotlander, Sandra
Another Country. *See* Mitchell, Julian
Antematter 226
Anthill 210. *See also* Australian Nouveau Theatre
Appetite. *See* Club Swing
Arabian Nights 154
Archer, Robyn 75, 99, 106, 149, 203; *The Pack of Women* 11; *A Star is Torn* 111
Arena Theatre Company 153, 154, 160, 163, 164, 210; *Fix It, Alice!* 162; *The Emperor's New Clothes* 164. *See also* Children's Arena Theatre
Arena Theatre Company (Llandudno) 159
Armfield, Neil 5, 7, 16, 19, 87
Arts Council (Great Britain) 20
Arts Victoria 162
As Is. *See* Hoffman, William M.
Asian Writers' Network 70
Ashton's Circus 216, 227
Ashton, Becky 216, 227
Ashton, Michelle 227
Ashton, Pepe 216, 227
Asialink 53, 54
Asia-Pacific Film Festival 53
Asia-Pacific Triennial of Contemporary Art 53
Asian Oranges. *See* Hibberd, Jack
Asian-Australian theatre festival (Playbox) 53, 54
Asian-Australian Young Playwrights' Award 54
Asian Theatre Festival (Belvoir Street). *See* Belvoir Street Asian Theatre Festival
ASSITEJ 153
Atlanta. *See* Murray-Smith, Joanna
ATTC. *See* Australian Theatre Training Conference
ATYP. *See* Australian Theatre for Young People
Australasian Drama Studies 10, 16, 149
Australasian Drama Studies Association 26
Australia Council 3, 7, 20, 22, 23, 32, 35, 53, 101, 152, 153, 154, 166, 183, 193, 208, 209, 211, 212
Australian (newspaper) 18
Australian Broadcasting Commission 56, 136, 140, 228
Australian Children's Theatre 154
Australian Dance Theatre. *Furioso* 223; *Possessed* 223
Australian National Playwrights' Centre 7
Australian Nouveau Theatre 10. *See also* Anthill
Australian Opera 21, 36. *See also* Opera Australia
Australian Performing Group 16, 105, 216
Australian Theatre Festival 140
Australian Theatre for Young People 155, 157; *Yukkety Yuk* 156
Australian Theatre Training Conference 26, 27
Away. *See* Gow, Michael

Back to Back Company 210, 227
Balodis, Janis 4, 10, 98. *My Father's Father* 130; *No Going Back* 130; *Too Young for Ghosts* 130
Bangarra Dance Theatre 146. *Ninni* 74; *Praying Mantis Dreaming* 74, 147
Barbagallo, Maria 227
Barking Gekko 160, 164. *See also* Acting Out

Barmaids. See Thomson, Katherine
Barnstorm Theatre 153, 160, 162, 209. *See also* Four's Company
Barungin. See Davis, Jack
Bauer, Ruth 228
Baxter, Virginia 223
Baylis, John 226
Beaton, Hilary 227. *No Strings Attached* 91,
Beauty and the Beast. See Holman, David
Becker, Jane 227
Belgrade Coventry TIE 159, 161, 165, 166
Bell, Christopher 133
Bell, David 220
Bell, Hilary 4, 14. *Fortune* 54
Belvoir Street Asian Theatre Festival 53, 54, 63, 67, 70
Belvoir Street Theatre 5, 7, 16, 85, 88, 100, 143, 148, 178- 181
Bennell, Eddie. *My Spiritual Dreaming* 88
Bennett, Roger 5. *Funerals and Circuses* 13, 73, 84, 86, 87
Bent Legs 226
Bent, Roxxy. *Waiting for Annette* 92; *Yellow Roses* 92
Betrothed. See Kooris in Theatre
Betty Can Jump 105
Beynon, Richard. *The Shifting Heart* 120
Bharatam Dance Company (Melbourne) 58
Bhatalaya School of Indian Classical Dance 58
Bicentenary (of Australia) 1, 2, 8, 71
Big Toys. See White, Patrick
Bidenjarreb Pinjarra 79
Bitches from Hell 199
Bizicircus 226, 227
Black Eyes. See Teck Tan
Black Sequin Dress, The. See Kemp, Jenny
Blackman Whiteman 88
Blackrock. See Enright, Nick
Blair, Ron. *The Christian Brothers* 18
Blake, Teresa 223, 228
Blanco, Raymond 193
Bleedin' Butterflies. See Clarke, Doreen
Blind Giant is Dancing, The. See Sewell, Stephen
Blind Salome. See Shotlander, Sandra
Blomfield, Thor 215
Blood and Honour. See Harding, Alex
Blood is Blue. See Da Costa, Suneeta
Blood Orange. See Death Defying Theatre
Blood Relations. See Malouf, David
Blyton, Enid. *The Magic Faraway Tree* 155; *Noddy in Toyland* 155
Boal, Augusto 197
Bobis, Merlinda. *The Cantata of the Warrior Woman Daragang Magayon* 12, 60-63, 70; *Ms Serena Serenata* 59
Boddy, Michael & Bob Ellis. *The Legend of King O'Malley* 18, 104
Body Slam. See Rock'n'Roll Circus
Bolton Octagon TIE 159
Bon Bons and Roses for Dolly. See Hewett, Dorothy
Bonner, Neokigai 78
Bosworth, Michael 148
Bouverie St TIE 160, 161, 162
Bovell, Andrew 4
Bowden Brompton Youth Circus. *See* Cirkidz
Bower, Ros 208
Bran Nue Dae. See Chi, Jimmy
Brand, Mona 105
Branded. See Corrugated Iron
Bray, Erroll 156, 157, 158
Bread Trap, The. See Kalamaras, Vasso
Brilliant Lies. See Williamson, David
Brink 226
Brisbane Biennial International Music Festival 142
Brisbane Festival 88
Broadway, Sue 217, 227
Broinowswki, Adam 228
Broinowski, Anna. *The Gap* 54, 70
Brolgas (TIE) 160. *See also* Roadworks
Brook, Peter. *Mahabharata* 191
Brown, Paul & WCAC. *Aftershocks* 7, 16, 17, 168-181
Brumby Innes. See Prichard, Katharine Susannah
Brunswick: The Musical. See O'Connell, Geoffrey
Burger Brain: The Fast Food Musical. See Watkins, Dennis & Chris Harriott
Burnett, Frances Hodgson 154
Burnt Wedding, The. See Sydney Front
Burying Mother. See Thorne, Mémé
Buzo, Alex 4, 10, 105

Cabaret Erratica 227
Cabral, Gabriela 186, 194
Cafe Hakawati. See Death Defying Theatre
Caffè Teatro. See Doppio Teatro
Cage, John 189
Call of the Wild. See Kemp, Jenny
Cameron Mackintosh organisation 31
Campbelltown Youth Action Group 144
Campo, Valeria 145
Canada Council 20
Canberra Youth Theatre, 12, 54, 153, 156
Canberra Youth Wind Ensemble 12, 54
Cantata of the Warrior Woman Daragang Magayon, The. See Bobis, Merlinda

Capricornia. See Nowra, Louis
Carclew Youth Arts Centre 153, 166
Carlin, David 154, 163, 164
Carnivale (Sydney) 54, 131, 143
Carousel 31
Carouselle (TIE), 164
Casella, Antonella 217
Cassidy Album, The. See Kenna, Peter
Cathcart, Sarah 203
Cathcart, Sarah & Andrea Lemon 112, 203. *The Serpent's Fall* 111, 130; *Tiger Country* 111; *Walking on Sticks* 112
Catherine. See Shearer, Jill
Cece. See Pirandello, Luigi
Celluloid Heroes. See Williamson, David
Chan, Kai Tai 58, 59
Chandabhanu 58
Chapel Perilous, The. See Hewett, Dorothy
Chaplin, Angela 76
Chaplin, Charlie 63
Chapman, Roger 160, 165
Charlton, Peter & Bill Just. *Cosmé* 158
Cheery Soul, A. See White, Patrick
Cherry Pickers, The. See Gilbert, Kevin
Cheeseman, Peter 181
Chi, Jimmy, 5. *Bran Nue Dae* 13, 18, 73, 81, 82, 84, 87; *Corrugation Road* 84
Chicago, Chicago. See Romeril, John
Childermas. See Keneally, Thomas
Children's Arena Theatre 159-160. *See also* Arena Theatre Company
Chin Kham Yoke. *Inflamed* 59
China Diary. See Yang, William
Christian Brothers, The. See Blair, Ron
Christian, Beatrix 4. *The Governor's* Family 14
Chronicles of Macbeth, The. See Suzuki, Tadashi
Churchill, Caryl. *Mad Forest* 143
Cianciulli, Leonarda 143
Ciccatosto, Emma & Michael Bosworth. *Emma: A Translated Life* 110, 147
Cinderella 154
Circus Archaos 220
Circus Oz 5, 18, 194, 197, 210, 217, 226, 227
Circus Under the Tin Top. See Rock'n'Roll Circus
Cirkidz 156-157
Ciszewska, Barbara 163
Civic Playhouse (Newcastle) 170
Clarke, Doreen. *Bleedin' Butterflies* 109; *Farewell Brisbane Ladies* 109
Clarkson, David 226
Clemente, Rosalba 113, 143, 148
Close to the Bone. See Manning, Ned
cLUB bENT 93
Club Swing 18, 220, 226. *Appetite* 218-219, 221
Coassin, Cinzia 145
Cockpit TIE (London) 159, 164
Coco Youth Theatre 156
Coffin, Lorrae 228
Cold Harvest. See Janaczewska, Noëlle
Collie, Therese 79, 80, 95
Come Out youth theatre festival 135, 153
Commitment. See Hibberd, Jack
Composto-Eberhard, Josie 137
Companion to Theatre in Australia 9, 10, 92-93, 94
Competitive Tenderness. See Rayson, Hannie
Conigrave, Timothy 5. *Holding the Man* 100-101
Connelli, Judy 91
Consiglio, Paolo 145
Contact Youth Theatre 156
Contemporary Performance Week 192
Conversations with Charlie. See Ta Duy Binh
Copeman, Peter. *Hearts and Minds* 12, 39-40, 51, 54; *Sinakulo* 54
Copping it Sweet 71
Coppola, Guido 145
Corrugated Iron (Youth Theatre) 156; *Branded* 165
Corrugation Road. See Chi, Jimmy
Così. See Nowra, Louis
Cosmé. See Charlton, Peter & Bill Just
Cotton, Julia 226, 227
Coustas, Mary 137
Craigie, Cathy & Therese Collie. *Murri Love* 79, 80, 95
Crea, Teresa 15, 133-152. *Windows* 144
Crichton, Pat 158
Crome 226
Crosswinds Theatre in the Community 160, 162
Crow. See Nowra, Louis
Crowley, Anthony & Luke Devenish. *Vincent* 158
Cult of Dionysus, The. See Zen Zen Zo
Currency Press 9, 157
Curtis, Penelope. *A Time to Kill* 39, 41
Curtis, Stephen 226
Cusack, Dymphna. *Morning Sacrifice* 105
Custodians, The. See Earley, Eric

Da Costa, Suneeta. *Blood is Blue* 59
Dahl, Roald 154
Daily Grind. See Reynolds, Vicki
Dallas, Helen 194
Daly, Timothy 4
Danceworks 211
Dark, The. See Rock'n'Roll Circus
Darwin Theatre Company 35
Darwin Theatre Group 39, 51
Davis, Jack 4, 9, 10, 88. *Barungin* 71, 73; *The Dreamers* 87; *First Born*

Trilogy 71, 88; *Kullark* 82; *No Sugar* 18; *Wahngin Country* 83, 86
Davy, Anni 218, 219
Dawson, Steven. *The Gathering of Vampires* 94
Daylight Saving. *See* Enright, Nick
de Castro, Angela 203
De Groen, Alma 4, 10, 14, 18, 112, 116. *The Girl Who Saw Everything* 108; *Going Home* 108; *The Rivers of China* 2, 97, 108; *Vocations* 108
Dead City. *See* Jose, Nicholas
Dead Heart. *See* Parsons, Nicholas
Death: The Musical. *See* Women's Circus
Death Defying Theatre 92, 133. *Blood Orange* 16; *Cafe Hakawati* 16
Deceit. See *Nowra, Louis*
Deck Chair Theatre 7, 88, 148
Desoxy 225, 226. *A Vulgar Ear* 223, 228
Devenish, Luke 158
di Cesare, Eva 143
Dickens, Charles. *Great Expectations* 214
Difficult Women. *See* Van Hek, Linn
Dimboola. *See* Hibberd, Jack
Dimech, Mary 120
Diving for Pearls. *See* Thomson, Katherine
Dobson, Dennis 160
Don Juan. *See* Sydney Front
Don's Party. *See* Williamson, David
Doppio Teatro 6, 7, 15, 110, 133-151. *Caffè Teatro* 137; *Il Cabaret dell' emigrante* 134-135; *Eremophilia: Pulcinella* 145-146; *Una festa di nozze* 140-144; *Just Call Me Jo* 135; *Love and Magic in Mamma's* Kitchen 143-144, 145; *La Madonna emigrante* 135-137, 139; *Naso bello, naso brutto* 140; *The Olive Tree* 139; *Pane e cipolla* 145; *Peppino* 139; *Preludes to an Exile* 150; *Presepio vivente* 137; *Un pugno di terra* 135; *Ricordi* 137-139, 141, 147; *Tinto di rosso* 140; *Le voci del silenzio (Filling the Silence)* 142, 150
Doyle, Matthew 88
Draffin, Robert 227
Dreamers, The. *See* Davis, Jack
Drink the Mercury 161
Drunken Boat. *See* Sidetrack
Dust Off Vietnam 39, 51

Eager Hope, An. *See* Kenna, Peter
Earley, Eric. *The Custodians* 79
Earth 226
Edinburgh Festival 218
Einstein on the Beach. *See* Wilson, Robert & John Cage
Elisha, Ron 4
Ellis, Bob 18 104
Ellis, Lois 113
Elston, Glenn 155
Embassy 56-57
Emerald City. *See* Williamson, David
Emerald Room, The. *See* Watkins, Dennis & Chris Harriott
Emma. *See* Pitts, Graham
Emma: A Translated Life. *See* Ciccatosto, Emma & Michael Bosworth
Emperor Regrets, The. *See* Radic, Therese
Emperor's New Clothes, The. *See* Arena Theatre Company
Enoch, Wesley 5, 87
Enoch, Wesley & Deborah Mailman. *The Seven Stages of Grieving* 8, 18, 83-84, 222
Enright, Nick 10, 13, 18, 166. *Blackrock* 6, 7; *Daylight Saving* 90; *Good Works* 89, 90, 100; *Mongrels* 4, 90, 101; *Playgrounds* 91, 101; *A Property of the Clan* 7, 90, 165; *The Quartet from Rigoletto* 90-91; *St James' Infirmary* 42, 48, 51-52, 90
Ensemble Theatre 92, 101
Entr'acte 54
Entwistle, Edwina 226
Eora Centre (Redfern) 79
Eremophilia: Pulcinella. *See* Doppio Teatro *and* Gatti, Elio
Esson, Louis 9
Etcetera 226-227. *In Which Case* 215-216
Evans, Ken 226
Exbendable. *See* Legs on the Wall
Export Oz 53

Face of Buddha, The. See Yang, William
Falling From Grace. *See* Rayson, Hannie
Family Portrait. *See* One Extra Dance Company
Fantin, Francesco 140
Farewell Brisbane Ladies. *See* Clarke, Doreen
Farr, Ian 226
FCAC. *See* Footscray Community Arts Centre
Federal Theatre (USA) 180
Festival of Australian Theatre 148
Festival of Contemporary Arts 166
Festival of Perth 104, 158, 193
FILEF 132, 138, 140
Filiki Players 132, 138
Filling the Silence. *See* Doppio Teatro
First and Final Warning. *See* Sydney Front
First Born Trilogy, The. *See* Davis, Jack
Fischer, Gerhard 73
Fischer, Margaret. *The Gay Divorcee* 92, 101; *Home Sweet* Home 144; *Wanted* 101 144

Fischer, Michael 121
Fitzroy Town Hall 88
Fix It Alice! See Arena Theatre Company
Flash Rat Company 106
Flinders University 26, 133
Floating World, The. See Romeril, John
Flores, Hernan 186, 194
Flying Ashtons 227
Flying Fruit Fly Circus 153, 159, 167, 197, 210, 217, 226, 227
FM Live 153. *On the Rocks* 162
Footscray Community Arts Centre 195, 203, 210-211
For Coloured Girls Who Have Considered Suicide When the Rainbow is Enuf. See Shange, Ntozake
Forth, Sally 201, 203, 227
Fortune. See Bell, Hilary
Forty Lounge Cafe, The. See Lyssiotis, Tes
Foundation South Australia 162
Four's Company 160. *See also* Barnstorm Theatre
Framework. See Shotlander, Sandra
Franceschi, Vincenzo. *L'innocente* 133-134
Freer, Wayne 226, 227
Freewheels TIE 7, 1534, 160, 164, 165, 166
Fright. See Sidetrack
Frontier Stories. See Sidetrack
Frumpus 226
Funerals and Circuses. See Bennett, Roger
Furioso. See Australian Dance Theatre
Furious. See Gow, Michael
Furtive Love. See Kenna, Peter
Future Tense. See Sidetrack

Gaal, Mark 157
Gaiety of Nations, The. See Seymour, Alan
Gallasch, Keith 145, 146, 150, 223
Gambit Youth Theatre 156
Gap, The. See Broinowski, Anna
Garbutt, Russell 226, 227
Gathering of Vampires, The. See Dawson, Stephen
Gatti, Elio. *Eremophilia: Pulcinella* 145
Gay and Lesbian Mardi Gras Festival. *See* Sydney Gay and Lesbian Mardi Gras Festival
Gay *Divorcee, The. See* Fischer, Margaret
Gay Theatre Company 93, 94
General, The. See Radic, Leonard
Geography of Haunted Places, The. See Hefferon, Erin
George, Emma 227
George, Rob. *Sandy Lee Live at Nui Dat* 41, 42, 49, 50, 51
Gibbs, May. *Snugglepot and Cuddlepie* 155
Gibson, Sophia 226
Gilbert, Kevin. *The Cherry Pickers* 80-81
Giles, Mike. *Rest and Recreation* 41
Gillot, Venetia 144
Ginivan, Garry 155
Girl Who Saw Everything, The. See De Groen, Alma
Girl with a Stone in Her Shoe, The. See Open City
Gladwin, Neill 5, 164, 226
Glass Mermaid, The. See Learner, Tobsha
Glen Street Theatre 226
Goh Chok Tong 69
Going Home. See De Groen, Alma
Golden Age, The. See Nowra, Louis
Golden Valley. See Hewett, Dorothy
Good Works. See Enright, Nick.
Gordon Frost organisation 31
Gorman, Clem. *A Manual of Trench Warfare* 96
Gorman, Peter 88
Governor's Family, The. See Christian, Beatrix
Gow, Michael 4, 9, 10, 13, 18, 95, 158; *1841* 2, 71; *All Stops* Out 157; *Away* 4, 18, 42; *Furious* 89-90, 91, 100, 101, 102; *The Kid* 2, 89; *Live Acts on Stage* 90
Grahame, Kenneth. *Wind in the Willows* 155
Grant, Clare 226
Gray, Oriel. *The Torrents* 105
Great Expectations. See Dickens, Charles
Great Moscow Circus 157
Greenwich Bowsprit TIE (London) 159
Griffin Theatre 101
Griffiths, Sophie 227
Grommitts. See Lette, Cathy
Guangzhou Acrobatic Company 157
Gunzburg, Darrelyn. *Water From the Well* 144
Gurr, Michael, 4. *Sex Diary of an Infidel* 54, 99, 130

Hall, Radcliffe. *The Well of Loneliness* 113
Ham *Funeral, The. See* White, Patrick
Hamlet. See Shakespeare, William
Handful of Friends, A. See Williamson, David
Handspan Theatre Company 152, 213, 226. *Lunatic Soup* 162; *We Repeat Ourselves* 162
Hanusiak, Xenia 228
Hard God, A. See Kenna, Peter
Harding, Alex, 5. *Blood and Honour* 13, 99-100; *Only Heaven Knows* 92
Harding, John 5

Hardy, Sara. 95. *Vita! A Fantasy* 91, 113
Hardy, Sara & Adele Saleem. *Radclyffe* 95, 113
Harmer, Wendy 111
Harpies Bizarre 226
Harriott, Chris 43, 91, 157
Hate. See Sewell, Stephen
Hatzimanolis, Adam 186, 188, 194
Havir, Michael 78
Healthway 162
Hearts and Minds. See Copeman, Peter
Heaven. See Sidetrack
Hefferon, Erin. *The Geography of Haunted Places* 8
Helpmann Academy 27
Here! Now! See Pitts, Graham
Hewett, Dorothy 4, 10, 14, 18, 98, 112, 116, 165. *Bon Bons and Roses for Dolly* 106, 107; *The Chapel Perilous* 106, 107-108; *Golden Valley* 164; *Joan* 107; *The Man from Mukinupin* 18; *Song of the Seals* 164; *The Tatty Hollow Story* 106-107
Hewett, Robert 4
Hibberd, Jack 4, 6, 10, 13, 18, 98, 99, 105, 141, 198. *Asian Oranges* 43; *Commitment* 40, 43, 49-50; *Dimboola* 141
High Society 31
High Vaultage (UK) 227
History of Water, The. See Janaczewska, Noëlle
Hodgson, John 155
Hoffman, William M. *As Is* 103
Holding the Man. See Conigrave, Timothy
Hole in the Wall 102
Holman, David 163. *Beauty and the Beast* 164; *No Worries* 164; *The Small Poppies* 164
Home Cooking Theatre Company 106
Home Sweet Home. See Fischer, Margaret
Honour. See Murray-Smith, Joanna
Hopgood, Alan, *Private Yuk Objects* 12, 38, 39, 42, 44-46, 49, 51
Hotel Sorrento. See Rayson, Hannie
How Does Your Garden Grow? See McNeil, Jim
Hunter Valley Theatre Company 170
Hunting Party 226

Icarus 226
Ilbijeri 71
Il cabaret dell'emigrante. See Doppio Teatro
Il pane e le rose. See Randozzo, Nino
In Cahoots 164
In the Pink Theatre Company 93
In the Winter Garden. See Janaczewska, Noëlle
In Which Case. See Etcetera
Inflamed. See Chih Kham Yoke
Industry Advisory Boards 37
Ingleton, Sue 106. *Near Ms's* 111
International Radio Festival (New York) 136
International Women Playwrights' Conference 131
International Year of Indigenous Peoples 71, 78
Is That You Nancy? See Shotlander, Sandra
Italian Folk Ensemble 140
Italo-Australian Theatre Company 132, 136
Ives, Derek 227

Jabo, Sawung. *Time's Journey* 59
Jacaranda Blue. See One Extra Dance Company
Jackson, Donna 195, 197, 199, 201, 202-203, 207, 217
Jamieson, Nigel 225
Janaczewska, Noëlle 150. *Cold Harvest* 120, 121-129, 131; *The History of Water* 54; *In the Winter Garden* 15; *Madagascar Lily* 54; *Yungaburra Road* 92
Jane Street 106
Janson, Julie. *Lotus War* 54
Japan-Australia Cultural Exchange Programme 19
J.C. Williamson (organisation) 30
Jellicoe, Ann 197. *TheRising Generation* 156
Jenkins, Warren 159
Jigsaw Theatre Company 153, 160, 164, 167
Jigsaws. See Rogers, Jennifer
Joan. See Hewett, Dorothy
John Curtin Youth Theatre 166
John, Rosemary. *Luck of the Draw* 40, 41, 42, 50-51
Johnson, Eva 5. *Murras*, 71; *What Do They Call Me?* 81, 96
Jones, Bill T. *Still/Here* 103
Joo-For Lee, John, *The Propitious Kidnapping of the Cultured Daughter* 58
Jose, Nicholas. *Dead City* 59
Joss Adams Show, The. See De Groen, Alma
Journey, The. See Lyssiotis, Tes
Joyride. See Zeal Theatre
Jugglers Three. See Williamson, David
Jungle, The. See Nowra, Louis
Just, Bill 158
Just Call Me Jo. See Doppio Teatro

Kabuki 73, 109
Kalamaras, Vasso, *The Bread Trap* 131
Keene, Daniel 4
Keepers, The. See Maza, Bob
Kellaway, Nigel 193, 226
Kelly, Gail 218, 220-221, 227

Kemp, Jenny 113, 203. *The Black Sequin Dress* 11-112; *Call of the Wild* 111-112; *Remember* 111-112; *The White Hotel* 111-112
Keneally, Thomas, *Childermas* 42, 43-44
Kenna, Peter 90, 95. *The Cassidy Album* 90, 101; *An Eager Hope* 101; *Furtive Love* 101; *A Hard God* 18, 95, 102; *Mates* 95
Keyes, Beth 214
Kid, The. See Gow, Michael
King and I, The 32
Kingham, Mike 158
Kirby, Margaret. *My Body, My Blood* 112
Kirkby, Emma 33
Kite (TIE) 161
Knee-High 226
Knox, Moira 218
Kooemba Jdarra Indigenous Theatre 7, 8, 71, 80, 82, 87, 222
Kooris in Theatre 71. *Betrothed* 83
Kosky, Barrie 6, 104
Kramer, Larry. *The Normal Heart* 103
Kreckler, Derek 193
Kuckles 73
Kullark. See Davis, Jack
Kummara Aboriginal Theatre Restaurant 87
Kurzer, Edie 85
Kushner, Tony. *Angels in America* 17, 97

L'innocente. See Pensa, Carlo Maria
La Boite Theatre 91, 101, 148
La Boite Youth Theatre 153, 156
La Madonna emigrante. See Doppio Teatro
La Mama 95
Lamb of God. See Summons, John
Langford, Barney 156
Lattuada, Laura 143, 145
Laurie, Robyn 194, 203, 218
Lawford, Josie Ningali. *See* Ningali Lawford, Josie
Lawler, Ray. *Summer of the Seventeenth Doll* 18, 98
Lecoq Mime School (Paris) 29
Le Gioie delle Donne (film) 131
Le Gioie delle Donne (choir) 148
Le voci del silenzio. See Doppio Teatro
Leapers 226
Leaping Loonies 226
Leaping The Wire. See Women's Circus
Learner, Tobsha 4, 14, 112, 116. *The Glass Mermaid* 113; *Mistress* 113; *Seven Acts of Love (As Witnessed by a Cat)* 114; *Quiver: A Book of Erotic Tales* 114; *SNAG* 113; *Witchplay* 113; *Wolf* 113-114
Lee Kuan Yew 69
Leeds Playhouse TIE 160
Leeming Youth Theatre 158, 166
Legend of King O'Malley, The. See Boddy, Michael & Bob Ellis
Legs on the Wall 18, 220, 225, 226. *Exbendable* 215; *All of Me* 225
Lemon, Andrea 111, 112, 130, 203
Lenza, Rosemary 148
Les Misérables 30
Leslie, Michael 78, 87
Lette, Kathy. *Gromitts* 157
Liebmann, Adrienne 203
Lindsay, Norman. *The Magic Pudding* 155
L'innocente. See Pensa, Carlo Maria
Littlewood, Joan 180
Living Newspaper (USA) 180
Live Acts on Stage. See Gow, Michael
Livermore, Reg. *Red Riding Hood, the Speed Hump and the Wolf* 92
Lloyd Webber, Andrew 30
Lloyd, Belinda 228
Lorenzin, Max 144
Los Trios Ringbarkus 164
Lotus War. See Janson, Julie
Love and Magic in Mamma's Kitchen. See Wertmuller, Lina *and* Doppio Teatro
Love Child. See Murray-Smith, Joanna
Lowdown 166
Lowe, Barry 93, 95. *Tokyo Rose* 41
Lu Guang Rong 217
Luck of the Draw. See John, Rosemary
Lunatic Soup. See Handspan
Lycos, Tom 194
Lyssa, Alison. *Pinball* 91
Lyssiotis, Tes 4, 131, 132. *The Forty Lounge Cafe* 110; *The Journey* 110, 138; *A White Sports Coat* 110

Mad Forest. See Churchill, Caryl
Madagascar Lily. See Janaczewska, Noëlle
Madame Mao. See Radic, Therese
Magic Faraway Tree, The. See Blyton, Enid
Magic Pudding, The. Se Lindsay, Norman
Magpie theatre company 153, 160, 164. *Verona* 5, 16, 164-165, 226
Mahabharata. See Brook, Peter
Mailman, Deborah 5, 8, 78, 82, 222
(M)alice 101
Malino, Catia 226
Malouf, David 98. *Blood Relations* 2
Mamouney, Don 182, 189, 191, 192, 193
Man from Mukinupin, The. See Hewett, Dorothy
Manning, Barbara 160
Manning, Ned. *Close to the Bone* 79
Mansfield, Katherine 108
Manual of Trench Warfare. See Gorman, Clem
Martin, Karen 203

Mastrantone, Lucia 135, 137, 140, 141, 142, 145
Mates. See Kenna, Peter
Mayhem Youth Theatre festival 137
Maza, Bob. *The Keepers* 71
McCaughey, James 154
McColl, Ewen 180
McCormick, Emily 226
McDonald, Meme 203
McGregor, Brent 170
McHenry, Jai 194
McNeil, Jim. *How Does Your Garden Grow?* 90; *The Old Familiar Juice* 90
Measure, The. See Sidetrack
Melbourne Comedy Festival 120
Melbourne Italian Arts Festival 132
Melbourne Theatre Company 27, 31, 32, 98
Melbourne Women's Theatre Group 105, 210
Melbourne Workers' Theatre 110, 138, 143, 210
Menon, Padma. *Relations: Of Mothers, Aunts and Other Memories* 59
Meyerhold, Vsevolod 201, 227
Midnight Youth Theatre 166
Midsumma Festival (Melbourne) 93
Midsummer Night's Dream, A. See Shakespeare, William
Miles, Maggie. *Branded* 165
Mill Theatre 209
Miller, Lydia 78
Mills, Hayley 32
Mimi. See Stalker Stilt Theatre
Mineur, Rudi 220, 227
Miss Haversham's Dream. See Theatre Physical
Miss Saigon 30
Mistress. See Learner, Tobsha
Mitchell, Julian, *Another Country* 102
Monash University 26. *See also* Alexander Theatre
Mongrels. See Enright, Nick
Moomba Festival (Melbourne) 199
Moore, John 79
Morgan, Sally. *Sistergirl* 80, 85
Morgillo, Antonietta 135, 136, 137, 139, 143
Morning Sacrifice. See Cusack, Dymphna
Morris, Mary 227. *Two Weeks With the Queen* 92; *All of Me* 225-226
Mother Tongue Interference. See Pollard, Deborah
Ms Serena Serenata. See Bobis, Merlinda
MTC. *See* Melbourne Theatre Company
Mudrooroo 88. *The Aboriginal Protesters* (etc*)* 73; *Wild Cat Falling* 81
Multicultural Theatre Alliance 133, 138
Müller, Heiner 73
Murras. See Johnson, Eva
Murray River Performing Group 157, 210
Murray, Peta 4, 14. *One Woman's Song* 78; *Wallflowering* 115
Murray-Smith, Joanna 4, 14. *Atlanta* 115; *Honour* 115; *Love Child* 114-115
Murri Love. See Craigie, Cathy & Therese Collie
Museum of Accidents, The. See Open City
Mushroom Troupe 209
My Body, My Blood. See Kirby, Margaret
My Father's Father. See Balodis, Janis
My Spiritual Dreaming. See Bennell, Eddie

Naked Gun, The. See Reade, Harry
Nancarrow, Brett 226
Nanjing Acrobatic Troupe 157, 217
Nantsou, Stefo 186, 194
Napier Street Theatre 228
Naso Bello Naso Brutto. See Doppio Teatro
National Institute of Dramatic Art 26, 27, 29, 36
National Script Centre. *See also* Salamanca National Script Centre
National Theatre, Perth. *See* Western Australian Theatre Company
Native Title Act 71
Naturals 226
Near Ms's. See Ingleton, Sue
Netherwood. See White, Patrick
Nevin, Robyn 98, 106
Newcastle Trades Hall Council 168, 170
Newcastle Workers' Club 168, 170-180
Newman, Guy 227
News of the World 218
Next Wave Festival 153
NIDA. *See* National Institute of Dramatic Art
Niesche, Kathryn 218
Night on Bald Mountain. See White, Patrick
Nimrod Theatre 91, 92, 106, 154, 210
Ningali. See Ningali Lawford, Josie
Ningali Lawford, Josie 13, 111. *Ningali* 76, 81, 83, 87
Ninni. See Bangarra Dance Theatre
No Condom, No Start. See Sidetrack
No Going Back. See Balodis, Janis
Noh 73, 109
No Strings Attached. See Beaton, Hilary
No Sugar. See Davis, Jack
No Worries. See Holman, David
Noddy in Toyland. See Blyton, Enid
Normal Heart, The. See Kramer, Larry
NORPA. *See* Northern and Regional Performing Arts Association
North, The. See Yang, William

Northern and Regional Performing Arts Association 32, 33
Norwood Concert Hall 145, 226
Nowra, Louis 2, 4, 5, 6, 9, 10, 13, 18, 19, 98, 129. *Capricornia* 71, 79; *Così* 6, 39, 42, 49; *Crow* 79; *Deceit* 103; *The Golden Age* 130, *The Jungle* 5, 90, 103; *The Price of Prayer* 103; *Radiance* 6, 79, 130; *Summer of the Aliens* 130; *Sunrise* 51

O'Brien, Simone 218
O'Connell, Geoffrey. *Brunswick: The Musical* 158
Oates, Kareena 217, 220, 227
Offord, Colin 8, 88
Ofria, Silvio 140, 194
Old Familiar Juice, The. See McNeil, Jim
Olive Tree, The. See Doppio Teatro
Oliver, Stephen 228
Olympic Games (Atlanta) 97; (Berlin) 202
On the Rocks. See FM Live
One Day of the Year, The. See Seymour, Alan
One Woman's Song. See Murray, Peta
One Extra Dance Company. *Ah Q Goes West* 58; *Family Portrait* 58; *Jacaranda Blue* 58; *Othello* 58; *People Like Us* 58; *Two Wongs* 58
Only Heaven Knows. See Harding, Alex
Oodgeroo (Noonuccal) 78
Open City 18, 223. *All That Flows: Out There* 228; *The Girl With the Stone in Her Shoe* 228; *The Museum of Accidents* 228; *Photo Play* 228; *Promiscuous Spaces: Mondo Lingo* 228; *Sense* 228; *Shop and the Necessary Orgy* 228; *Tokyo/Now/Thriller* 228; *Tokyo Two* 228
Opera Australia 21
Orientalia. See Sussman, Sally
Othello. See Shakespeare, William *and* One Extra Dance Company
Oxford Children's Theatre 155
Oxford Playhouse Team 159

Pack of Women, The. See Archer, Robyn
Pact Youth Theatre 133, 156
Page, Stephen 87
Palmer, Vance 9
Pane e cipolla. See Doppio Teatro
Panozzo, Dina. *Varda che Bruta ... Poretta* 15, 120, 121-129, 131, 143
Papademetriou, Nicholas 140, 148
Parker, Brett 227
Parker, Trina 163, 226
Parr, Mike 13, 194
Parsons, Nicholas. *Dead Heart* 6, 79, 82-83, 85
Parsons, Philip 92
Party Line 220, 226
Passion. See Sydney Front
Patch Theatre 153, 164
Pearce, Jill 228
Pearls Before Swine. See Watkins, Dennis & Chris Harriott
Peking Opera 193
Pell, Kelton 79
Pensa, Carlo Maria. *L'innocente* 133
People Like Us. See One Extra Dance Company
Peppino. See Doppio Teatro
Performance Space 95, 184, 225, 226
Performing Older Women 207
Perkins, Elizabeth. *A Squeaking of Rats* 48-49
Perth Playhouse 107
Perry, Dein 7
Perth Institute of Contemporary Arts 8
Phoenix (theatre company) 17
Photo Play. See Open City
Pigarm, Darlisa 228
Pinball. See Lyssa, Alison
Pinocchio 139, 154, 155, 159
Pirandello, Luigi. *Cece* 133; *Six Characters in Search of an Author* 144-145
Pitts, Graham. *Emma* 7, 110, 148-149; *Here! Now!* 158
Plane Truth — A Show About an Airport and Other Low Flying Acts. See Sidetrack
Playbox Theatre 19, 53, 54, 58, 91, 102, 113, 116, 148, 154
Playgrounds. See Enright, Nick
Playing With Time Festival 114
Playlab 7
Playworks 7, 109, 116
Pollack, Linsey 138, 142
Pollard, Deborah. *Mother Tongue Interference* 54, 69
Polyglot Puppet Theatre 164
Pope, Deborah 227
Popular Theatre Troupe 16
Pornography of Performance. See Sydney Front
Port Youth Theatre 156
Porter, Cole 30
Possessed. See Australian Dance Theatre
Post Arrivalists 226
Powerhouse Youth Theatre 156
Pram Factory 216
Praying Mantis Dreaming. See Bangarra Dance Theatre
Precarious 217, 227
Preludes to an Exile. See Doppio Teatro
Presepio Vivente. See Doppio Teatro
Price of Prayer, The. See Nowra, Louis
Prichard, Katharine Susannah, *Brumby Innes* 18, 105

Priscilla - Queen of the Desert 70
Private Yuk Objects. See Hopgood, Alan
Promiscuous Spaces: Mondo Lingo. See Open City
Property of the Clan, A. See Enright, Nick.
Propitious Kidnapping of the Cultured Daughter, The. See Joo-For Lee, John
Public Lending Right 21

Q Theatre 102
QTC. *See* Queensland Theatre Company.
Quartet from Rigoletto, The. See Enright, Nick
Queensland Cultural Centre 31, 32, 37
Queensland Performing Arts Trust 37
Queensland Philharmonic Orchestra 36
Queensland Theatre Company 27, 31, 32, 36, 37, 78, 106
Queensland Theatre Summit 96
Queensland University of Technology 26, 27
Qui tutto bene. See Franceschi, Vincenzo
Quiver: A Book of Erotic Tales. See Learner, Tobsha
QUT. *See* Queensland Institute of Technology

Radclyffe. See Hardy, Sara & Adele Saleem
Radiance. See Nowra, Louis.
Radic, Leonard. *The General* 42; *Sideshow* 42
Radic, Therese. *The Emperor Regrets* 109; *Madame Mao* 109, 227
Radikal Thesbian Theatre Company 96
Randazzo, Nino, 132. *Il pane e le rose* 136
RaRazo (UK) 227
Rare Earth 161
Rayner, Joan and Betty 154
Rayson, Hannie 4, 14, 114. *Competitive Tenderness* 115; *Falling from Grace* 115; *Hotel Sorrento* 6, 115
Reade, Harry. *The Naked Gun* 42, 50
Readman, Mark. *Rubber, Steel and Confidence* 165-166
Rebound Acrobat 226
Red Riding Hood, the Speed Hump and the Wolf. See Livermore, Reg
Red Shed 164
Regan, Bernadette 215
Relations: Of Mothers, Aunts and Other Memories. See Menon, Padma
Remember. See Kemp, Jenny
Removalists, The. See Williamson, David
Rest and Recreation. See Giles, Mike
Return, The. See Ta Duy Binh
Reynolds, Vicki. *Daily Grind* 110
Richards, Ernest 155
Ricordi. See Doppio Teatro
Rising Generation, The. See Jellicoe, Ann
Rivers of China, The. See De Groen, Alma
Roadworks (TIE) 160. *See also* Brolgas
Robert Lepage company (Canada) 194
Robin Hood 154
Robins, Gavin 215
Rock 'n' Roll Circus 6, 18, 99, 197, 217, 225, 226, 227. *Body Slam* 220; *Circus Under the Tin Top* 220; *The Dark* 99, 220, 221
Rodgers and Hammerstein 30
Rogers, Jennifer. *Jigsaws* 96, 102
Roland, Betty. *The Touch of Silk* 18, 120
Romeo and Juliet. See Shakespeare, William.
Romeril, John 4, 10. *Chicago, Chicago* 42; *The Floating World* 18, 19, 109
Royal National Theatre (UK) 31
Royal Shakespeare Company (UK) 24, 31
Rubber, Steel and Confidence. See Readman, Mark
Run For Your Wife 22
Russell, Carlos 226, 227
Ryan, Chris 226

Sadness. See Yang, William
Salamanca National Script Centre 153, 166. *See also* National Script Centre
Salamanca Theatre Company 71, 153, 160, 164
Saleem, Adele 95
Sanctuary. See Williamson, David
Sandy Lee Live at Nui Dat. See George, Rob
Sato, Makato 19
SBS Television 144
Season at Sarsaparilla, The. See White, Patrick
Secret Garden, The 32
Sedgwick, Katrina 226, 227
Self-Raising Theatre 164
Sense. See Open City
Serpent's Fall, The. See Cathcart, Sarah & Andrea Lemon
Seven Acts of Love (As Witnessed by a Cat). See Learner, Tobsha
Seven Stages of Grieving, The. See Enoch, Wesley & Deborah Mailman
Sewell, Stephen 2, 4, 9, 10, 18. *The Blind Giant is Dancing* 42; *Hate* 5, 71
Sex Diary of an Infidel. See Gurr, Michael
Seymour, Alan. *The Gaiety of Nations* 42; *The One Day of the Year* 18
SGLMG. *See* Sydney Gay and Lesbian Mardi Gras

Shakespeare, William 7, 37. *Hamlet* 5; *A Midsummer Night's Dream* 96; *Othello* 58; *Romeo and Juliet* 157, 164; *The Tempest* 87; *Twelfth Night* 79
Shange, Ntozake. *For Coloured Girls Who Have Considered Suicide When the Rainbow is Enuf* 138
Sharman, Jim 19
Shaw, George Bernard 2
She (magazine) 211
Shearer, Jill 4, 14. *Catherine* 109; *Shimada* 54, 109
Shifting Heart, The. *See* Beynon, Richard
Shimada. *See* Shearer, Jill
Shop and The Necessary Orgy. *See* Open City
Shopfront Theatre for Young People 156
Shotlander, Sandra 95, 111, 112, 115. *Angels of Power* 113; *Blind Salome* 113; *Framework* 92, 113; Is *That You, Nancy?* 92, 102
Sideshow. *See* Radic, Leonard
Sidetrack Theatre Company 6, 17, 132, 138, 140, 152, 182-194. *Adios Cha-Cha* 185-188; *Drunken Boat* 191; *Fright* 193; *Frontier Stories* 193; *Future Tense* 193; *Heaven* 189; *The Measure* 190; *No Condom, No Start* 192-193; *Plane Truth - A Show About an Airport and Other Low Flying Acts* 193; *sit.com* 193; *Whispers in the Heart* 182, 185
Sidetrack Performance Group 182-194 *passim*
Silver's Circus 227
Silvio D'Amico Accademia Nazionale dell'Arte 133
Sinakulo. *See* Copeman, Peter
Singapore Arts Festival 141
Sista-web 226
Sistergirl. *See* Morgan, Sally
sit.com. *See* Sidetrack
Six Characters in Search of an Author. *See* Pirandello, Luigi
Skids. *See* St Martin's
Skylark (TIE) 164
Slice of Ice (youth theatre) 156
Small Poppies, The. *See* Holman, David
Smith, Kevin 87
SNAG. *See* Learner, Tobsha
Snugglepot and Cuddlepie. *See* Gibbs, May
Solitary Animals. *See* Acworth, Elaine
Song Ngoc Water Puppetry Troupe 12
Song of the Seals. See Hewett, Dorothy
Sons of Cain. *See* Williamson, David
Sound of Music, The 31
South Australian Theatre Company. *See* State Theatre Company of South Australia
South Australian Youth Arts Board (Carclew Centre) 153
Southwest Arts Project 156
Space Theatre 146
Spare Parts (TIE) 164
Splatto 226
Splinter 226
Spolin, Viola 155
Spooner, Michelle 226
Spring Awakening. *See* Wedekind, Frank
Sproul, Linda 14
Spruce, Phil 145
Squeaking of Rats, A. *See* Perkins, Elizabeth
St James' Infirmary. *See* Enright, Nick
St Martin's Youth Arts Centre 153. 157, 158. *Skids* 165-166
Stables Theatre 121, 131
Stalker Stilt Theatre 215, 226. *Mimi* 227-228
Star is Torn, A. *See* Archer, Robyn
State Theatre Company of South Australia 3, 27, 31, 32, 91, 106, 131, 144, 160
STC. *See* Sydney Theatre Company.
STCSA. *See* State Theatre Company of South Australia
Steps Youth Dance Company 158
Still/Here. *See* Jones, Bill T.
Strange Fruit 226
Strathie, Angus 221
Stretchmark 2, 226
Subiaco Theatre Centre 153
Suitcase Theatre 166
Summer of the Aliens. *See* Nowra, Louis
Summer of the Seventeenth Doll, The. *See* Lawler, Ray
Summons, John. *Lamb of God* 42, 46-48
Sunrise. *See* Nowra, Louis
Sussman, Sally. *Orientalia* 54
Suzuki, Tadashi. *The Chronicles of Macbeth* 54
Swain, Rachael 226, 228
Sweet FA 226
SWY Theatre 81, 88
Sydney Festival 87
Sydney Front 18, 183-184, 193, 213. *The Burnt Wedding* 226; *Don Juan* 226; *First and Final Warning* 194, 226; *Passion* 194, 226; *Pornography of Performance* 226; *Waltz* 226
Sydney Gay and Lesbian Mardi Gras Festival 6, 13, 89, 91, 92, 93, 97, 100, 102, 227
Sydney Multicultural Theatre Festival 183
Sydney Opera House 21, 31, 92
Sydney Theatre Company 5, 7, 10, 27, 31, 32, 91, 92, 96, 101, 103
Sydney Woman Action Theatre 106

Ta Duy Binh. *Conversations With Charlie* 12, 63-65; *The Return,* 59
Tait, Peta 227
Talonga, Richard 228
Tankard, Meryl 18, 223
Tap Dogs 7, 32, 33
Tasmanian TIE 160. *See also* Salamanca Theatre Company
Tatty Hollow Story, The. See Hewett, Dorothy
Taylor, Jean 207
Tempest, The. See Shakespeare, William
Temptation of St Anthony, The. See Wooster Group
Terracini, Lyndon 32, 33, 35
Teck Tan & David Zhu. *Black Eyes* 59
Theatre Centre (London) 159
Theatre de Complicité (London) 194
Theatre Now! 156
Theatre of the Deaf 153
Theatre Physical 18, 215. *Miss Haversham's Dream* 214-215
Theatre Royal (Sydney) 37
Theatre South 39
Theatreworks 210
Theatre Workshop (UK) 180-181
Third World Blues. See Williamson, David
Thomson, Katherine 4, 14. *Barmaids* 114; *Diving for Pearls* 114
Thorne, Mémé 66. *Burying Mother* 67-68
Threadbare Theatre 166
TIE/DIE 160, 161, 162
Tiger Country. See Cathcart, Sarah & Andrea Lemon
Time to Kill, A. See Curtis, Penelope
Time's Journey. See Jabo, Sawung
Tinto di rosso. See Doppio Teatro
Toe Truck Theatre 35, 153, 160
Tokyo Rose. See Lowe, Barry
Tokyo/Now/Thriller. See Open City
Tokyo Two. See Open City
Too Young for Ghosts. See Balodis, Janis
Top Silk. See Williamson, David
Toppano, Peta 143
Torrents, The. See Gray, Oriel
Touch of Silk, The. See Roland, Betty
Travelling North. See Williamson, David
Troika (TIE) 160, 161, 162
Tsoutas, Nicholas 194
Twelfth Night. See Shakespeare, William
Two Weeks with the Queen. See Morris, Mary
Two Wongs. See One Extra Dance Company

Un pugno de terra. See Doppio Teatro
Una festa di nozze. See Doppio Teatro
Under the Skin 144
Universal Theatre 95, 131
University of Tasmania School of Visual and Performing Arts 27
Unley Youth Theatre 154, 158

Valentine, Alana 92
Van Hek, Linn. *Difficult Women* 111
Varda che Bruta. See Panozzo, Dina
Vawter, Ron 184
VCA. *See* Victorian College of the Arts
Vella, Maeve 153, 226
Verona. See Magpie
Vertigo 226
Victoria State Opera 31, 36
Victoria Theatre (Stoke-on-Trent) 181
Victorian Arts Centre 31
Victorian College of the Arts 26, 27
Victorian Health Promotion Foundation 162
Victorian Ministry of School Education 162
Vincent. See Crowley, Anthony & Luke Devenish
Vita! A Fantasy. See Hardy, Sara
Vitalstatistix 92, 95, 101, 106, 110, 144
Vocations. See De Groen, Alma
Vulcana Women's Circus 217, 226
Vulgar Ear, A. See Desoxy

WA Youth Jazz Orchestra 158
Wahngin Country. See Davis, Jack
Waiting for Annette. See Bent, Roxxy
Walking on Sticks. See Cathcart, Sarah
Wallflowering. See Murray, Peta
Waltz. See Sydney Front
Wanted. See Fischer, Margaret
Warringah Youth Theatre 156
Water from the Well. See Gunzburg, Darrelyn
Water Stories 12, 54
Watkins, Dennis 102, 158
Watkins, Dennis & Chris Harriott. *Burger Brain: The Fast Food Musical* 157; *The Emerald Room* 91; *Pearls Before Swine* 43, 51
Watt, David 16, 17
Way I Was, The. See Enright, *Playgrounds*
Way, Brian & Warren Jenkins. *Pinocchio* 159
WCAC. *See* Worker's Cultural Action Committee
Webber, Andrew Lloyd 30
We Repeat Ourselves. See Handspan
Wedding Feast, A. See Doppio Teatro
Wedekind, Frank. *Spring Awakening* 158
Well of Loneliness. See Hall, Radclyffe
Wertmuller, Lina. *Love and Magic in Mamma's Kitchen* 143, 144, 145
West (company) 209
West Side Story 31
Western Australian Academy of the Performing Arts 27

Western Australian Theatre Company, 36 160
Westwood, Chris 3, 96, 106, 144
Wharf, The 31, 101, 137
What Do They Call Me? See Johnson, Eva
What If You Died Tomorrow. See Williamson, David
Where Are We Now? See Enright, *Playgrounds*
Wherrett, Richard 96, 103, 156
Whispers In the Heart. See Sidetrack
White Hotel, The. See Kemp, Jenny
White Sports Coat, A. See Lyssiotis, Tes
White, Celia 218, 226, 227
White, Patrick 4, 10, 18, 90, 97, 98. *Big Toys* 96-97; *A Cheery Soul* 19; *The Ham Funeral* 19; *Netherwood* 96; *Night on Bald Mountain* 19; *The Season at Sarsaparilla* 18, 19
Whitton, Dan 223, 228
Who (magazine) 211
Wicked Women 103
Wigman, Mary 202
Wild Cat Falling. See Mudrooroo
Wilson, Lee 214
Williamson, David 1, 4, 6, 7, 10, 115; *Brilliant Lies* 6, 13, 91, 95; *Celluloid Heroes* 95; 102; *Don's Party* 18; *Emerald City* 6; *A Handful of Friends* 97; *Jugglers Three* 42, 50; *The Removalists* 18; *Sanctuary* 98; *Sons of Cain* 2; *Third World Blues* 42, 50; *Top Silk* 2; *Travelling North* 6; *What If You Died Tomorrow?* 95
Williamson, J. C. 30
Wilson, Matt 227
Wilson, Peter 226
Wilson, Robert & John Cage. *Einstein on the Beach* 189
Wimmin's Circus 226
Wind in the Willows, The. See Grahame, Kenneth
Windows. See Crea, Teresa
Witch Theatre 94
Witchplay. See Learner, Tobsha
Wogs out of Work 120, 132, 137, 138
Wolf. See Learner, Tobsha
Wollongong Trades Hall Council 193
Woman's Day (magazine) 211
Women and Theatre Project 92, 106, 210
Women Directors' Workshop 106
Women's Circus, 6, 17, 116, 195-212. *Death: The Musical* 198-199; *Leaping the Wire* 199, 203
Women's Theatre Group 106, 211
Woolly Jumpers (youth theatre) 153, 209
Wooster Group (USA) 184, 194
Workers' Cultural Action Committee 170, 193

Yang, William, *China Diary* 70; *The Face of Buddha* 70; *The North* 8, 12, 70; *Sadness* 8, 12, 66-67
Yellow Roses. See Bent, Roxxy
Yirra Yaakin Youth Theatre 71
Yock, Daniel 84
Yothu Yindi 78
Youth Performing Arts Association 153
Yukkety Yuk. See ATYP
Yungaburra Road. See Janaczewska, Noëlle

Zeal Theatre. *Joyride* 165
Zen Zen Zo 37. *The Cult of Dionysus* 54
Zhu, David 59
Zootango Theatre Company 103

Fig. 1

Adam Broinowski, Daniel Witton, Teresa Blake (top); Michael Newbold (bottom) in Magpie's *Verona*. at Glen Street Theatre, Sydney, 1996. Photo: Branco Gaica, courtesy State Theatre Company of South Australia.

Fig. 2

Zen Zen Zo in *Unleashed* at Princess Theatre, Brisbane, 1996. Photo Rachel Konyi, courtesy Zen Zen Zo.

Fig. 3

Song Ngoc Water Puppetry Troupe's *Water Stories* at Canberra Youth Centre, 1997. Photo: David Morrow, courtesy Canberra Youth Theatre.

Fig. 4

Merlinda Bobis in *Cantata of the Warrior Woman Daragang Magayon* at Asian Theatre Festival, Belvoir Street Theatre, Sydney, 1994. Photo: John Borthwick, courtesy Merlinda Bobis.

Fig. 5

Denice Kickett, Ta Duy Binh, Kerry Cassey in Ta Duy Binh's *Conversations With Charlie* at Asian Theatre Festival, Belvoir Street Theatre, Sydney, 1996. Photo courtesy Ta Duy Binh.

Fig. 6

William Yang in *Sadness*, 1992. Photo: Peter Elfes, courtesy William Yang.

Fig. 7

Margaret Harvey, Bill Sandy in Jack Davis's *The Dreamers*. Kooemba Jdarra Indigenous Theatre at Festival Space, Brisbane, 1996. Photo: Michael Taylor, courtesy Kooemba Jdarra.

Fig. 8

Jaylene Riley in Sally Morgan's *Sistergirl*. Black Swan Theatre & Melbourne Theatre Company, 1992. Photo: David Dare Parker, courtesy MTC.

Fig. 9

Deborah Mailman in Kooemba Jdarra's *Seven Stages of Grieving*, 1995. Photo: Tracey Schramm, courtesy Kooemba Jdarra.

Fig.10

Lillian Sansbury, Paul Kelly, Kate Roberts, Wayne Anthoney in Roger Bennett's *Funerals and Circuses* by Magpie Theatre at Theatre 62, Adelaide, 1992. Photo: Lisa Tomasetti, courtesy State Theatre Company of South Australia.

Fig. 11

Helen Moulder, Caroline Kennison in Sarah Hardy's *Vita! A Fantasy* at La Boite, Brisbane, 1993. Photo: Christabelle Baranay, courtesy La Boite.

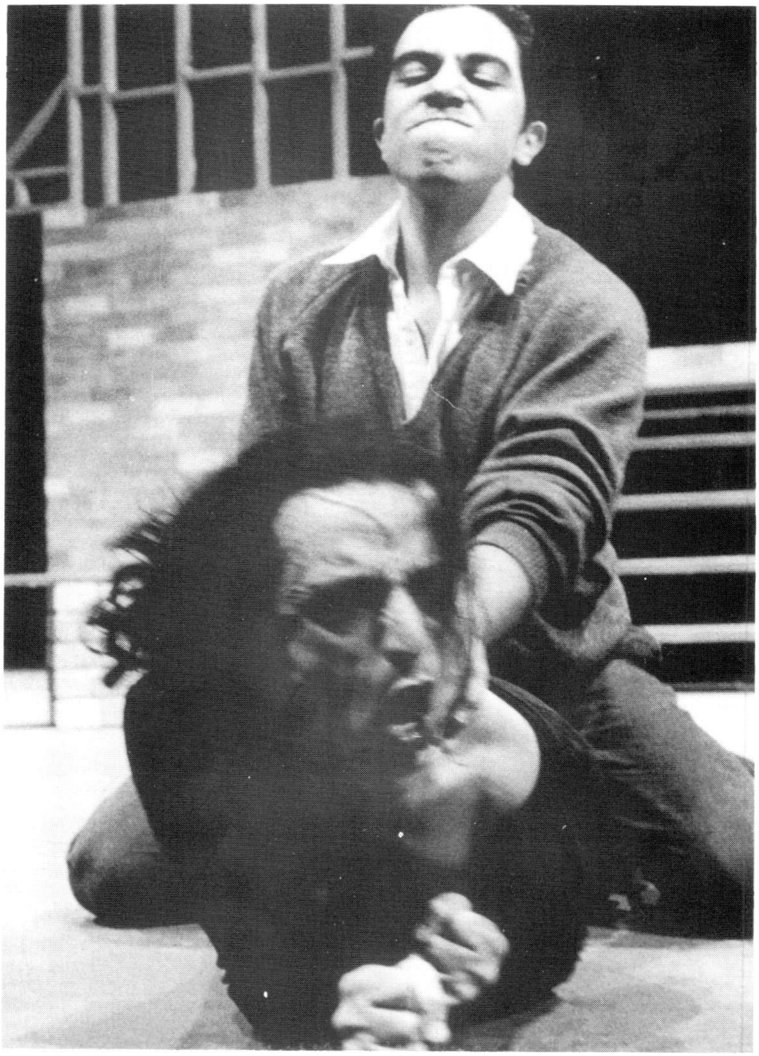

Fig. 12

Wadin Dona (above) and Paul Capsis in Nick Enright's *Playgrounds*. Sydney Theatre Company at The Wharf, 1996. Photo courtesy Tracey Schramm.

Fig. 13

Reg Livermore in *Red Riding Hood, the Speed Hump and the Wolf* at Ensemble Theatre, Sydney, 1996. Photo courtesy Steve Moorehouse.

Fig. 14

Glen Ryman and Philip Ross in Jill Shearer's *Shimada* at Queensland Theatre Company at Cremorne Theatre, Brisbane, 1990. Photo: Chris Ellis, courtesy QTC.

Fig. 15

Natasha Herbert, Mark Pegler, John Diedrich in Tobsha Learner's *Wolf* at Playbox Theatre, Melbourne, 1992. Photo: Jeff Busby, courtesy Playbox.

Fig. 16

Dina Panozzo in *Varda Che Bruta...Poretta*. Sydney Festival at Stables Theatre, Sydney 1992.
Photo: Sandy Edwards, courtesy Dina Panozzo.

Fig. 17

Doppio Teatro's *Pane e cipolla* at Adelaide Italian Club, Ruggero Centre, © 1995. Photo: Peter Heydrich, courtesy Doppio Teatro

Fig. 18

Antonino Gorgone, Eva Di Cesare, Antonino Lo Giudice, Andreas Constantinou in Doppio Teatro's *Una festa di nozze* at Newcastle, Australian National Tour, © 1996. Photo: Peter Heydrich, courtesy Doppio Teatro.

Fig. 19

Crosswinds Theatre in the Community in *Blurgon the Bunyip*, 1979. Photo courtesy Geoffrey Milne.

Fig. 20

Steven Smith, Irene Jarzabek, Josie Eberhard in Arena Theatre's *Three Stories High*, 1990. Photo: Jeff Busby, courtesy Geoffrey Milne.

Fig. 21

Aftershocks at Civic Playhouse, Newcastle, 1991. Photo courtesy Paul Makeham.

Fig. 22

Sidetrack Performance Group's *Adios Cha-Cha* (rehearsal). Sydney 1986. Photo courtesy Tom Burvill.

Fig. 23

Sidetrack Performance Group in *The Measure*. City Square, Melbourne, 1994. Photo courtesy Tom Burvill.

Fig. 24
Women's Circus in the 'Women and Sport' show, Melbourne 1993. Photo: Viv Mehès.

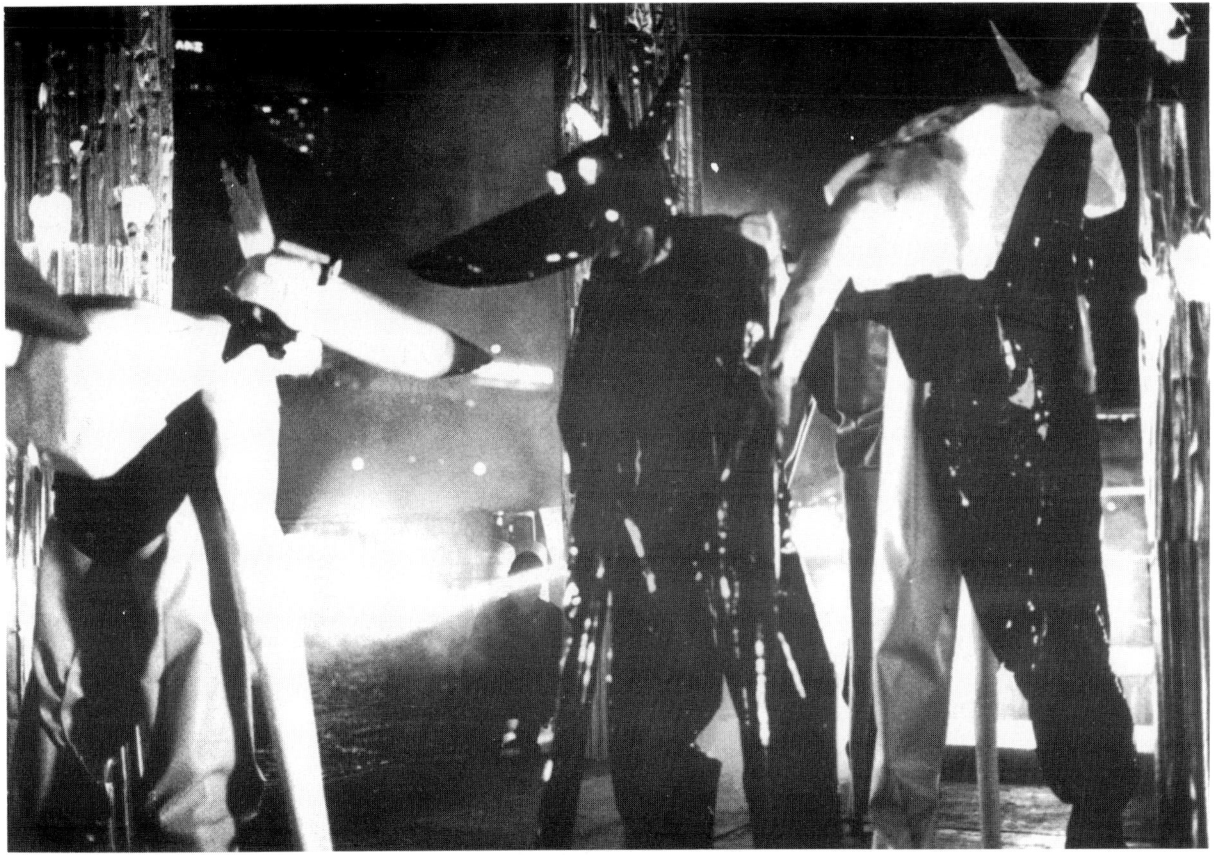

Fig. 25

Women's Circus as the Bitches from Hell, Moomba River Pageant, Melbourne, 1994. Photo: Viv Mehès.

Fig 26

Kareena Oates, Steve Brown in Rock'n'Roll Circus's *Body Slam*, Sydney, 1994. Photo courtesy Angela Bailey.

Fig. 27

Thor Blomfield, Gavin Robins, Kirsty Hilhouse, Bernie Regan in Legs on the Wall's *Temptation*, Sydney. Photo: Scott Barnett, courtesy Legs on the Wall.

Fig. 28

Kareena Oates, Matt Wilson, Rudy Mineur in Rock'n'Roll Circus's *The Dark* at Princess Theatre, Brisbane, 1995. Photo Ponch Hawkes

Fig. 29

Annabel Lines and Matt Wilson in Rock'n'Roll Circus's *The Dark*. Princess Theatre, Brisbane, 1995. Photo: Ponch Hawkes.

Fig. 30

Celia White and Anni Davey of Club Swing at Southgate, Melbourne International Festival, 1996. Photo courtesy Angela Bailey.

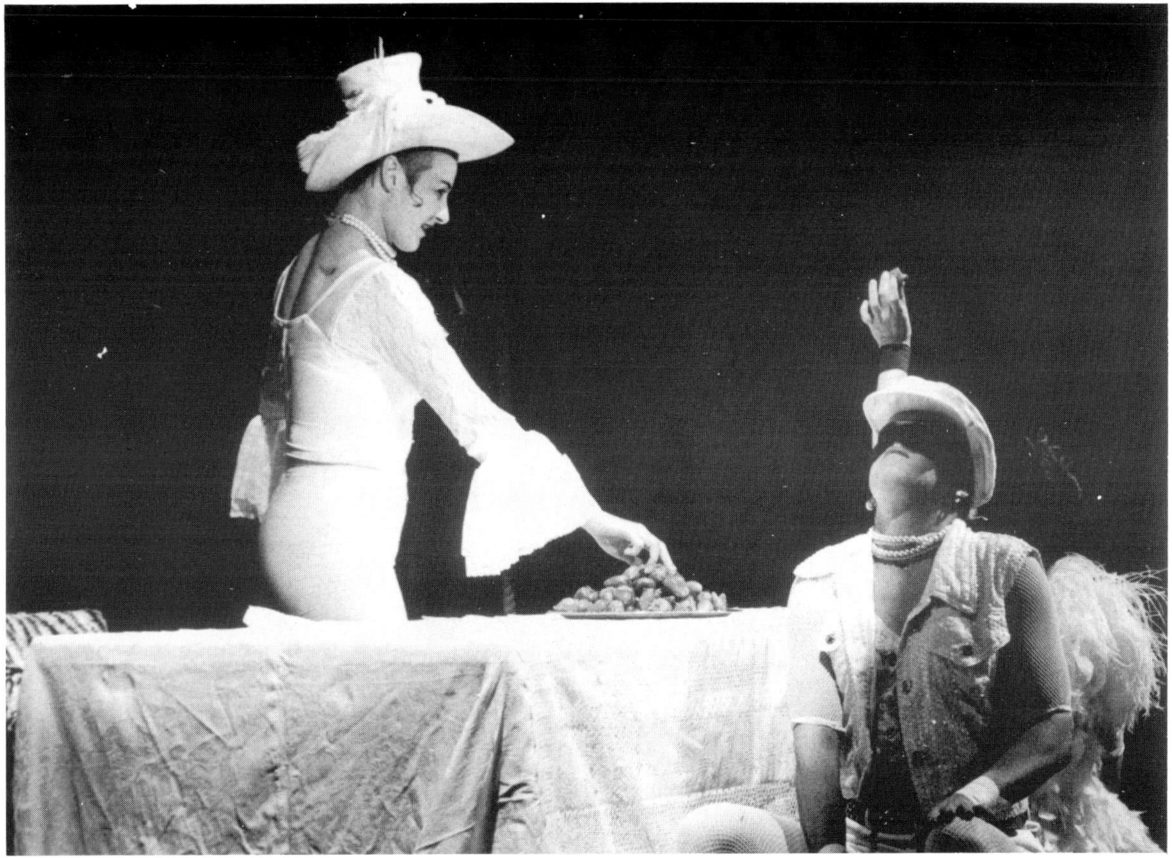

Fig. 31

Anni Davey and Simone O'Brien in Club Swing's *Appetite*. Metro, Melbourne, 1996. Photo courtesy Angela Bailey.

Fig. 32

Mia Mason and Grayson Millwood in Meryl Tankard's *Furioso* at Adelaide Festival Centre, 1995. Photo: Régis Lansac, courtesy Meryl Tankard Australian Dance Theatre.